غرافيتي عربية

Arabic Graffiti

پاسكال زغبي
دون كارل ـ ستون

FROM HERE TO FAME
PUBLISHING

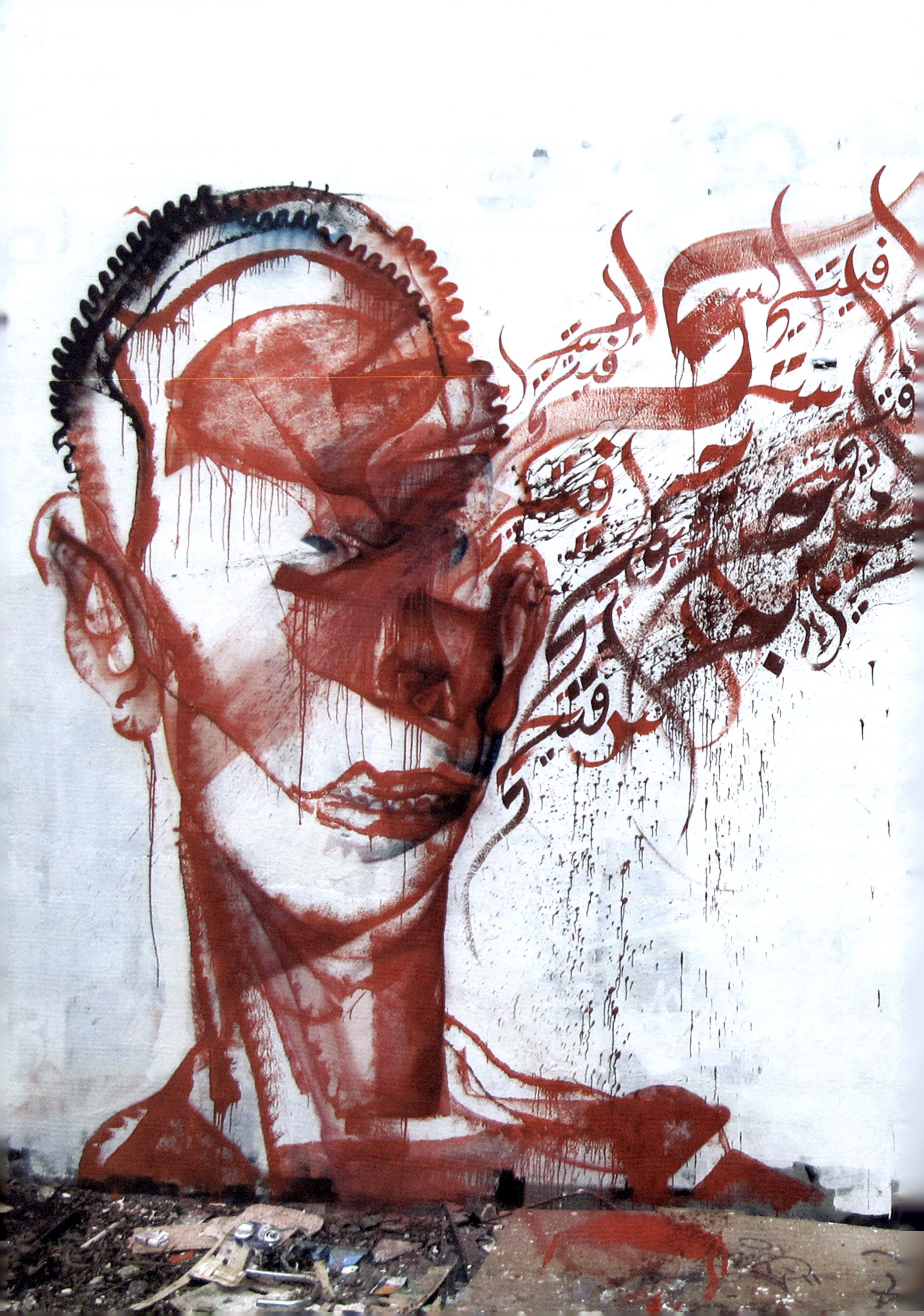

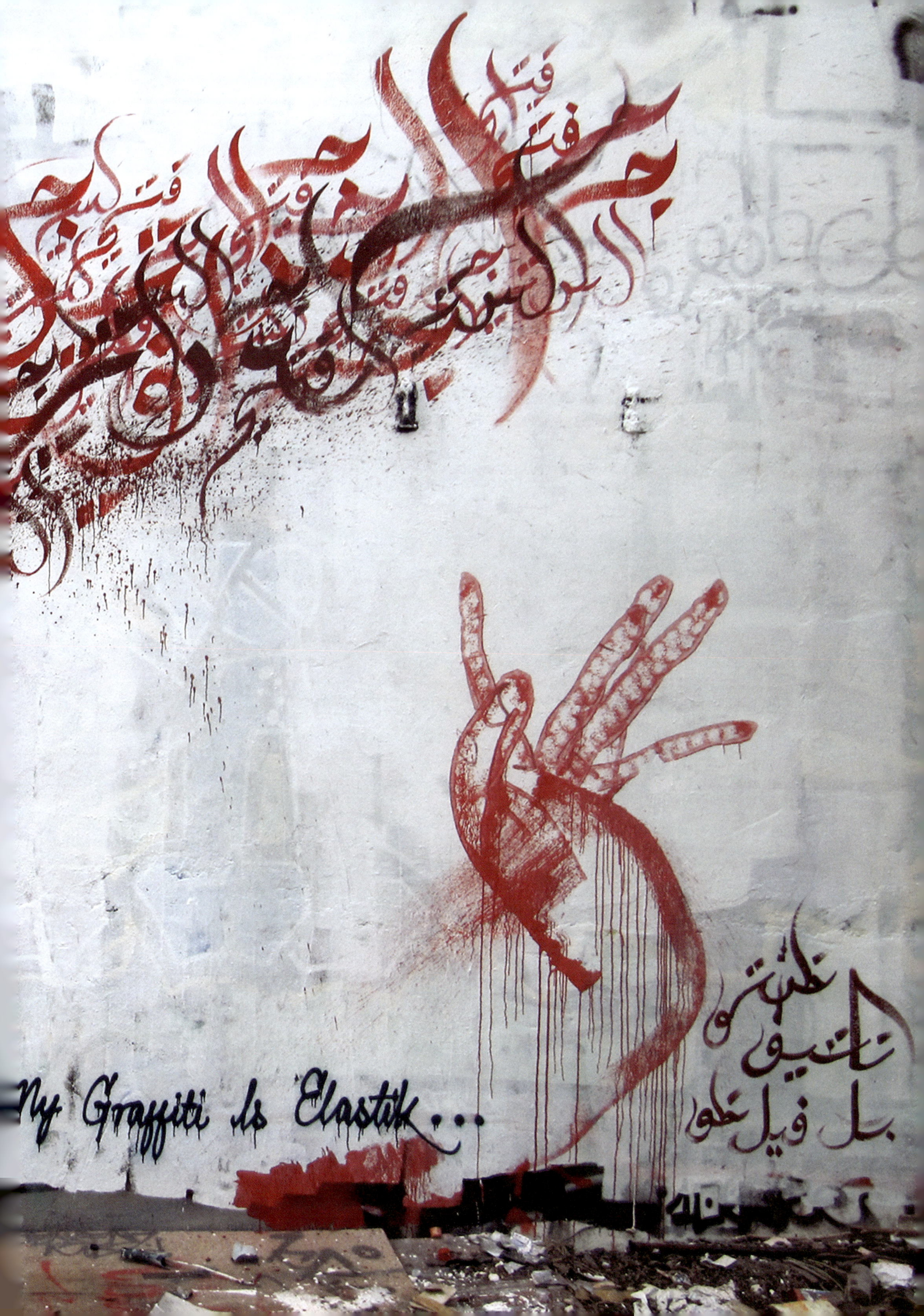
Graffiti Is Elastik ...

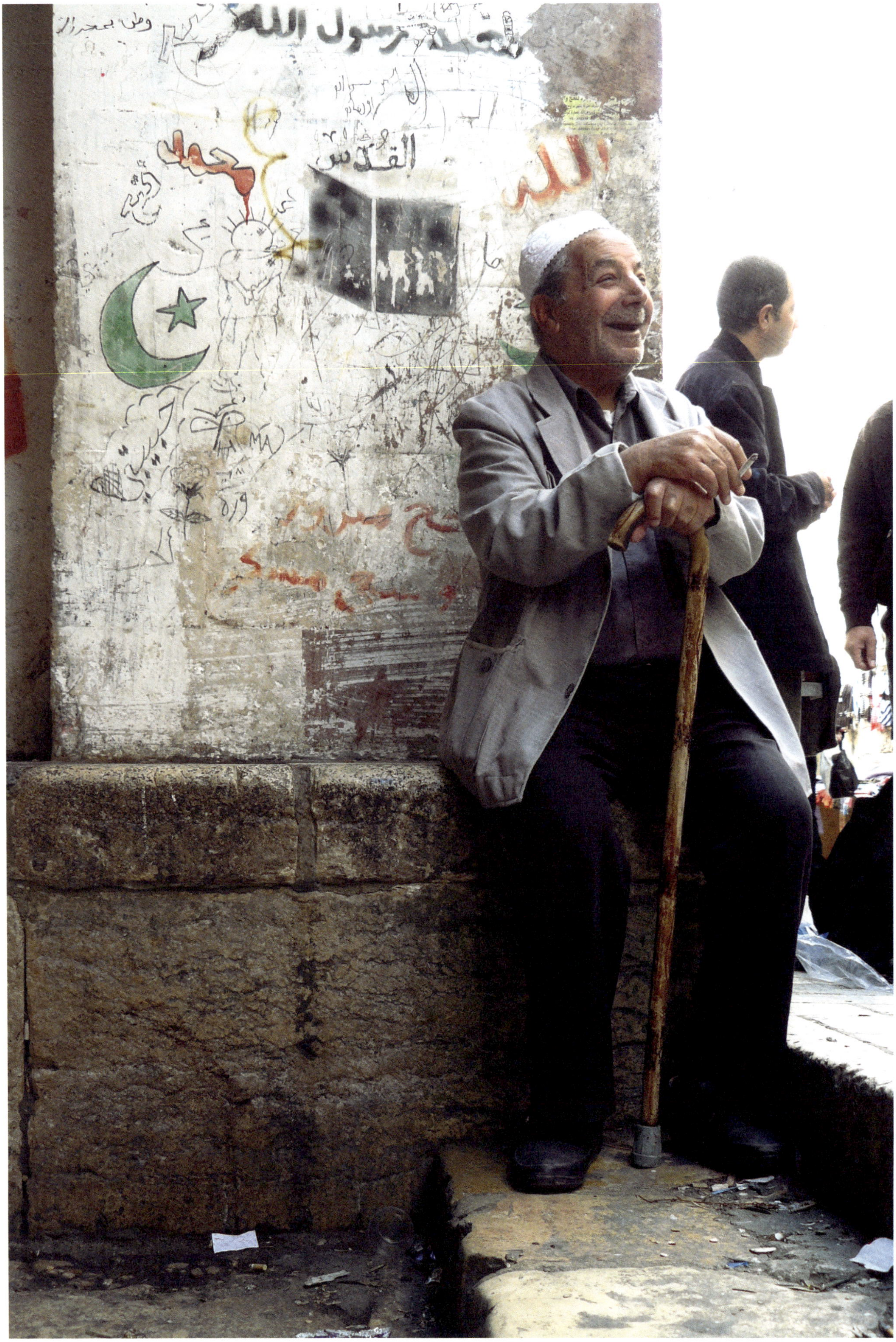
رسول الله
القدس

Contents
المحتويات

الخميس في 17 شباط 2005. الساعة الثانية بعد الظهر.
إجتمع عدد من الأصدقاء غير الحزبيّين في وسط المدينة،
ساحة الشهداء، دون هدف محدّد سوى
التعبير عن حجم الجرح الذي يجمعهم.
الساعة الثانية والنصف بعد الظهر،
إنتشال أحد المعتصمين لافتة بيضاء
بقياس ميترين عن الأرض،
وكتب بما تيسّر من أقلام حبر جاف
أو أحمر شفاه كلمة «إستقالة».
تمّ وضع الافتة على الأسفلت في مواجهة الضريح،
حيث صادف مرور رجل مسنّ،
أخرج طبشوراً أخضر من جيبه
وكتب بحروف كبيرة كلمة
«إستقيلوا».
الساعة الثالثة والنصف بعد الظهر.
أحضر أحد المعتصمين عبوة سبراي أسود
وأعاد تخطيط العبارتين بشكل أوضح.
أخذ أحدهم قلماً ووقّع الافتة التي ملأتها
التواقيع والعبارات خلال ساعات معدودة،
فتنبّه المعتصمون أنّهم أمام عريضة
يجب التوقيع عليها كما وجبت الإستعانة
فوراً بلافتة بيضاء أخرى من المكان عينه.

سَار: سَيراً، تَسيَاراً، مَسِيراً، مَسِيرَةً، سَيرُورةً: ذهب في الليل. سارَهُ وسارَ به: جعلهُ يسير.

05 إستقلال. بيروت في 14 أذار.
إن الحياة إنتصار للأقوياء في نفوسهم ولا للضعفاء.
إنهضي يا مدينة بيروت.
من منا أختار مذهباً أو ديناً، هكذا ولدنا بشراً.
معارض. شوكة في صدورنا.
كفانا دماء، كفانا ضياع،
كفانا ظلم. بدنا لبنان!

1

Previous pages 2 & 3:

Arabic graffiti, NATIVE & ZENTWO, La Forge, Belleville, 2010

Previous page 4:
Street corner, Arab Quarters, Old City Jerusalem, Palestine, 2009

1. Massira Type Family, Type & Media, KABK, the Netherlands, 2006. The design of the type family is inspired by the writings on the Lebanese Petition in 2005.

• PASCAL ZOGHBI,
Arabic type designer and typographer, is the founder of 29letters, an Arabic type design and typography firm in Beirut. He earned his master's degree in type design at KABK (The Royal Academy of Arts) in the Netherlands. His work ranges from creating contemporary Arabic fonts and corporate identities to print publications and other ventures. Pascal teaches typography courses in graphic design departments at AUB (American University of Beirut) and LAU (Lebanese American University). He frequently gives lectures and workshops and runs a highly regarded blog about Arabic type and typography.

Authors' Preface

مقدمة المؤلفين

Analyzing the written graffiti words or sentences and tracing back the political, economic and social factors behind them illustrates the art piece in a different perspective. During the mass demonstration in Beirut that took place in Martyr's Square in 2005, hundreds of people wrote their thoughts and messages on an enormous petition and on the temporary wooden walls that surrounded the space. Photographing the Lebanese Petition and the walls made me realize the power of the written words and the different personalities of the people expressing their thoughts with their own unique handwriting. By then, most of the urban graffiti sprayed in Beirut consisted of political sentences which were still remnants of the civil war.

After that, while I was pursuing my postgraduate studies in the Netherlands, I realized the richness of the urban street art there and all over Europe. Whenever I was traveling to a new city, I would photograph the graffiti and analyze its meaning and connotations. When it came to choosing a topic for my final year project at Type and Media, which is a postgraduate course in type design, I decided to refer back to the photos I took in Beirut during the demonstrations and create an Arabic typeface inspired by the handwriting of the Lebanese people. After analyzing the writings and the tools used to create the Lebanese Petition, I developed the Massira type family, which consisted of Normal, Ballpoint and Spray.

Returning to my home nation in 2007 made me aware of the urban graffiti scene in Beirut and the lovely calligraphic writings on cargo trucks and old shops. Since then, I have been documenting the graffiti scene and analyzing the socio-political messages behind it. I noticed that graffiti in Beirut was still at an earlier stage of development compared to the European counterpart, but the socio-political messages behind it were to a great extent more powerful. What is also interesting is that Beirut has two opposing kinds of graffiti: the political graffiti and the underground graffiti. The politicians support the former and the youth artists who have a counter message about the political and the economic situation in Lebanon create the latter.

Lebanese graffiti is still in the process of finding its forms because it is distant from Arabic calligraphy and it is still imitating the Western style. Most of the graffiti is done in English and very little is created in Arabic. In my view, Lebanese artists should become more familiar with the Arabic script and its calligraphic styles and start creating Oriental writings with a unique style inspired by the Arabic art and culture.

In 2008 I participated in "Bombing Beirut", a graffiti workshop organized by Stone (Don Karl), in which I created my first piece of Arabic graffiti, "Who is the Arab". In the workshop I met most of the Lebanese graffiti crews and started listening to Lebanese rap and Hip Hop songs. Since then, Don and I have shared our interest in the Arabic graffiti scene. This book is the fruit of our collaboration.

At first we considered documenting Arabic graffiti in every country of the Middle and Far East using the Arabic script and analyzing the difference between each nation, but we quickly noticed that while a powerful graffiti scene exists in places such as Lebanon, Tehran and Palestine, it is still shy or totally absent in other nations. Hence the chapters of this book focusing on actual urban art or graffiti scenes mostly feature examples of graffiti in Lebanon and Palestine, especially Beirut and Gaza consequently, alongside other public arts associated with calligraphy. Besides the Middle Eastern nations, we noticed that some Arabic and Persian artists living abroad in the Diaspora are doing very elaborate Arabic graffiti on the streets and in the studios of Paris, Montréal and London etc. We also discovered Western artists who, due to growing up in multicultural societies or out of sheer love for Arabic calligraphy, found their link to integrate those styles into their own art. Finally, in the last section of the book we explore typographic and artistic works that are inspired by the urban street art movement and how modern graphic design is linked to graffiti.

The aim of this book is to document the Arabic graffiti scene and to help develop a stronger connection with the local artists, as well as an awareness of the Arabic calligraphic side of the art, which will lead to a mature Oriental graffiti scene. Our second goal is to introduce the Arabic graffiti scene to the Western public.

Pascal Zoghbi, Beirut, January 2011

1. STONE, "Bombing Beirut" workshop, Beirut, 2008

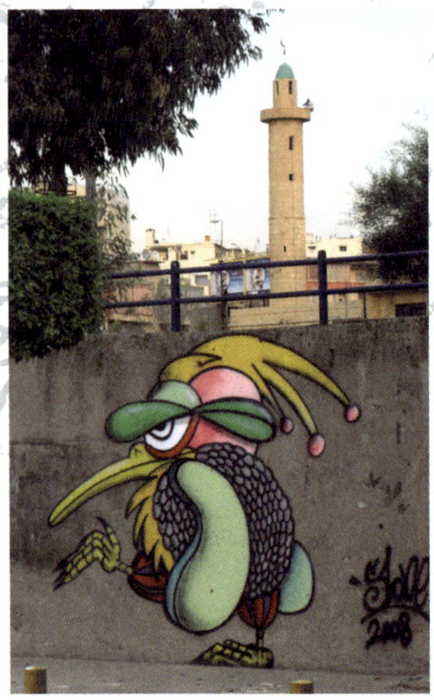

1

• STONE AKA DON KARL

is a style writer, author, publisher and cultural activist. He started to write graffiti in 1983 and published his first book on train writing in 1986. Many books and articles have followed since. He has participated in and curated various international urban art exhibitions and projects, such as Cubabrasil (cubabrasil.net). Stone runs the publishing house From Here To Fame and the Common Ground Gallery in Berlin.

While a boy in Iraq or Syria who discovered his love for letters could step onto a millennia-old path and learn his skills in Arabic calligraphy, there was nothing similar around when I started writing letters in Germany nearly thirty years ago. Graffiti or "style writing" had just cautiously begun to spill over towards Europe. And instead of teachers who conveyed thousands of years of mastery, I had nothing more than my own imagination and some rumors about that strange and wonderful writing movement that was coloring the subways of New York City. It was this fascination, shared by hundreds and hundreds of youngsters across Europe, that soon led to an avalanche of bright and happy letters on the trains and walls of our cities.

Like many style writers before me, I discovered the powers that lie within the Latin alphabet and later, that also in our European culture there were links from what I did to ancient traditions: to the art of writing and symbolism. Graffiti now has its own traditions, merely forty-five years of them, but in our fast-paced times, this is already a long way gone for a contemporary art movement. And over time it has assimilated additional centuries of knowledge. Naturally, I was always fascinated by calligraphies made in scripts other than the Latin script, like Japanese Sho or the beautiful scripts of Arabic calligraphy.

When graffiti continued its conquest towards Asia, I met some kids from Tokyo in Los Angeles. Completely taken in with American urban culture, they were convinced that wearing baggy jeans was the only way to be real. They painted graffiti with the same attitude. We talked about this and I asked them why they did not write in Japanese letters, having this beautiful calligraphy just in front of them in Japan. "Calligraphy? That is for old men!" they replied. Today, less than twenty years later, they have been proven wrong. Japan is rich with beautiful graffiti writings and larger scale murals that make elaborate use of the Japanese script. And there are style writers who learned their basic skills from those "old men" and after mastering them, translate them into their own new graffiti styles.

Since the viral phenomenon of graffiti writing does not seem to stop anywhere, it has long since arrived in the Middle East as well. The Middle East is a treasure box for a graffiti writer who seeks true knowledge about the origins of the letters that he has spent years to master. After all, the Arabic, Latin, Greek and Hebrew alphabets all have the same mother: the Phoenician alphabet, which was developed and used 3000 years ago in today's Lebanon, Syria and Palestine. Thus, graffiti in the sense of "write your name and leave a mark on a wall" existed in the Orient long before anyone in the Occident even learned what writing was.

When I first came to Beirut, I was planning a mural project called "Living Alphabets". My aim was to arrange a meeting between masters of Arabic calligraphy and expert Latin graffiti writers with local graffiti artists and then basically wait and see what happens. I expected to find some of the local writers already experimenting with Arabic calligraphy in their styles, but I found none. Instead, there too I ran into a familiar answer: "Calligraphy? That is only used for wedding cards and done by old men! It has nothing to do with our culture." Well, what could I say to this? I am not one of Edward Said's Orientalists, who think they know more about someone else's culture than themselves. And there is obvious truth to what they said, when Western influences and computer graphics had all but marginalized the use of Arabic calligraphy in everyday culture. But I definitely know my bit about style writing and how it has worked and developed over decades in similar ways — in country upon country and all around the globe.

My thesis that style writing is a perfect host for Arabic calligraphy wasn't wrong and by doing some research, I found more and more artists in different places around the world who were already way ahead with their idea of Arabic graffiti and had completed the convergence. We are honored that so many of those artists agreed to participate in this book.

Without Pascal Zoghbi's expertise in Arabic letters, this book would not have been possible. Unlike me, he actually speaks, reads and writes Arabic. So while I concentrated more on the mere abstract aesthetic messages in the artwork we selected, for him the message of what was actually written was of greater significance. Interestingly enough, some of the Arabic graffiti writers, notably Muslims, put the message before the traditional (and egocentric) aim of writing ones name and getting fame for it. Being able to read the letters of a calligraphy or graffiti style inevitably changes its structures and dynamics to the eye of the beholder. Very much like the famous optical illusion of Rubin's Vase, which can also be seen as two faces. So in order to comprehend and translate the styles and codes of Latin graffiti into Arabic graffiti and vice versa, a deep understanding of both scripts and their rules is a prerequisite.

Judging from the enthusiastic response that we got from artists and the outstanding authors who contributed their essays to the book, it seems that the topic has struck a chord. The movement of Arabic graffiti will continue growing in the years to come and I won't be surprised if many young writers jump at the opportunity to get some proper teaching from their local calligraphy masters.

Stone, Berlin, January 2011

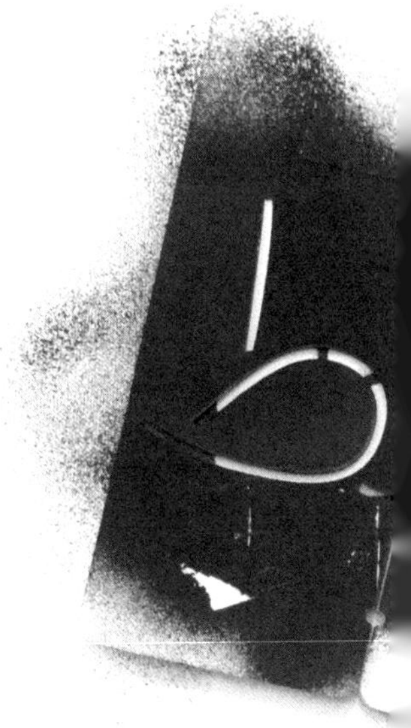

Arabic Script & Calligraphy

1

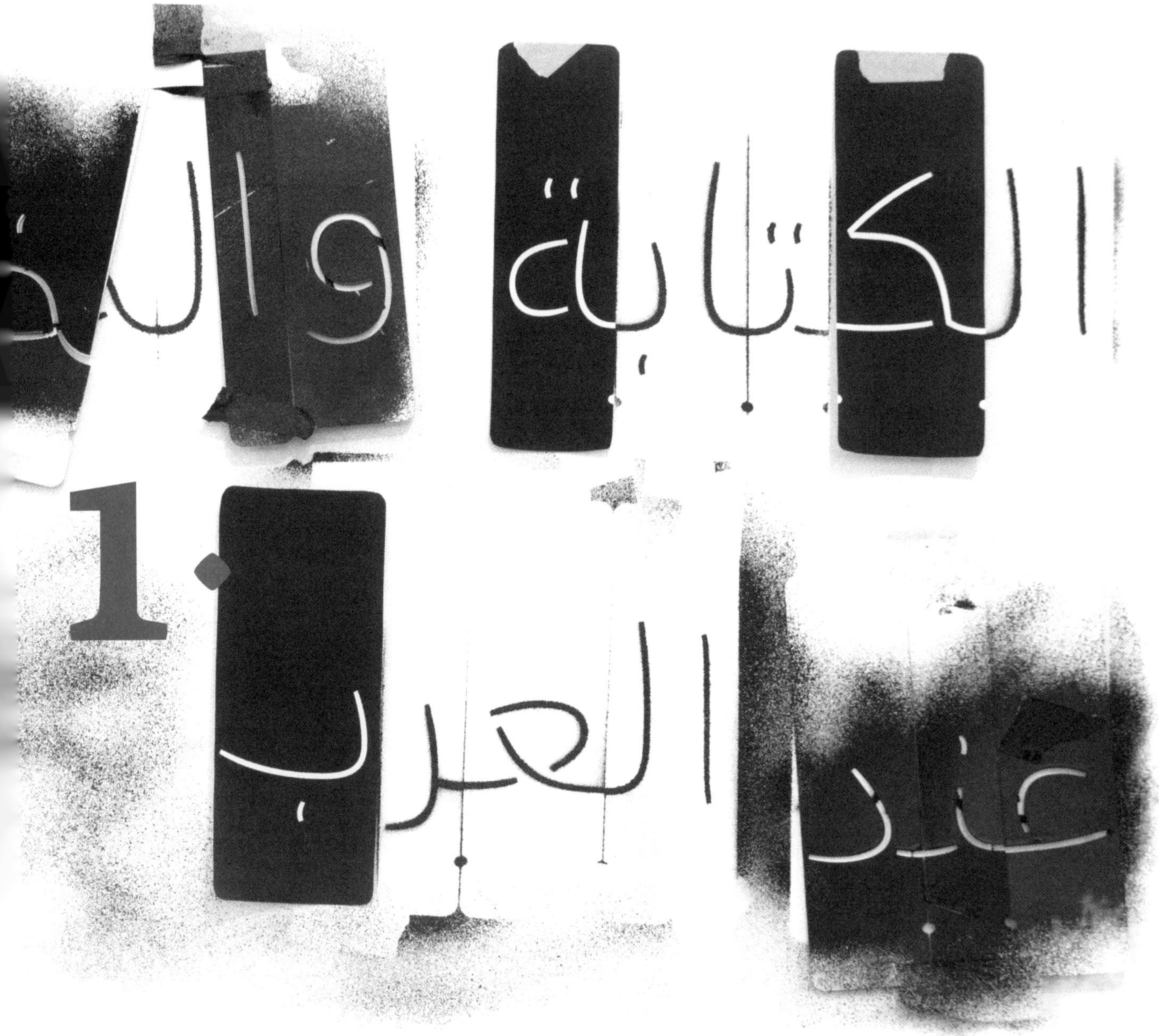

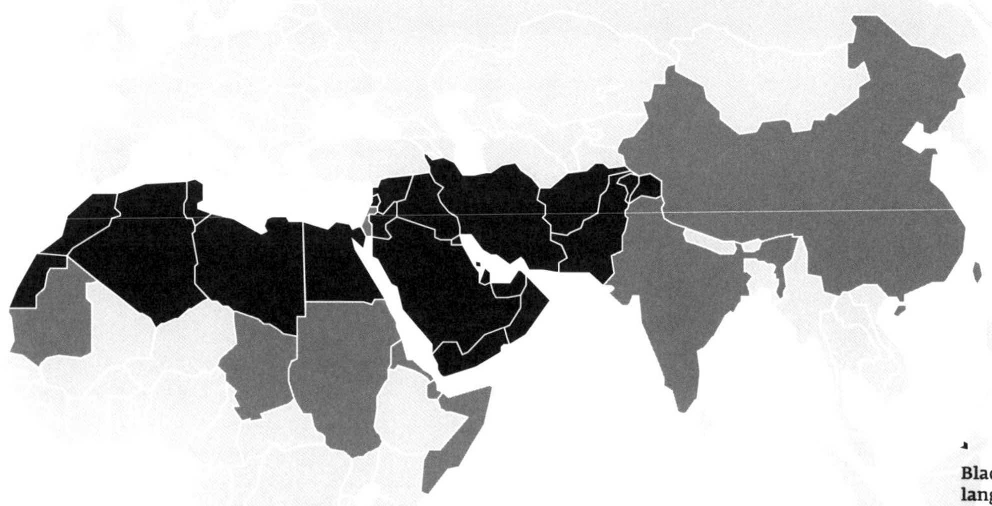

Black: Nations that have the Arabic language as their official language and use the Arabic script.

Dark Gray: Nations that speak non-Arabic languages but use the Arabic script.

Light Gray: Nations that have select areas that use the Arabic script.

غ غغغ	ع ععع	ظ ظظظ
Ghayn • g / gh	Ayn • —	Zah • z / zz

ك ككك	ق ققق	ف ففف
Kaf • k / c	Qaf • q	Fa' • f

ه ههه	ن ننن	م ممم	ل للل
Heh • h	Noon • n	Meem • m	Lam • l

ء	لا لا	ي ييي	و و
Hamza • —	Lam Alef • la	Ya' • y / i	Waw • w / o / u

1·1
The Arabic Alphabet
الأبجدية العربية

ث ثثث ت تتت ب ببب أ ا

Tha' • th | Ta' • t | Ba' • b | Alef • a

خ خخخ ح ححح ج ججج

Kha' • kh | Ha' • h | Jeem • j

س سسس ز ـز ر ـر ذ ـذ د ـد

Seen • s | Zay • z | Ra' • r | Zal • dh / z | Dal • d

ص صصص ش ششش

Sad • ṣ / ss | Sheen • sh / ch

ط ططط ض ضضض

Tah • ṭ / tt | Dhad • ḍ / dd

The Arabic alphabet consists of twenty-nine letters. There are nineteen base glyphs and with the added diacritic dots, there is a total of twenty-nine letters. The script is written from right to left and is connected. The shape of the letters changes depending on their position in the word, whether they are initial, medial, final or isolated. Some letters have only isolated and final shapes, while the rest have four alternative forms in initial, medial, final and isolated shape. Letters that do not have initial and medial forms interrupt the connectivity of the word.

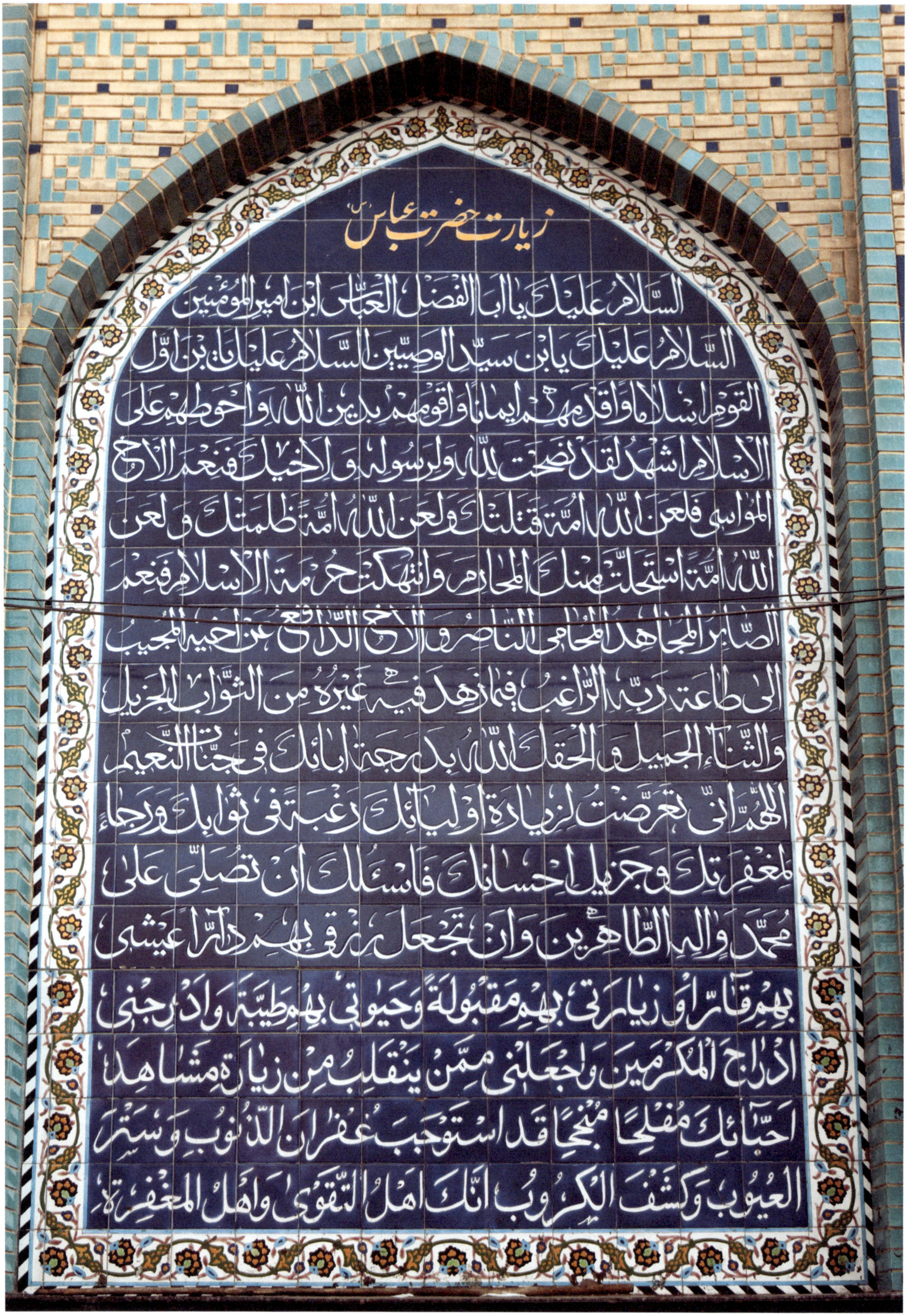
زيارت حضرت عباس ع
السلام عليك يا ابا الفضل العباس ابن امير المؤمنين
السلام عليك يا ابن سيد الوصيين السلام عليك يا ابن اول
القوم اسلاما واقدمهم ايمانا واقومهم بدين الله واحوطهم على
الاسلام اشهد لقد نصحت لله ولرسوله ولاخيك فنعم الاخ
المواسي فلعن الله امة قتلتك ولعن الله امة ظلمتك ولعن
الله امة استحلت منك المحارم وانتهكت حرمة الاسلام فنعم
الصابر المجاهد المحامي الناصر والاخ الدافع عن اخيه المجيب
الى طاعة ربه الراغب فيما زهد فيه غيره من الثواب الجزيل
والثناء الجميل والحقك الله بدرجة ابائك في جنات النعيم
اللهم انى تعرضت لزيارة اوليائك رغبة في ثوابك ورجاء
لمغفرتك وجزيل احسانك فاسئلك ان تصلي على
محمد واله الطاهرين وان تجعل رزقي بهم دارا عيشى
بهم قارا وزيارتي بهم مقبولة وحيوتي بهم طيبة وادرجني
ادراج المكرمين واجعلني ممن ينقلب من زيارة مشاهد
احبائك مفلحا منجحا قد استوجب غفران الذنوب وستر
العيوب وكشف الكروب انك اهل التقوى واهل المغفرة

1

1·2
Brief History of the Arabic Script
تاريخ مختصر للكتابة عند العرب

by Huda Smitshuijzen AbiFarès

1. Prayer inscribed on tiles in a mosque. Title written in Farsi script, prayer in Thuluth script. Iran

The rich Arabic calligraphic tradition has had a long and influential history in shaping and regulating the visual aspect of the Arabic script. Originally conceived to represent the holy scriptures of the Koran, the Arabic script became an emblem of the Islamic religion, and therefore, its perceived beauty and reproduction became a matter of religious piety. Not only used for representing religious text, its use in profane texts and its function as ornamentation on everyday objects and architecture testifies to its special status within the Arab/Islamic cultures. It is a part of a holistic life philosophy in which artistic expression plays a vital role.

The Arabic alphabet evolved by first borrowing from neighboring civilizations and then developing in its own right as an independent script. With the collective contribution of many talented individuals and the influences of various cultures, calligraphy developed into a form of communication that balanced clarity with beauty in an art form that embodied disciplined freedom. The Arabic alphabet, like most alphabetic writing systems in use today, has its roots in the first developed alphabetic writing system invented around 1300 BCE by the Phoenicians. The Phoenicians developed a simple and limited set of phonetic characters that were easy to learn and adapt to various languages. As traders, the Phoenicians managed to spread the alphabet across their trade routes and port cities. The invention of the alphabet spread westward via the Greeks and eastward via the Aramaeans as far as India, and was adopted as a writing system by various Semitic, Indo-European and other languages. The Arabic alphabet, born in Arabia, is the last of the Semitic scripts (c. 500 CE). From its origin on the Arabian Peninsula, the Arabic language spread via the Islamic conquests to neighboring nations, into what constitutes the Arab/Islamic nations of today. As a language, it has replaced a number of native languages and was adopted by non-Arabic languages as a visible cultural allegiance to the Islamic faith. The Arabic language became a unifying cultural force, and its visual representation through calligraphy became the supreme artistic achievement of Islamic art.

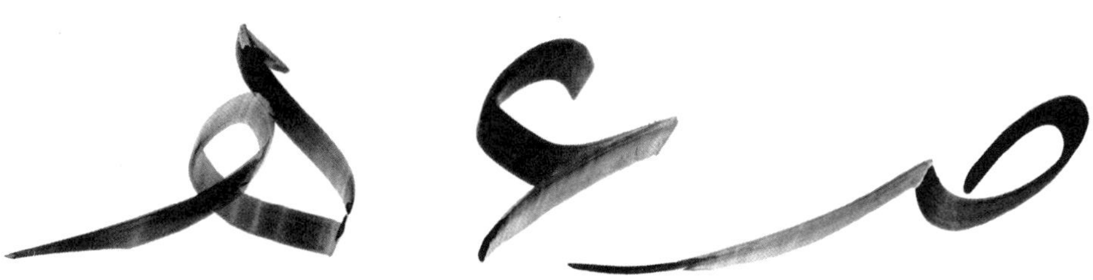

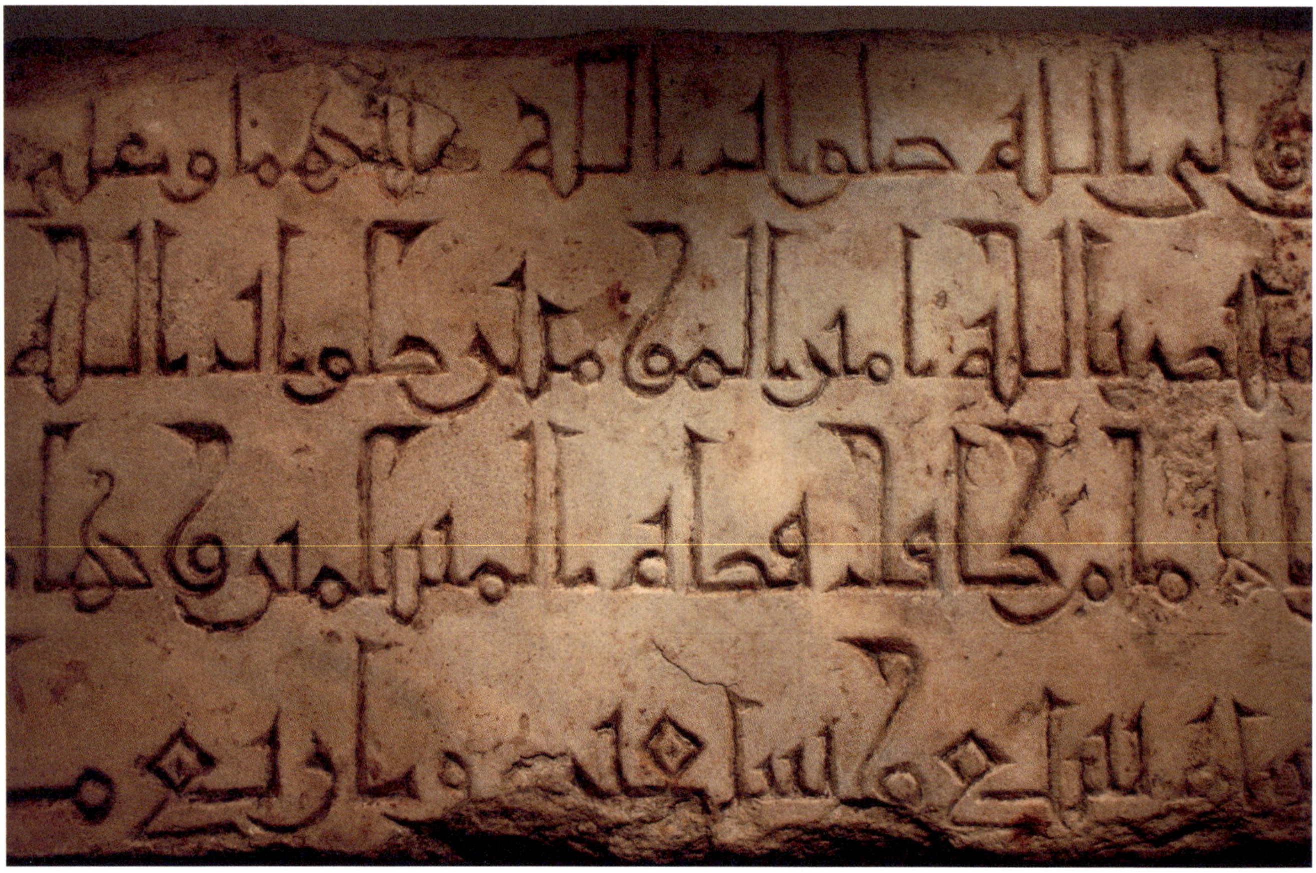

1

Calligraphy can only flourish when a civilization is at the peak of its cultural activities and prosperity. The initial development of Arabic calligraphy took place in the first Arab empire in Iraq in the 7th century, namely in Hira, where the Naskh style was developed, and during the Abbasid Dynasty in Baghdad, where the style later to be known as Kufic was developed. Both the Kufic and Naskh styles were to definitively influence Arabic calligraphy by creating the two broad categories for the classification of Arabic calligraphic styles. The script then flourished as a higher art form in the 10th century in the eastern and western parts of the Arab empire. It finally reached its climax of refinement under the auspices of the Ottoman sultans in the 18th century.

1) The original Kufic style (c. 7th–9th century) was the oldest and most refined Arabic script; it reached a high level of formal perfection in the 8th century, which made it the unrivaled style worthy of transcribing the Holy Koran — a tradition that persisted for the following 300 years. In its original form, it was a rather austere style which grew more ornate as the Arab empire grew more prosperous. It developed in two main directions: the smoother, curvilinear Maghrebi styles in the western regions of the empire (North Africa and Spain), and the angular styles of the Eastern Kufic in the eastern part of the empire. From the 11th century onwards, more ornate variations were developed by extending the letters into decorative endings (ranging from floral to arabesque motifs) and became the Square Kufic style, which was used as architectural ornamentation, often covering whole facades of building.

2) The cursive styles, starting with the Naskh style, are based on fluid handwriting. These styles, pre-dating the Islamic era, were originally used strictly for secular documents. Their development into calligraphic styles began with the Caliph Abdelmalek's decree to legislate the use of cursive scripts for official documents. In the 10th century, the cursive scripts were further developed and refined by the vizier and calligrapher Ibn Muqlah, who gave the cursive styles standardized proportions and calligraphic rules which put order and structure into the roughly twenty calligraphic styles that were in use at the time. The classical cursive styles laid down the foundations for a number of other styles. A brief list of cursive styles includes the Thuluth, the Naskh, the Muhaqqaq, the Rayhan, the Tawqii, the Ruqaa, the Behari, the Diwani, the Nastaaliq, the Shikasteh, and a few others.

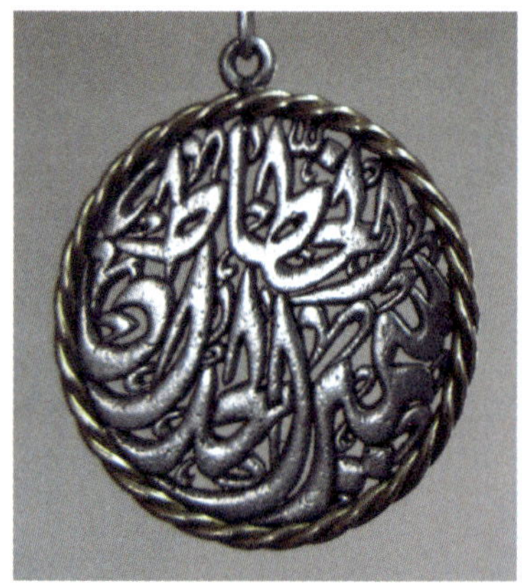

2

1. Stone carved Kufic script

2. Silver engraved Diwani script, jewelry, Lebanon

3. Stone carved Thultuh script, fragments of a tombstone, Turkey

4. Thuluth script, Bab-i Hümayun gate, Topaki Palace, Istanbul

Following pages 18 & 19:

Calligraphy by ALI ASSI which shows the Thuluth, Naskh, Farsi, Diwani, Ruq'ah scripts and two freestyles of Arabic calligraphy. The text is from the socio-political writer Fouad Sleiman and taken from his writings entitled "Tamouziyat".

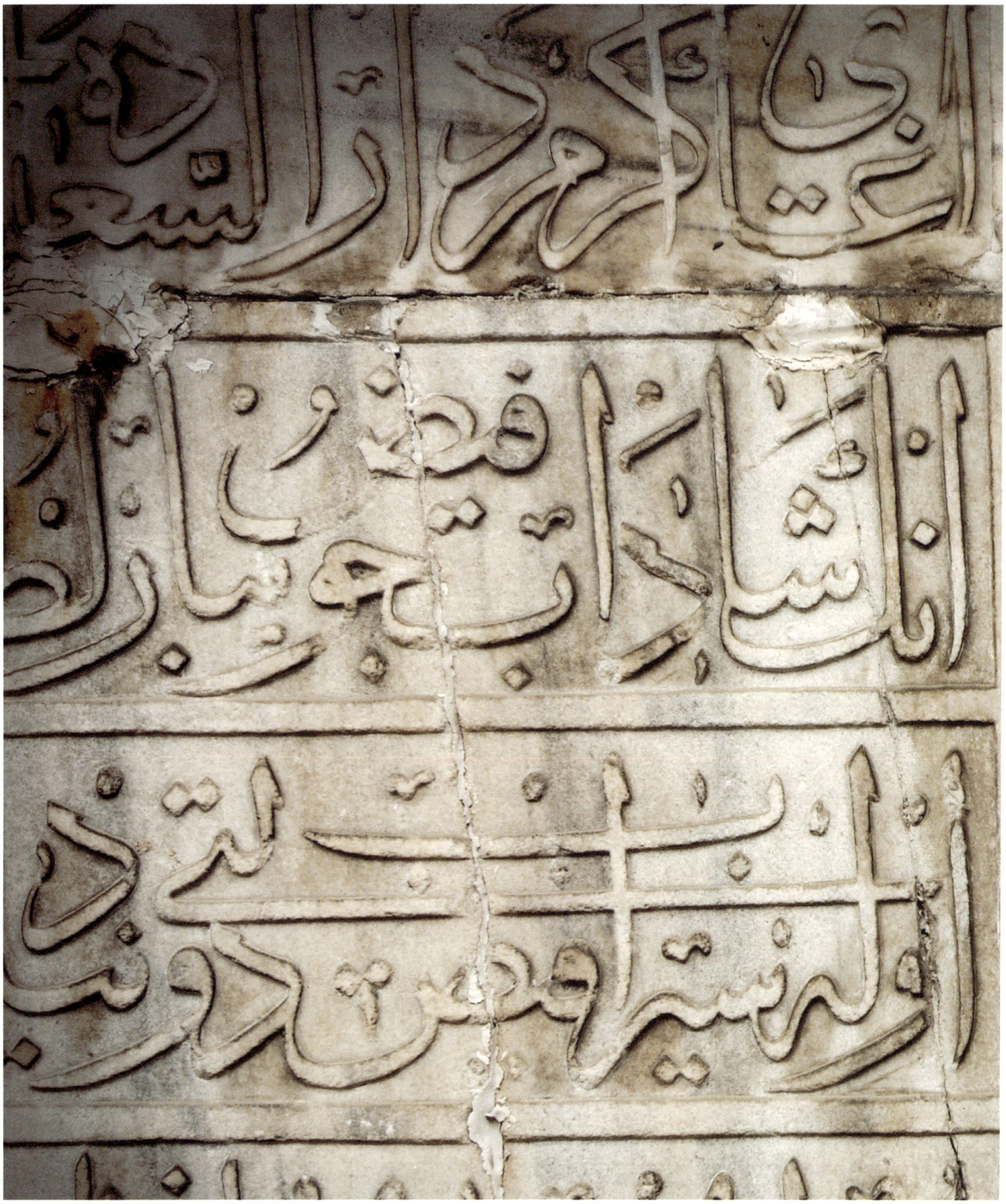

3

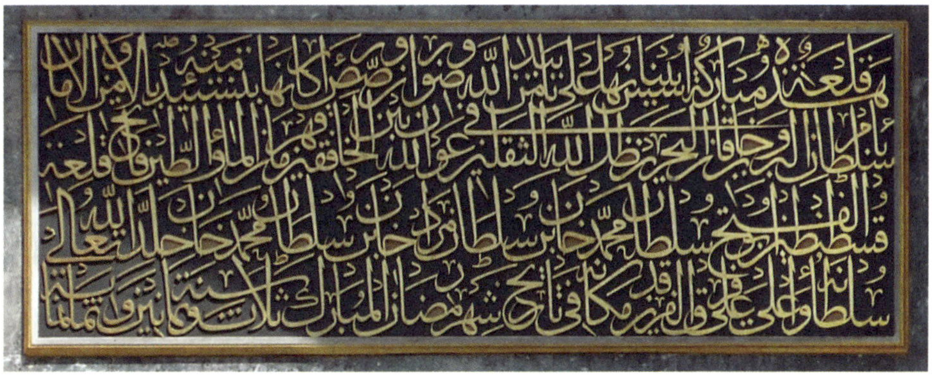

4

بست حبرًا عندنا وإنّما هي قطعٌ من القلب،

ألوانًا وكانت أنغامًا، وهكذا نريدُها، لونًا من القلب

سنا بالحديد والرصاص، يصرع ويصرع ولا ترتدُّ له يد، ولا

جة وأولاد كان للموت عندنا ثارات ... رنا من هتف

ن في وجهه يتلوّى ... يا زغردات الدماء في أعراس الحريات! والحروف

قطع من القلب، سلخناها نحن، من اللحم والدم

لب ونغمًا من الدم.

فؤاد سليمان

تمّوزيّات

وَالحُرُوف هَذِهِ، هَذِهِ الحُرُوف الصَّغِيرَة المُنَمَّقَة

Thuluth

سَلَخنَاهَا نَحنُ، مِنَ اللَّحم وَالدَّم. فَكَانَت لَنَا الحُرو

Naskh

ونغمًا من الدم ... كان الموت أمس ضيفًا ثقيلًا في أرضنا، ح

Farsi

يرتجف له عرق! كان الموت قاسيًا مرًّا، فلا أشفق ع

Diwani

ومزّق هتافه الأليم، ومنامه صمت، فلا هتف ولا شكى، ب

Ruq‘ah

هذه، هذه الحروف الصغيرة المنمقة. ليست حبرًا عندنا وإن

Ali Assi Freestyle 01

فكانت لنا الحروف ألوانًا وكانت أنغامًا، وهكذا نريدها، لونًا

Ali Assi Freestyle 02

• ARABIC TYPOGRAPHY

When the printed Arabic typographic book was first introduced in the Middle East by the Roman Church for religious and political reasons, the emphasis was put mainly on making the type look as similar as possible to the calligraphic styles that were most popular at the time. The later versions of Arabic printing types, whether of European or Middle Eastern origin, hardly deviated from that formula. Though there were some movements in the 1930s to 'modernize' the Arabic script and adapt it to modern means of type production, these ideas were neither widely popular nor implemented in the mainstream visual culture.

Formal experiments in Arabic type design came to their highest point with Letraset's invention of the dry-transfer type. The low cost and flexibility of this production medium brought type design close to Arab designers, as opposed to the high cost typesetting machines of that period, which were exclusively in the hands of Western manufacturers, and were primarily conceived to typeset Latin fonts. This was also the reason why the groundbreaking digital technology had little influence on Arabic type design. Fortunately, this situation has dramatically changed with the advent of the Internet, and the growing awareness of the potential market benefits of a global world culture.

The latest widespread communication media have empowered many people around the globe. The rapid and efficient exchange of ideas and products at low cost and high speed has created a fluid global society. With the spread of the Internet computer network, textual information has regained its front-row importance, and the boundaries of type representation have widened towards uncharted territories. The manipulation of type and our constant interaction with textual information have become commonplace. The potential of typography's communication power has grown exponentially with the recent technological advancements and has come to represent our modern world. Though the affluent Arab nations have taken an active part in this global culture, their script has remained poorly represented in the digital media.

1. Contemporary Arabic fonts from the 29letters collection created by PASCAL ZOGHBI. The collection shows fonts based on the Naskh and Kufic calligraphic scripts. From top to bottom: Arabic for Universe (FedEx Kinkos), Baseet, FF Seria Arabic (Sada), Droid Naskh (Google), ADA Arabic (Abu Dhabi Airport Terminal 3), Arabic Metal Type and Bukra (Ibn Battuta Mall).

• FRESH PERSPECTIVES IN SEARCH OF A NEW GLOBAL DESIGN AESTHETIC

In the last decade of the 20th century, a number of educational programs emerged in the Middle East, and they have been actively graduating a new generation of well-educated graphic designers. These young designers entering the design profession have had to face the fact of the limited choice of quality Arabic fonts. The problem they face is how to design a contemporary-looking bilingual piece using antiquated-looking Arabic fonts, especially when these fonts are paired with modern Latin fonts, which is an inevitable requirement for most design pieces produced in the multicultural communities of the Middle East. It has become essential to put the design of Arabic type back into the hands of the young people directly involved in shaping the contemporary Arab visual culture, and to encourage them to experiment with typography in their native languages. The emerging generation's 'do-it-yourself' attitude shows a desire to establish a modern type design trend in the Arab world. These type designs aim to address on one hand the new global design aesthetic, and on the other hand to provide design solutions for the needs of modern communication media. The experimental aspect of these new type designs lies in the fact that they intentionally break away from the conventional calligraphic styles and move towards a new design that does not strictly abide by the rules of pen-drawn letterforms.

• LEGIBILITY VERSUS VISUAL NOVELTY

Since the 1990s, the number of stylistic experiments has taken the design world by storm, shaking up conventions and questioning the common practice. They have left their imprint on the global trends of visual communication. For instance, the number of stylistic variations on the traditional font family has gone beyond the different weight and proportional variations to include illustrative or unusual hybrid variations, as well as idiosyncratic ligatures and letter combinations. Regardless of nationality, the need to be unique is at the root of every designer's motivation. The novelty of the Arabic fonts lies in the creation of new styles that do not fit into the traditional classifications. These designs vary from the modernist approach of 'form follows function', or the opposite, which puts form before any other consideration. Some type design trends include display fonts that are expressive and playful, designed for special purposes, and often inspired by popular culture. These range from personal formal experiments to representations of vernacular street art, cartoons and comic strips. The challenge, however, remains in testing the limits of legibility.

These fonts play an important role in instigating discussion about the formal and conceptual developments of future Arabic type design. When we design Arabic fonts, we must assume the responsibility of taking creative risks that challenge the rules of the old establishment; of recognizing present realities of contemporary design and visual branding; of being ready to constantly question what we take for granted; and of setting the stage for constructive discussions about the future of Arabic typography.

• HUDA SMITSHUIJZEN ABIFARÈS
is an Amsterdam-based typographer, designer, writer, and Founding Director of the Khatt Foundation (khtt.net). She is the author of "Arabic Typography" and has recently published "Typographic Matchmaking in the City" (Khatt Books, Amsterdam 2011). She writes on design and typography from the Middle East. She was born in Beirut and has traveled and worked in the Middle East since 1994.

غرافيتي عربية في الشرق الأوسط

غرافيتي عربية في الشرق الأوسط

غرافيتي عربية في الشرق الأوسط

غرافيتي عربية في الشرق الأوسط

غرافيتي عربية في الشرق الأوسط

غرافيتي عربية في الشرق الأوسط

1 غرافيتي عربية في الشرق الأوسط

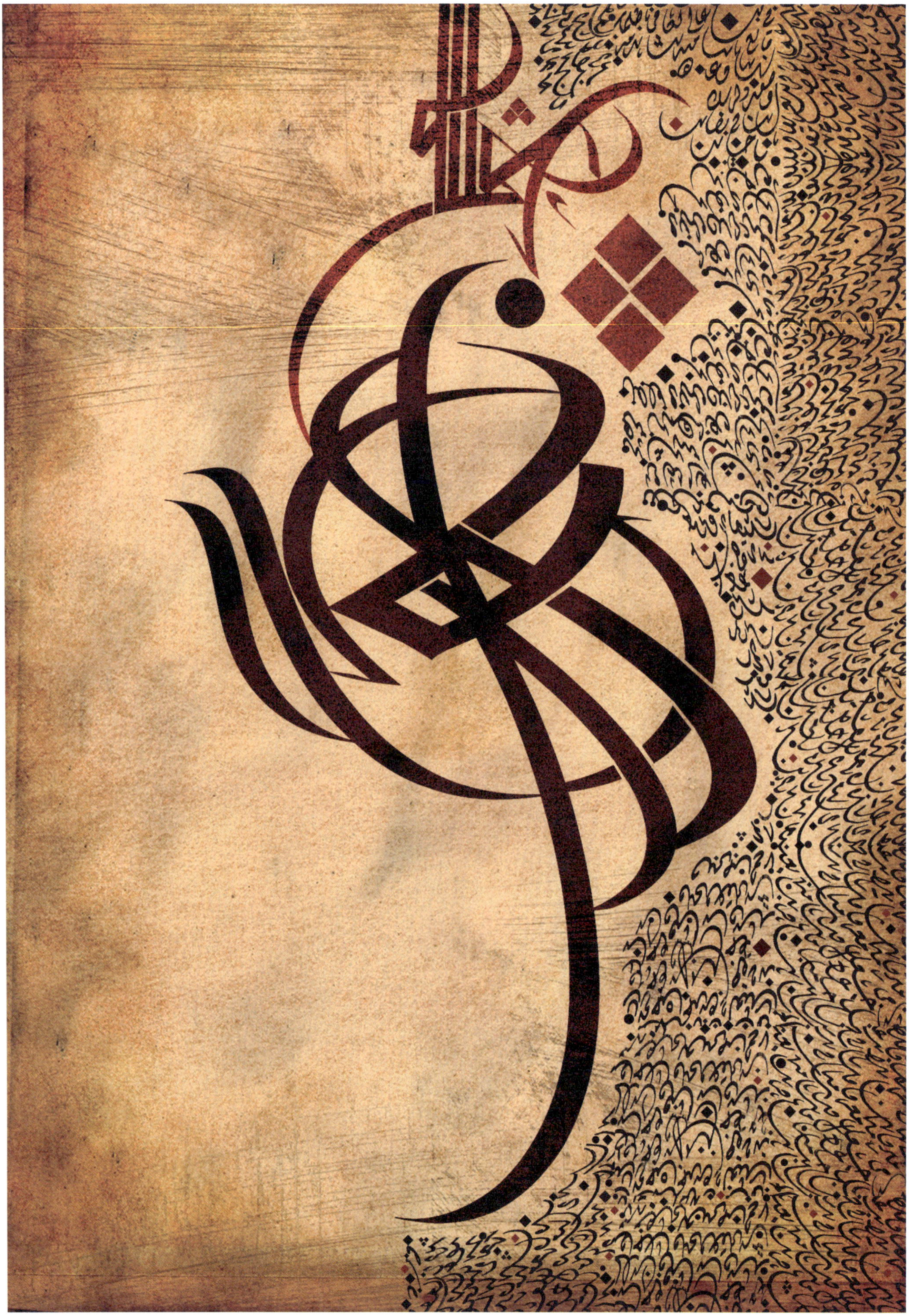

1

1·3
Contemporary Arabic Calligraphy
الخط العربي المعاصر

by Malik Anas Al-Rajab

A thousand years ago, a man who lived in Baghdad, Ibn Muqlah (886–940), designed and developed many of the calligraphic styles that we know today as the Six Pens Styles. Since then, all further amendments to Arabic calligraphy (within the Arab world's territories) have been mere enhancements of the original work of Ibn Muqlah. A few more styles were added from Persia and Turkey (Ottoman Empire).

The tradition of learning and teaching the secrets of the Arabic letters is something that takes three to ten years to master, depending on how much time you invest daily in practicing how to draw the letters, and apprentices are taught how to draw the letters exactly as the old masters did. There are very strict rules to follow: measurements, ratios, combinations etc.

A true master of calligraphy would accept you as a student for free, simply by agreeing to see you, usually on a weekly basis. He would ask you to write a few letters in a basic style (some of them would ask you to start by practicing drawing a single dot for a week!) and the next week you would show up with your lesson on a piece of paper with your homework drawn in colored ink (no black ink for you at this stage). Your master would evaluate it and rewrite it for you on the same paper as you follow his hand movements in a breathtaking process that would reveal to you the secrets of this beautiful art.

You would keep repeating this training for as many weeks — sometimes months — until your letters met the requirements of your master's trained eyes. Then, one day he would look at your lesson, take a different pen, dip it in pure, shiny black ink and he would write 'Ahsant' (Arabic for 'well done') and sign his name and write down the date. You can now move on to the next lesson. You should feel very proud of yourself that day, for it means you passed this lesson!

Along the way, you would not only gain your master's skills but also his perception of art, how he prefers his coffee and — if you are lucky enough — his passion for the craft. After learning all the secrets, letters, paragraph structures and how to prepare the pen and ink, you would ask your master to grant you a certification (Ijazah), which is a work of art on its own. You would write selected verses from the Koran or Hadith, usually in Thuluth style (the most complex and difficult style in Arabic calligraphy) and in Nuskh style, and you would leave a space down below your artwork for your master to state in his own writing that your writings have met the mastery requirements and you are now officially a master

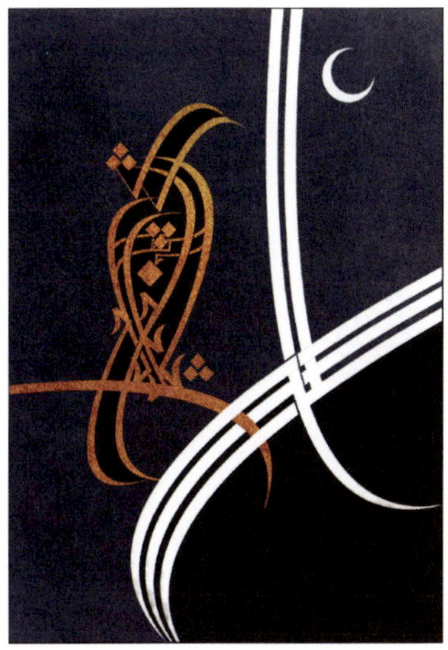
2

1. "The Oriental Pages Collection", MALIK ANAS AL-RAJAB, abstract composition, mixed media, 21 × 29.7 cm

2. "The Oriental Pages Collection", p.56, MALIK ANAS AL-RAJAB, abstract composition, digital artwork, 21 × 29.7 cm

calligrapher. From now on you can sign your own name under your writings. For you the journey has just begun, as you must keep practicing to perfect your craft and become ready to teach other students the secrets that you've been granted.

This rich tradition kept the spirit, the essence of Arabic calligraphy alive for centuries; at the same time it made it difficult for many master calligraphers to accept change. As far as I know, the attempts to develop new styles have not been so popular among calligraphers, for they see change as a threat to this solid tradition. It seems that it would certainly take much more time for master calligraphers to be more open to new experiments and incorporate their classical techniques into contemporary artworks. A few did just that and the results were sublime!

The unique form and structure of Arabic script makes it necessary to learn the basics of traditional Arabic calligraphy as a starting point to the infinite world of contemporary calligraphy. This solid foundation of tradition and understanding the spirit of the letters would give so much power, relevance and most of all depth to any experimental or contemporary approaches. I experienced the joy of studying traditional calligraphy almost fifteen years ago under the best calligraphers in Baghdad at the time (Hameed Al-Saadi and Hayder Rabee); and yes, I was also asked to practice single, double and triple dots for a week for starters! And I still have close relations with my masters today. If you ask me what the most important outcome of this journey has been I would reply: a trained eye for good calligraphy. Knowing the way of the masters and being exposed to some of their craft secrets and passion gave me an awareness of what is considered good calligraphy, typography and lettering, which are the most important aspects that you need to specialize in this fascinating art form.

1. "The Oriental Pages Collection" p.23, MALIK ANAS AL-RAJAB, abstract composition, digital artwork, 21 x 29.7 cm

It was a surprise for me as to realize that the same approach applies to many Latin calligraphers as well. Most of the best contemporary calligraphers in the Western world received their traditional training before going on to create some of my all-time favorite pieces of contemporary calligraphy. At the same time, I noticed that many calligraphy masters in the Arab world could take much from contemporary art. Knowing more about it and developing an eye for good art would make it much easier for them to use their knowledge in more contemporary pieces and would lend their calligraphy work a balance between past and present. I'm not suggesting that we should abandon this rich and great tradition; on the contrary, I'm asking that we do much more with it, as it has the power and flexibility to grow and to serve the artist in a unique way.

If we focus on a contemporary approach to Arabic calligraphy, we can see that it is not new: many brilliant master calligraphers tried to contribute their share to this evolution over the centuries, and I can mention a few of the recent contributions as a sample. All of these attempts were conducted by calligraphers who started their journey by studying and/or practicing traditional calligraphy at first, calligraphers like Mohamed S. Al-Saqar (Iraq), who designed a set of calligraphic fonts, some of which we are still using on our computers today. Some of his artworks were important steps towards contemporary calligraphy. Also, the late Khalil Al-Zahawi (Iraq) did a beautiful combination of traditional pieces composed in a contemporary layout. Khalid Al-Saee (Syria) did brilliant contemporary artworks based on Arabic letters. Of course, Hassan Massoudy (Iraq) is a name without which we could not speak of a modern contemporary calligraphy movement. His unique experience in this field, his brave stokes, elegantly composed pieces and vibrant color palette made it possible to introduce Arabic calligraphy to many — especially in the Western world — in a new, fascinating way. His works were inspirational to many, including myself. And the list could go on and on. And there is what can be considered the most promising, established, advanced and coherent contemporary contribution to Arabic calligraphy today, which came not from within the Arab world but from outside. It came from Iran, where we can find a perfectly balanced wave of contemporary art that made use of all the richness of both worlds, calligraphy and contemporary art. This movement can be very interesting to observe, learn from and follow as well.

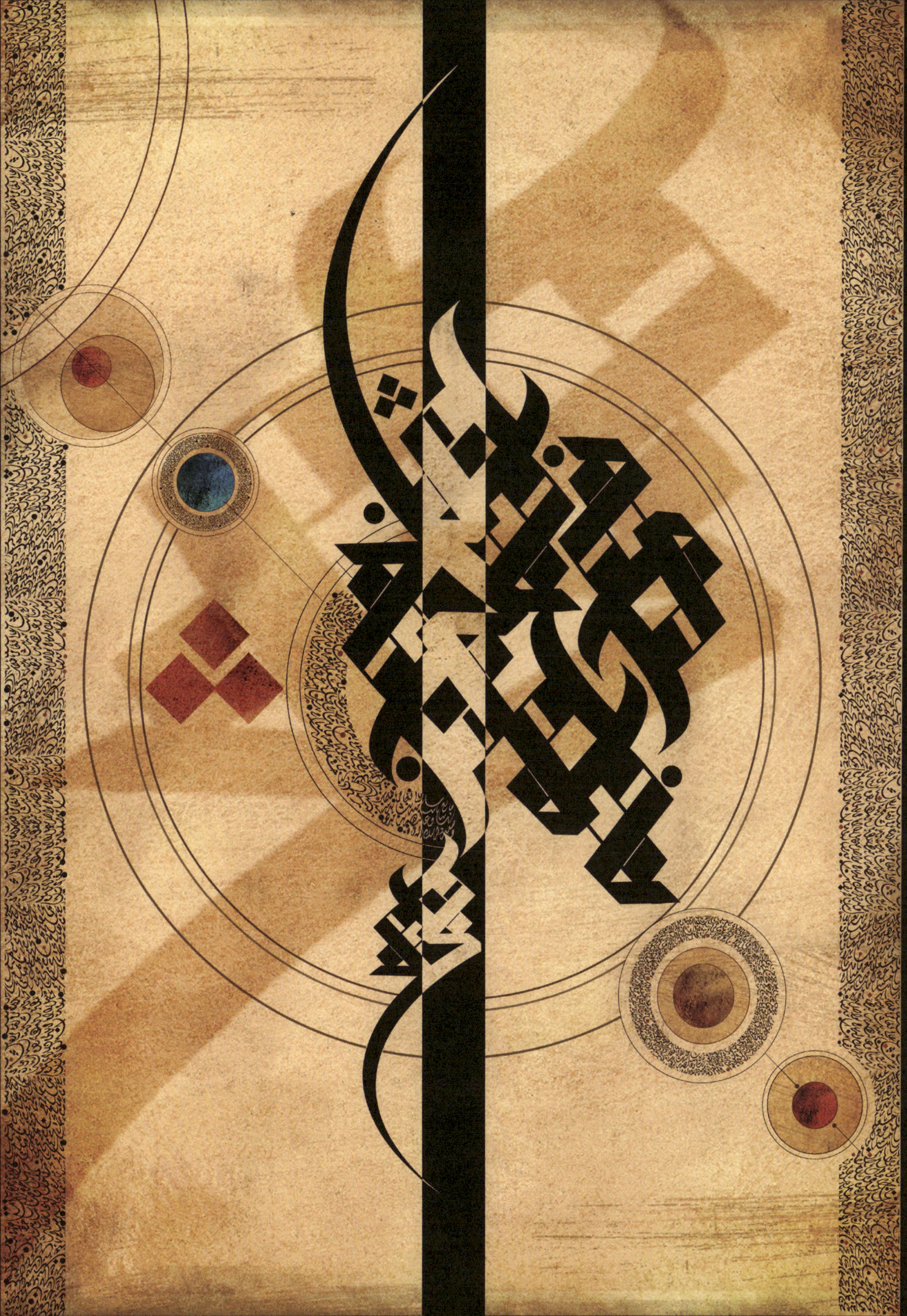

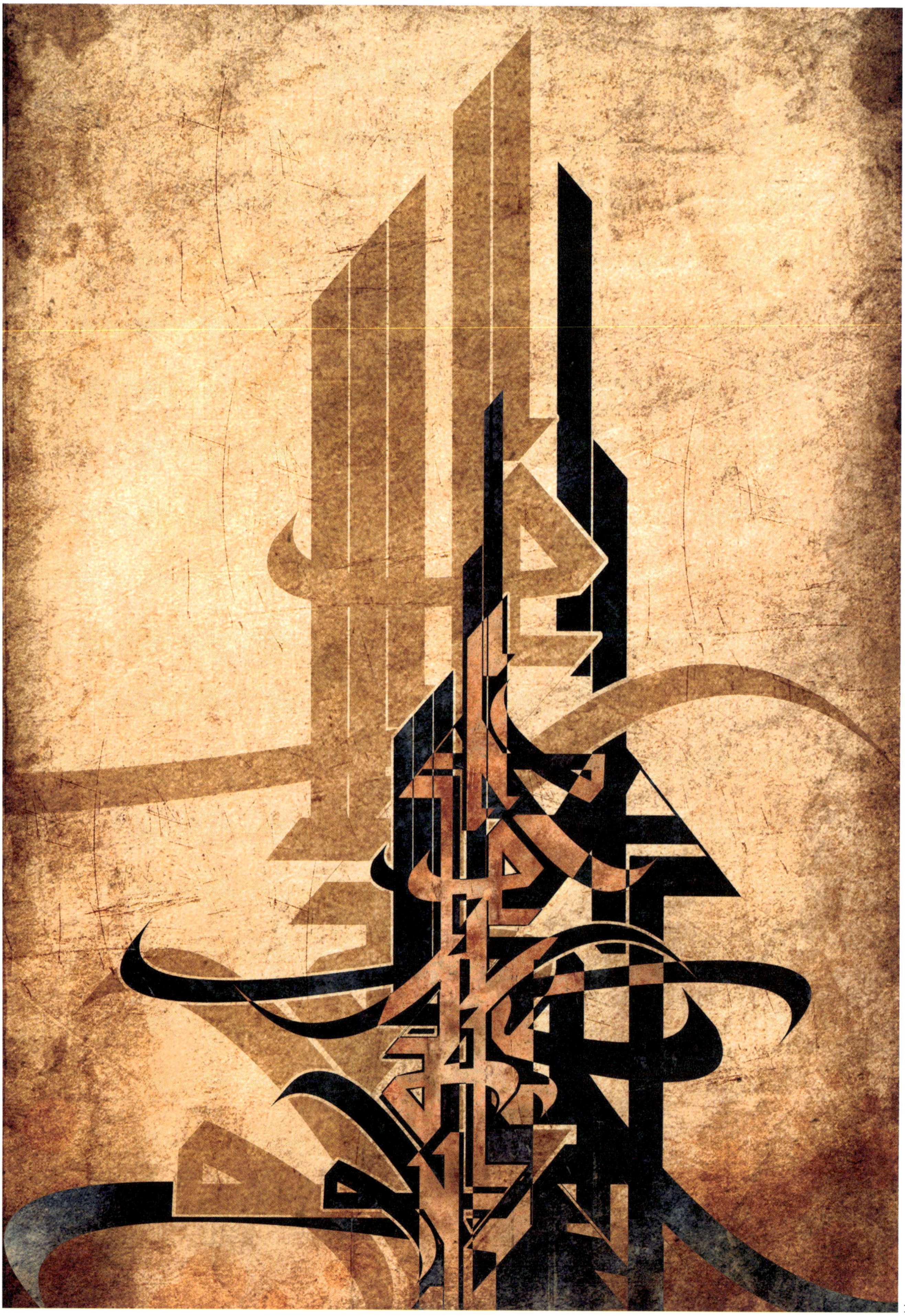

1

In recent years one can sense a growing interest in typography and contemporary calligraphy as a medium of expression and an art form. This interest paved the way (in the Arab world, Persia and Turkey) for some artists to try to do more explorations with the help of digital art, which grew immensely and provided an excellent platform for art and graphic design. The result was an interesting combination of traditional and new approaches fused together in a different yet promising contemporary/experimental calligraphy.

Yet the growing interest that I'm pointing out here is different from what was it like twenty years ago, as it is coming from a younger generation of artists who discovered the potential of their tradition at an early stage and have bravely tried to do more experimental variations on the subject. The pace of this movement is slow yet steady and has been gaining speed over the years, as we are able to share our thoughts, work and experiments. Now more than ever before, we are witnessing more and more of this contemporary art form, in which calligraphy plays the lead role.

Graffiti is certainly an important aspect and result of this marriage between old and new. It's a growing phenomenon in some Arab countries as a form of art and expression, and I believe that Arabic calligraphy has the flexibility to add to this growing form of art. However, we will enjoy it much more if we first develop our understanding of, appreciation for and sensibility towards the beauty of Arabic calligraphy.

1. "The Oriental Pages Collection", p.60, MALIK ANAS AL-RAJAB, abstract composition, digital artwork, 29.7×42 cm

2. "The Oriental Pages Collection", p.65, MALIK ANAS AL-RAJAB, abstract composition, digital artwork, 29.7×42 cm

Following pages:

1. "The Oriental Pages Collection", p.22, MALIK ANAS AL-RAJAB, abstract composition, mixed media, 21×29.7 cm

الإنسان الخيّر محق وعادل ولكن ليس جامداً
ولا متحجرا ، يعرف كيف ينثني دون ان ينحني

2. "The good man is right and just, but not stiff and inflexible, and he knows how to bend but not bow." Quote by Confucius, HASSAN MASSOUDY, calligraphy on paper

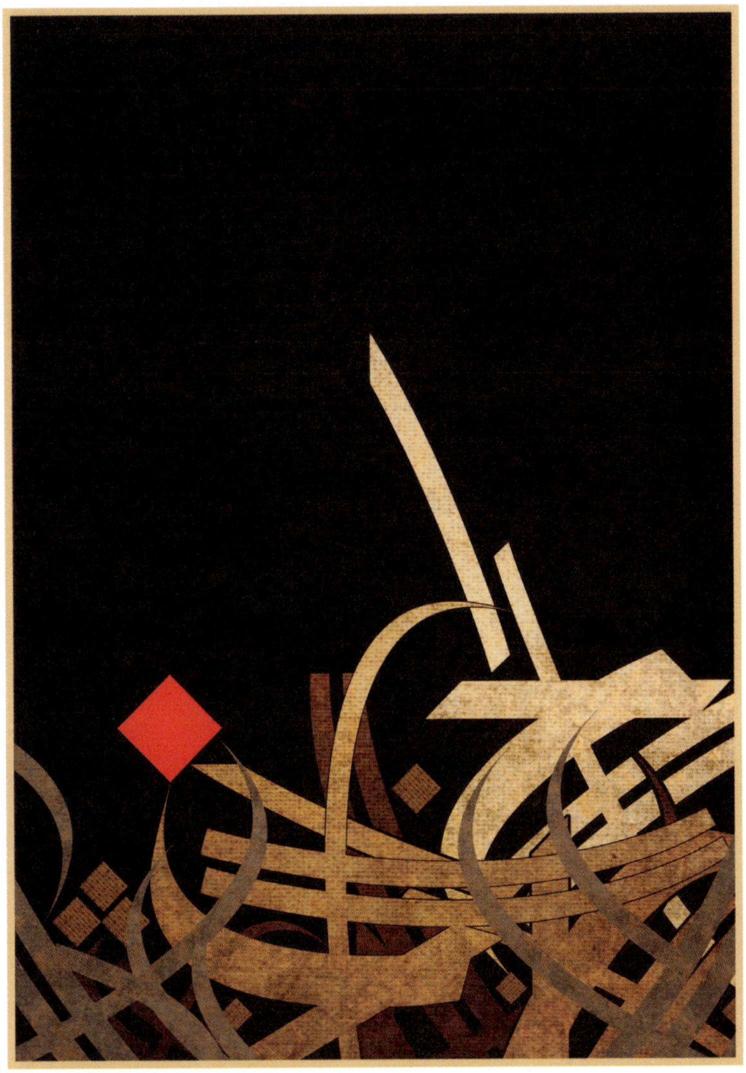
2

• MALIK ANAS AL-RAJAB

Born 1976 in Baghdad, Iraq

Malik Anas Al-Rajab is a contemporary calligrapher, art director and graphic designer. He is a member of the Society of Iraqi Calligraphers. His personal experience with contemporary calligraphy began after years of working with traditional calligraphy. Eventually he became interested in graphic design, and while learning the tools, he noticed the potential of using graphic design techniques together with his previous experience as a calligrapher. He started to appreciate contemporary art in general and contemporary calligraphy of the Arabic, Latin and Asian scripts. This increased his already strong appreciation and feel for the abstract components of the art of writing. The act of leaving a human trace through calligraphy and writing is something that he has always been fascinated with. In some works he does the basic layout by brush first and then puts digital finishes on it. Over the years he has developed his methods and is able to do most of his artwork using a digital pen. His works are abstract compositions that resemble Arabic letters and words. He wants to break the language barrier and tries to make several interpretations of a single artwork possible to the eye of the beholder. At the same time, he focuses on the Oriental spirit in his art, which has become one of his most important goals.

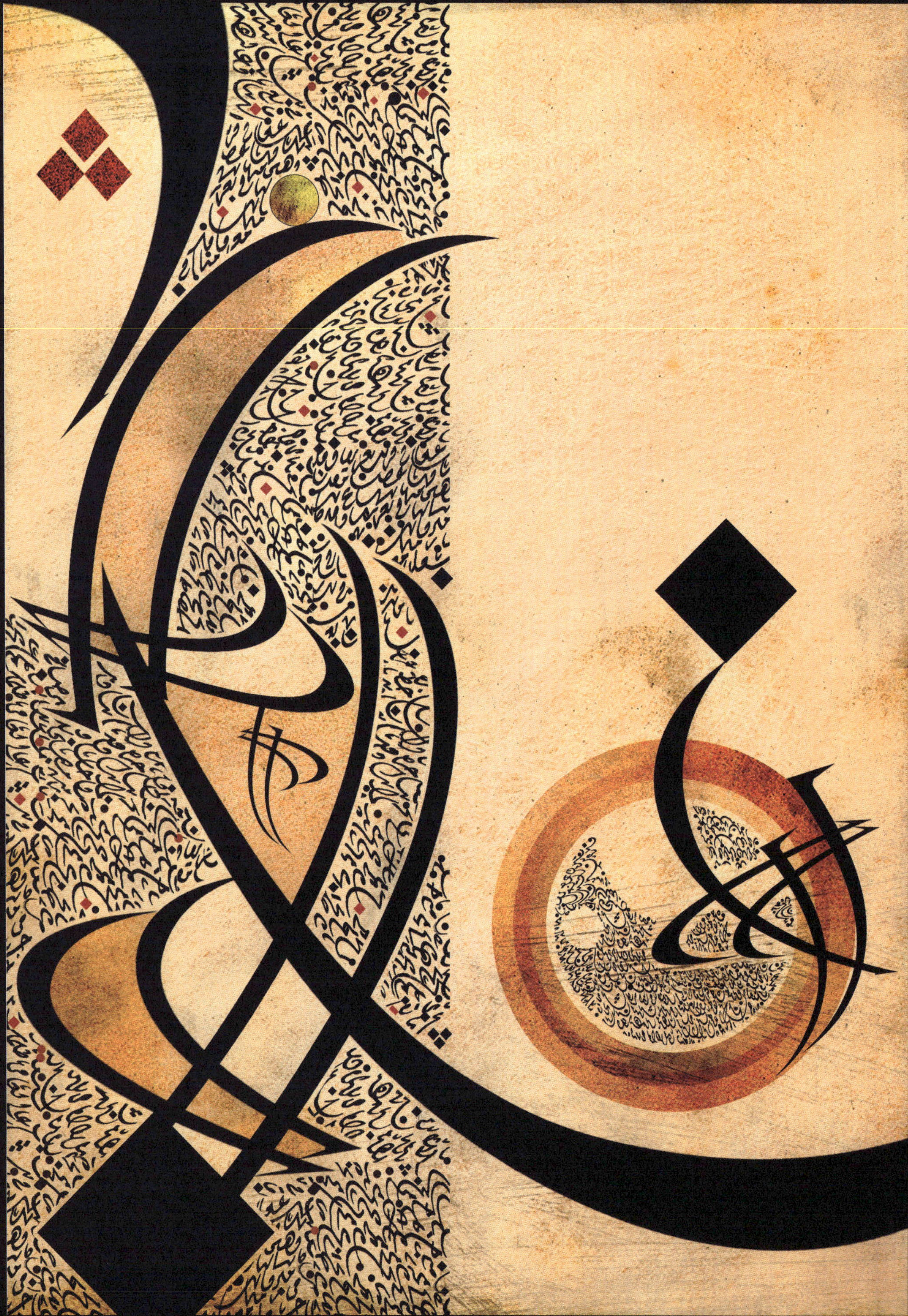

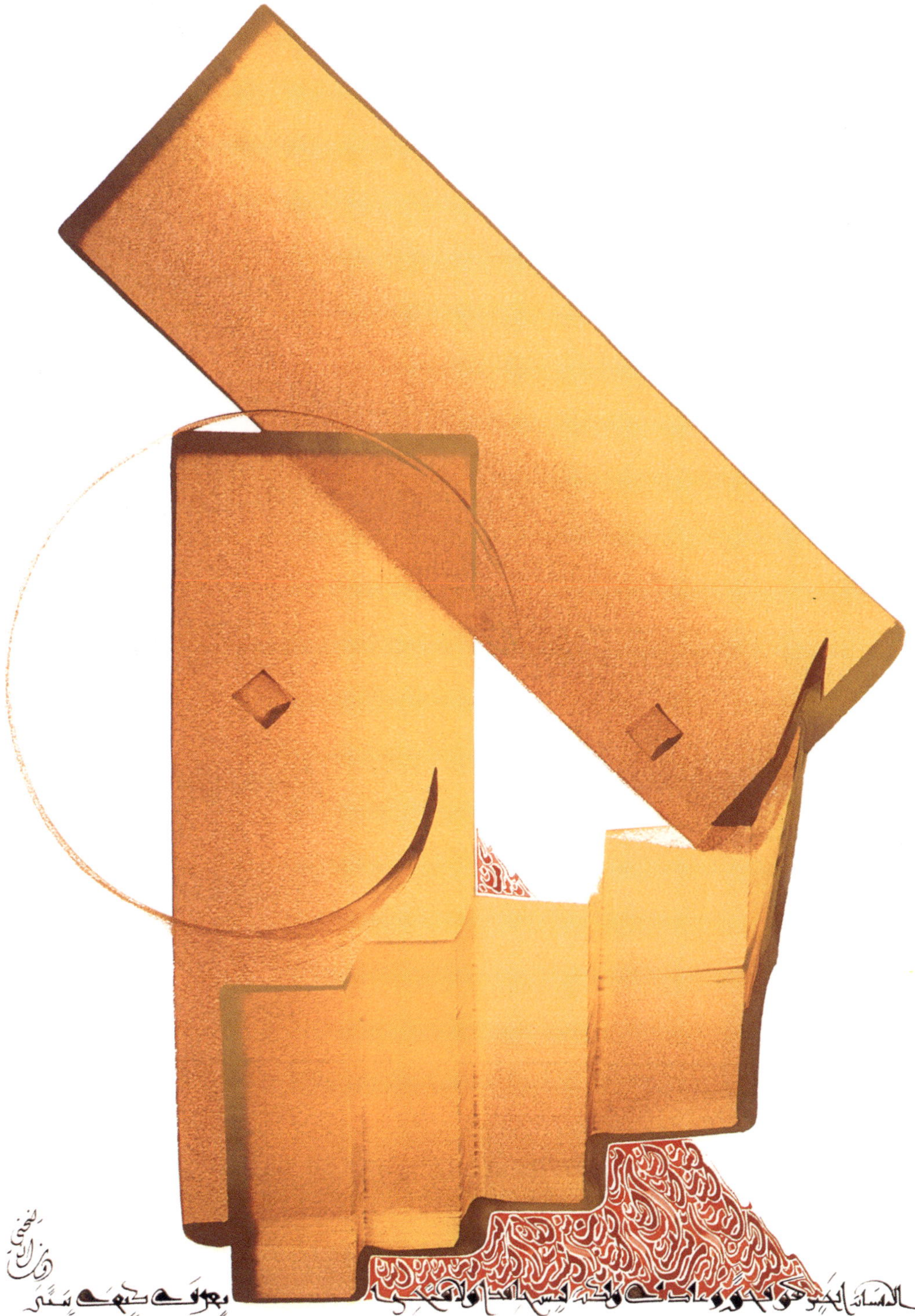

2

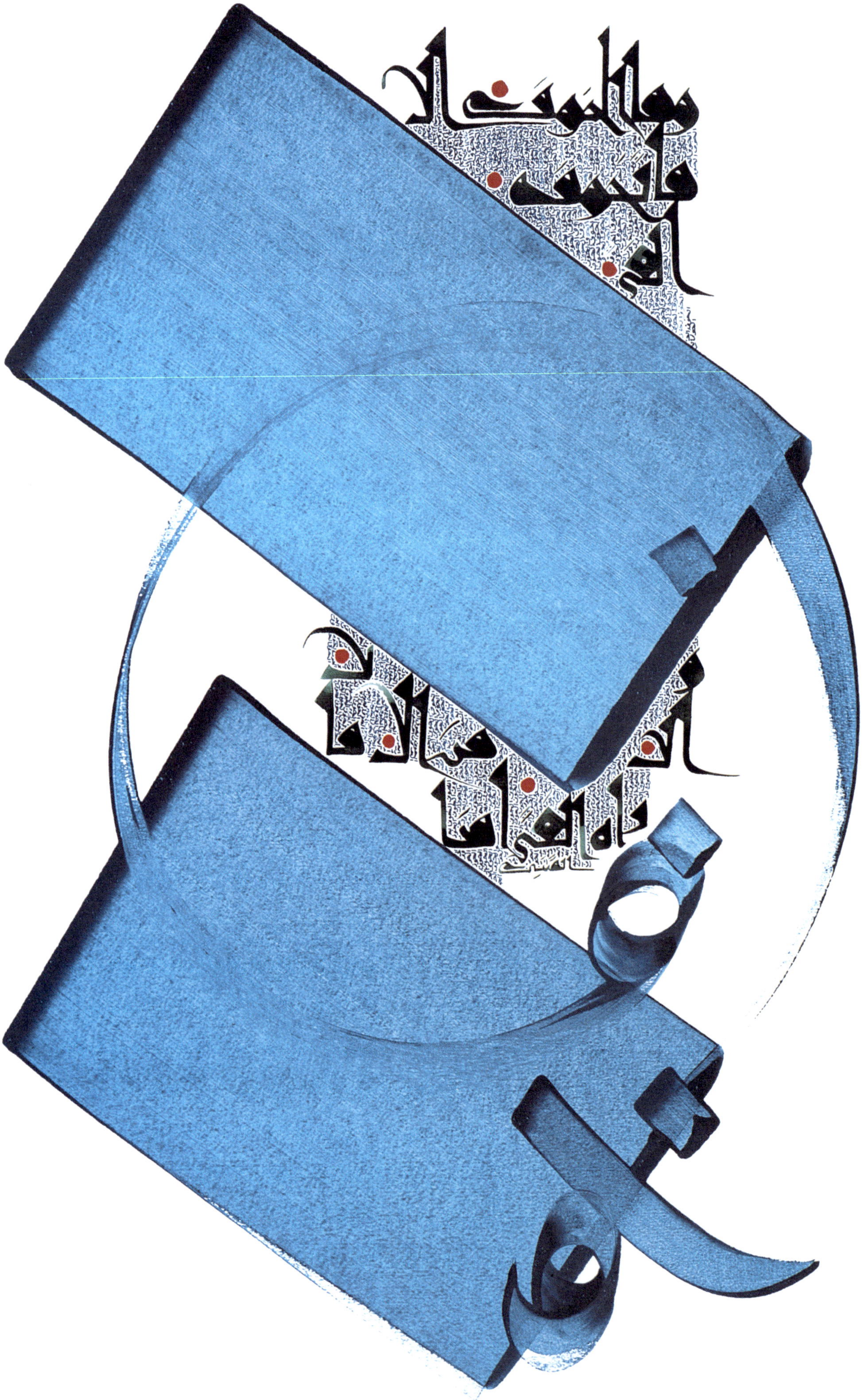

1

1·4
Two Daughters of the Same Parents
ابنتان للوالدين نفسيهما

Hassan Massoudy

وما الخوف إلا ما تخوَّفَهُ الفتى،
ولا الأمن إلا ما رآه الفتى أمنا. (المتنبّي)

1. "Fear is what is imagined by man, and security is what is deemed secure by him." Quote from al-Moutanabbi, HASSAN MASSOUDY, calligraphy on paper

The Arabic calligraphy I do literally comes directly from the heart, the movement of my arm and the heartbeat work together. When I direct the brush, I stop breathing. This also limits the size of the calligraphy: a brushstroke cannot last longer than it takes my heart to beat. So most Arabic calligraphy is limited to a diameter of maybe one, two meters. If the writing becomes any bigger, it has to be constructed and thus it is not calligraphy anymore, but a design. Other limitations are the size of the paper and the tools. When I painted a mural with the French graffiti writer Marko 93 — the only time I did try to do actual graffiti — I discovered the fluidity of the spray can, which suddenly allowed me to do a continues gesture of five meters before stopping a stroke.

Arabic calligraphy and graffiti are two daughters of the same parents. They live their separate, independent lives, but they are related in many ways. Obviously both are about the use of letters and their alphabets, and their center of gravity is the beauty of writing. For both, a letter is more than just a letter and they fill them with emotions. The use of empty space and composition within this space is something else they have in common. The resemblance of Arabic calligraphy and graffiti is most obvious in tags, because here the tools — ink and pen — are quite the same. Gestures are also done with the whole body and are in sync with breathing. The movement of writing graffiti leaves the restrictions of the paper — it is like a dance in front of a wall.

Arabic calligraphy is the more conservative sister, bound to thousands of years of tradition and knowledge. When I started to do my contemporary calligraphy, there were some who did not like what I did, because I also bent the rules, starting with the colors and freeing myself from the strict forms of the letters. Over the years my art became more and more accepted, also by conservative calligraphers. Graffiti has more freedom from traditions, even if it is not without rules.

Calligraphy plays a social and political role in society, but graffiti does this in a more forceful way. Calligraphers are accepted and integrated in society, whereby graffiti writers act against the law; they impose and take over the streets, thus becoming more powerful. This power can be good for our society, with accomplished artists who offer their art for free and creative kids expressing themselves in a society where artistic education plays a far too little role.

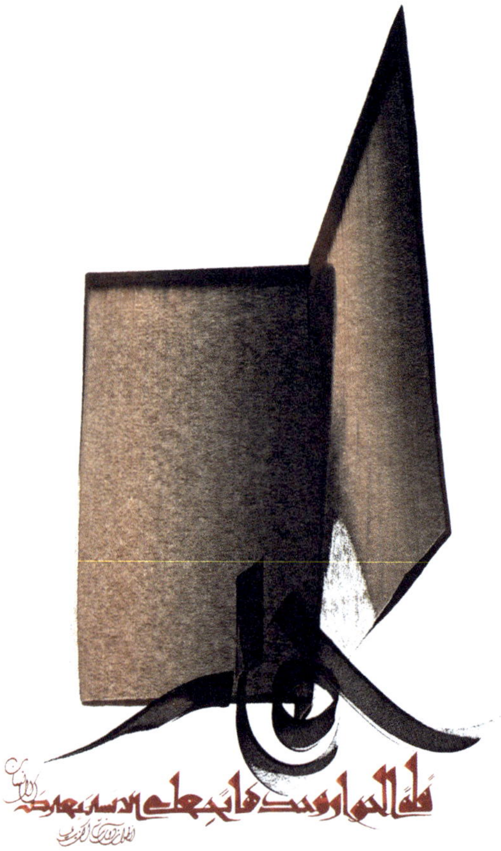

1

قلة الحوار وحدها تجعل
الإنسان يعارض الإنسان

1. "Only an insufficient language opposes the people to each other, for what they wish does not vary." Quote from Saint Exupéry, HASSAN MASSOUDY, calligraphy on paper

لقد دأب العنف على إنجاب العنف

2. "Violence breeds violence", quote from Aeschylus, HASSAN MASSOUDY, calligraphy on paper

يولد الإنسان حراً ولكنه مقيدٌ
في الحديد. (جان جاك روسّو)

3. "Man is born free and yet everywhere he is in chains." Quote from Jean-Jacques Rousseau, HASSAN MASSOUDY, calligraphy on paper

Following pages 34 & 35:

Graffiti mural inspired by Hassan Massoudy, FANTOM, ETHER & STARE, Al-Omah Al-Islamiah Mosque, Montréal, 2005

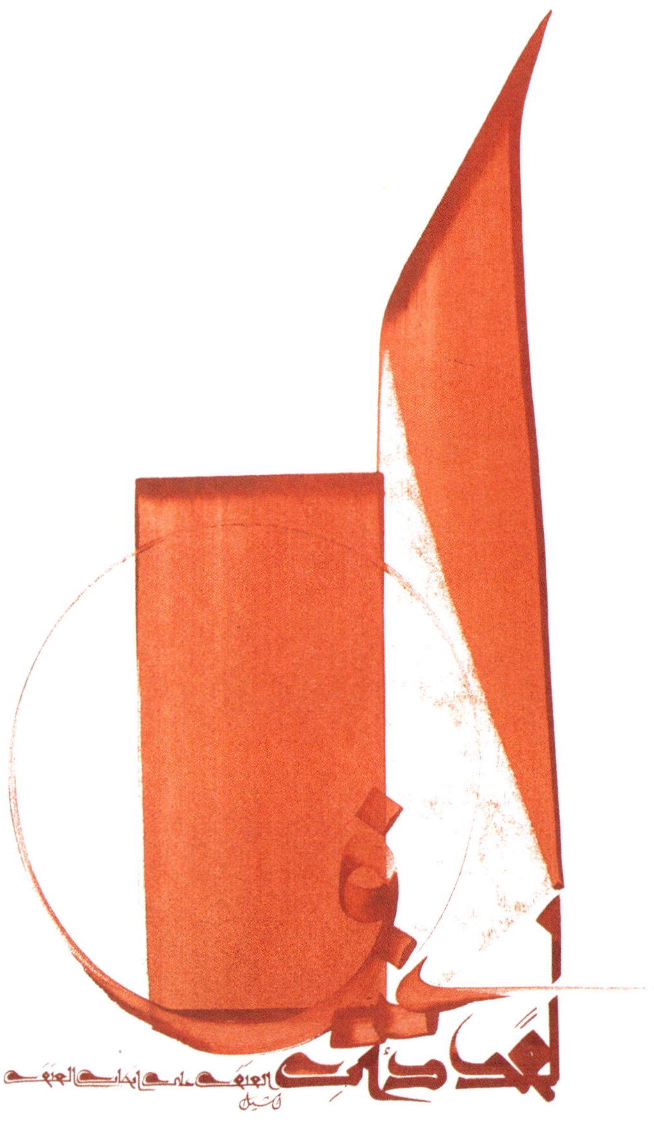

2

• HASSAN MASSOUDY

Born in 1944 in Najef, Iraq, lives in Paris

Hassan Massoudy grew up in the scalding heat of the desert, in a traditional Iraqi society characterized by strong religious beliefs, a sense of solidarity and a love for festive gatherings. As a youngster, in this town where all images were prohibited, he fulfilled his passion for art by making drawings and calligraphy while investing his energy in getting materials.
In 1961 he left for Baghdad and started working as an apprentice for various calligraphers. He was fascinated by modern art and started to dream of studying art. The unfolding political events and ensuing dictatorship prevented him from doing so. He eventually left Iraq for France in 1969, freed from the oppressing regime but heartbroken. He studied at the Ecole des Beaux-Arts in Paris. In 1972, he created the show "Arabesque" with the actor Guy Jacquet, and a few years later the musician Fawzy Al Aiedy joined. "Arabesque" was a performance combining music and poetry together with calligraphy projections. They performed across France and Europe over a period of thirteen years.
This marked a definite turn in Hassan Massoudy's work. His calligraphy became swifter and his gesture richer. He continued to be involved in performance with his show "Calligraphie d'ombre et de lumiere" (calligraphy of light and shadow), in which calligraphy was created for live audiences. The aesthetic, geometry and rhythms of the calligraphy were unveiled, giving birth to poetry. He created the design of the stage set for the ballet "Selim" with the dancer Kader Belarbi from the Opera de Paris and the singer Houria Aichi. In 2005 he met the dancer and choreographer Carolyn Carlson, and the musician Kudsi Erguner. Together with three other dancers and musicians, they created the show "Metaphore", a harmony of music, dance and calligraphy.
Creations from Hassan Massoudy are a subtle mix of present and past, Oriental and Occidental art, tradition and modernity. He perpetuates tradition while breaking from it. Over the years he has purified and simplified the lines of his drawing. The words and phrases he draws come from poets and writers from all over the world or sometimes simply from popular wisdom. All of his work is strongly inspired by a humanistic interest.

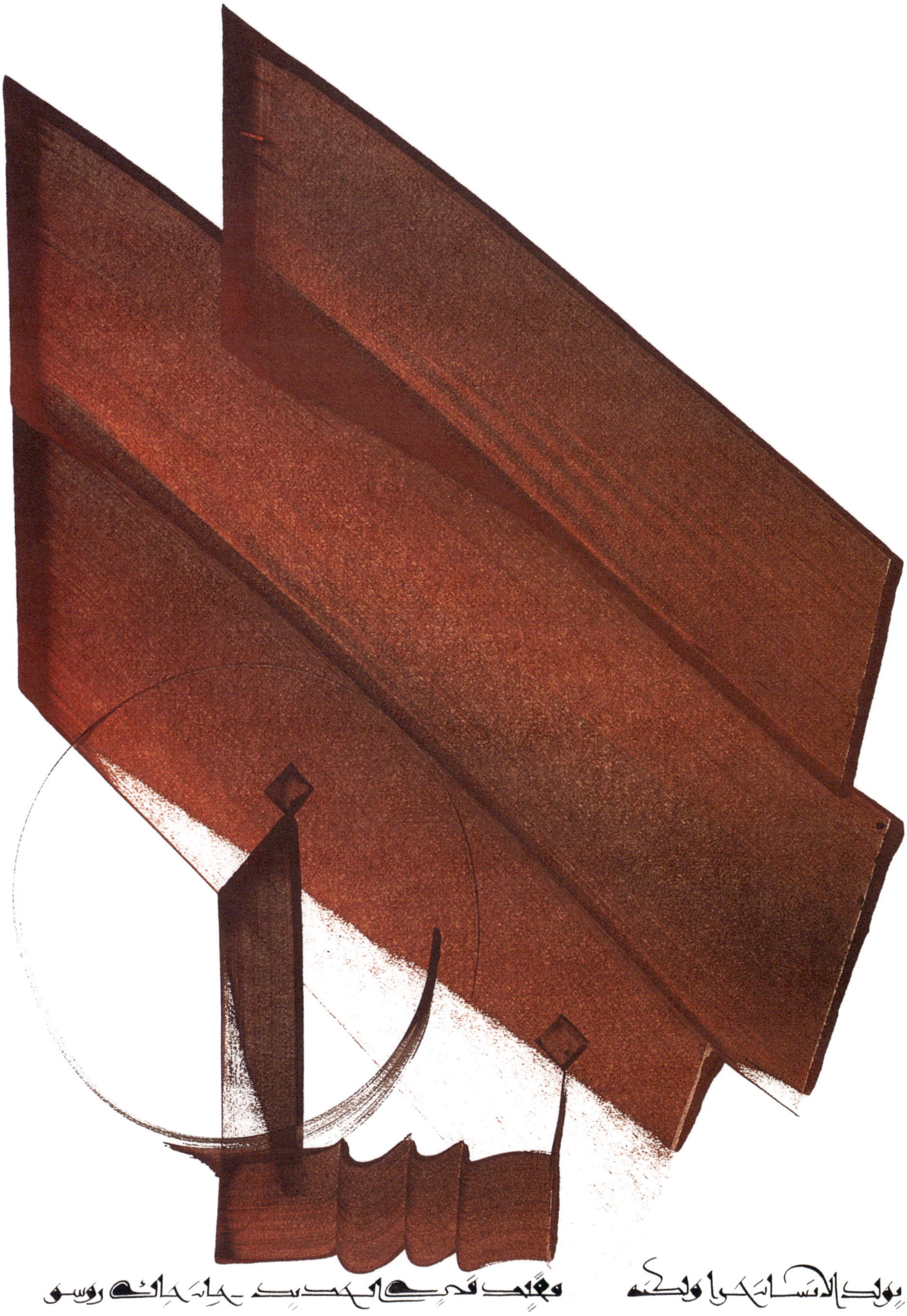

3

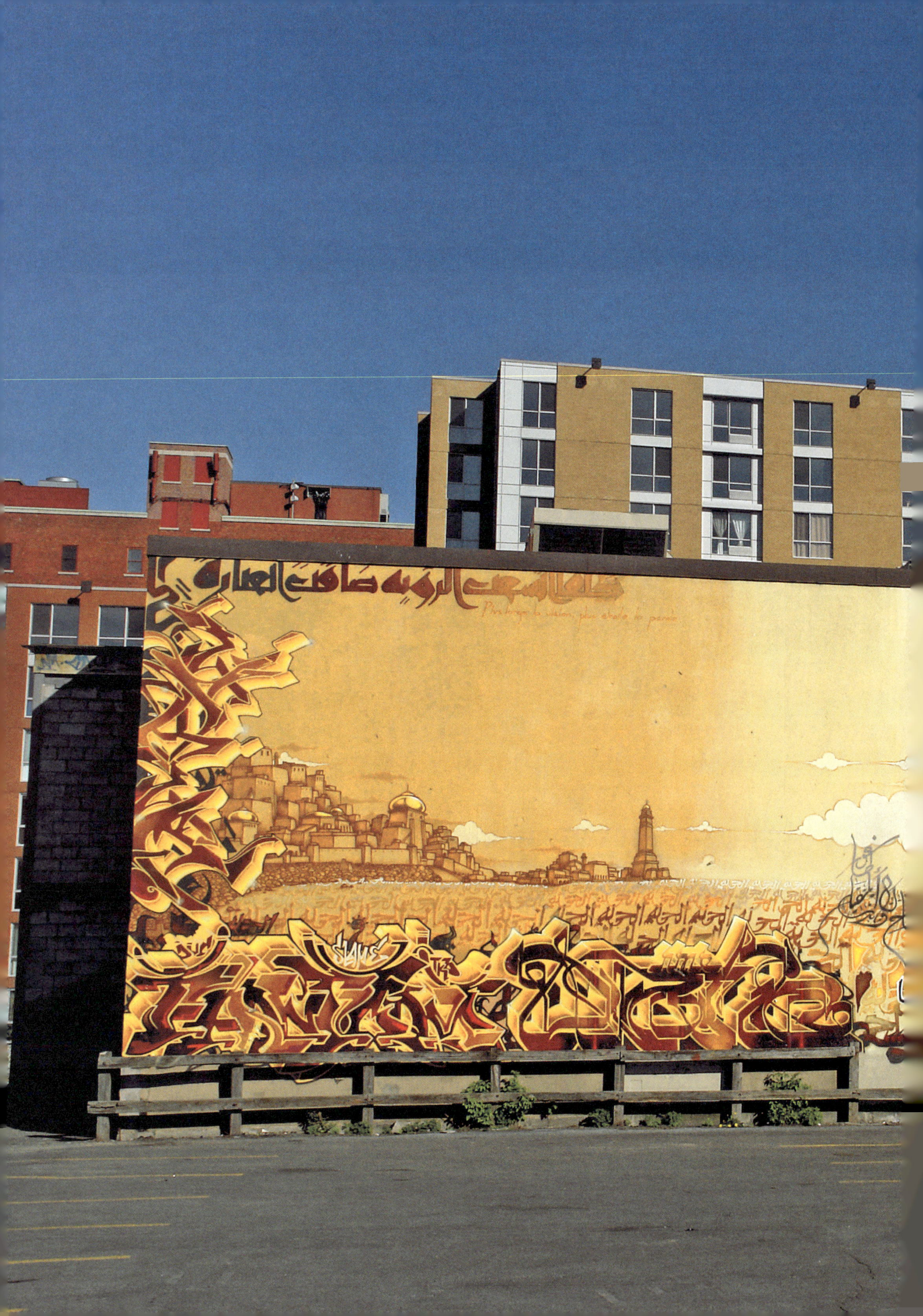

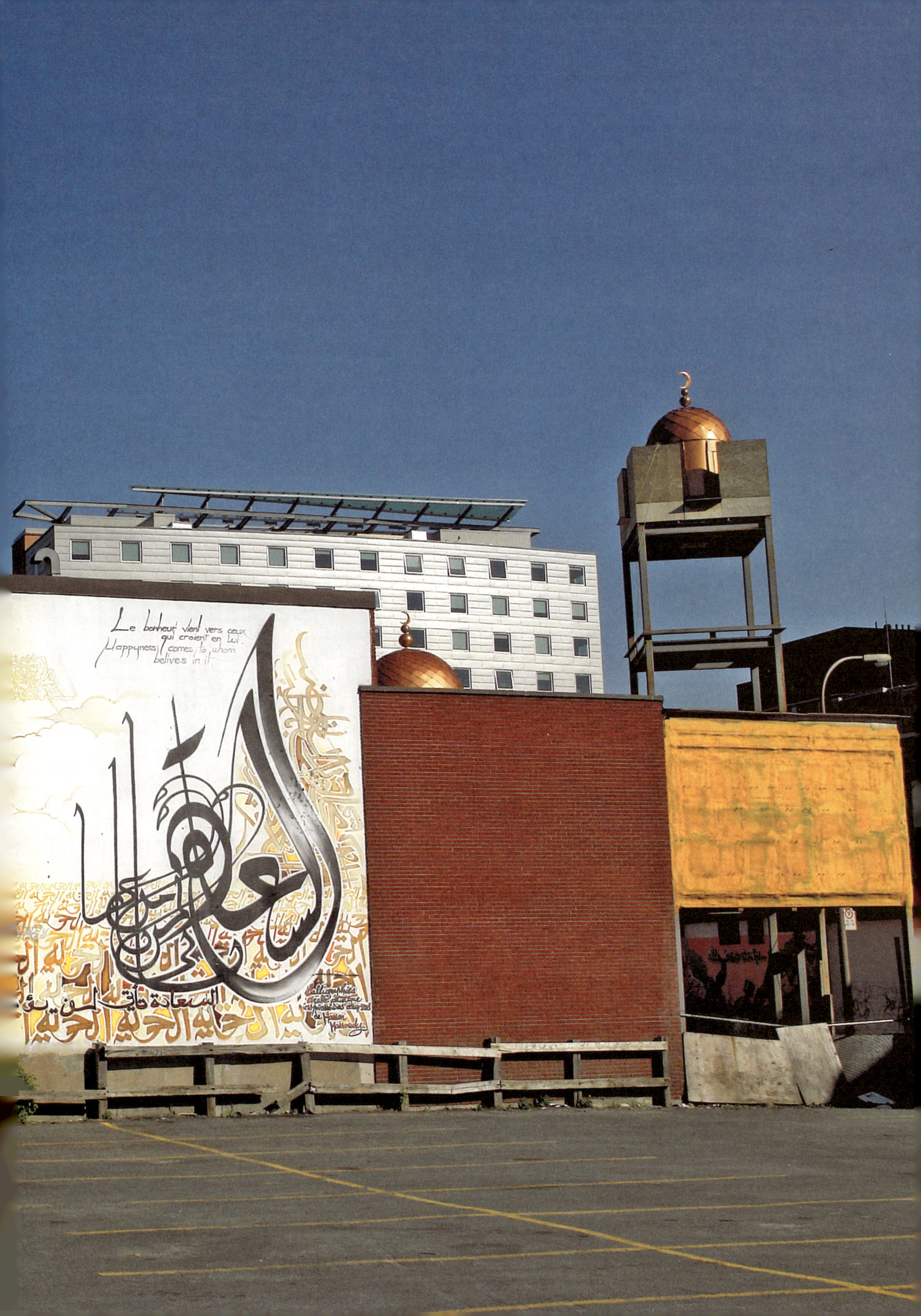
Le bonheur vient vers ceux qui croient en lui.
Happyness comes to whom belives in it.
السعادة تأتي لمن يؤمن بها

Public Art & Graffiti in the Middle East

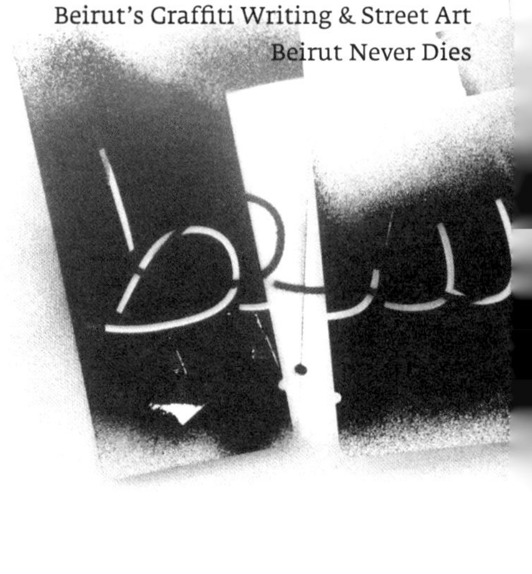

2.

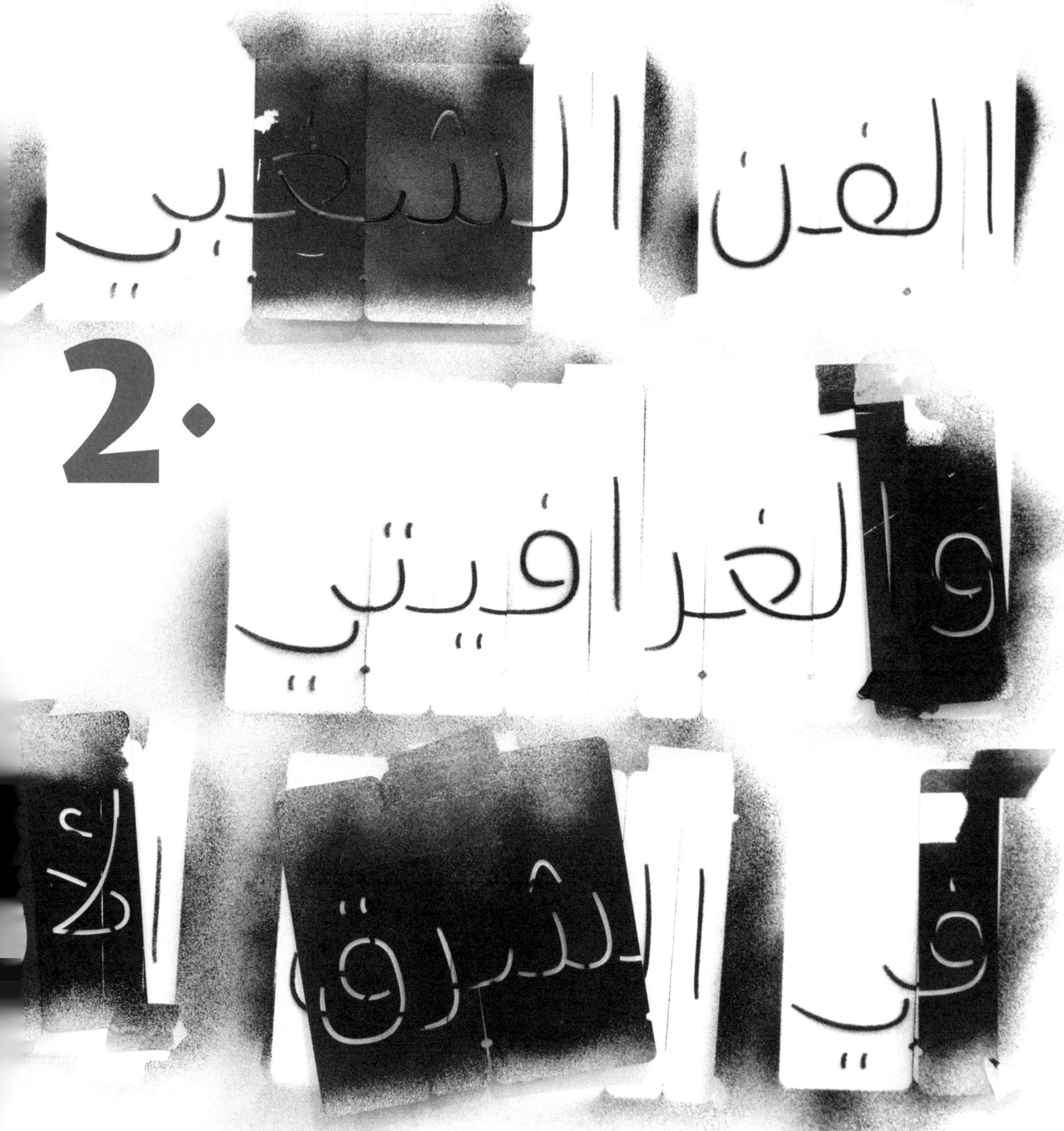

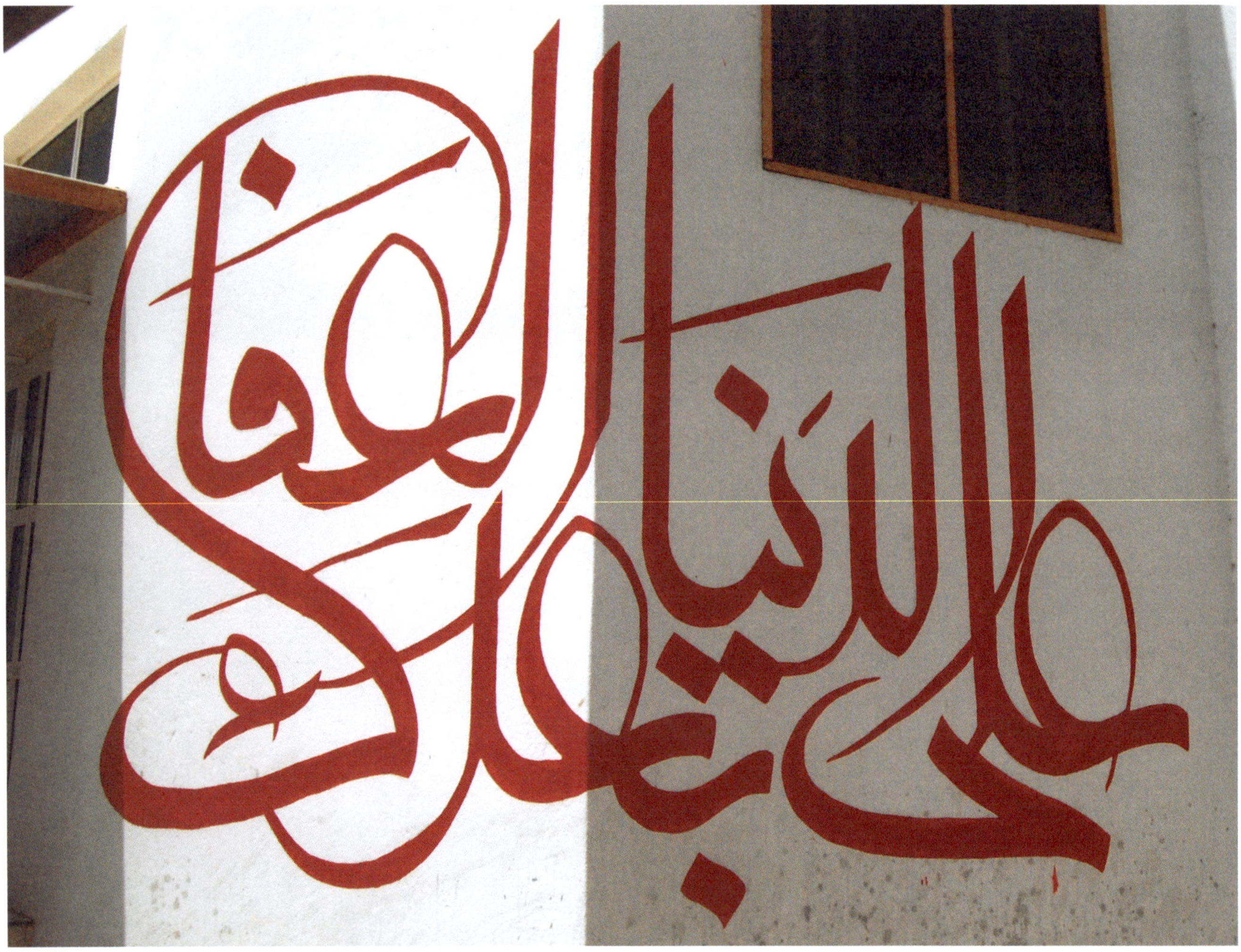
1

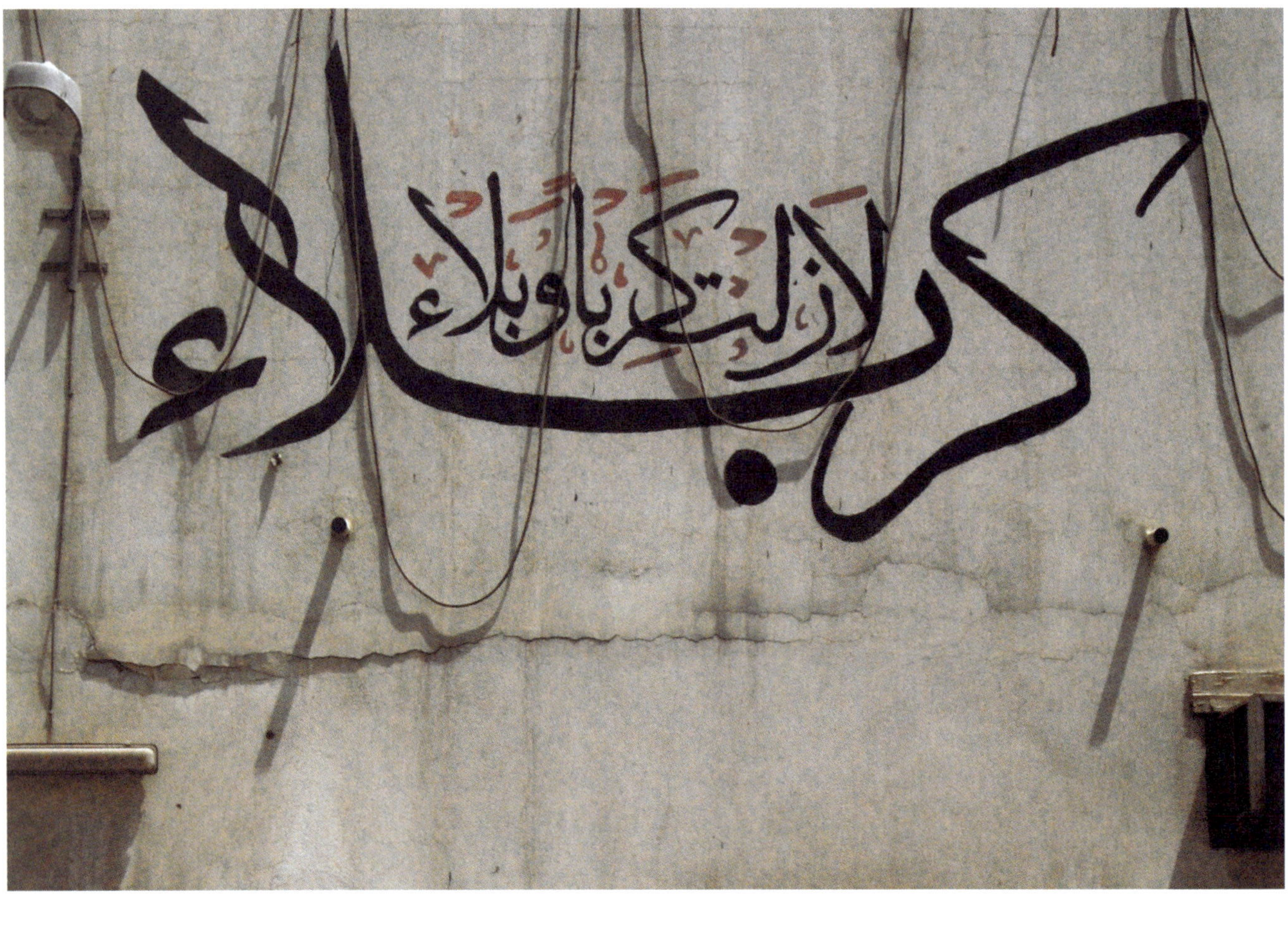
2

2·1
Bahrain's Calligraphic Messages
رسائل التخطيط البحرينية

Rana Jarbou

In this small desert kingdom in the Persian Gulf, stories from the present and past can be found on the walls of its hidden village communities which highlight an obvious territorial divide in its urban space. On the main roads, only signs and advertisements can be found on the clean, white walls. At times, angry cries are written on these walls, though they are instantly painted over. These expressions have found a temporary medium for venting social outrage, which is in constant flux. This medium then becomes a silenced narrative of a vital and much-needed discourse. Ultimately these expressions cannot be subdued as they are driven back to their sources, only to be uttered time and again.

In the closed off village communities, the expressions on the walls are left uncensored, reaching their different audiences despite the intention of some to address the authorities. The letters take on human characteristics, as graffiti shapes and fonts are conceptualized according to their different motives. Religious scriptures, aphorisms and historic references are written in colorful calligraphy. Influences range from the resistance in Lebanon, to stories from Karbala, to idols in Iran. A sense of belonging is manifested in these calligraphic writings, as graffiti writers reveal their identities and mark their existence through them. There is an abundance of glorifications of Hussain, the 'martyr of martyrs' and symbol of resistance, and commemorations of the battle of Karbala in the villages. These emphasize the Shiite identity and its affiliations, which continue to inspire their present day resistance and struggles. Their ultimate sacrifice for the ultimate cause, human dignity, is beautifully painted in different decorative forms.

على الدنيا بعدك العفاء
1. "After you, let dust cover this world", unknown artist, Abu Saiba, Sar, Bahrain, 2008

كربلاء لازلت كربا و بلاء
2. "Karbala, you are still an agony and scourge", unknown artist, Abu Saiba, Bahrain, 2008

لا يوم كيومك يا أبا عبد الله
3. "There is no day like your day, O Aba Abdullah", unknown artist, Abu Saiba, Bahrain, 2008

يا حسين
4. "O Hussain", unknown artist, Abu Saiba, Bahrain, 2008

3
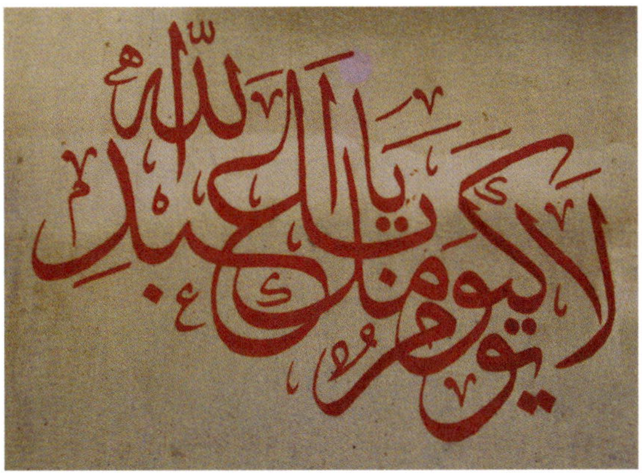

4
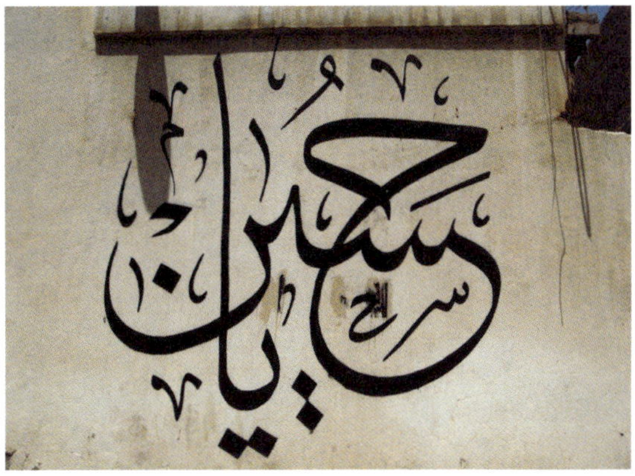

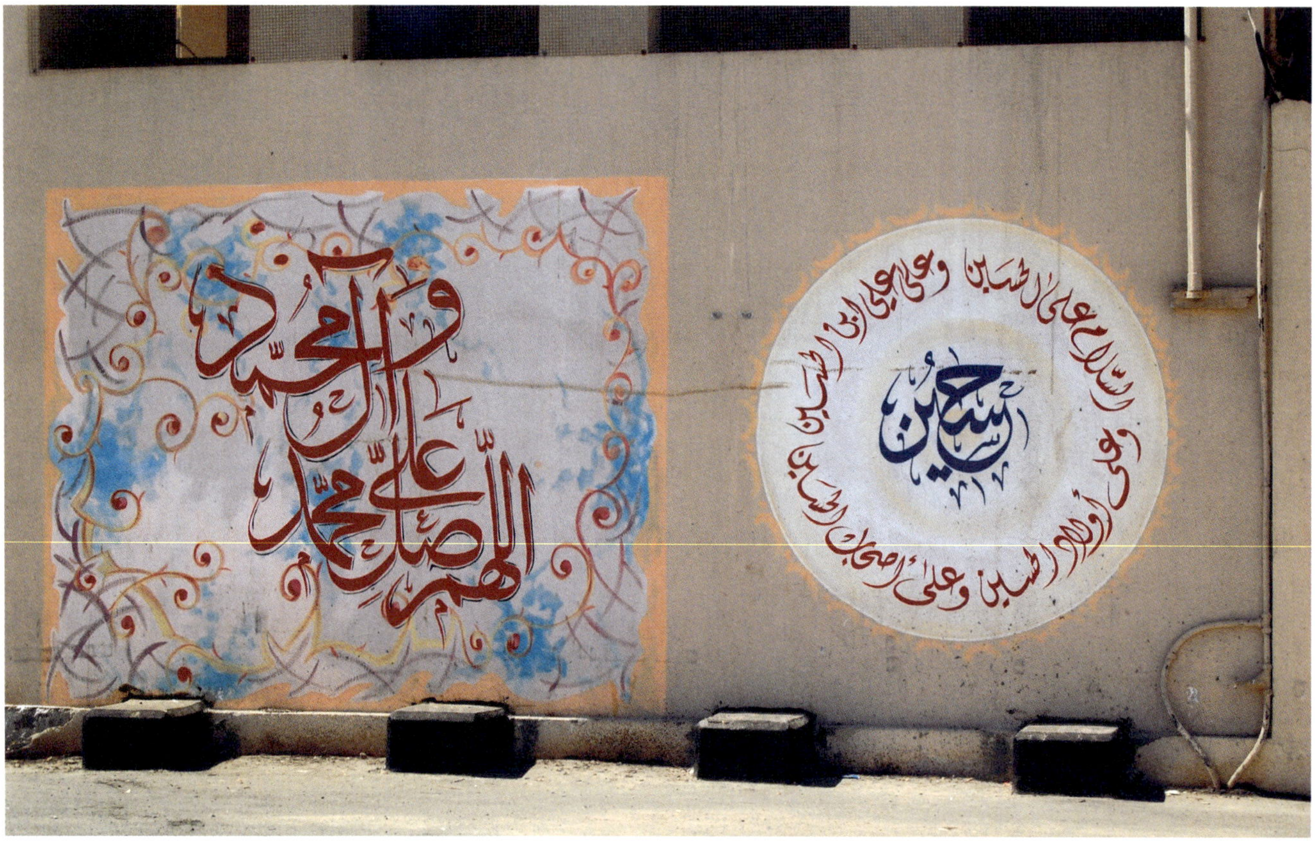

1

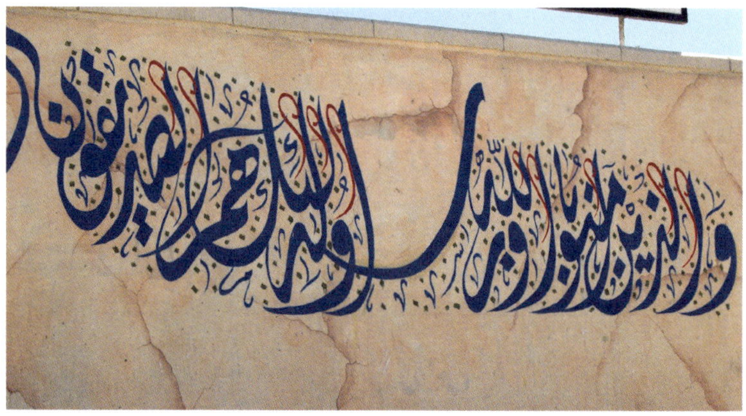

2

Messages such as "the Bahraini Hezbollah will not stop", written on a wall along with references honoring Hezbollah leader Hassan Nasrallah, imply yet another seed of influence and motivation. The large format supplication "here I am at Thy service, O Nasrallah" is neatly written next to a painted Hezbollah flag in the heart of Manama. On the upper half of the wall, a Palestinian flag is painted with the saying "Jerusalem is ours". Broad support of Ayatollah Khomeini is also apparent in the island's capital. These regional influences signify the impact of the historical transitions on this young country.

Dissenting graffiti is characterized by the anger and destructiveness visible in its vivid written form. Sectarian tensions between a marginalized Shiite majority and a Sunni elite and ruling minority are expressed on walls. In a general sense, the sectarian nature of written dissent displays the unequal education and employment opportunities among Bahrainis as well as their undermined representation and participation in the political process. More specific are demands for the release of political prisoners. Stenciled graffiti images of Hasan Mushaima, the leader and secretary general of the opposition group Haq Movement for Liberty and Democracy, were repeatedly sprayed on the walls during his imprisonment in 2009 with slogans such as: "Free our prisoners", "Al Mushaima is the red line", "Mushaima is the voice of the deprived", "In the hearts, O prisoner, victory is near" etc. Mushaima is merely a symbol and one of many political prisoners.

Demands to free the prisoners as well as torture claims have often been discounted and regarded as barbarous and uncivilized, though they seem to be in line with international human rights organizations such as Amnesty International and Human Rights Watch. The authorities call it corruption and terrorism in an attempt to avoid confrontation. Yet problems with division have been further intensified recently, demonstrating that the notion of identity is at stake with respect to power sharing. "Free the innocent people" is repeatedly sprayed on the walls along with posters of new detainees.

اللهمّ صلِّ على محمد وآل محمد

1. Left side: "O God bestow your blessing upon Mohammad and the family of Mohammad"

السلام على الحسين وعلى علي ابن الحسين
وعلى أولاد الحسين وعلى أصحاب الحسين

Right side: "Peace be upon Hussain and Ali son of Hussain and the children of Hussain and the friends of Hussain", unknown artists, Sar, Bahrain, 2008

والذين آمنوا بالله
ورسوله أولئك هم الصدّيقون

2. "And those who believe in God and His Messenger, they are the righteous ones", unknown artist, Sar, Bahrain, 2008

3. Stencils of Ahmed Issa Qassim & Al Jamri, unknown artist, Diraz, Bahrain, 2008

4. Stencil of Abdul Amir al Jamri, unknown artist, Diraz, Bahrain, 2008

سجونهم مليئة بالأنفس البريئة

5. "Their prisons are filled with innocent lives", unknown artist, Sar, Bahrain, 2008

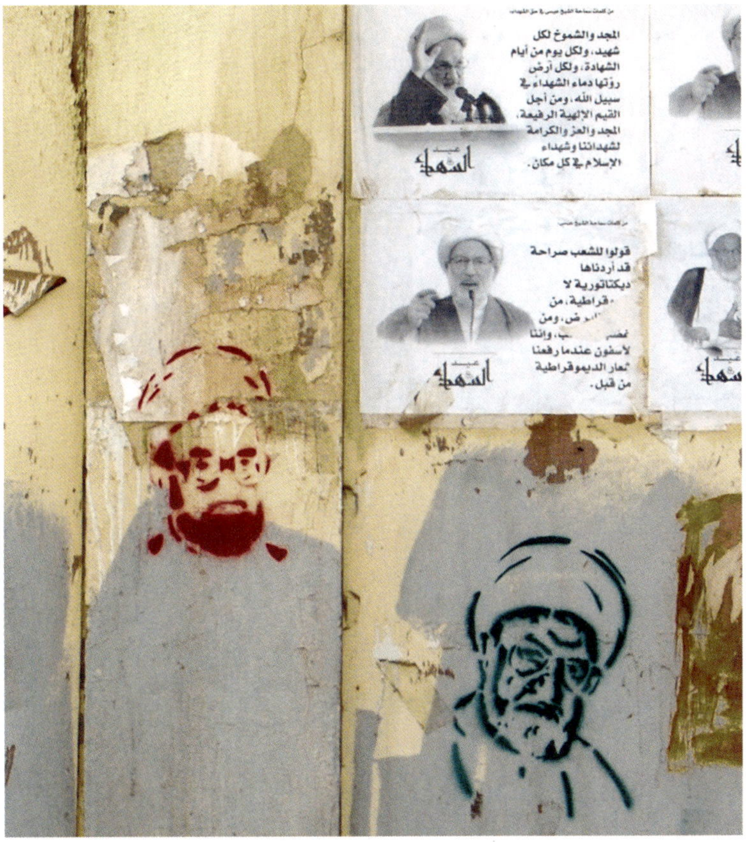
3

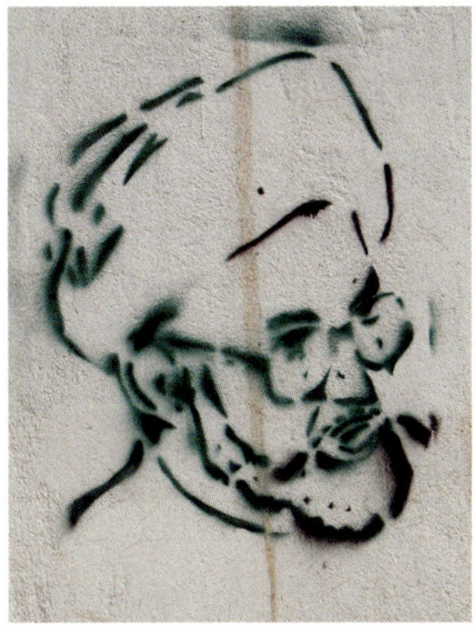
4

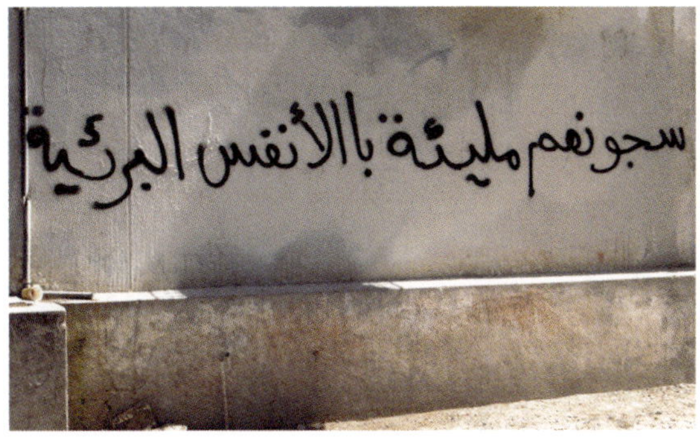

5

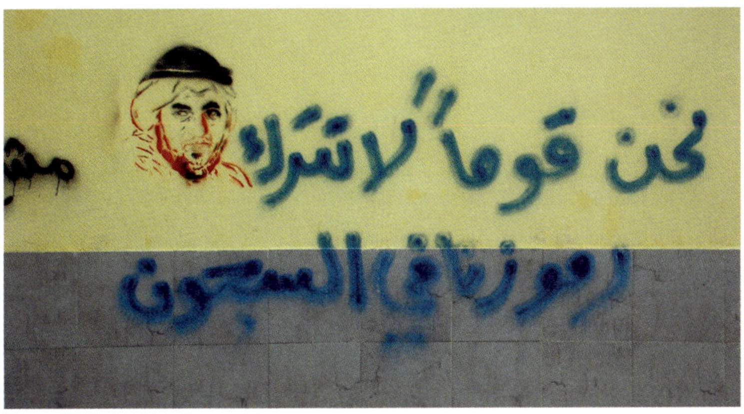

6

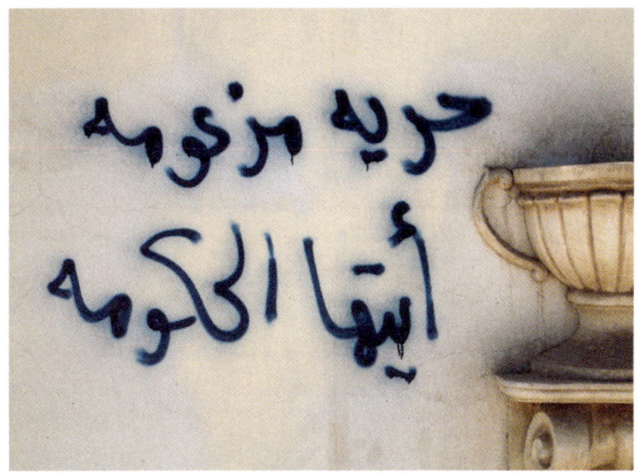

7

نحن قوماً (كذا) لا نترك رموزنا في السجون
6. "We are a people whose leaders are not left in prisons", stencil of Hasan Mushaima, unknown artist, Sar, Bahrain, 2009

حرية مزعومة أيتها الحكومة
7. "Alleged freedom, O government", unknown artist, Sar, Bahrain, 2009

Other notable stencil graffiti is that of the Bahraini cleric Sheikh Issa Ahmed Qassim, particularly in the Shiite village of Diraz, where words from some of his speeches and sermons are also printed. The most prominent figure idolized in most villages is Abdul Amir al Jamri, who was the 'spiritual leader' of Bahrain's Shiite population and of the 1990s uprising. "Al Jamri in our hearts", "we will not forget you, O Jamri", "we are following your path, O Jamri..." are a few of the frequent mentions across the island. Reminiscences of Al Jamri illustrate the need to hold onto memories in order to keep them from being diffused or altered. The importance of a culture's collective memory signifies the need to preserve a narrative and historical account, to which graffiti writers have made a great contribution.

There is no doubt that the graffiti scene in Bahrain is unique and distinguishable from those of its neighboring Gulf countries. Struggle seems to be the main motivator for graffiti writers to pick up a spray can or pen and take their stand on the walls. For some passers-by, these expressions may be simple, ordinary distractions, which they learn to overlook. Undermining this dialogue is a sign of disengagement from a major faction of society and sheer indifference to bitter truths. The truth is in the medium, and the silenced medium is the message. The writing is, after all, on the wall.

• RANA JARBOU
Saudi-born Rana Jarbou recently embarked upon a calling in artistic expression, leaving behind her background in banking and finance. Equipped with a camera and an eagerness to explore repressed socio-political issues, Jarbou's latest project had her travel across eleven Arab countries documenting graffiti in an attempt to give voice to society's silent cries. Her book "Arabian Walls" will be published in 2011.

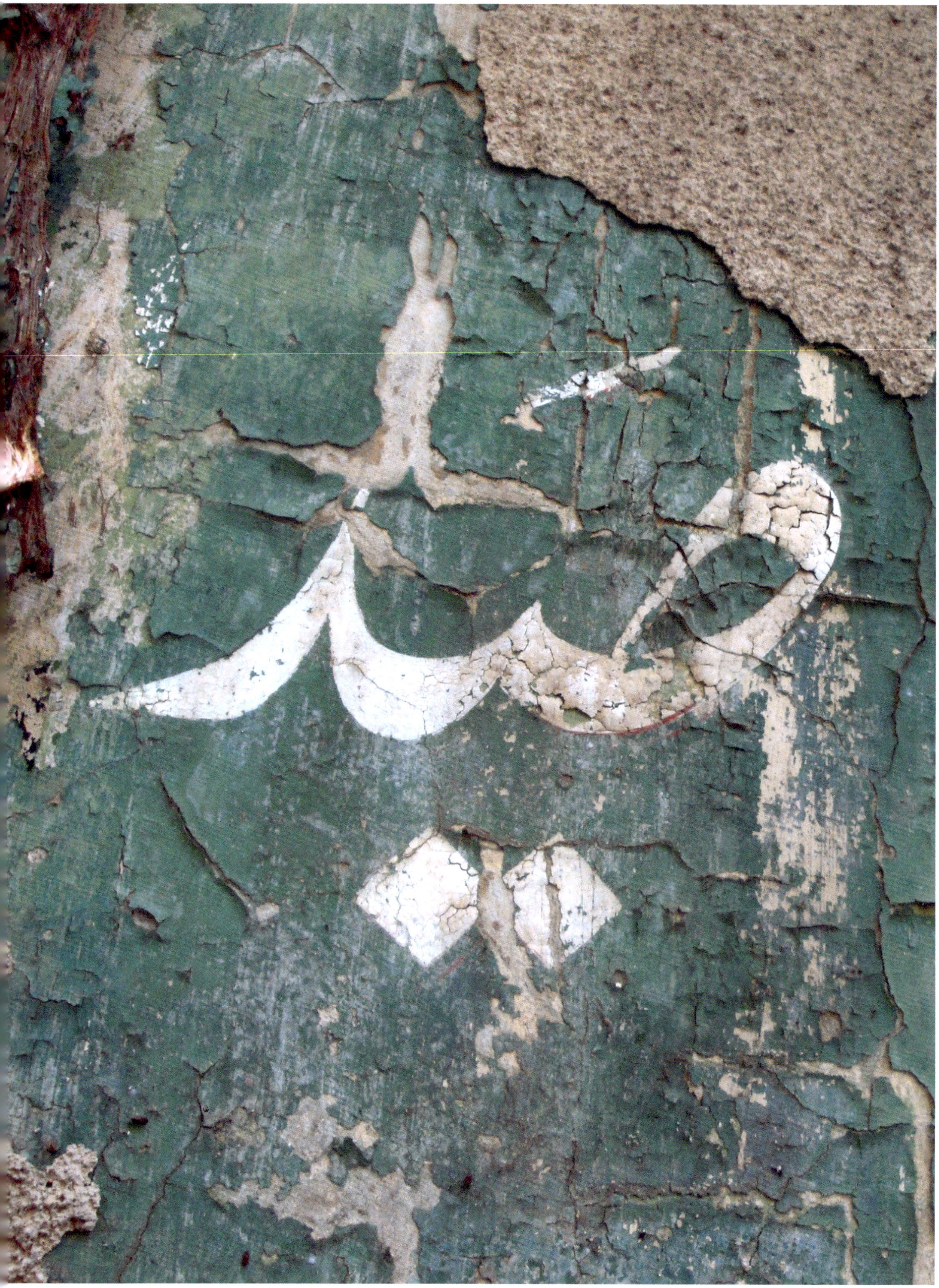

1

2·2
Calligraphic Shop Signs
التخطيط على لافتات المحال التجارية

Pascal Zoghbi

صيدلية
1. Pharmacy shop's old calligraphic sign, Bliss Street, Beirut, Lebanon

مؤسسة الصراط لتجارة الالبسة
2. Clothing store, Tripoli, Lebanon

Up until the 1980s in the Arab world, calligraphers were regularly commissioned by shop owners to write the name and description of shops on newly painted, white walls. The size, the calligraphic style and the color of the sign was all the information needed. No need to choose between metal, aluminum or plexi structures, as you do with modern shop signs, no backlit signs or neon lights. No need for a logo or a corporate typeface, the calligraphy on the wall becomes the identity of the shop. The sign is amendable when any additional information (phone number, service, brand etc.) needs to be added to the wall. Consequently, it is fragile and exposed to weather conditions and vandalism. Sun, rain and humidity affects the paint and roughens its texture. The wall starts to get dirty and the white background darkens. Furthermore, a passerby might intervene by writing on the calligraphy, thus changing the context and environment of the calligraphy over time, which does not happen to modern shop signs. When a shop promotes its identity, the owners do not acknowledge the value of the calligraphic lettering. They cover it with paint or rough cement textures and replace the calligraphy with standard current shop signs.

With the presence of the new materials and new technology for manufacturing shop signs, hand painted calligraphic signs are disappearing and the identities of the Arabic shops are losing their uniqueness. Even though the new, glittery shop signs might use the Arabic script, the chosen typefaces are mostly rigid in structure or Latinized. Most of the modern signs lose their traditional spirit to become standardized like international shop signs.

Two decades ago, handwritten signs were utilized all over Arabic cities. However, they have almost vanished from the developed urban regions and are only found in rural areas, where they are still the norm.

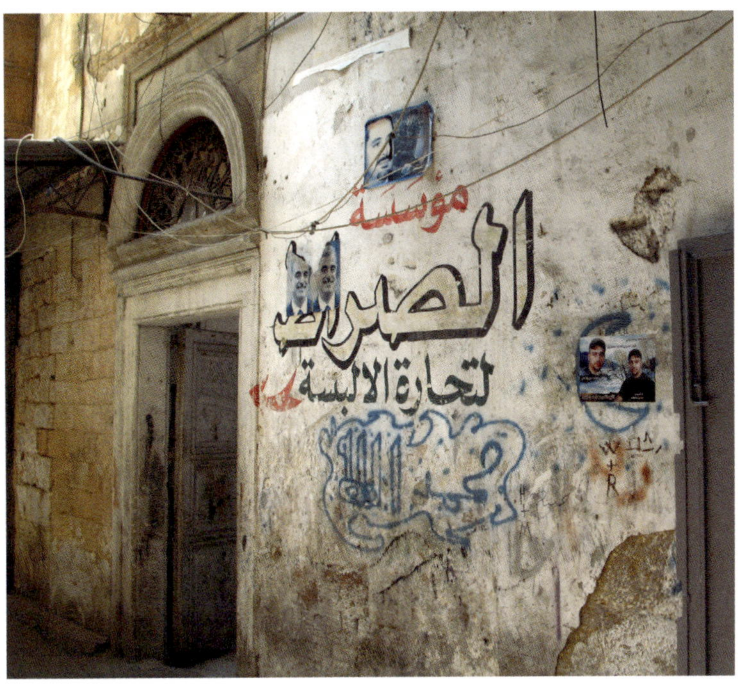

2

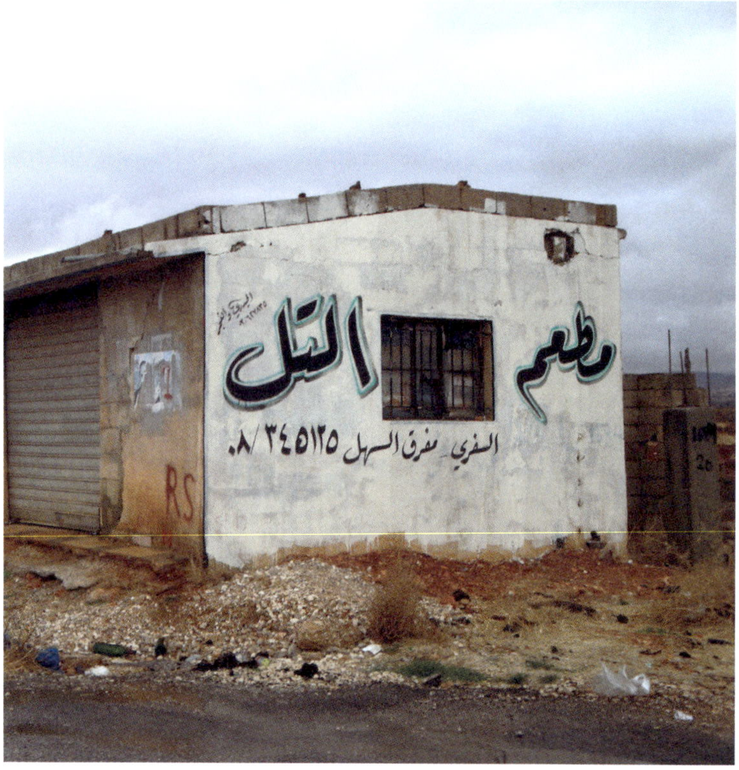

1

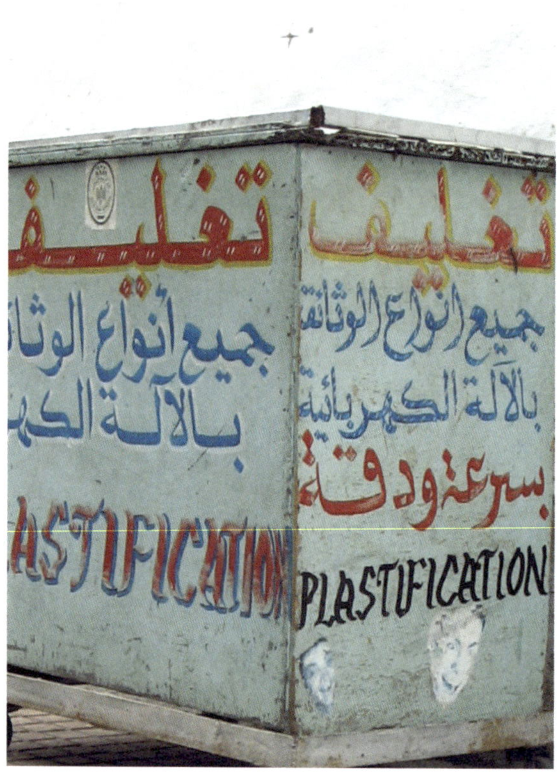

2

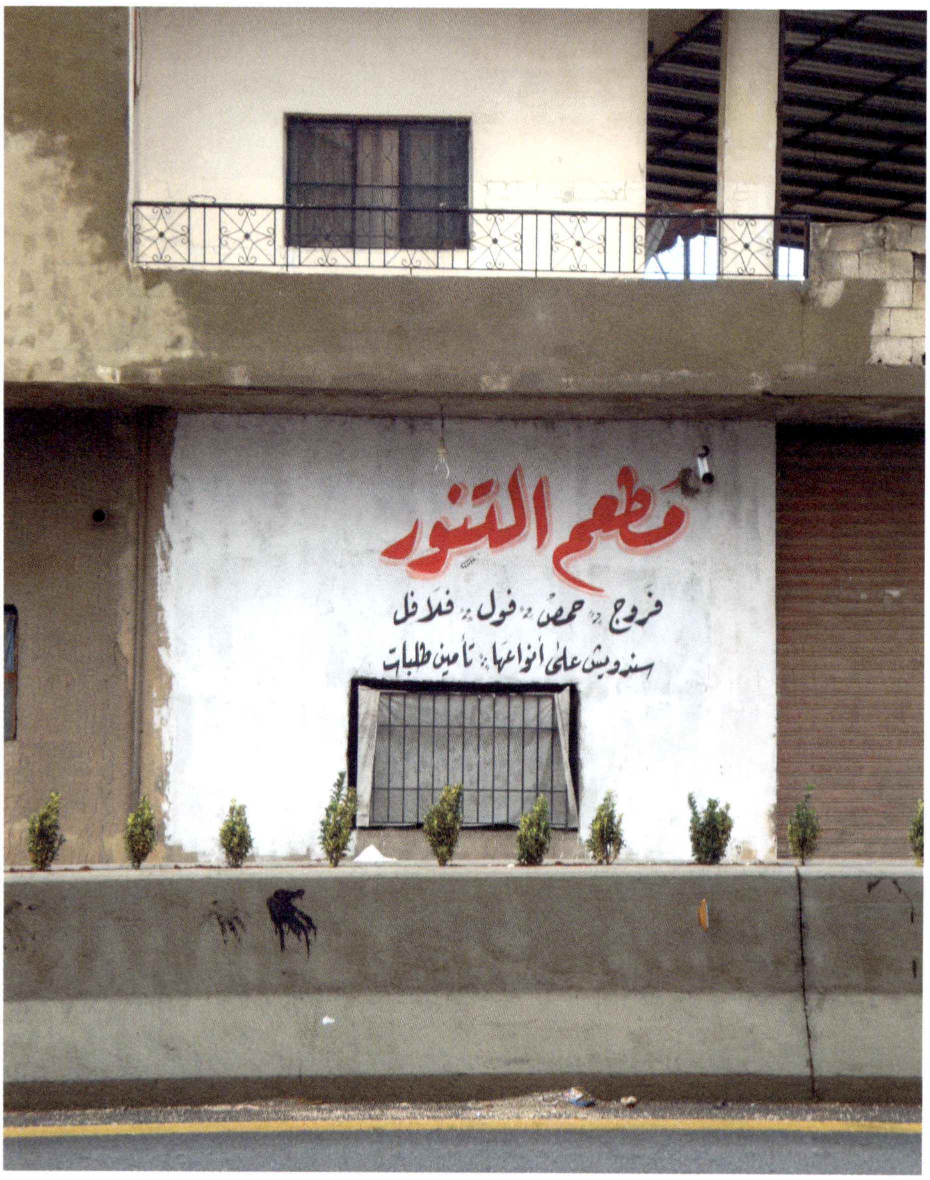

3

مطعم التل
1. “At-Tall Restaurant” advertisement, Beqaa, Lebanon

تغليف
2. “Plastification” mobile shop, Rabat, Morocco

مطعم التنور
3. “At-Tanour Restaurant” shop sign, Beqaa, Lebanon

مخلات / موقف
4. Shop and parking signs, Tripoli, Lebanon

محلات صالح
5. “Saleh’s Garage” sign, Beqaa, Lebanon

Following pages:

1. Several mini-market stores with calligraphic shop signs, Old Souk, Tripoli, Lebanon

بيبسي، كل ما تتمناه
2. Pepsi name and slogan in Arabic, Beqaa, Lebanon

3. Detail of mini-market sign, Beqaa, Lebanon

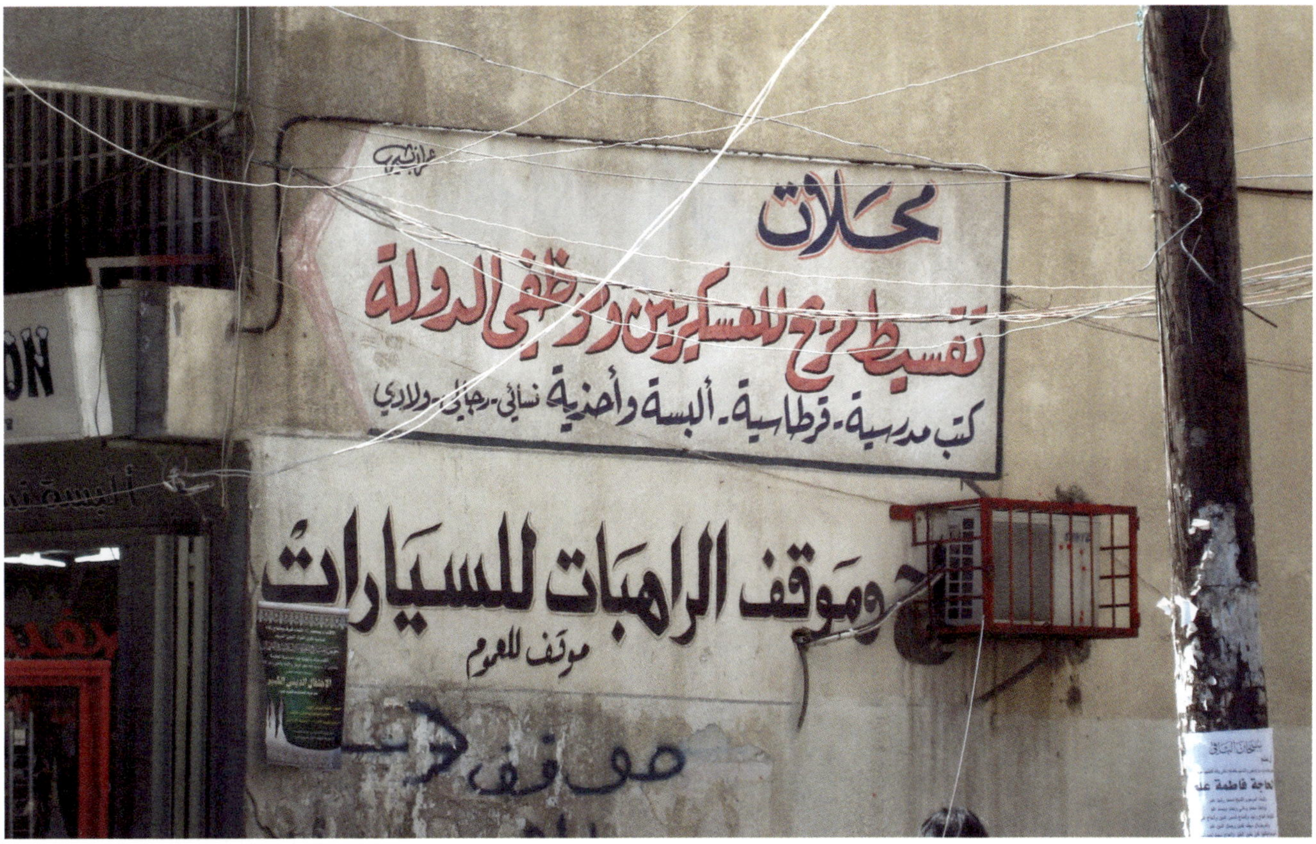
محلات
تقسيط مريح للعسكريين وموظفي الدولة
كتب مدرسية - قرطاسية - ألبسة وأحذية نسائي - رجالي - ولادي
وموقف الراهبات للسيارات
موقف للعموم

4

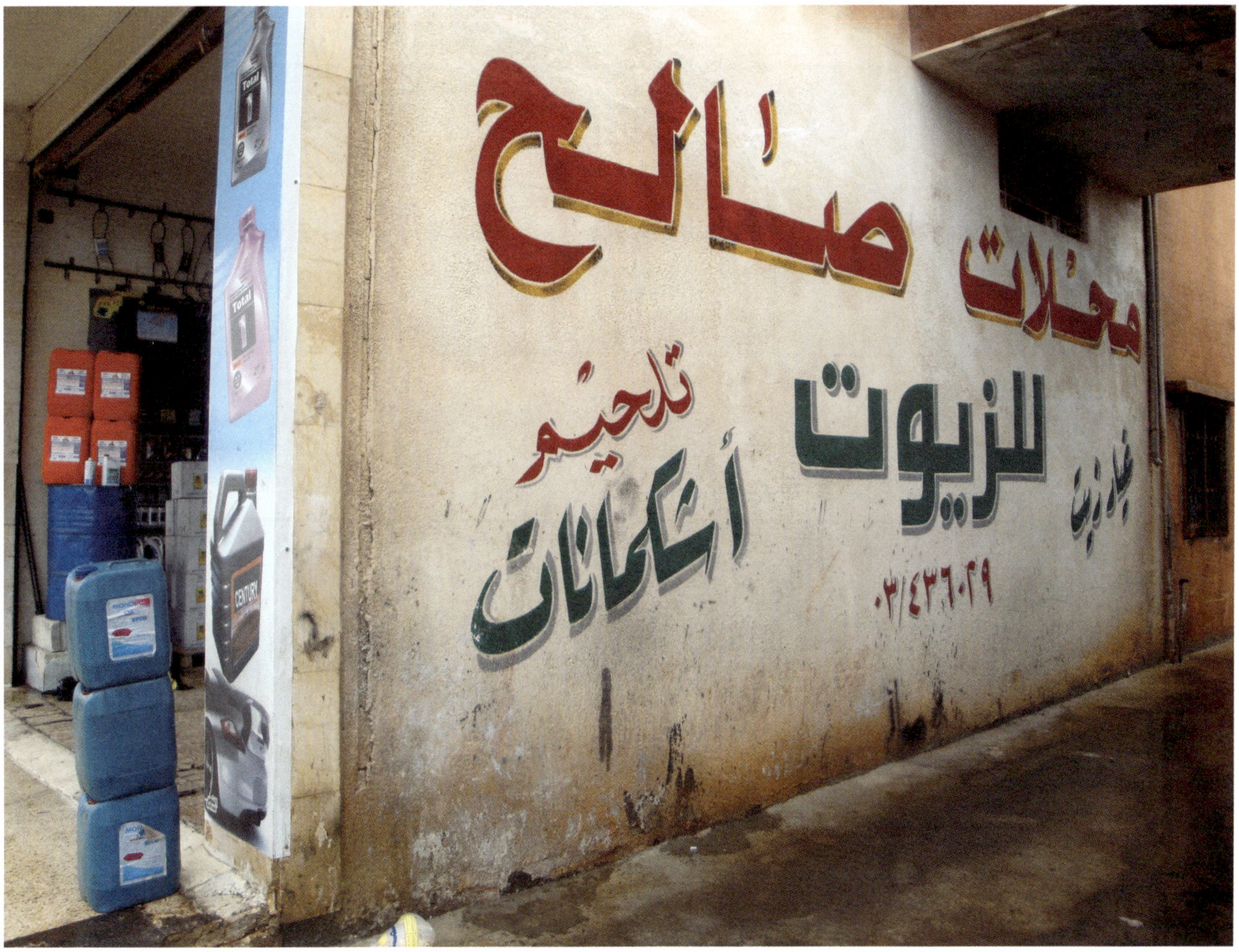
محلات صالح
للزيوت
تلحيم
أشكمانات
غيار زيت
٠٣/٤٣٦٠٢٩

5

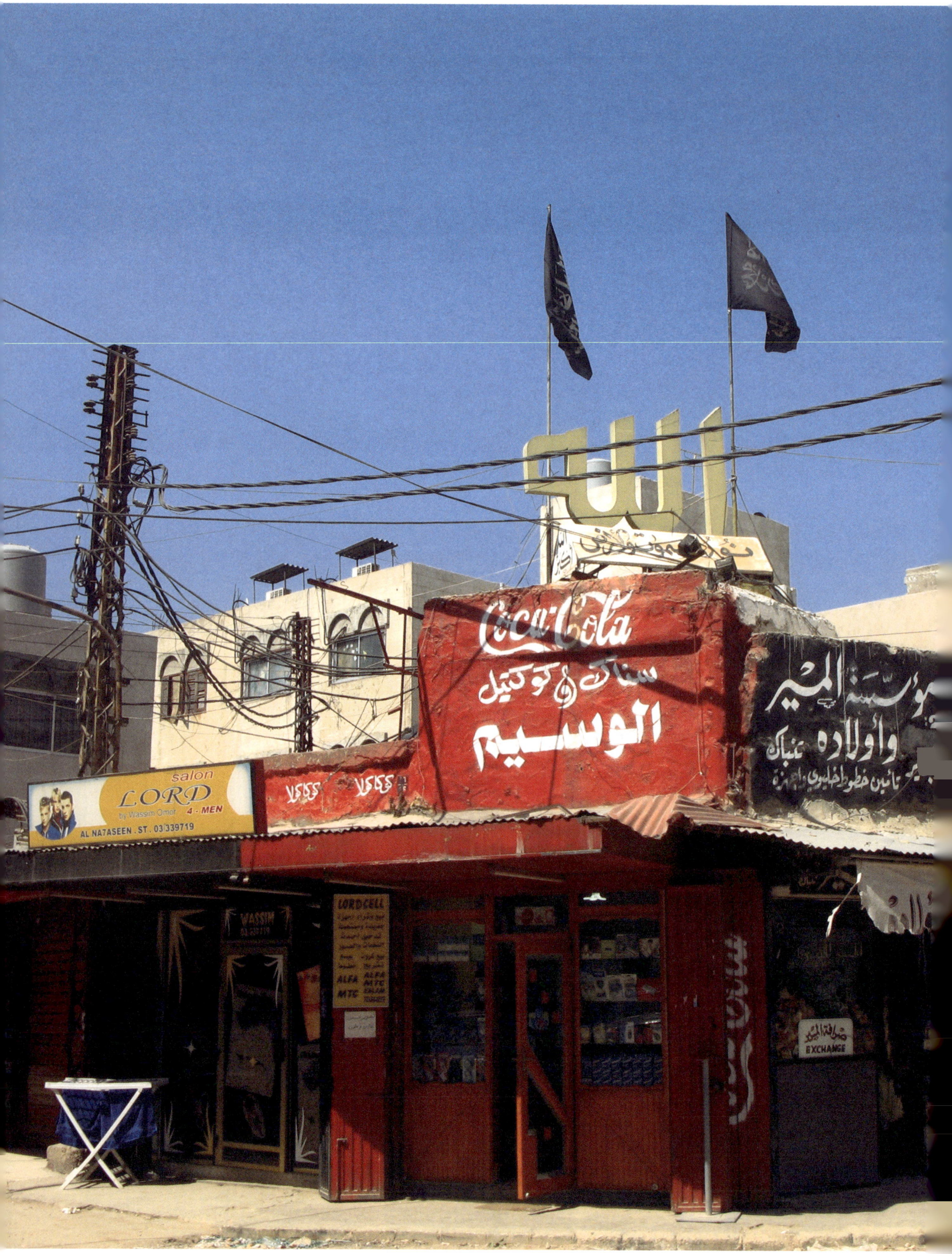
Coca-Cola
سناك و كوكتيل
الوسيم
salon
LORD
4 - MEN
AL NATASEEN . ST. 03/339719
LORDCELL
ALFA
MTC
WASSIM
EXCHANGE

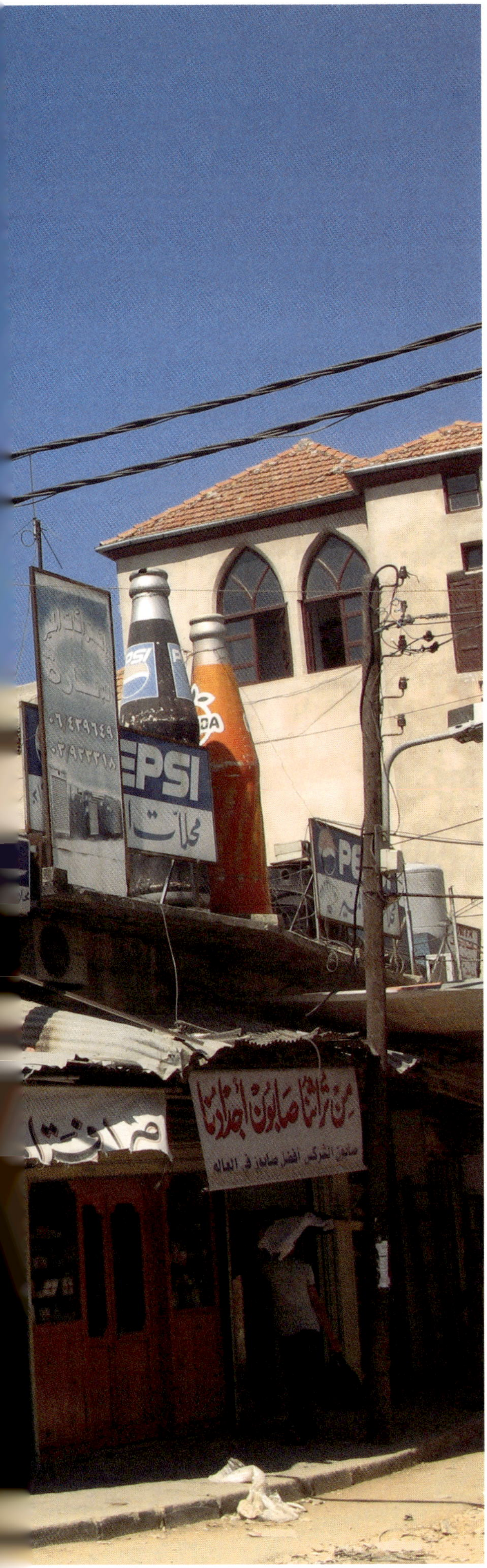

1

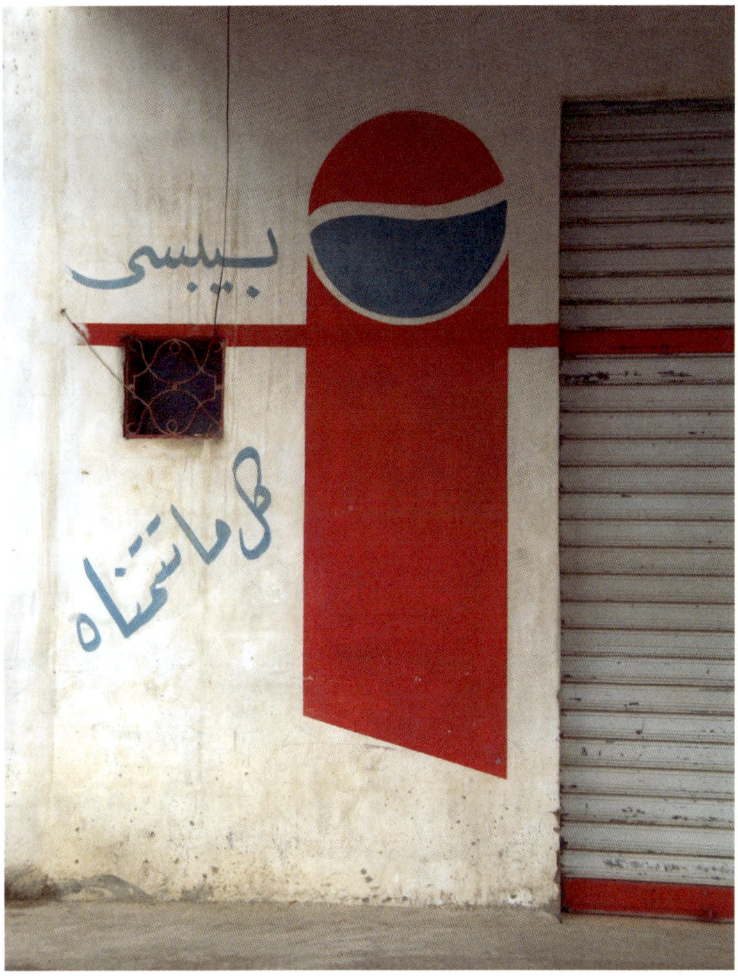

2

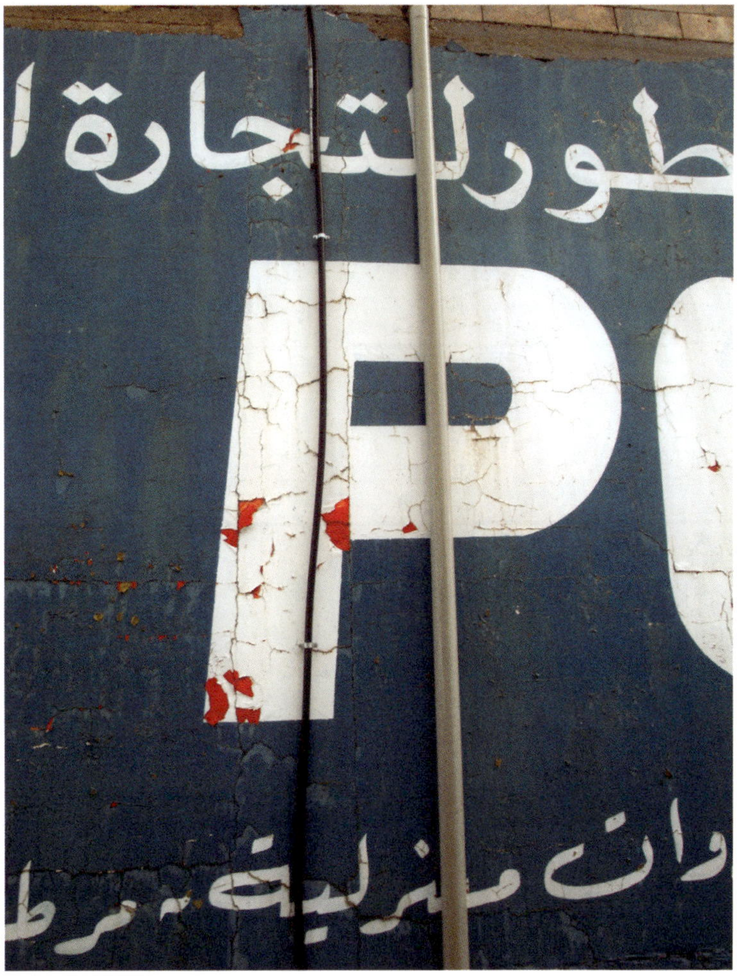

3

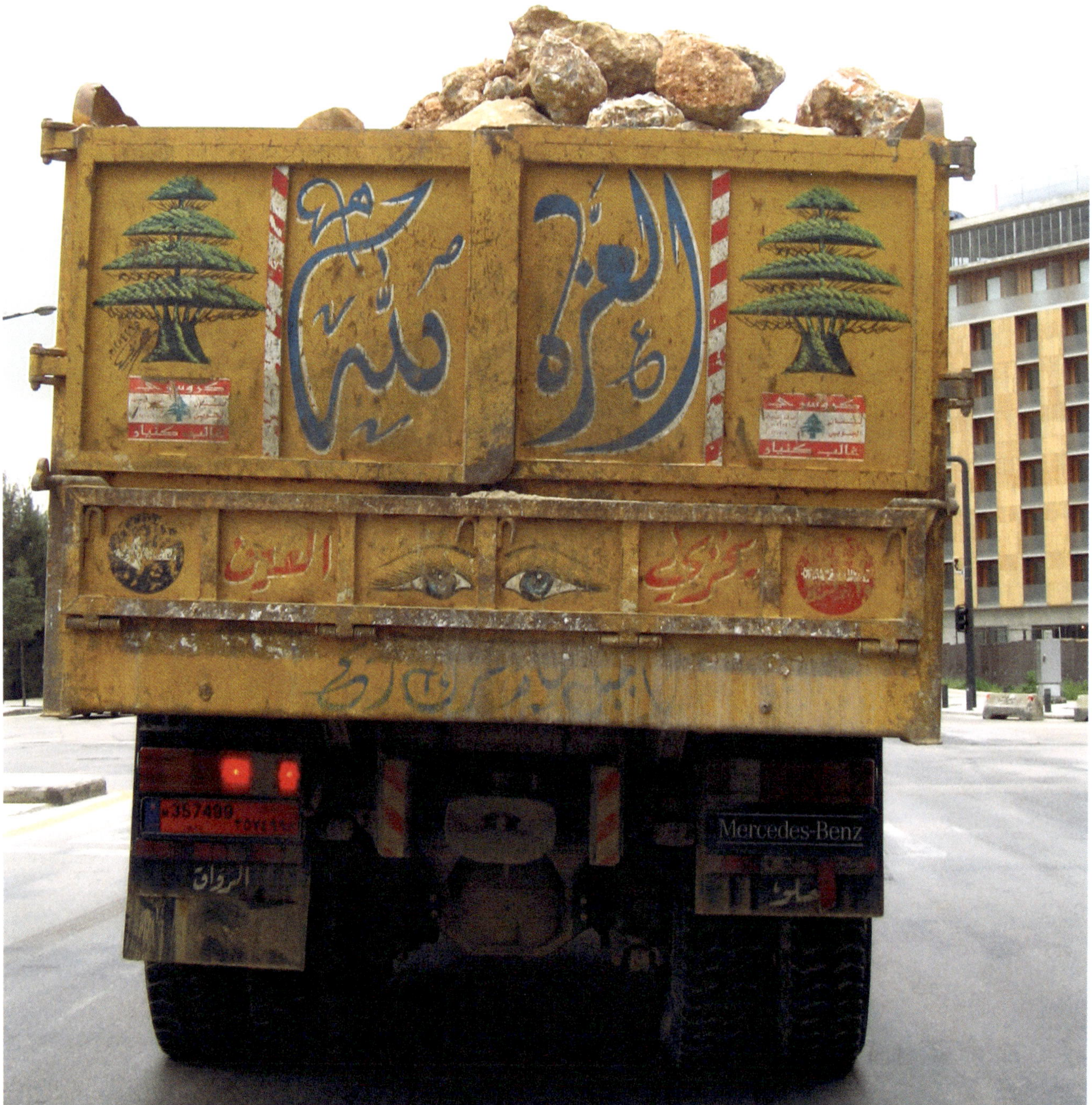

1

2·3
Calligraphy On Trucks
التخطيط على الشاحنات

Houda Kassatly

العزة لله \ يخزي العين

1. Cargo truck with calligraphy, back view, Beirut, Lebanon

2. Front view of a cargo truck

Trucks registered in Lebanon as well as medium weight pickup trucks mainly utilized by farmers for shipping products from various areas of Lebanon to the marketplaces of Beirut and other cities, as well as passenger buses or vans, frequently carry a multitude of expressions on their side faces. Indeed, it is rare to observe any of these vehicles bereft of all adornments, be it a sticker, a drawing, or above all, calligraphy. The latter is so omnipresent that you can even find it on cab windshields.

Far from being the privilege of Lebanon, this practice is common in most Arab countries in this region. In Syria, Egypt, Jordan and surrounding countries, quite rich calligraphies are traded on trucks. Decorated trucks are likewise a tradition in numerous other countries. But if there is something that distinguishes trucks in Arab countries, it is that this region is definitely the favorite haunt of those who occupy themselves with the calligraphy of vehicles.

It was in the 1950s when the first trucks — American brand — showed up on the roads of Lebanon. In their tracks a new tradition was born, which consists of transferring calligraphies onto the bodies of vehicles. The ancient convention of adorning pack, draft and riding animals with items to keep away various lurking dangers should be considered in light of truck calligraphy. The numerous objects against the evil eye recognizable on trucks include: hands of Fatima, a blue eye, horseshoes, blue pearls and stones, shoes, etc., as well as the protective content of a large part of phrases which confirm that they are meant to protect the truck, its driver and other occupants against hazards of the street, accidents of destiny, strokes of fate, but most of all against jealous glances.

Studying the calligraphies on trucks reveals that these primarily show the machinery of fear of the evil eye. As a matter of fact, on trucks one can find more than sixty expressions manifesting the existence of this fear, its power and the instruments used for deliverance. Actually, throughout all of these calligraphies the truck driver always aims to avert the unfortunate eye by averting the gaze of the envious person. The truck is often the most valuable property of the driver and the ownership of an item, even though expensive, obviously holds the risk of attracting the envy of others.Facing this fear, the truck driver arranges his faith in God like a protective wall. Faith he expresses in diverse ways by carrying the names of God, petitions, the profession of faith, verses of the Koran or excerpts of the Gospel, by invocation for protection through saints, particularly the saints of the local pantheon: Saint Sharbel, Mar Elias, Mar Gerios... and by praying for intercession of the Virgin, the prophets and the holy persons of the Shiites: Ali, Fatima, Husayn, Zaynab, etc.

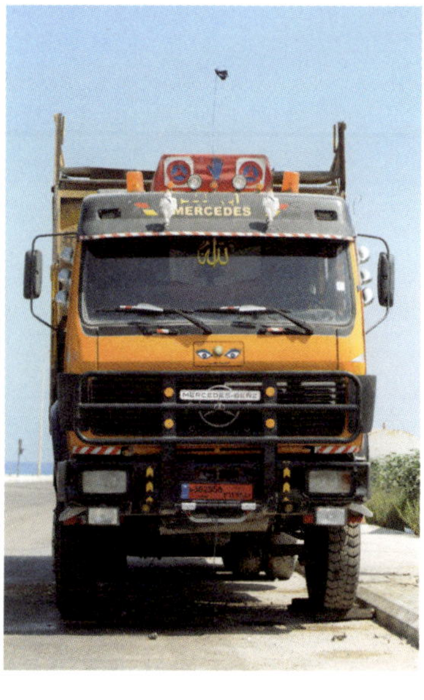

2

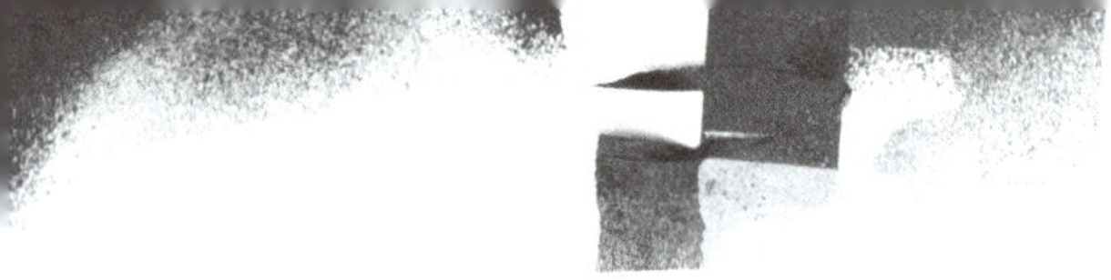

If the protective function remains the leading function, one should not forget the others: aesthetic and decorative, practical, cultural, expressing identity, etc. The reason is that over the course of time the practice of writing on trucks did spread and democratize itself. Two factors have contributed to this change: on one hand the emergence of calligraphers specialized in truck calligraphy and on the other hand the usage of decals, which are less expensive and much easier to apply. The truck, alter ego and eternal companion of the driver, who spends more time with it than by himself, has become the medium of his anxieties and his fears but also his method of social, political and amorous expression. Hence the bloom of sentences put into calligraphy, which confide to us the amours of the truck driver, his philosophy, his fond feelings, his deceptions, his taste in music, his ethics, and all this through fiery declarations to his belle, proverbs, aphorisms, maxims, finding a favorite place on the metal sheets of vehicles. The truck driver gives his feelings free run and in this country, where tolerance and permissiveness are still largely suppressed, he quite frankly enunciates about love, tells of his misfortunes, complains, makes his truck the medium of his dreams and his fantasies, yet his confidant. In addition, when you conduct a historical study of calligraphies, these can be considered as a barometer of public life, notably a barometer of social relations. In that way, Jacques Berque's concept of emotional preoccupation with the mother is revealed in the Arab world: "Below the feet of mothers runs the river of paradise" [1], "Speed up, don't worry, the ambulance will collect you, but only your mother will cry about you" [2], "I'm not afraid of death, I'm afraid of the tears of my mother" [3], "Rather a thousand eyes crying than the eye of my mother shedding one tear" [4]... Likewise on trucks are references to friendship, or the truck driver's perspective of women, boasting with an informative misogyny : "Girls are beautiful, but they all are liars" [5], "Beautiful and deceitful" [6], "Betrayal is the nature of women" [7], "Neither trust kings, even if they honor you, nor women, even if they adore you" [8], "Entrust a secret to a mute woman and she will speak" [9]... And finally the trucks show the measure of intimacy that can exist between the sons-in-law and their mothers-in-law, a recurrent social conflict. Whereas the

طق دوب / يخزي العين / محروسة

1. Some of the phrases written: "Snip and melt", "May the [evil] eye be thwarted", "The protected"

أبو هادي / الله يحميكي (كذا) / موفقة

2. The name of the truck driver is written on the highest point of the truck and then followed by words of protection and pride

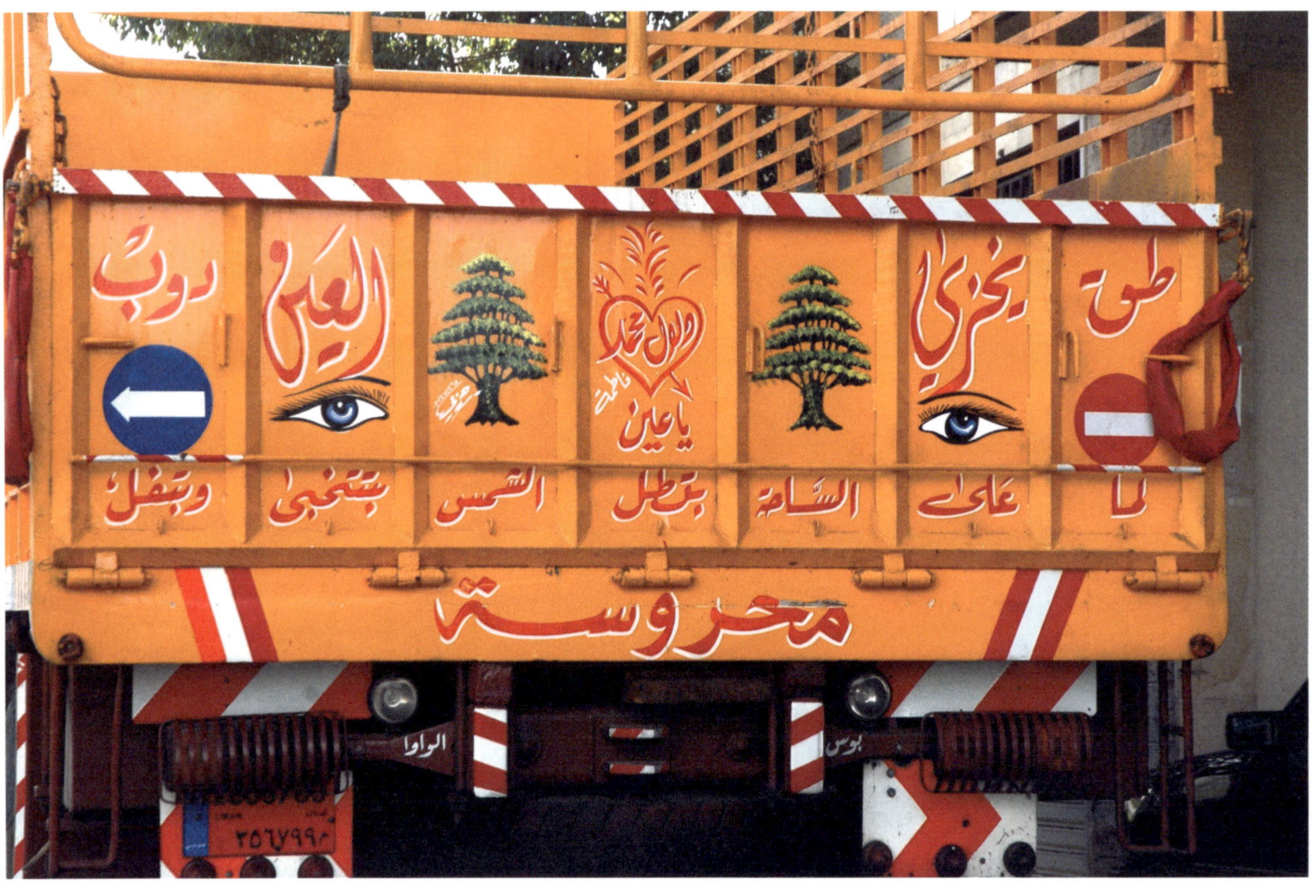

1

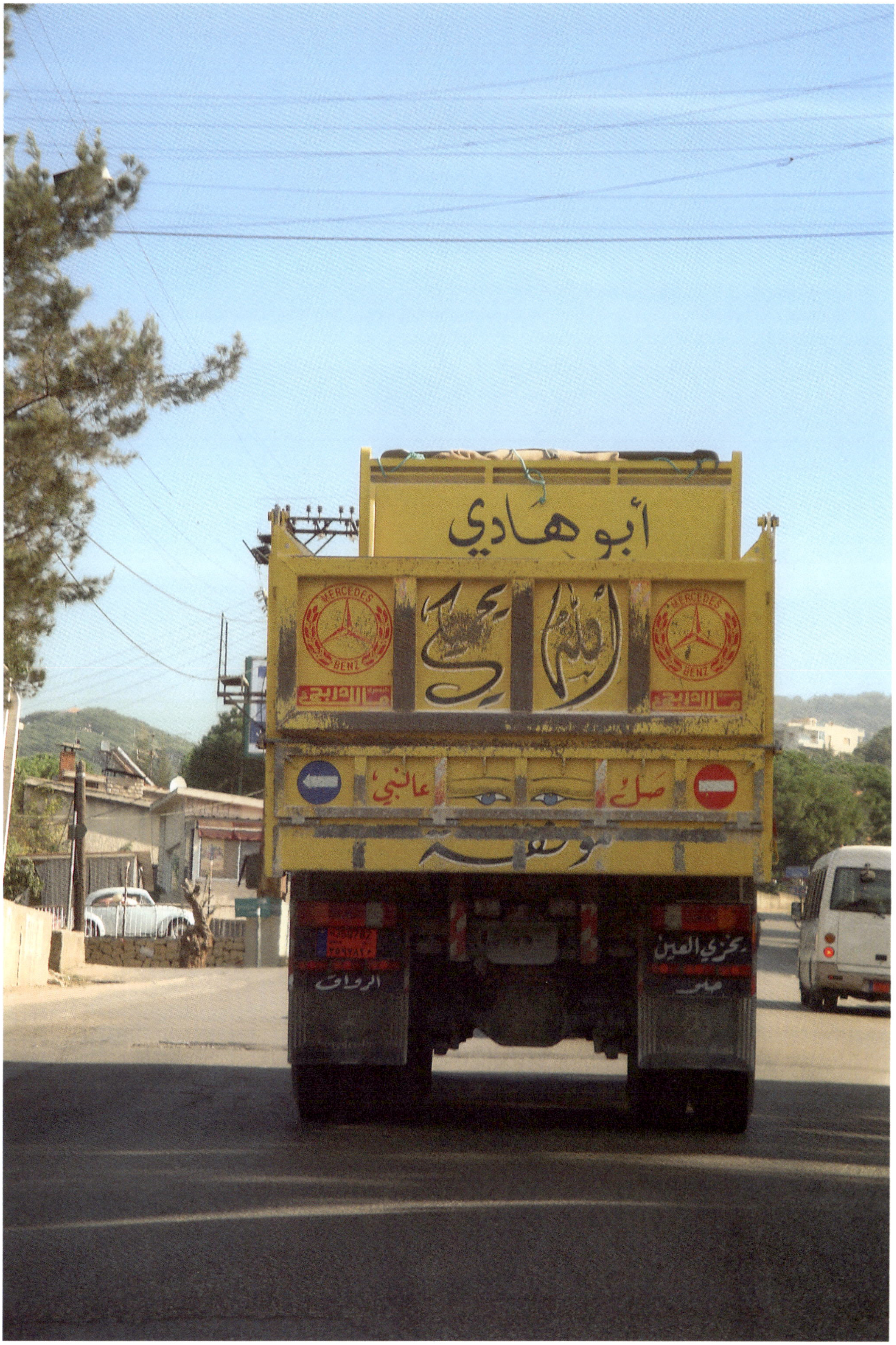

2

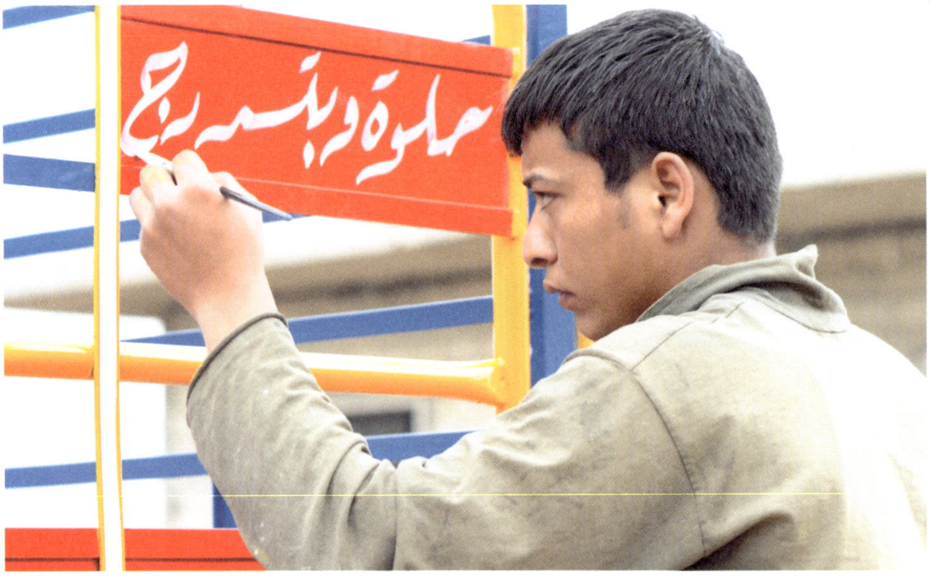

1

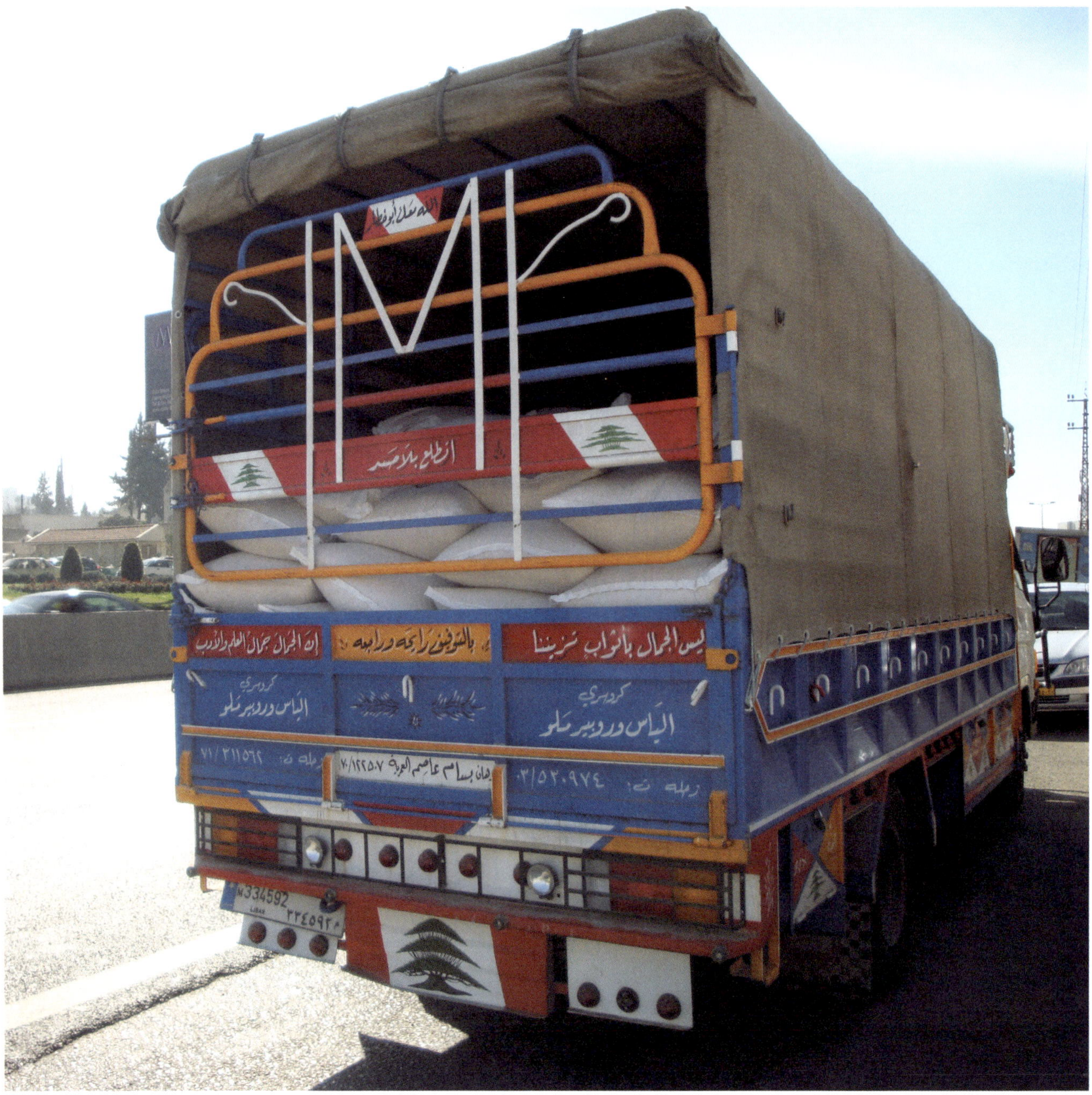

2

mother-in-law is depicted by some as "a moon amidst the stars", she is rejected by the majority of truck drivers, who write: "My wife is a beauty, my mother-in-law a calamity"[10], "I love you O my mother-in-law, but I wish to forget about you, throw you out the window and throw your daughter after you".[11]

According to his movements, the truck driver makes these calligraphies voyage, which he confides to the gaze of all those he meets and even establishes a dialogue with his fellow men stuck in traffic jams, a dialogue that can be comforting and contain advice to prudence: "Conduct is art, savoir vivre and courtesy" [12], "Have mercy on yourself and others, don't drive while using your cell phone" [13], "If you want to arrive at your destination, drive according to the rules" [14], "Don't go fast, death will go faster" [15], "Drive slowly, your parents await you" [16], "Travel easy, life is precious" [17], or to the contrary contain warnings, challenges and threats: "Don't try to play with me" [18], "Stay away" [19], "May God damage those who damage" [20], "Don't approach the eagle, oh dove" [21], "I am the wolf, don't play with me" [22], "Do not mess with me" [23], "I defy you" [24], "Don't make me throw my virility on you" [25], "Those who will mock us, their blood we drink in a cup" [26], "Pass and pass by, but look out if you challenge me" [27], "You want to see the stars in broad daylight? Follow me" [28], "Those who want death follow me" [29].

The previous quotes prove to what extent the vehicle is a medium of the male speech. This way, on the truck which constitutes his exclusive domain, a man can loosen up, let loose, truly and strongly say what he's thinking and above all unload his anger and his rage. In short, the truck allows him to release all his accumulated angers and all daily resentments.

حلوة وبتدرج

1. Young calligrapher decorating a small cargo truck with Arabic calligraphy, "Beautiful and trendy"

2. Back view of a decorated small cargo truck with Arabic calligraphy

بعيد عنّك حياتي عذاب
هي بتتغنج عالكل، حلوي وبتشوف بحالا
مين أدّك

3. Some of the sentences written: "I'm miserable when I'm away from you", "She is a beautiful coquette and arrogant", "Who can compare with you"

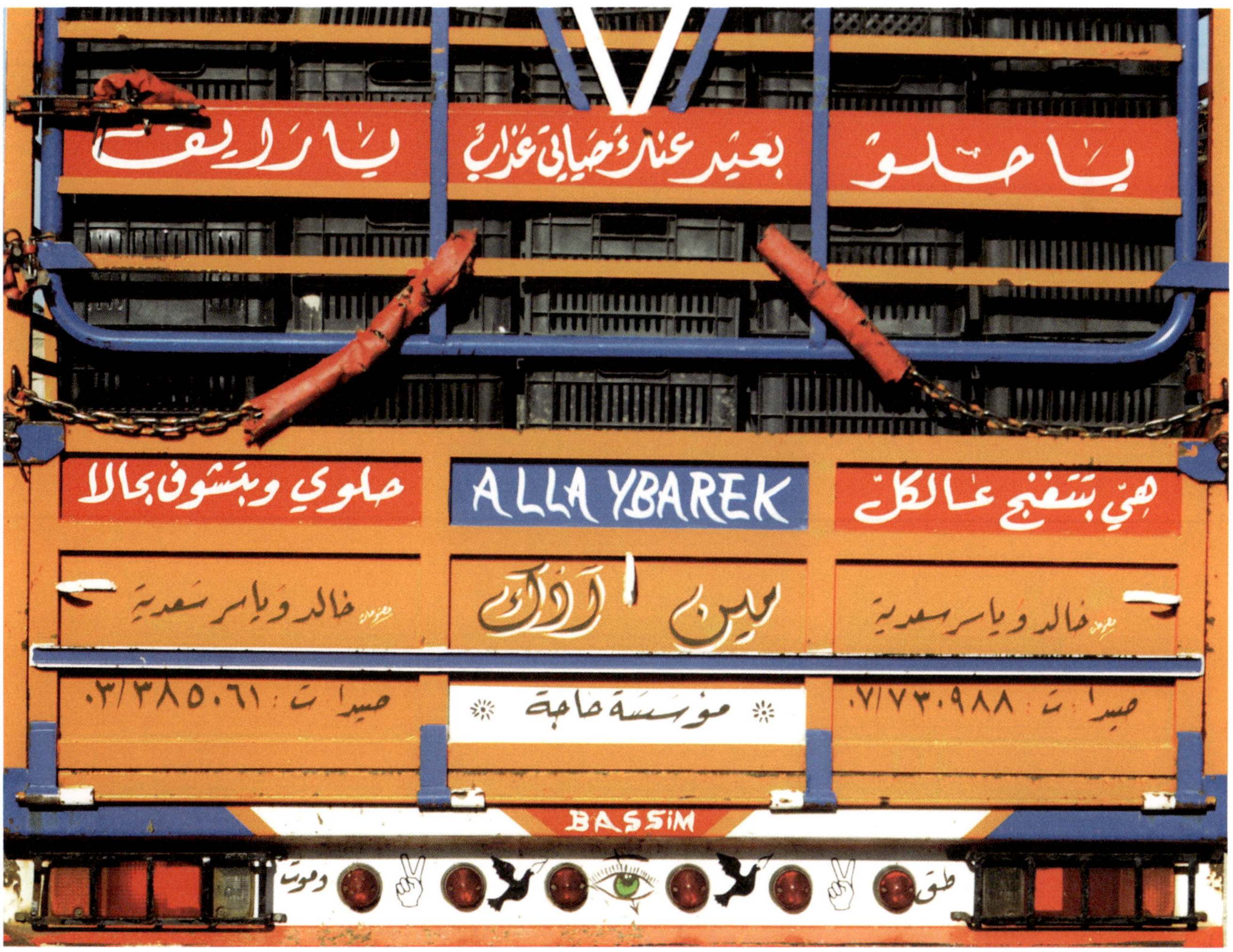

3

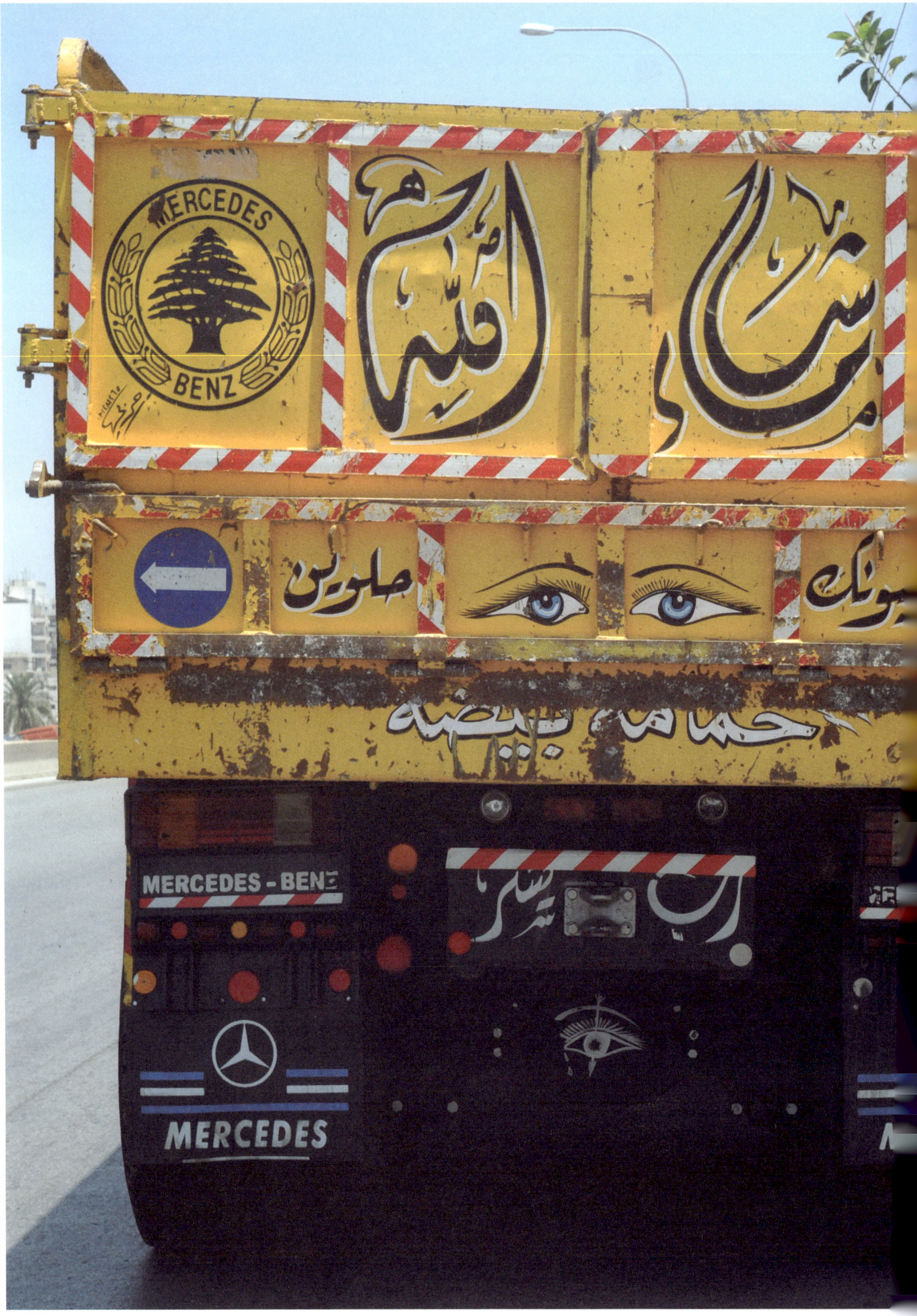

1

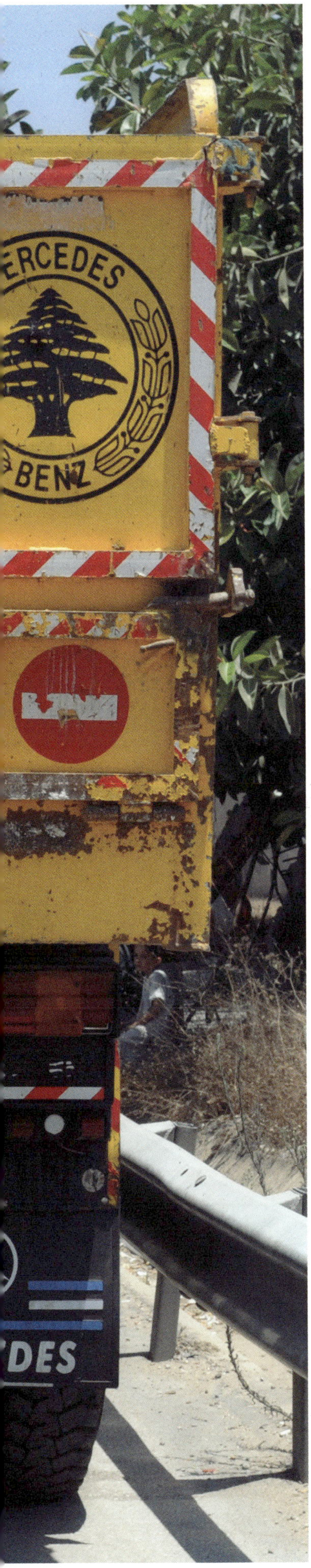

And even if the truck driver expresses his deceptions and his blackest ideas, he also shows humor and displays how he is not disappointed in himself and the life he is leading. Permanently on the road, somehow cursed to be inconstant and flighty, he carries on his car's body quite personal advice directed to women: "Marry a man loaded with debts, but don't fall in love with a truck driver" [30], "Pretty girl: love a poor genius but don't love a truck driver" [31], "Take these millions but don't marry a truck driver" [32], "Marry anyone, but not a truck driver"[33].

So in the end, the truck is the great developer of cultural tendencies in their progress, the developer of beliefs and the philosophy of life of a fringe of Arab society, of social relations, of the emergence of social rapports. In short, it's a cultural and social indicator of Lebanon and it could prove even more worthy to undertake an ongoing study of calligraphies, which will add to the known corpus and enrich it with consistency.

ماشاء الله / عيونك حلوين
حمامة بيضة (كذا) / رب يسّر

1. Some of the sentences written: "The will of God", "Your eyes are beautiful", "White Dove", "God facilitates"

2. Clutch design inspired by Lebanese cargo trucks, Sarah's Bag

1. الجنة تحت اقدام الامهات
2. اسرع ولا يهمك الاسعاف بتلمك وما حدا بيبكي عليك غير امك
3. لا يخيفني الموت لكن تخيفني دمعة امي
4. الف عين تبكي ولا عين امي تدمع
5. حلوين البنات بس كلن كذابين
6. حلوة وكذابة
7. الخيانة طبع النساء
8. لا تأمن للملوك لوملكوك ولا للنساء لو عبدوك
9. اعطي سرا لامرأة خرساء تنطق
10. مراتي حلوة وحماتي بلوة
11. اهواكي يا حماتي واتمنى لو انساكي وارميكي من الشباك وارمي بنتك وراكي
12. القيادة : فن وذوق واخلاق
13. ارحم نفسك والناس ما تسوق وتحكي بالسوليلير
14. اذا اردت الوصول فامشي عالاوصول
15. لا تسرع الموت اسرع
16. امشي عمهلك ناطرينك اهلك
17. خلي السفر هادي لان العمر غالي
18. English on the truck
19. خليك بعيد
20. الله بضر يلي بضر
21. لا تقرب من الصقر يا طير الحمام
22. English on the truck
23. English on the truck
24. بتحداك
25. Literal translation: "Don't let me curse by my mustaches". The mustaches constitute a sign of virility and of magnificence, as can be proved with a law that once awarded a bonus for all members of law enforcement who wore this male attribute and gave it jealous care.
26. يلي بدو يتحدانا منشرب دمو بالفنجان
27. مر وعدي اوعى التحدي
28. ...بدك تشوف نجوم الظهر؟ الحقني
29. الي يريد الموت يلحقني
30. تجوزي مديون ولا تعشقي شوفير كميون
31. يا حلوي حبي عفريت ولا تحبي شوفير ترانزيت
32. خذي مليون ولا تاخدي شوفار كميون
33. تجوزي كيف ما يكون بس لا تتجوزي شوفار كميون

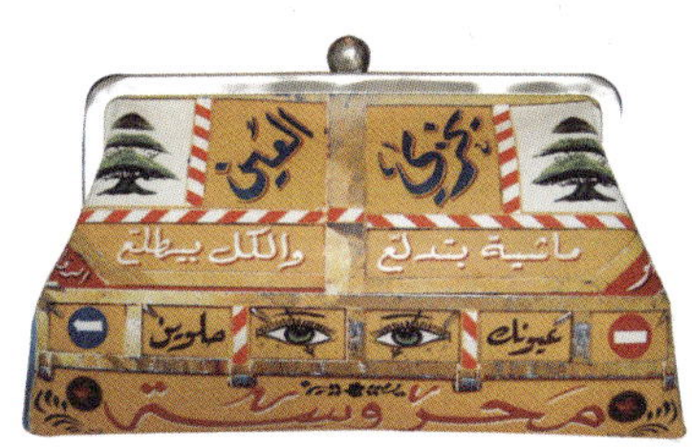
2

• HOUDA KASSATLY,
anthropologist, photographer and research associate in the Memory Unit Research at Saint Joseph University, is the author of several books and articles on Lebanon and the Middle East.
She recently published "Les camions peints du Liban d'aujourd'hui", a book on paintings and calligraphy by Lebanese truck drivers, and has also recently founded the Al Ayn publishing house, which specializes in Arab world heritage.

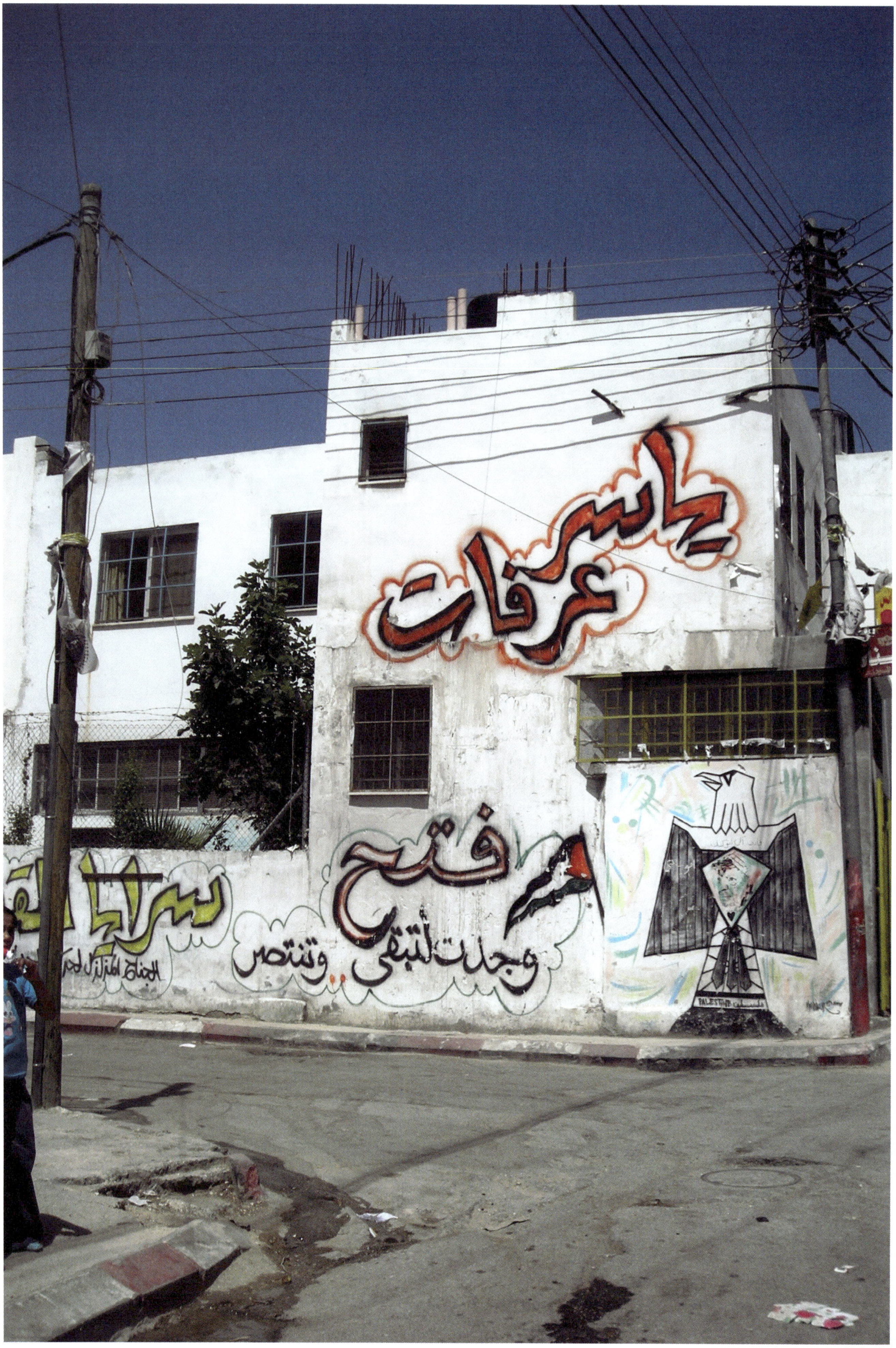

1

2·4 Palestinian Graffiti
الغرافيتي الفلسطيني

Pascal Zoghbi
& Stone

ياسر عرفات / فتح
1. "Yasser Arafat" (above) and "Fatah" (below) written beside the Palestinian Eagle, Askar refugee camp, Nablus, West Bank, Palestine, 2007

Long before street artists from all over the world flocked to the West Bank to leave their marks and signs of solidarity on the huge barrier walls, graffiti was already abundant in occupied Palestine and in the streets and alleys of the refugee camps in the neighboring countries of Jordan, Syria and Lebanon. The history of using their walls as an irreplaceable medium for all kinds of messages is as old as the Palestinian struggle itself.

The visuals present in Palestine have various styles, which range from casual, everyday scribbling and quickly sprayed slogans to elaborate calligraphic writing and colorful scenic murals. The themes of the stencils, simple writings or fine calligraphy are likewise diverse. They include anything from poetry — even recitations in Zajal (Arabic form of poetry) — to strong political or religious texts.

Palestinian house owners themselves or commissioned professional artists decorate the walls with colorful, festive paintings to celebrate religious holidays, welcome pilgrims back from the Hajj or to congratulate newly wedded couples. Idealizing murals commemorate the traditional Palestinian peasant life, which gives the residents a stronger national unity and a nostalgic memory.

Depictions of the Al Aqsa Mosque in Jerusalem and the Al Kaaba in Mecca are probably some of the most common motifs adorning Palestine. Most local residents of Gaza and the West Bank can only dream of being able to visit them one day. Stencils of those icons, applied again and again beside stencils of religious writings, occasionally cover whole walls and alleys as an expression of people's religious devotion and faith. They are especially common in the Muslim Quarter in the Old City of Jerusalem.

Hanzala, the hugely popular cartoon character of a barefoot refugee boy with patched clothing shown from the back, can be spotted on virtually every corner. The Hanzala figure was created by the Palestinian cartoonist Naji Al Ali, who was later assassinated.

The narrow alleys of Palestine echo the voices of the Fatah and Hamas movements, the Islamic Jihad and others, all spreading their slogans and mourning their martyrs. Stencils or paintings of the names of these martyrs, who have over time become national heroes, are painted all over.

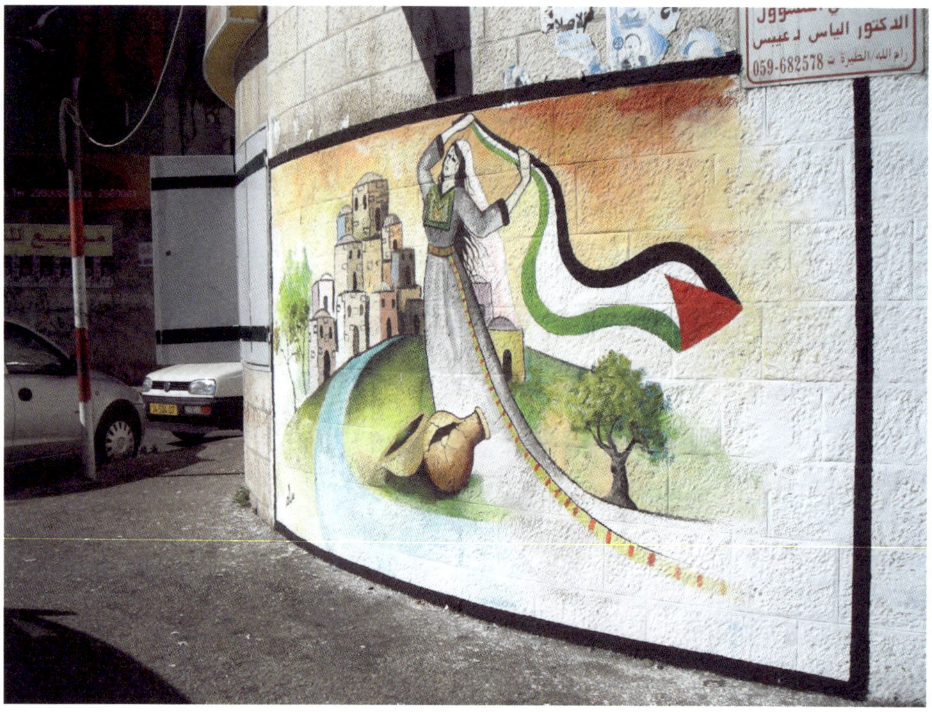

1

Palestinian graffiti writing grew increasingly throughout the Intifada, since it was the quickest method to spread news. It was used by all Palestinian factions without exception. In the beginning it was limited to quick sketches, which gradually evolved into beautiful artistic visuals. The lavish graffiti of Gaza held a very special place in this development for many years. What is outstanding about the graffiti of Palestine is the fact that the artists get training in Arabic calligraphy from their respective political or religious factions until the time comes for them to start creating murals.[1] For Hamas, this practice was of great importance because of their common use of sacred religious texts, whose display needed careful attention. This attitude towards beautification through graffiti and the competition of Fatah and Hamas in Gaza led their artistic endeavors to heights unseen in other parts of Palestine.

The use of traditional Arabic calligraphic styles in the creation of the graffiti lends Palestinian street art a unique Arabic style. Compared to graffiti in other Arab nations, which is mostly still inspired by Western graffiti, we can say that the Palestinian graffiti is a true Arabic urban art intervention.

1. Mural of the traditional Palestinian villages and folkloric clothing. Nostalgic drawing of Palestine before the Israeli occupation, Ramallah, West Bank, Palestine, 2007

حق العودة حق لا يموت

2. "The right to return is a right that will never die", West Bank separation wall, Abu Dis, Palestine

حج مبرور وسعي مشكور وذنب مغفور

3. Hajj greetings, stencils of the Al-Aqsa Mosque in Jerusalem and the Al Kaaba of Mecca alongside their stenciled names and olive branches. Arab Quarters, Old Town Jerusalem, Palestine

4. Al Kaaba and prayers are drawn on the wall of a small alley, Askar refugee camp, Nablus, West Bank, Palestine

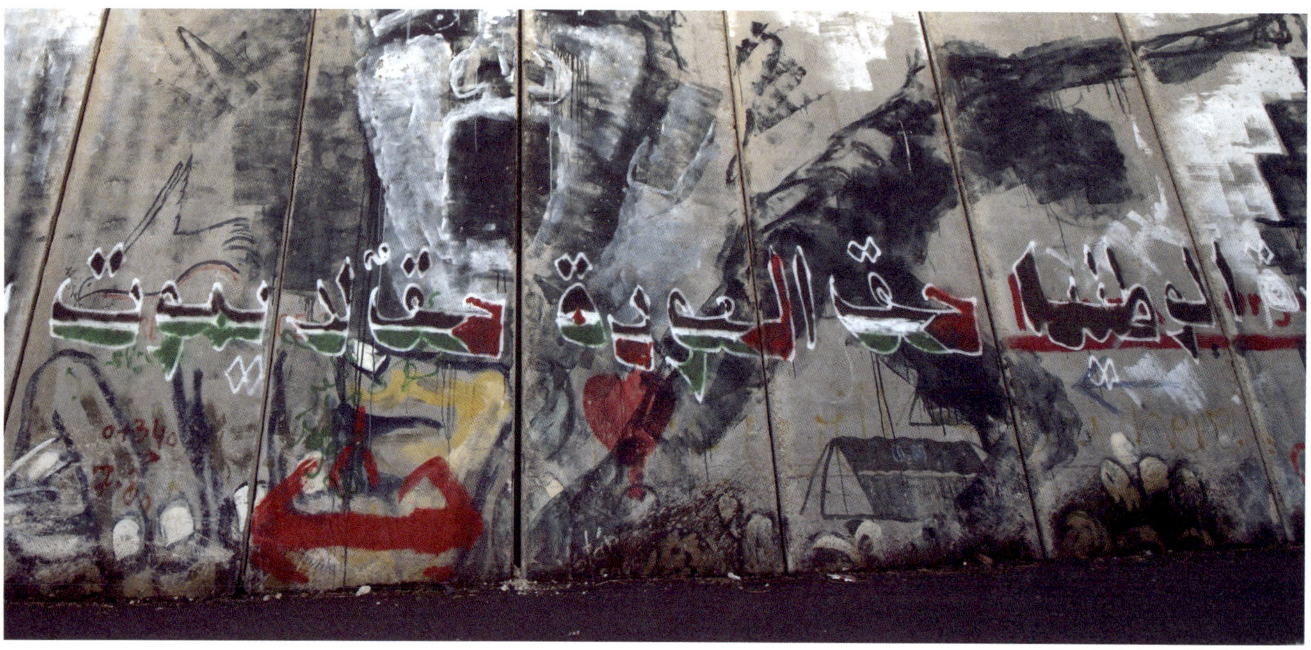

2

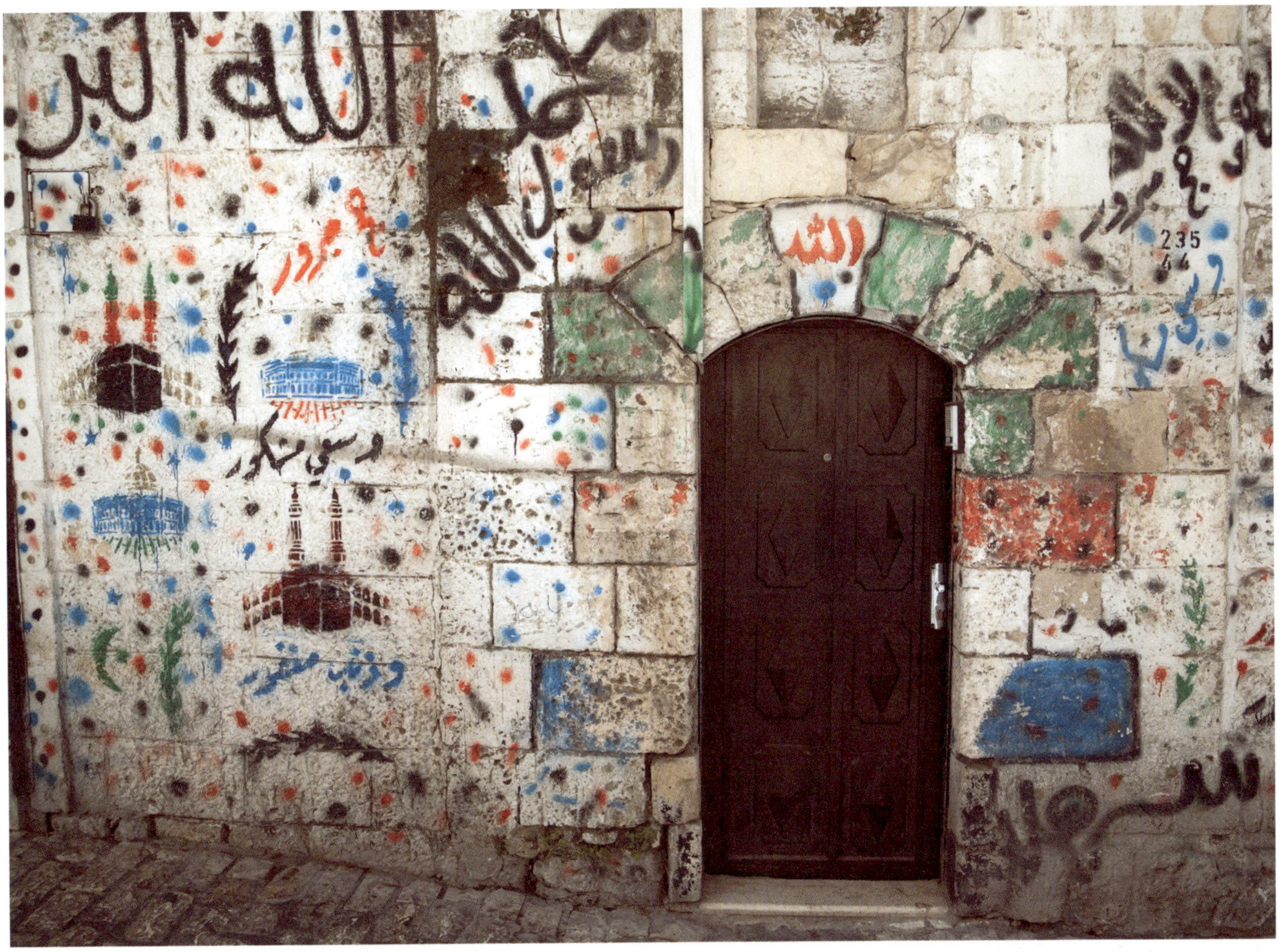

3

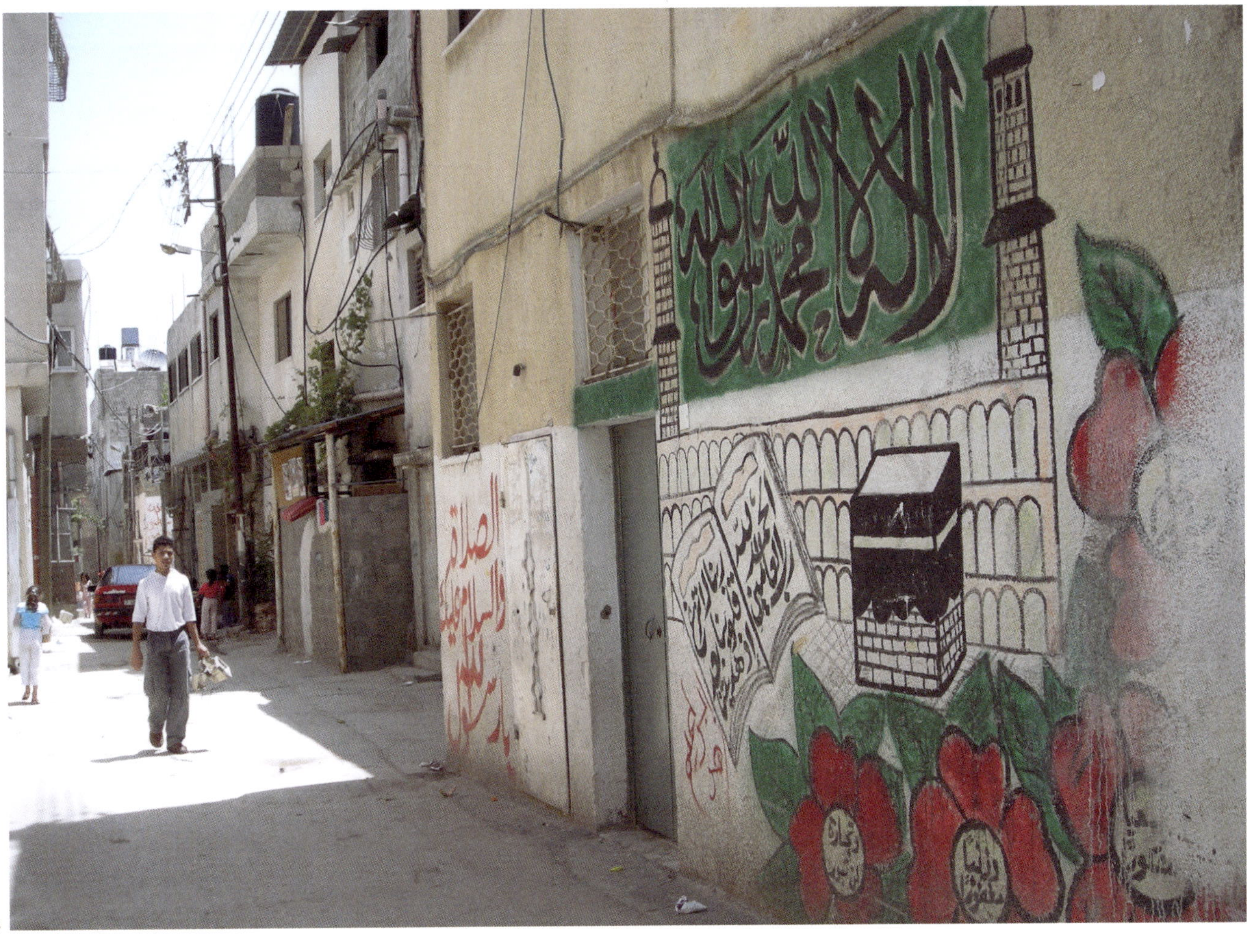

4

Gaza has witnessed strong political and religious local graffiti painted by Palestinian fighters and residents. No Western graffiti art is present, since it is practically impossible for a foreign artist to enter Gaza. Before the withdrawal of Israel from the Gaza Strip, graffiti artists were either fighters themselves or often accompanied by Palestinian fighters, who guarded them from the Israeli soldiers.

The popularity of this medium of communication, which transformed walls into a channel no less important than newspapers, was due to the trust and confidence that people put in graffiti. Certain factors contributed to the popularity of some locations among graffiti artists. Typically, the safest regions gave them more freedom to work. However, other less secure locations were also explored; depending on the occasion, artists would paint on occupier's headquarters, army posts or even their vehicles. Sometimes certain shops were painted to warn their owners against violating directives. Another preferred location for artists are the populated areas, as these guarantee a wider reach. Most artists are excited when groups gather around them to see the work evolving into a beautiful artistic piece, and they can instantly grasp the reception of their work. An additional appeal of graffiti to artists is the fact that it is a collective work, which opens up more possibilities for creative expression to them.

Artists are able to express the population's concerns, worries and even joys, while transforming blocks of concrete into works of art. Since Palestinian graffiti is intended to be seen

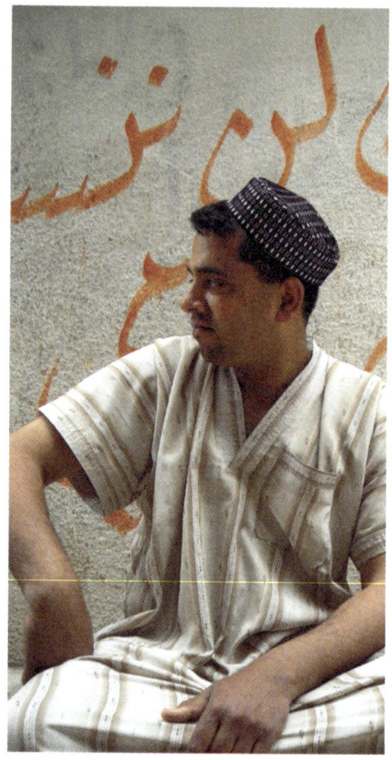

1

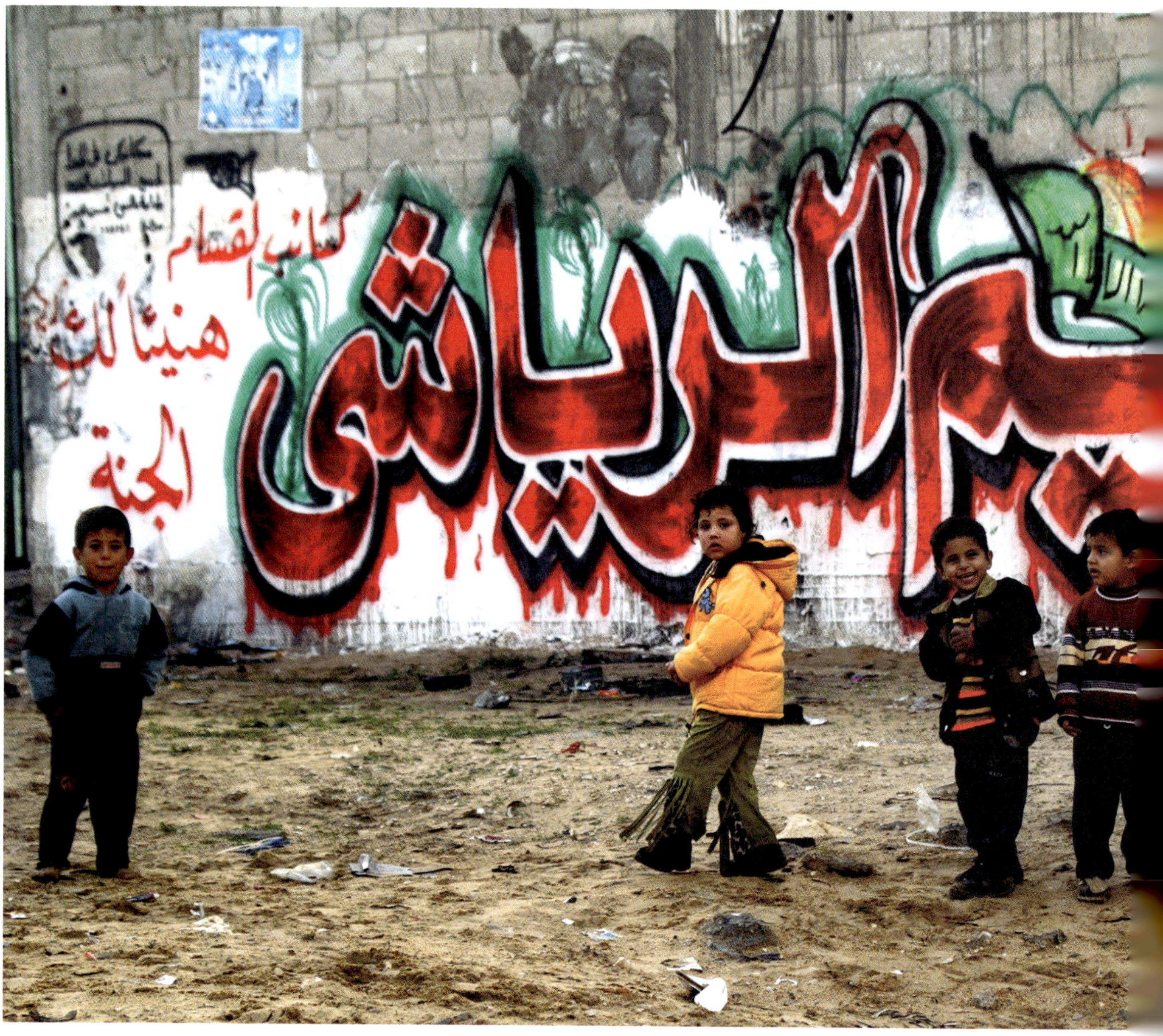

4

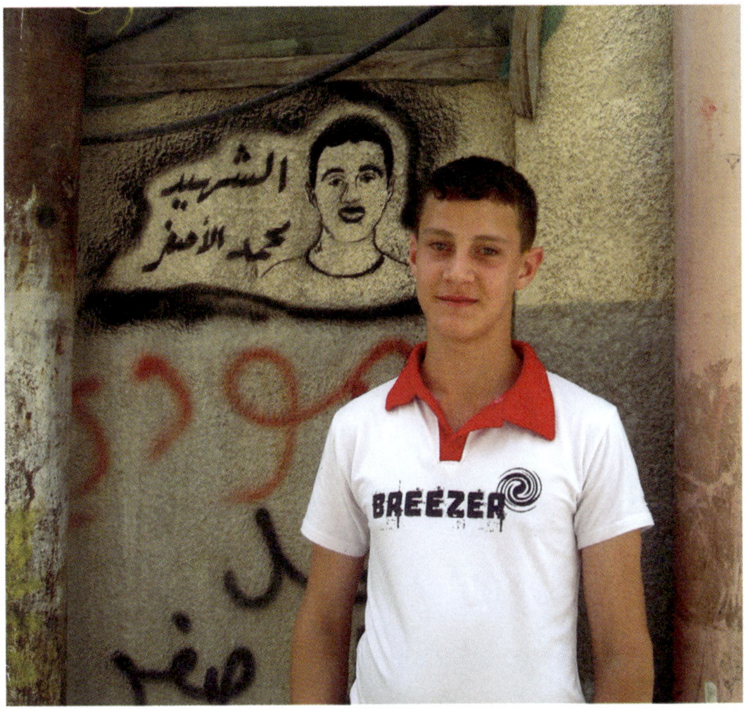

2

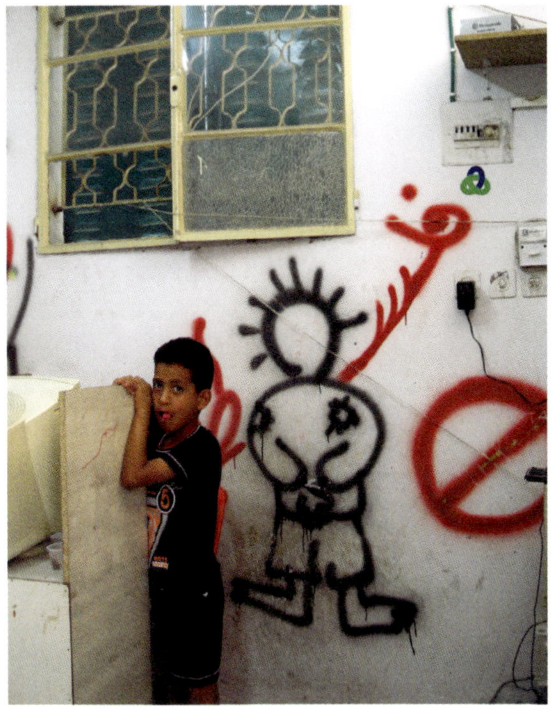

3

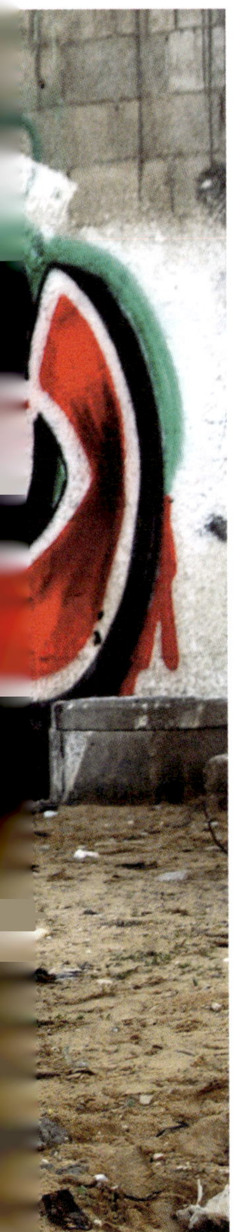

by all layers of society, its language, design and content must be clear, simple and legible, which naturally guarantees its increasing popularity.

The Israeli occupiers as well as the Palestinian factions themselves attempted to take control of graffiti many times and for many different reasons. The Oslo Peace Process went along with municipal clean up attempts by Fatah, and martyr portraits were banned by Hamas out of fear of idolization.[2] But whitewashed walls were usually quickly replaced by newly painted graffiti. After Hamas took control of the Gaza Strip, however, Fatah could only keep their presence on the walls with non-political messages.

Graffiti in the West Bank reflects both the local and the international graffiti scene. Palestinian residents and renowned graffiti artists from around the globe intervene on the barrier wall and in the alleys. However, there is widespread opposition from the Palestinian art community as well as the general Palestinian public to painting the wall. For Palestinians, the graffiti by international artists beautifies the barrier and renders it acceptable. They argue that the wall should instead be left untouched as an eyesore.[3] Artists are only able to write on the Palestinian side of the barrier. On the Israeli side this is impossible, as it is heavily barricaded by barbed wire and is under constant patrol. Israeli soldiers do patrols along the Palestinian side as well, but only occasionally stop graffiti artists.

Several graffiti workshops and mural projects are regularly organized for children and young artists in refugee camps with the help of UNERWA and other organizations. International and local graffiti artists organize the events with a school or institution in the refugee camp and collaborate with UNERWA to carry out the workshops. They are aimed to help the children express their pain and feelings through drawings and express their national Palestinian identity.

1. & 2. "Gaza Graffiti", Mia Gröndahl, The American University in Cairo Press
3. "The Aesthetics of Space: West Bank Graffiti and Global Artists", Hugh Lovatt

لن ننسى
1. "We will never forget" written on a wall, part of a long text, Askar refugee camp, Nablus, Palestine, 2007

الشهيد محمد الأصفر
2. "The martyr Mouhamad al-Asfar", a teenager standing in front of a stencil of his dead brother, Askar refugee camp, Nablus, Palestine, 2007

فلسطين / حنظلة
3. Hanzala figure sprayed looking at the word "Palestine", Askar refugee camp, Nablus, Palestine, 2007

ريم الرياشي، هنيئاً لكِ الجنة
4. "Reem Al Riyasheh", name of a female suicide bomber painted by a pro-Hamas militant group, Gaza City, Palestine, 2004

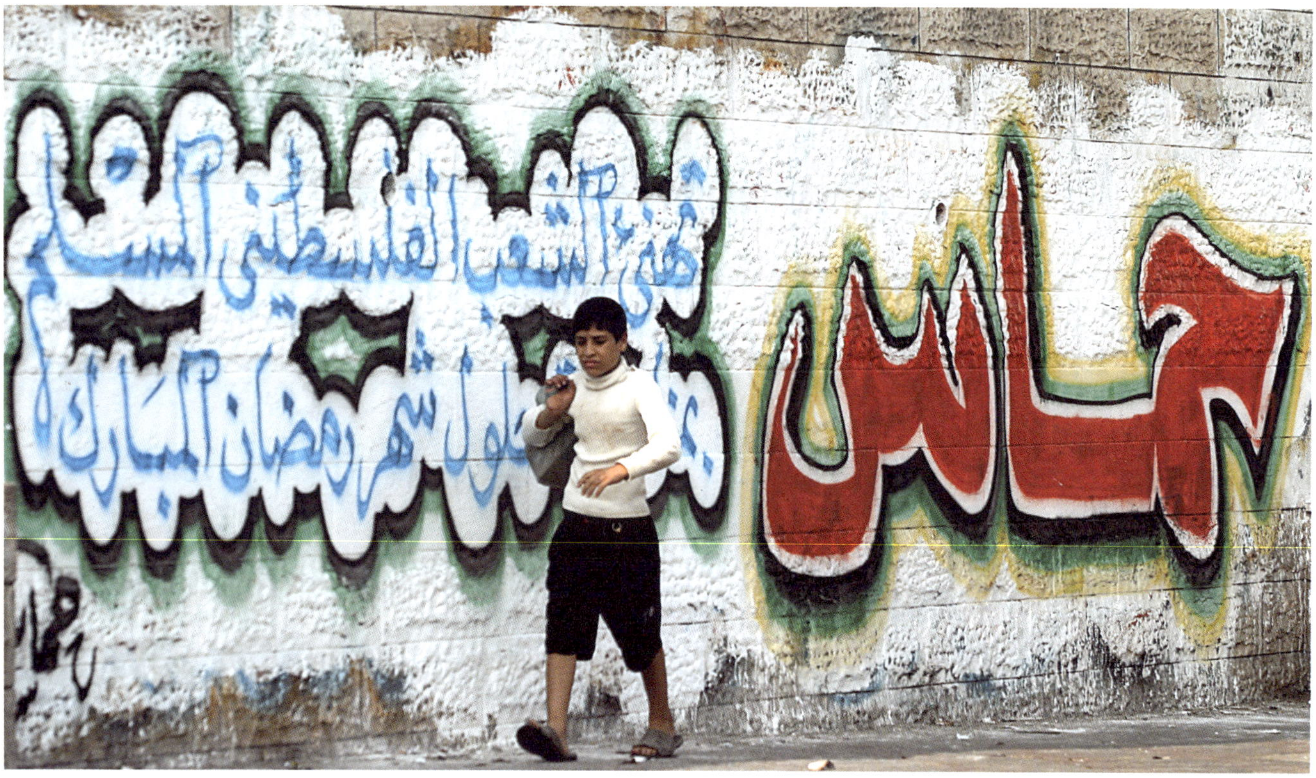
تهنئ الشعب الفلسطيني المسلم
حلول شهر رمضان المبارك
حماس

1

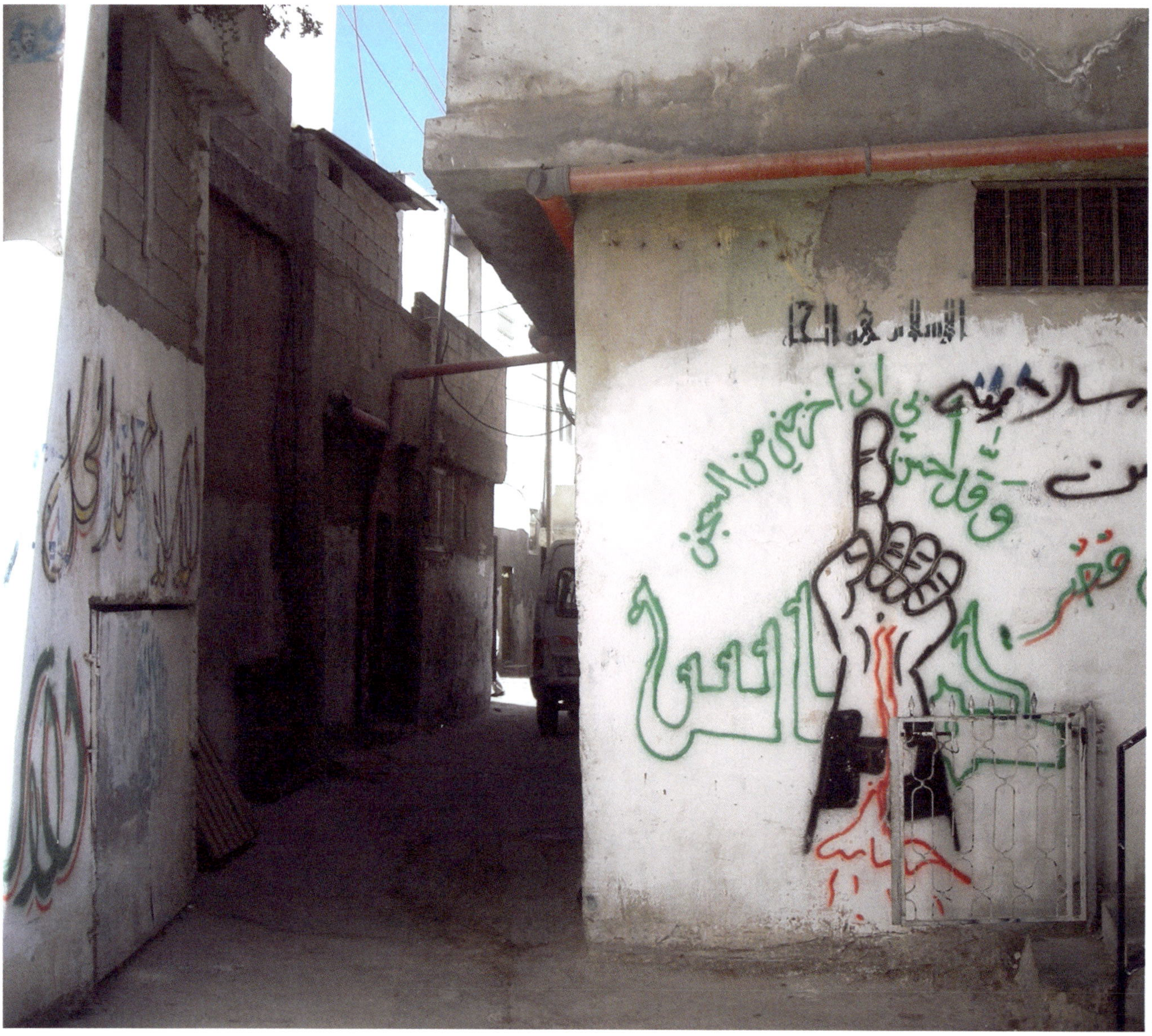
الإسلام هو الحل
وقد احسن بي اذ اخرجني من السجن
حماس

2

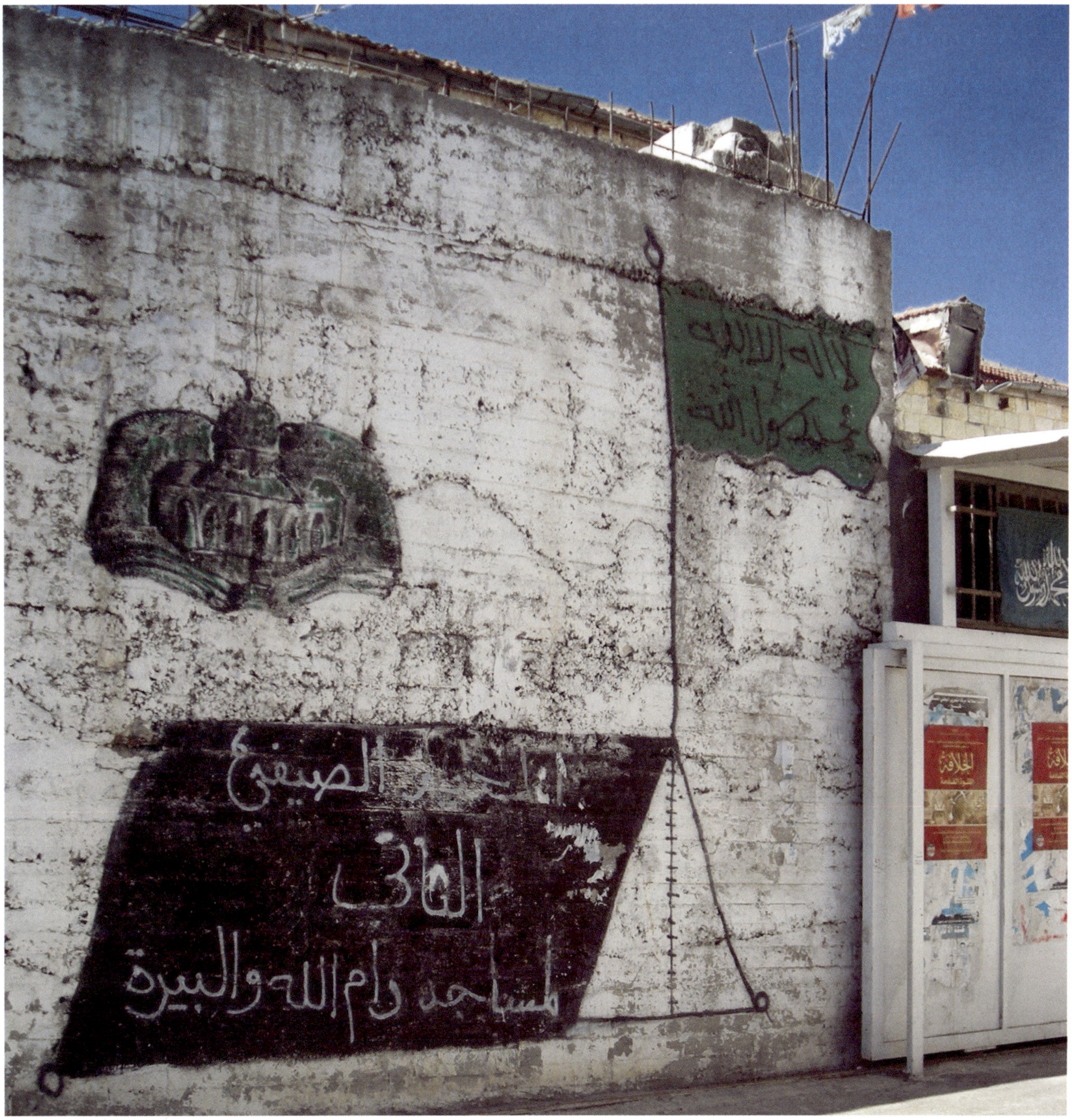

3

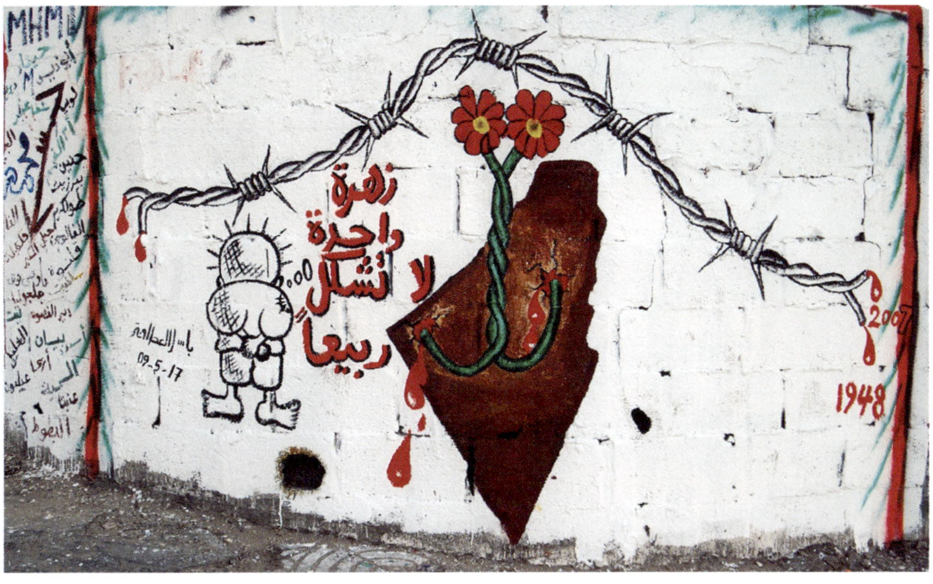

4

حماس / ...رمضان مبارك
1. "Hamas" is written beside Ramadan greetings, Jabalia refugee camp, Gaza, Palestine, 2004

حماس
2. The Palestinian resistance hand is drawn on top of "Hamas", Al Amari refugee camp, Ramallah, Palestine, 2008

3. Drawing of a refugee camp tent during the biggest Palestinian exodus, "Al Nakba", Ramallah, Palestine, 2007

زهرة واحدة لا تشكل ربيعاً
4. "One flower does not make spring", written between the Hanzala character and the map of Palestine, Gaza, Palestine, 2007

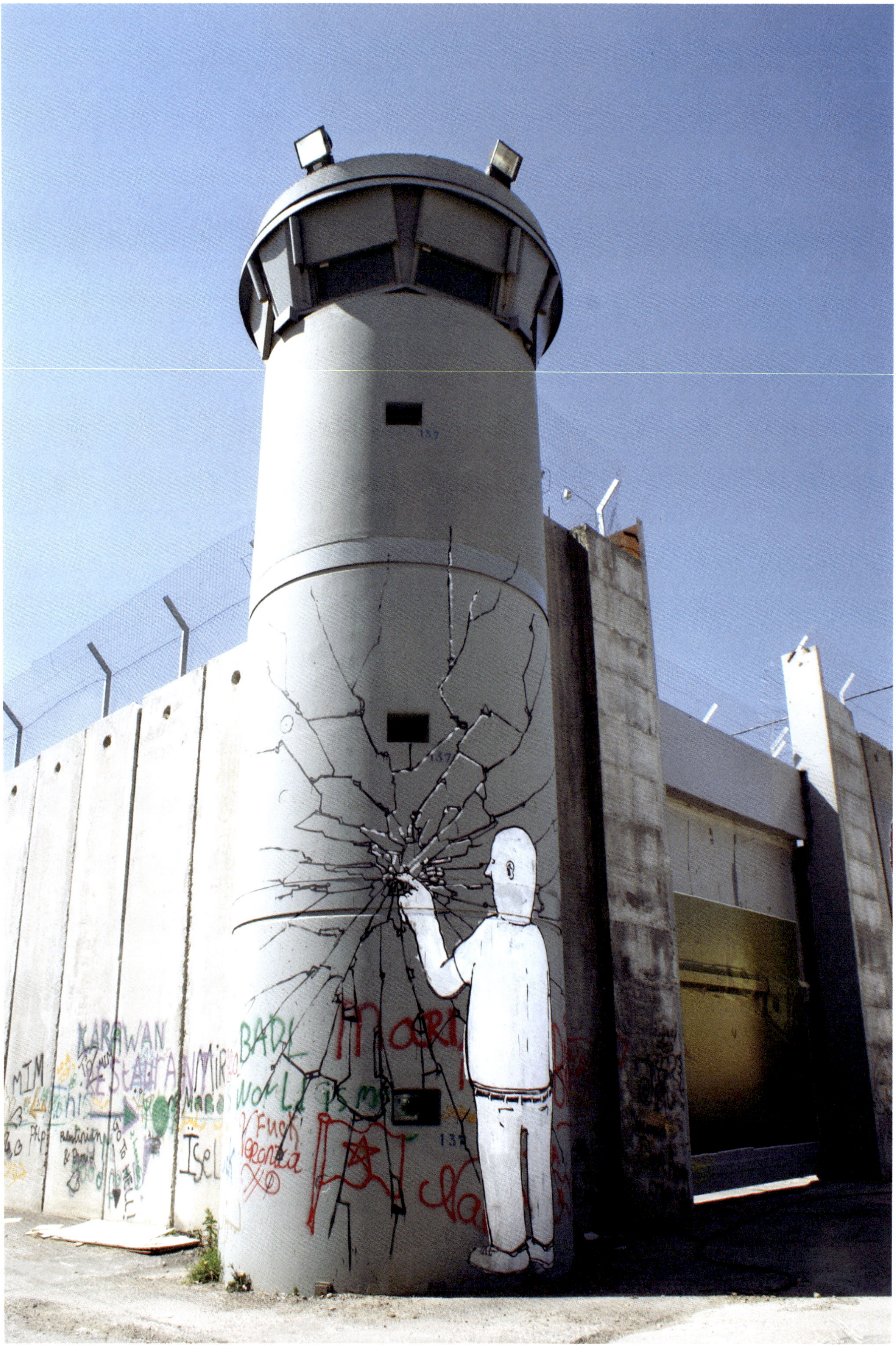

1

2·5

The Art of Resistance

فن المقاومة

William Perry

1. **Mural by BLU, watchtower at Rachel's Tomb, West Bank, Palestine, 2007**

Is the spray can mightier than the sword? The spray can hasn't forced Israel to stop building its highly controversial wall, but in the skilled hands of street artists like Banksy, Blu, Swoon and dozens of others, it's a formidable weapon in the struggle for hearts, minds and justice. In the case of Banksy, the most famous one to have registered his views on the wall, his artwork cuts to the heart of a contentious issue with thought-provoking wit, immediacy and appeal.

Banksy and Co.'s street art in Bethlehem and in the suburbs of Jerusalem has engaged a Western audience and contributed to an awareness of the reality on the ground and the asymmetrical power struggle between Palestinians and Israelis. Banksy's images in particular communicate this to a mass audience via the media and Internet with flabbergasting economy and efficiency. That ability to challenge Israel's narrative and to influence the Western public's perception of the wall and the broader conflict is as rare as it is invaluable.

Although Banksy and other renowned artists account for a modicum of the artwork on the wall and generate the most attention, interest and influence, there are thousands of other anonymous people from around the world who have traveled to Palestine to mark their individual protest against Israel's wall and their own governments' complicity, and to lend their idiosyncratic support through words and images to a people penned in by the wall. The wall has become an enormous visual petition, an ephemeral forum, a pictorial rant and reprimand calling for resistance, justice, freedom and solidarity, and a plea for understanding and humanity.

There are moving murals depicting a dove being nailed to the wall and a snake consuming all life in its path. There are numerous depictions of Jerusalem, Palestine's spiritual, religious, cultural and economic capital, which is now inaccessible to 3.6 million Palestinians from the West Bank and Gaza because of the wall. There are poignant, rhetorical questions to Israel's Jews, many of whom have endured inhuman suffering, asking how they and their descendants can now dispossess and imprison another people. There are quotations from Shakespeare, the Bible, and freedom fighters like Gandhi and Nelson Mandela, which are used to challenge the inhumanity of Israel as occupier and oppressor. And there are symbols central to Palestinian identity, denoting resistance, liberation, affinity to the land, Palestinian refugees' "right to return" and national unity. Some of the artwork is beautiful and moving; some conveys more spirit than artistic talent. Humor is often used to assuage or deflect the pain and naked barbarity of the wall. And there is no shortage of inane dross. One defining message that runs up and

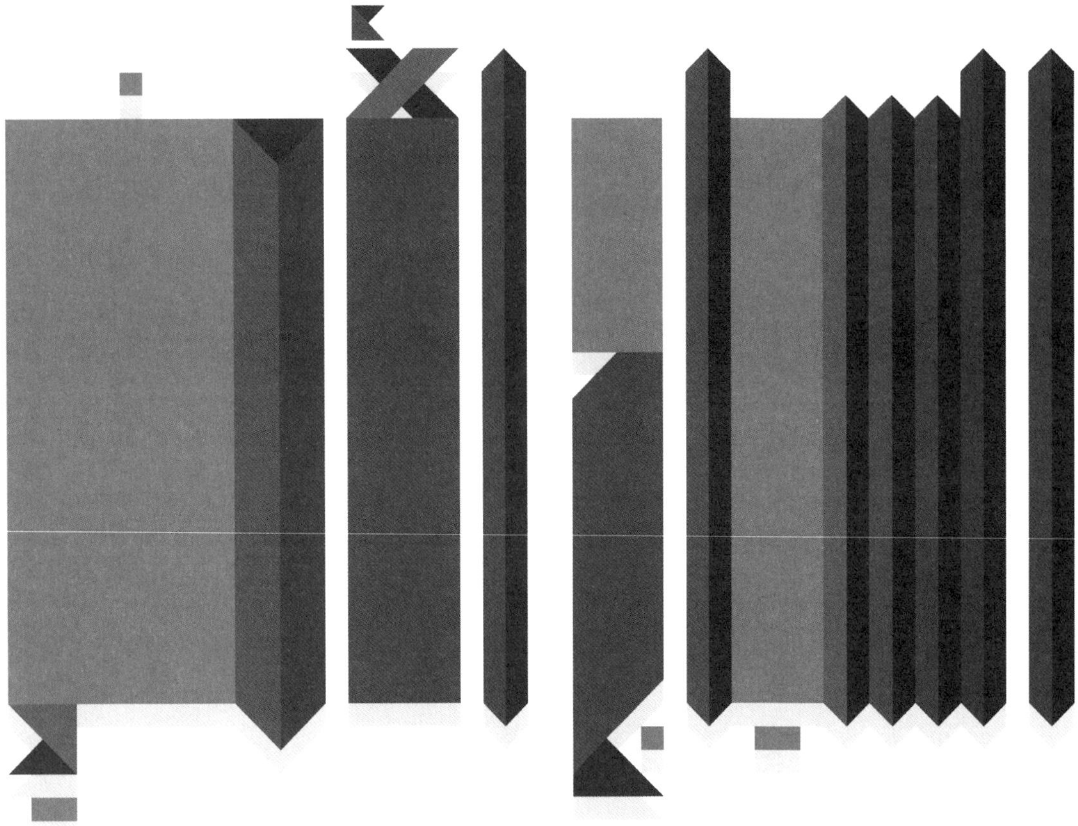

1

السياج الأمني

1. “Security Fence”, MUIZ ANWAR, typography

2. Black: Palestinian land
Gray: Israel and its colonies

3. “CTRL + ALT + DELETE”, FILIPPO MINELLI, near Qalandiya checkpoint

down the wall in the West Bank, however, is this: ‘To exist is to resist.’

Most Palestinians don’t object to Israel giving the world’s graffiti and street artists the largest canvas on the planet: what is primarily objected to is its route — it doesn’t follow the Green Line, the internationally recognized Palestine-Israel border. If you insist on building a wall, they say, build it along the internationally recognized border that we share. Fair enough.

But Israel hasn’t, and refuses to. The Green Line is 315 km long. The wall will be 709 km long when it is completed, and about eighty-five percent of that will be built on West Bank land. Consequently, its route will annex ten percent of the West Bank to the Israeli-controlled side. This insidious path, Palestinians assert, is a de facto land grab by Israel.

The reason for this circuitous route? Since 1967, successive Israeli governments have encouraged the establishment of illegally built Jewish-only colonies, euphemistically called ‘settlements’, on Palestinian land that Israel has illegally occupied for over forty years. Every one of Israel’s 220 colonies and outposts (fledgling colonies) in the West Bank is illegal under international law. The colonies themselves occupy just three percent of the West Bank; however, the complex security apparatus and infrastructure that serves these illegal colonies and their 500,000 Jewish settlers, and connects them to Israel, requires Israeli control over a staggering forty-five percent of the Palestinian West Bank.

But it’s much more than just a land grab. The impact that the wall is having on Palestinian lives, livelihoods, businesses and communities is, Palestinians and others insist, designed to isolate the West Bank’s communities economically, socially and culturally — and thereby strangle them. The wall divides major Palestinian population centers into fragmented “Bantustans” (this was the term used by a recent Israeli Prime Minister, Ariel Sharon). Critically, it amputates the West Bank’s major cities from Jerusalem, the economic hub of the West Bank, as well as the Palestinian cultural and spiritual capital. Without Jerusalem, the surrounding cities will wither.

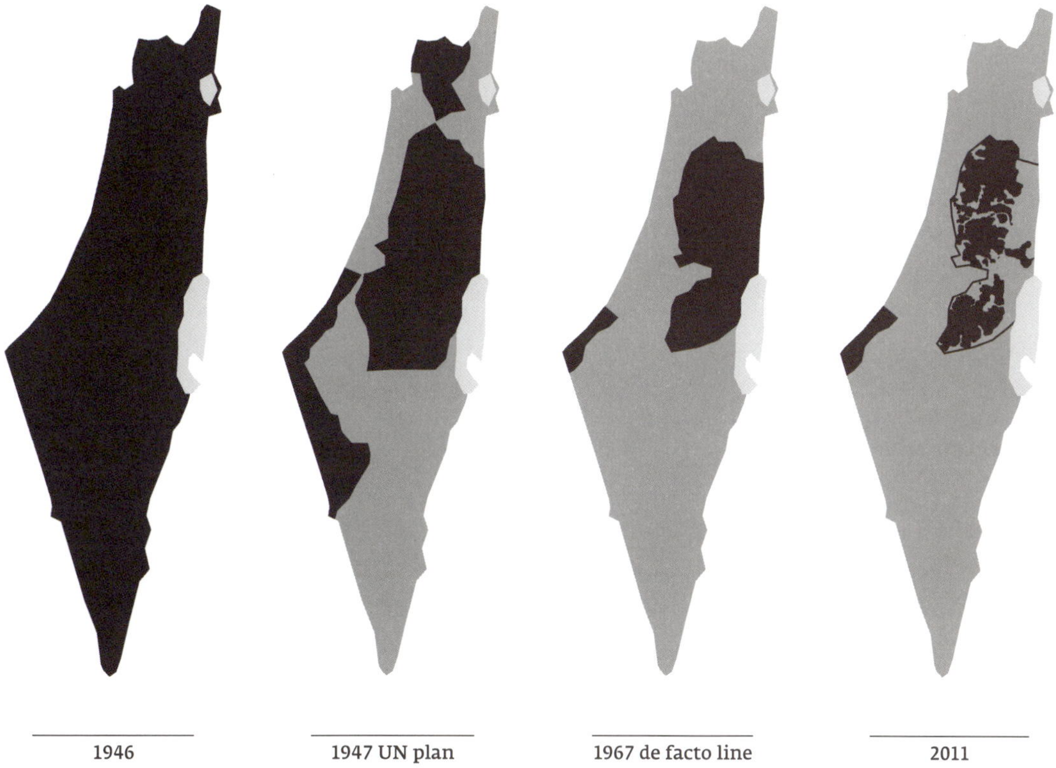
1946
1947 UN plan
1967 de facto line
2011

2

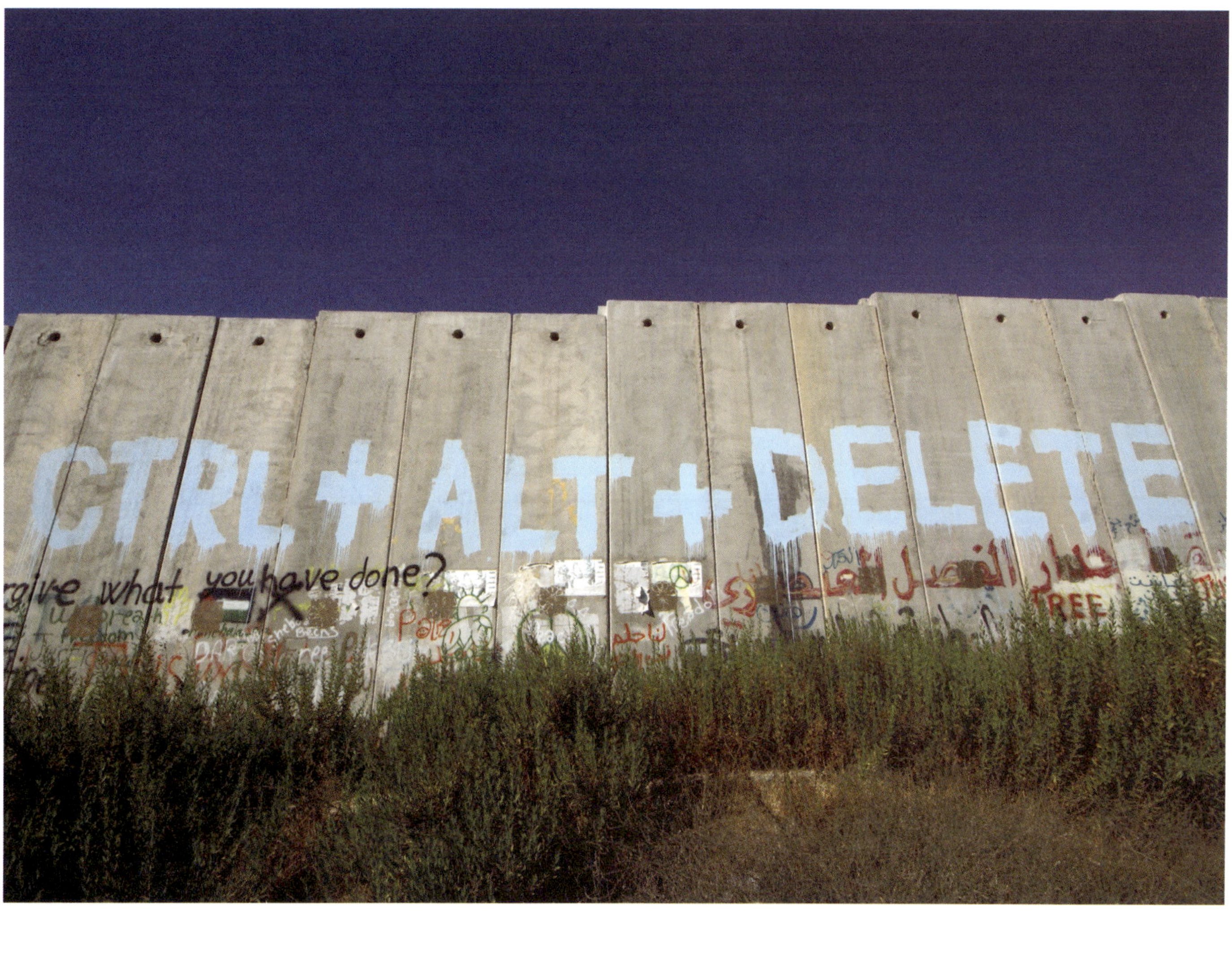
CTRL + ALT + DELETE
what you have done?
FREE

3

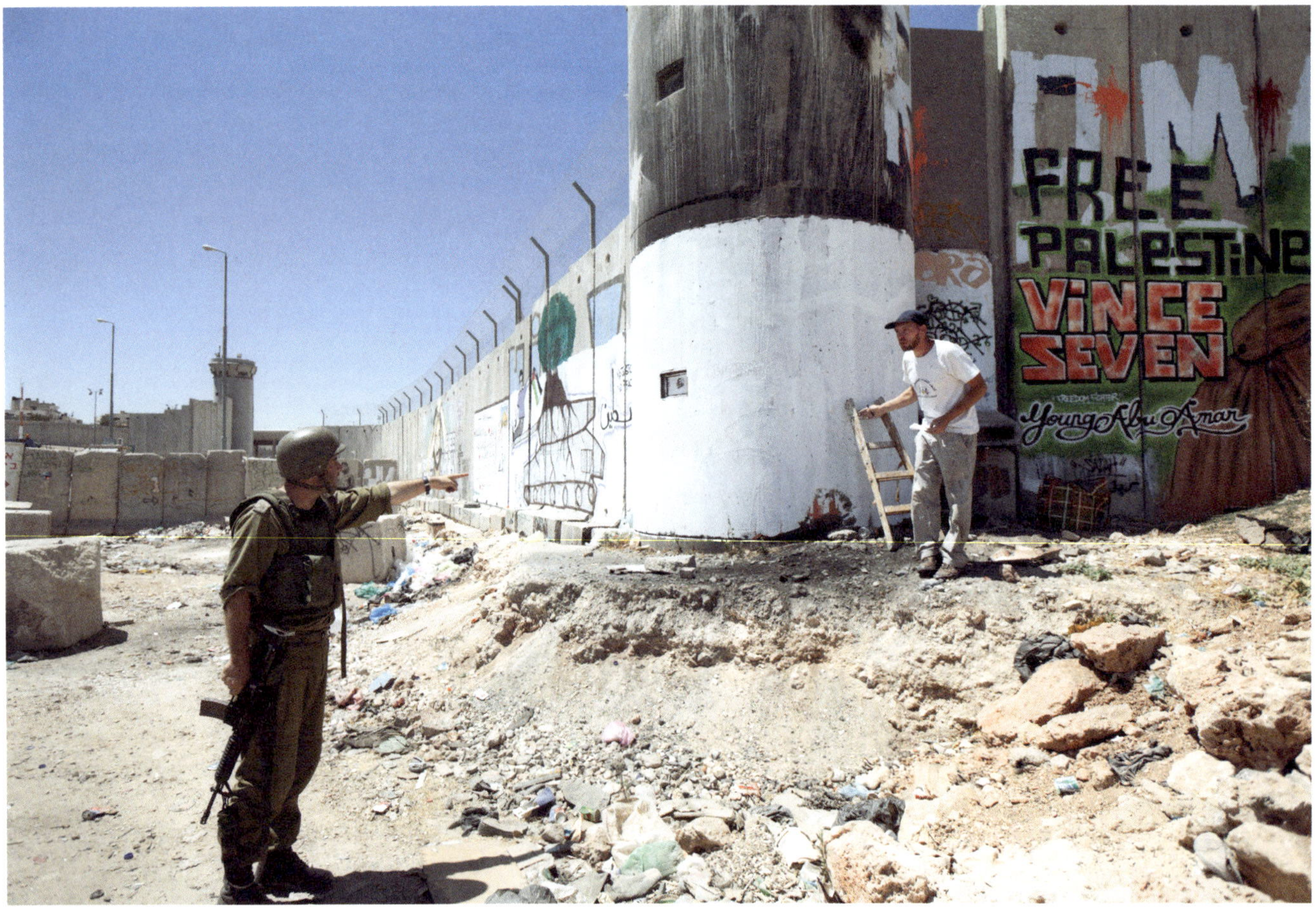

1

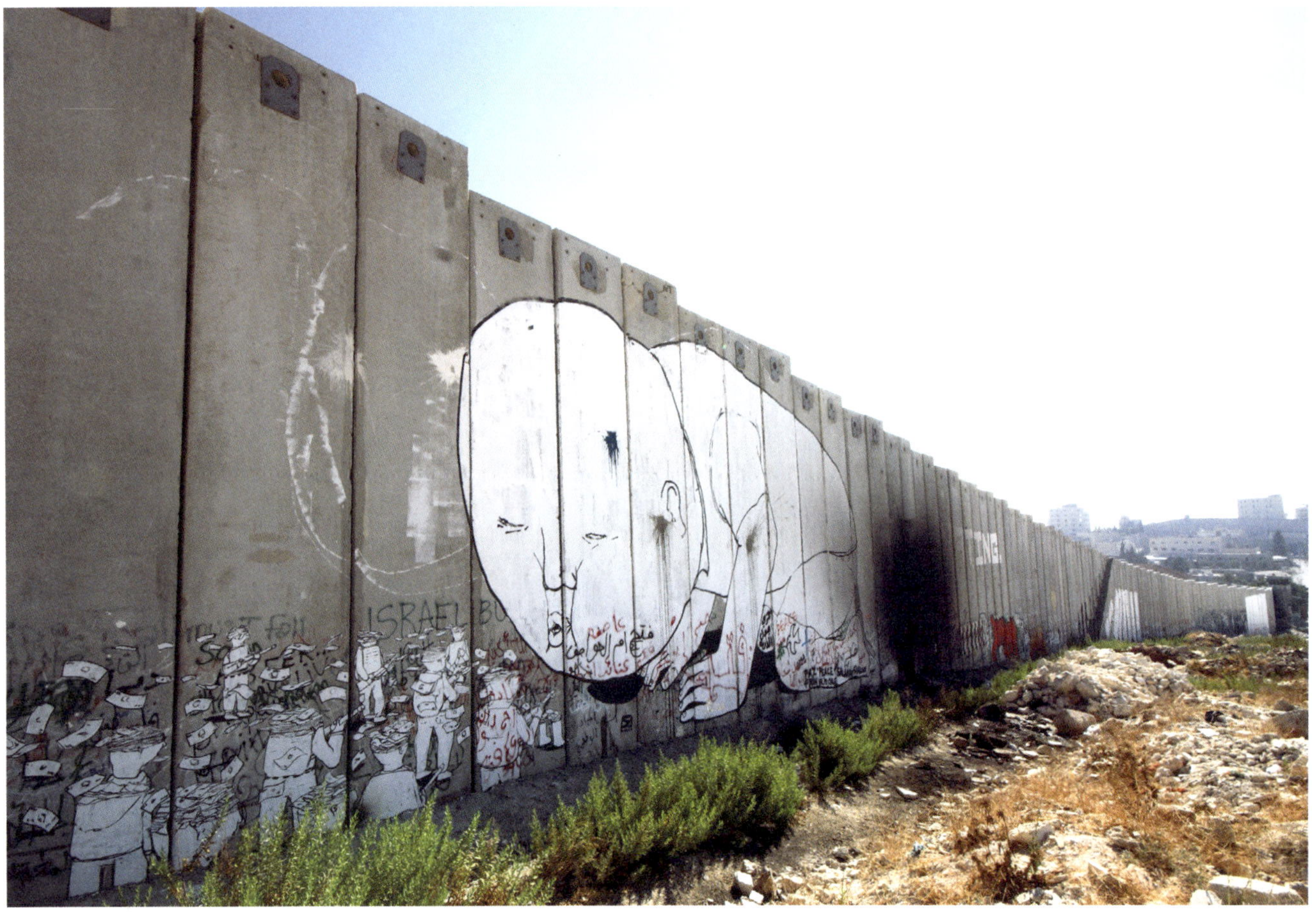

2

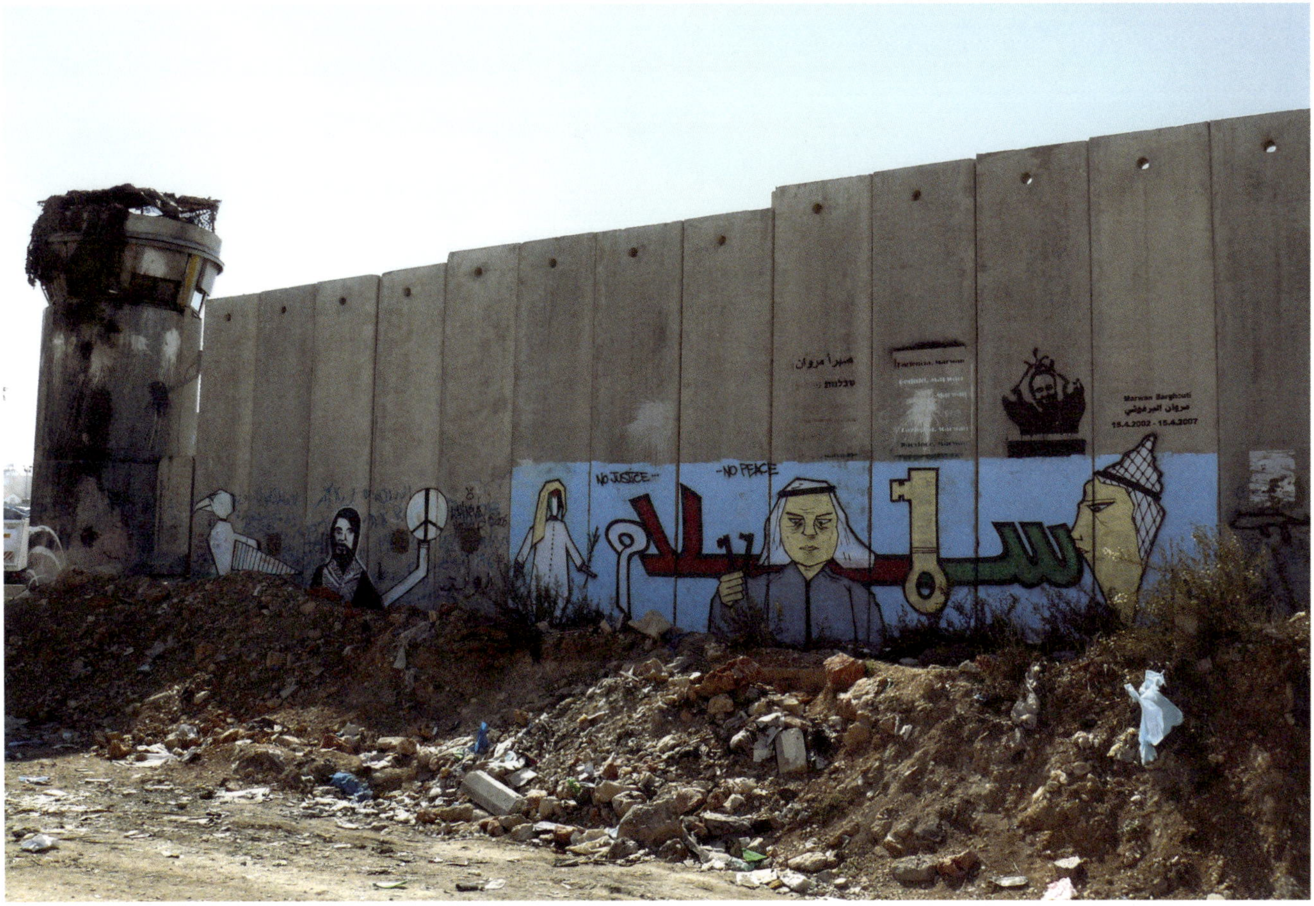

3

Palestinian land owners are made to apply for a 'visitor' permit to access their farmland, their olive groves, their greenhouses from the Israelis, who then determine who 'qualifies' for a permit. This permit regime has separated eighty percent of Palestinian farmers from their land and livelihoods in parts of the West Bank, and it regulates the few hours that they can access their land (some permits only allow weekly or seasonal access).

The wall is about separating families from their communities, their schools, their places of worship, from their clinics, hospitals and specialist facilities. It makes accessing them, via military checkpoints, difficult, time-consuming and humiliating. It makes Palestinians, as they say, refugees in their own land. One is left with the impression that it has been meticulously and methodically planned in order to impair the fabric of Palestinian life and society — and it appears ruthlessly effective.

So is the graffiti effective?, critics ask, with many quoting the one old local man who told Banksy to go home, saying that Palestinians don't want the wall to be made beautiful. Many don't, but most appreciate the international show of solidarity the artwork and graffiti represent, and the foreign interest it generates. If it attracts people who part with some tourist dollars on souvenirs and in Bethlehem's hotels and restaurants — and who also witness the reality — then it's worth it.

And for those who travel to the West Bank to leave their mark on the wall, it's a small way of expressing solidarity. Cynical about the effectiveness of writing to elected representatives, it's a means of voicing one's dissent in a way that will be read by hundreds of other visitors — until it is scribbled over by someone doing likewise — that's what graffiti is all about. Like boycotting Israeli products in the supermarket, or taking direct action through the Free Gaza convoys and flotillas, it is another example of the growing number of ways in which civil society is leading where leaders — for decades — have failed.

1. Askar, a European artist, is stopped from painting on the wall by an Israeli soldier, 2008

2. Painting of a giant baby blowing away soldiers made out of money, BLU, near Aida refugee camp, 2007

سلام

3. "Peace", ASKAR, Qalandiya checkpoint, 2008

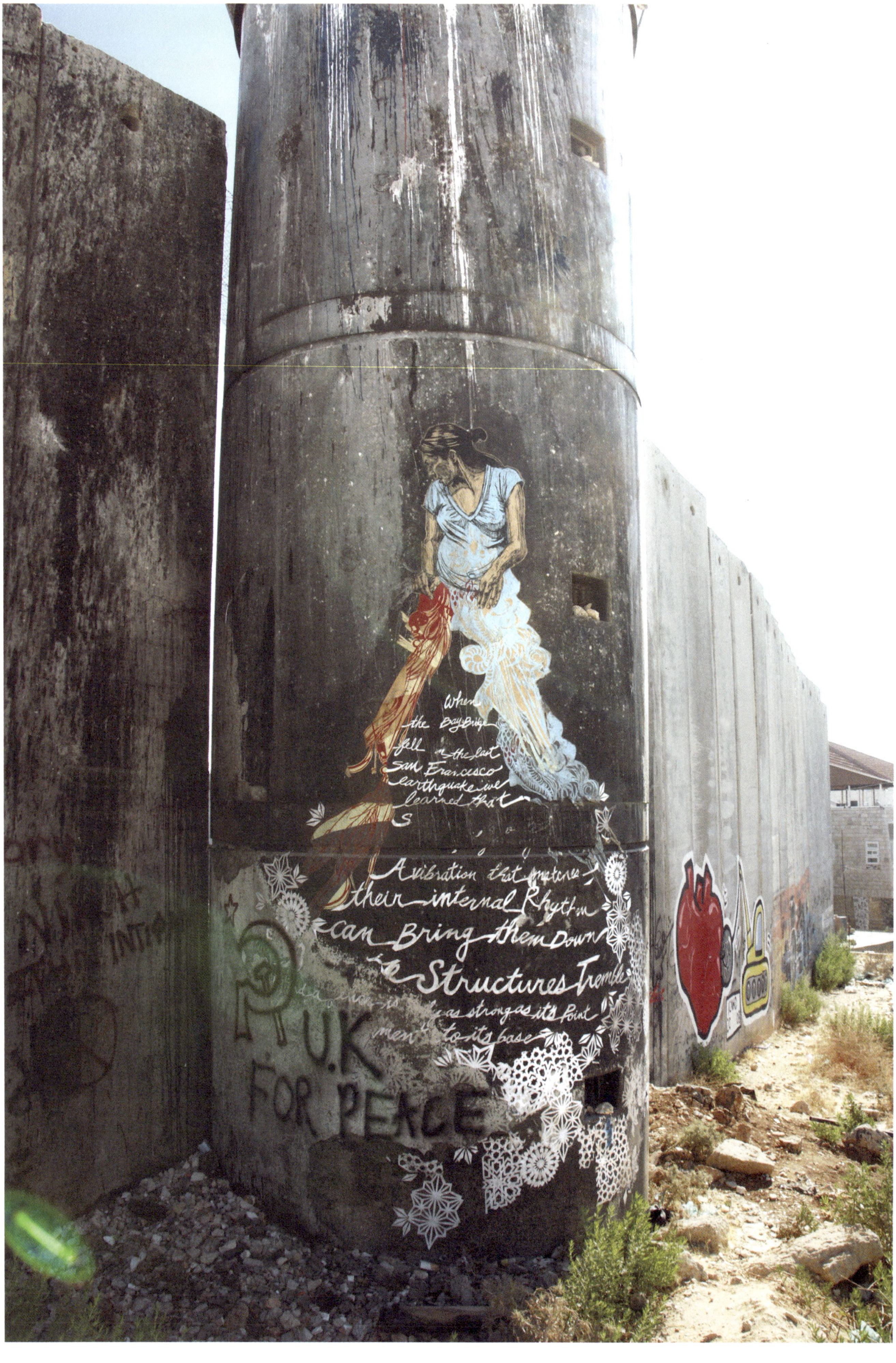
When the Bay Bridge fell in the last San Francisco earthquake we learned that
A vibration that matches their internal Rhythm can Bring them Down
Structures Tremble
as strong as it's Point
to its base
U.K
FOR PEACE

1

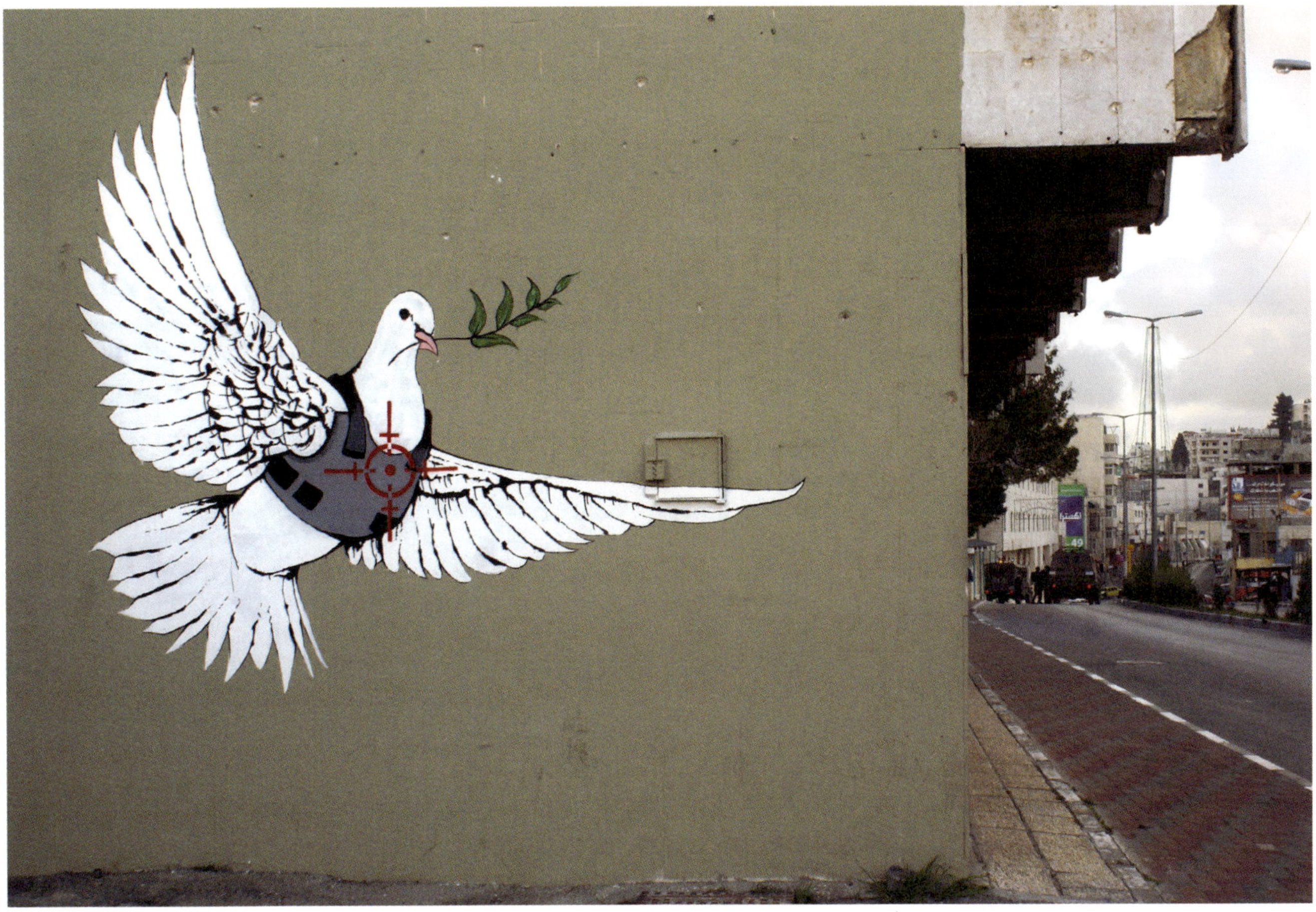

2

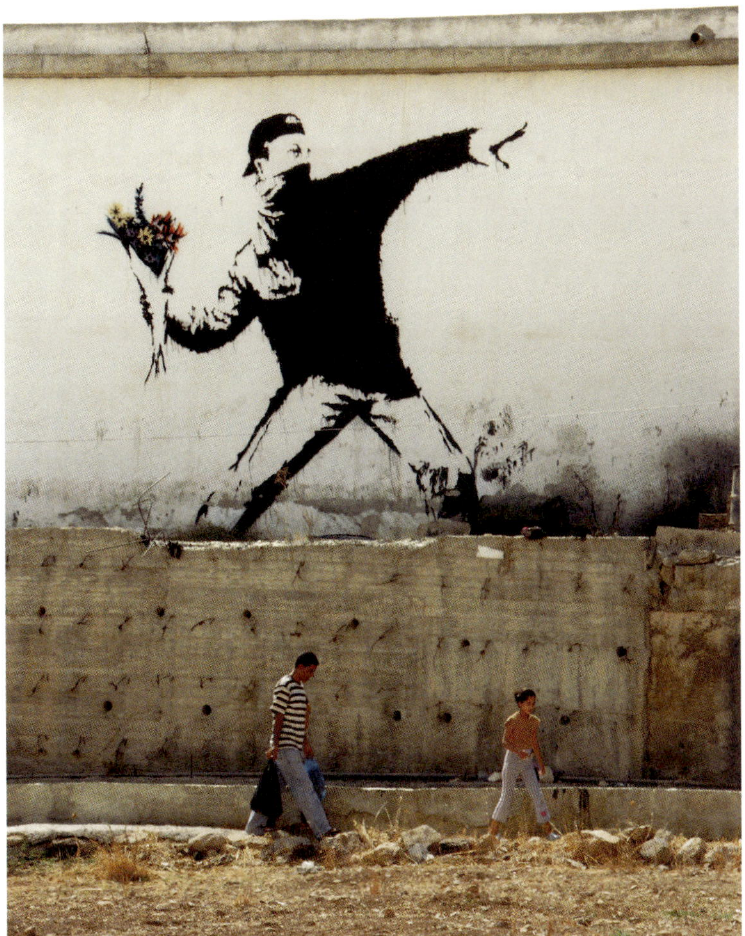

3

1. Paste up by SWOON, opposite Aida refugee camp, 2007. The image of a woman contains a quote about how, by matching the resonant frequency of any structure, it is possible to bring it down without using so much force. The spot was stained by a protest fire because it was there that a 17 year old boy climbed the wall to hang a Palestinian flag. He was imprisoned for 8 years for this simple act.

2. BANKSY, West Bank, 2007

3. BANKSY, Bethlehem, 2007

• WILLIAM PARRY
is a London-based freelance journalist and photographer who has published in The Guardian, The Independent and elsewhere. He recently published the book "Against the Wall: the art of resistance in Palestine" about the protest art on the West Bank Barrier. He has worked and traveled extensively in the Middle East.

"Against the Wall: the art of resistance in Palestine", published by PlutoPress
ISBN 978-0-7453-2917-8

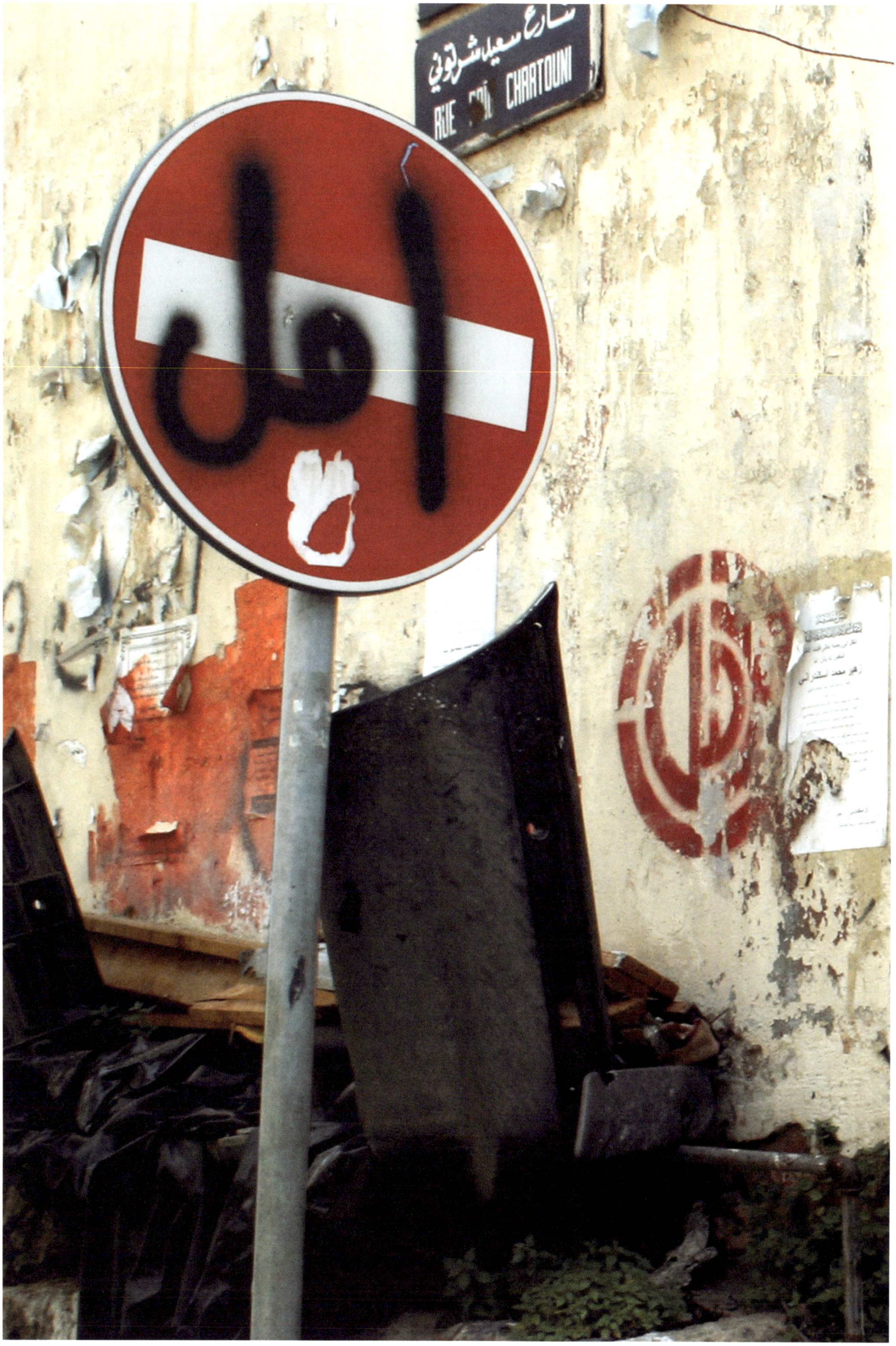

1

2·6
Marking Beirut
وسم بيروت

Tala F. Saleh

1. Amal stencil and slogan (on traffic sign), Patriachate, Beirut, 2007

After thirty years of civil war, and Israel's war on Lebanon in 2006, the people of Beirut began to express their thoughts, feelings, ideologies, and political affiliations on the walls of their city. The graffiti in Beirut provides insight into the functions and practices of Beirut's political and social communities, and serves as a tool to understand community activities and involvements.

In Beirut, the graffiti culture is a "spray it, don't say it" type of culture. What would perhaps not be openly spoken about in a public arena is sprayed on the city walls, ensuring that everyone and anyone will be able to see it, read it, understand it, and perhaps comment on it in the same manner.

Graffiti is a practice that originated within Western cultures; it is a form of self-expression and a sign of existence. It covers a wide range of techniques, from simple markings to tags, logos, colorful, complex stencils and murals. Today, graffiti has become attractive to many artists, who paint and stencil more than just tags and signatures, but it also consists of posting political and social commentaries on city walls and criticizing and satirizing current issues. Graffiti occurs at certain times and about specific topics, usually where there is incongruence between two or more sides, be it an individual versus an establishment, or two political groups competing with each other for territory.

Graffiti uses the wall as its medium and the streets as its canvas to provide artists, individuals and communities with a unique platform where they can express their opinions with the same amount of visibility as an official message. In her book "The Subversive Imagination", Carol Becker emphasizes: "it is in these rare spaces where artists and individuals can free themselves from the expectations of the art market and contingents of economic reality to immerse themselves in the making of their artwork." [1]

A type of graffiti mostly associated with revolutions and wars and a type that was extremely abundant in Beirut is stencil graffiti. Its immediacy and ability to communicate ideas in a powerful form of expression transformed stencil graffiti into a true art form. It allowed it to become the most widespread form of graffiti found in many major cities, especially those like Beirut, cities with a history of civil strife.

Throughout the Lebanese civil war (1975-1990), stencils and slogans were sprayed around the city on the walls and were used to mark territory and express demands and opinions. These writings and stencils were not only particular to a specific group during a particular

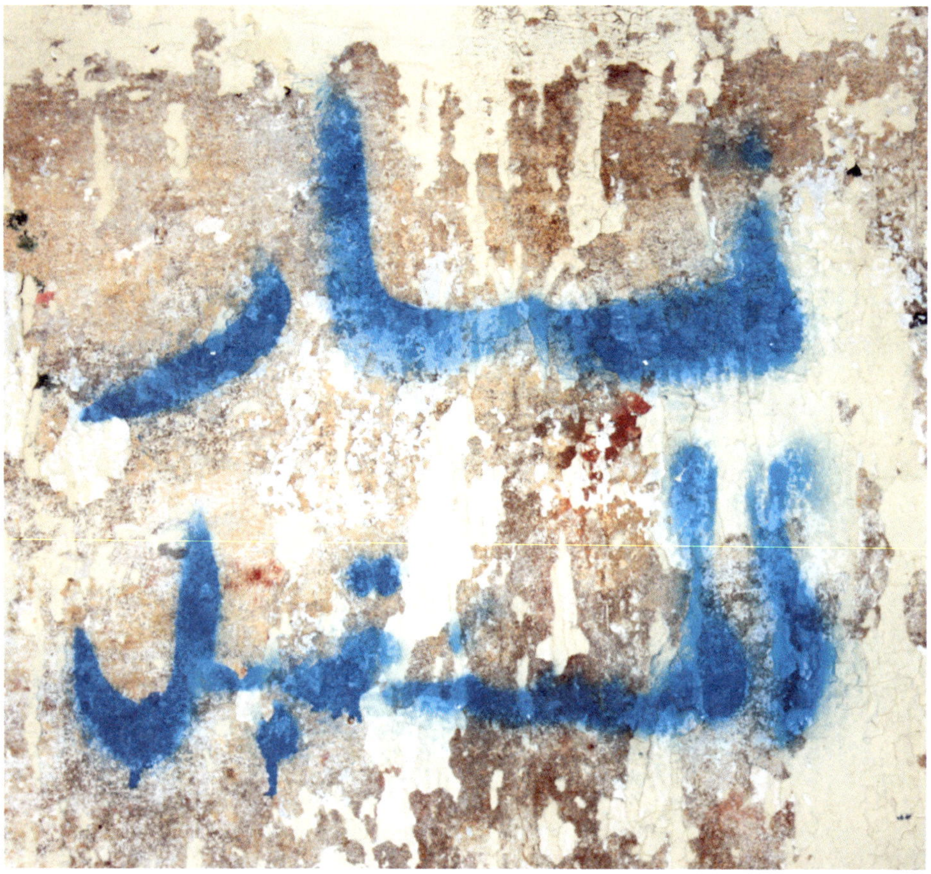

1

1. Tayyar Al-Mustaqbal (Future Movement) stencil, unknown artist, Sanayeh, Beirut, 2007

2. Kataeb (Phalange Party) and Bashir Gemayel stencil, unknown artist, Mar Nicolas, Beirut

3. Lebanese Phalange stencil, unknown artist, Mar Nicolas, Beirut, 2007

4. P.S.P. stencil, Hamra, Beirut

5. Lebanese Phalange on a building, unknown artist, traditional Lebanese house, Monot, Beirut

6. Kataeb and Lebanese forces stencils, unknown artist, Achrafieh, Beirut

situation, they were an official form of communication for every single political party during this time. The graffiti spoke the truth of the situation and was a way of recording exactly what was going on in the hearts and minds of those directly involved in the war. The language of graffiti allowed for the expression of hopes, dreams, demands, and political goals. Graffiti became the language of civil strife in a war in which much went unspoken.

With its stencils and slogans, the practice of graffiti in Beirut segregates the city along territorial lines. Every faction within the political community marks its space by use of graffiti to make the boundaries evident to outsiders. In Beirut, what is most noticeable is the abundance of political logo stencils which belong to the official political parties of Beirut, marking territories and dividing the streets. During the civil war in Beirut, graffiti took on a public role as a means of communication, a silent war between the political parties. These stencils were a proof of existence, marking territory and informing passersby whose territories they were entering.

These stencils proved to be very useful throughout the beginning of the civil war. The political stencils and logos were abundantly sprayed around every avenue and street corner of Beirut. By marking the public arena within every area of the then divided city, each faction marked its territory and kept viewers aware of their location, as well as strengthening party support among followers. Graffiti served as a system or

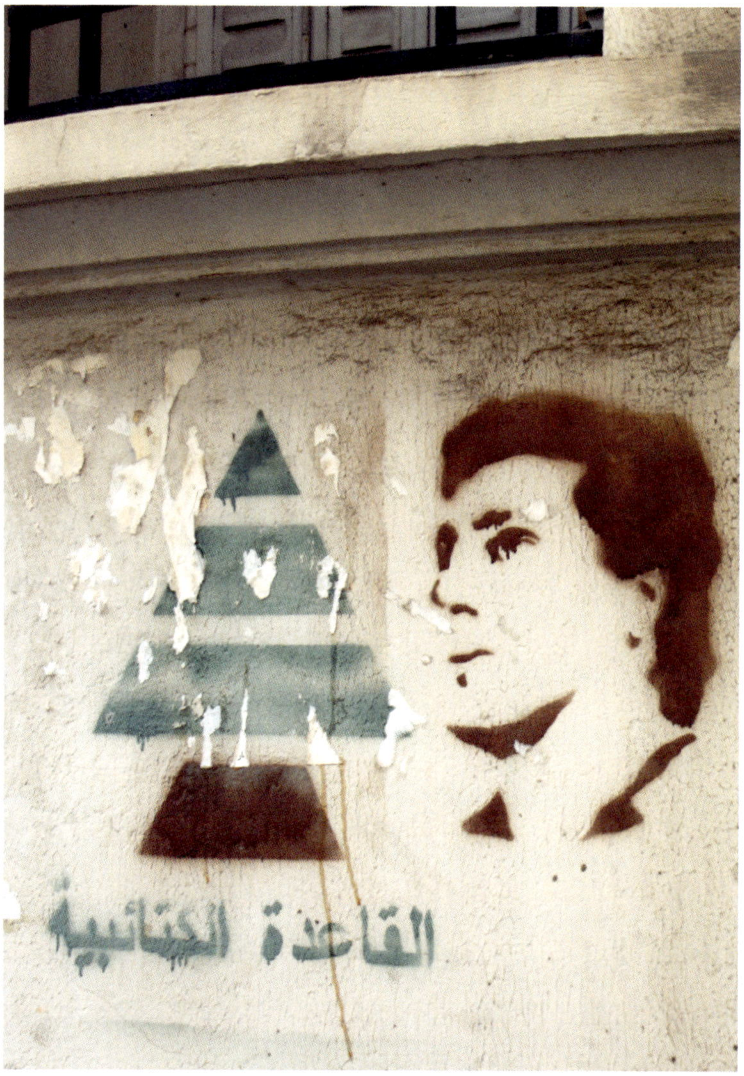

2

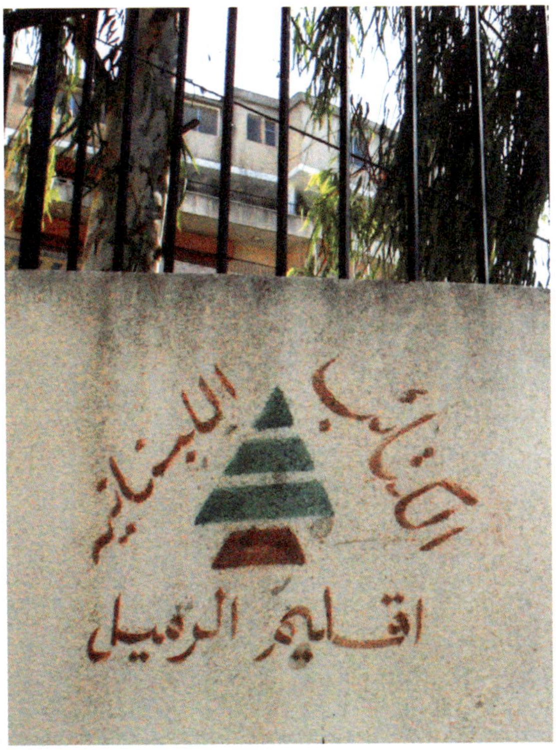
الكتائب اللبنانية
اقليم الرميل

3

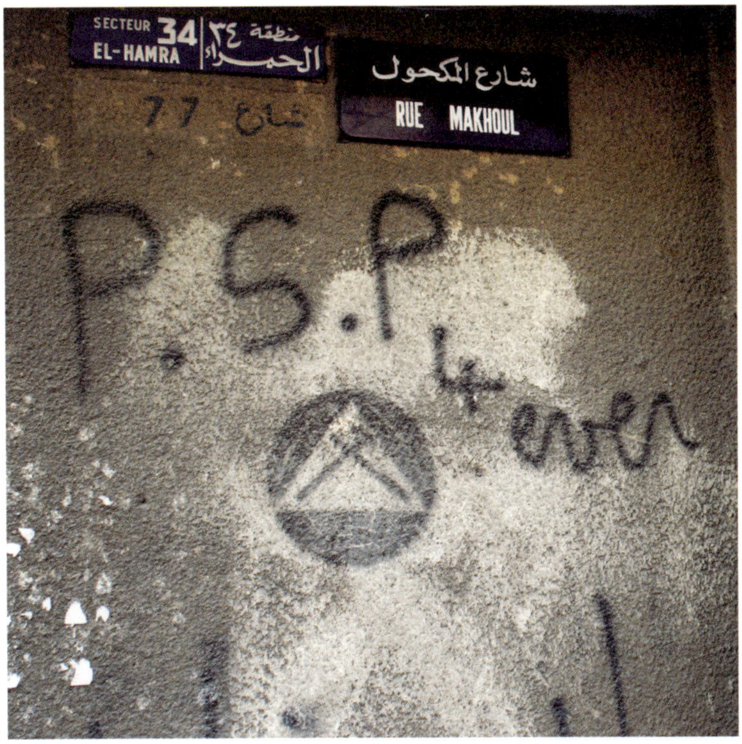
SECTEUR 34 منطقة ٣٤
EL-HAMRA الحمراء
شارع المكحول
RUE MAKHOUL
P.S.P
4 ever

4

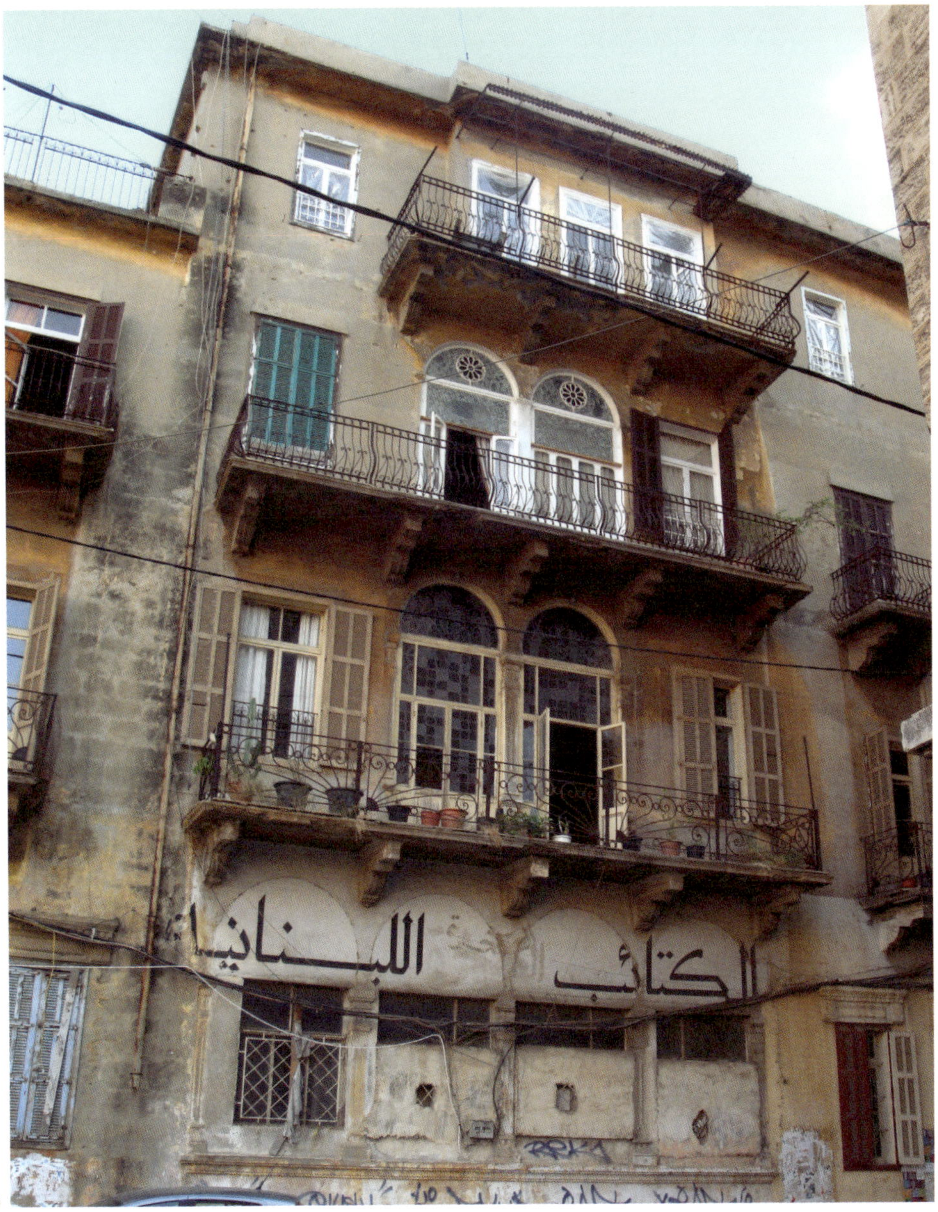
الكتائب اللبنانية

5

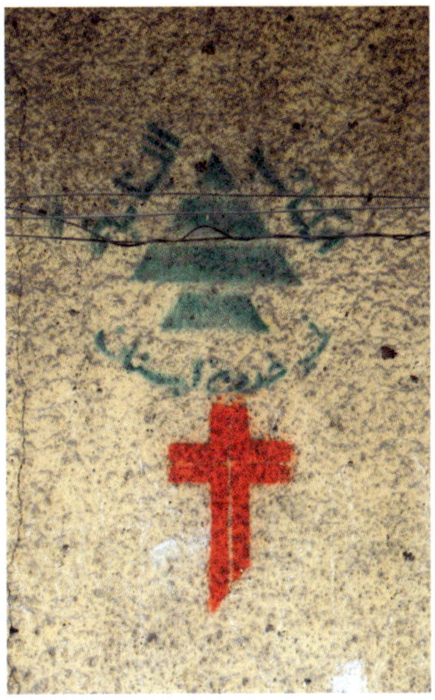

6

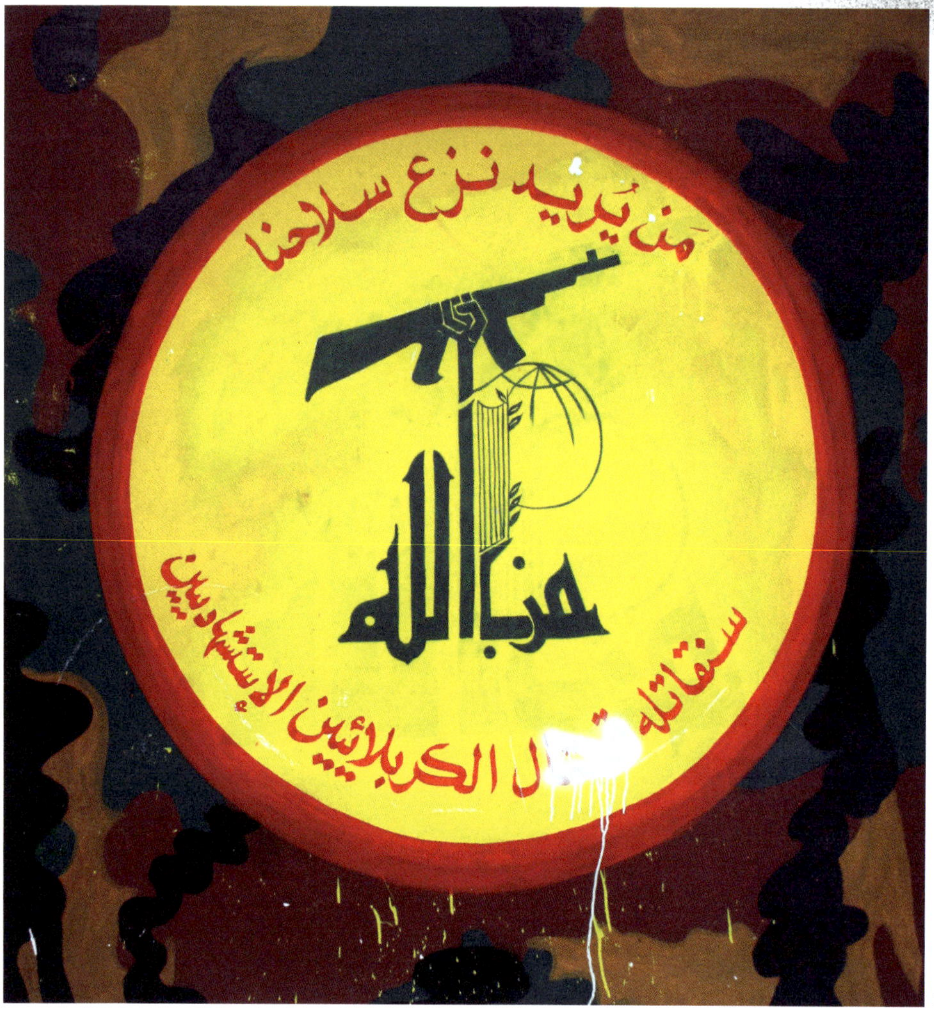

1

medium that freed expression from the restrictions of war and thus allowed different political parties to openly express their allegiances and ideologies.

Thirty years after the war started and about fifteen years after it ended, these stenciled logos still remained, and the practice of spraying and marking territory with these logo stencils was still popular among political parties in Beirut. The stencils silently marked territory and confirmed the ongoing existence and activities of many political parties that were under threat of dying out after the civil war. The street canvas of logos highlights the endless struggle for power, and the ongoing pursuit for recognition, whether from the state, political party followers, or the general public.

Comparable to the tagging of New York or Los Angeles gangs, which started in the late 1960s, the political logos within Beirut's vernacular politically set apart every area from its neighbor. While walking through Hamra (prior to 2008) or taking a stroll around Clemenceau, both primarily Muslim areas, one could see that most of the main walls were covered in political logos. Most of them belonged to Amal and the Lebanese Communist Party. They announced who this area belonged to, their ideologies, and who was in control, keeping a tightly knit, tribe-like neighborhood.

The stencil graffiti in Beirut speaks to multiple audiences and provides an astute image of the actions of the Lebanese political communities. Every political party has supporters in specific areas within Beirut's communities, and these areas are marked by the use of political stencils. Walkers and readers know where they are and under whose control a given area is simply by the sheer density of graffiti and signatures.

In addition to political stencils and logos, there are two other types of graffiti evident in the Beirut vernacular: social stencils and street art. Social stencils provide social commentaries

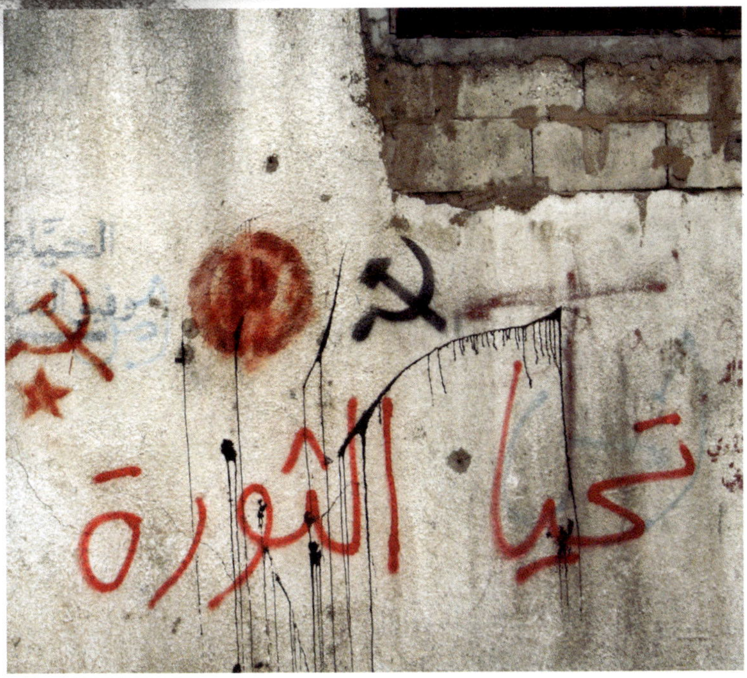

2

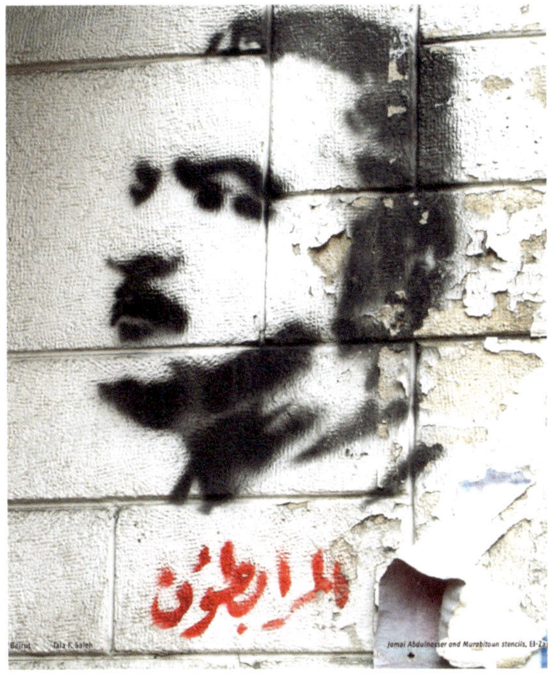

3

or satire on current events within Beirut's society. It is a form of graffiti that is critical of political conflicts and comments on social issues and current events in a humorous manner. In Beirut, this type of graffiti is primarily found in centers of nightlife and entertainment such as Gemmayzeh and Monot.

Street art is a form of graffiti that has become popular and more noticed in the city from 2008 and onwards. In May of 2008, with the crisis in Lebanon unsolved for three years, tensions were high after intense street level clashes between pro-government forces and the Hezbollah-backed opposition. After having reached an agreement in Doha, Lebanese political leaders ordered the removal of all political signs from the streets of Beirut in an attempt to ease tension. This resulted in a redirection of graffiti towards the artistic and patriotic context, towards street art.

Street art is technical and artistic; it is larger in scale than stencils and slogans, and more likely to be painted on larger walls on main roads for greater visibility. Street art has the capability to shock and awe, a powerful form of art that is very attractive in most cases. In Beirut, street art is a call for recognition, attention, and a response to current events in the country and surrounding Arab world. The difference between street art and the stencil graffiti in Beirut is that street art is not divided, it is patriotic, localized, colloquial, and most importantly found and drawn in Arabic letterforms and typography, something very specific to Lebanon. Beirut street art calls out for unity rather than division, calling for "One Lebanon" with no sectarianism.

Graffiti everywhere in the world is a tool of grassroots 'expansionism', an instrument or medium through which to be heard, and one that is easy to spread fast. In Beirut, and very uniquely for Beirut, it was used to mark territory and to affirm people's right to exist. This clearly revealed an amazing fact: that every party in the Lebanese war was fighting to protect their own identities and right to exist. Beirut's graffiti told the story of division, war, and social struggles; it spoke of its history in a way Lebanon's many history books could not.

---

1. Becker, Carol. "The Subversive Imagination; Artists,Society, & Social Responsibility". London: Routeledge, 1994. (essay # 8)

1. Mural with Hezbollah logo, Bachoura, Beirut, 2007

2. "Long live the revolution" slogan, Lebanese Communist stencils, Amal stencil, behind Spears St., Beirut, 2007

3. Gamal Abdel Nasser and Murabitoun stencils, El-Zarif, Beirut, 2007

Following pages 78 & 79:

Lebanese flag with Amal stencils, Patriachate, 2007

• TALA F. SALEH
is a Saudi freelance graphic designer based in Khobar, Saudi Arabia and Beirut, Lebanon. She graduated with a BFA in Graphic Design from AUB in Beirut and an MA in Graphic Branding and Identity from the London College of Communication in the UK. Her "Project de Diplôme" was the book "Marking Beirut: A City Revealed Through its Graffiti", which has received extensive press. Tala has attended several design conferences to present her work. She now works with many clients in the Middle East.

"Marking Beirut: A City Revealed Through its Graffiti", www.markingbeirut.com
ISBN 978-9586446402

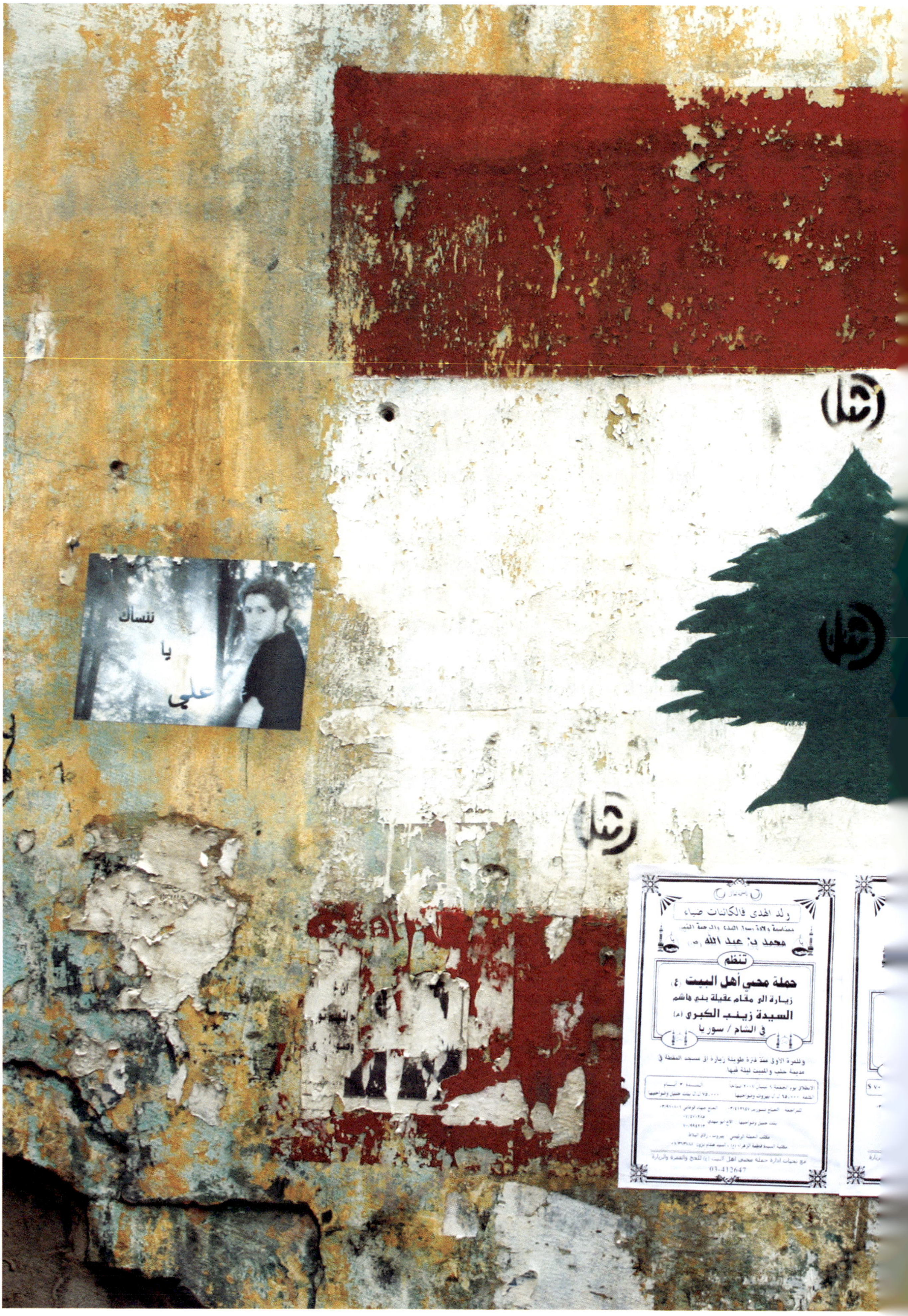
نساك
يا
علي
ولد الهدى فالكائنات ضياء
محمد بن عبد الله (ص)
تنظم
حملة محبي أهل البيت (ع)
زيارة الى مقام عقيلة بني هاشم
السيدة زينب الكبرى (ع)
في الشام / سوريا
03-412647

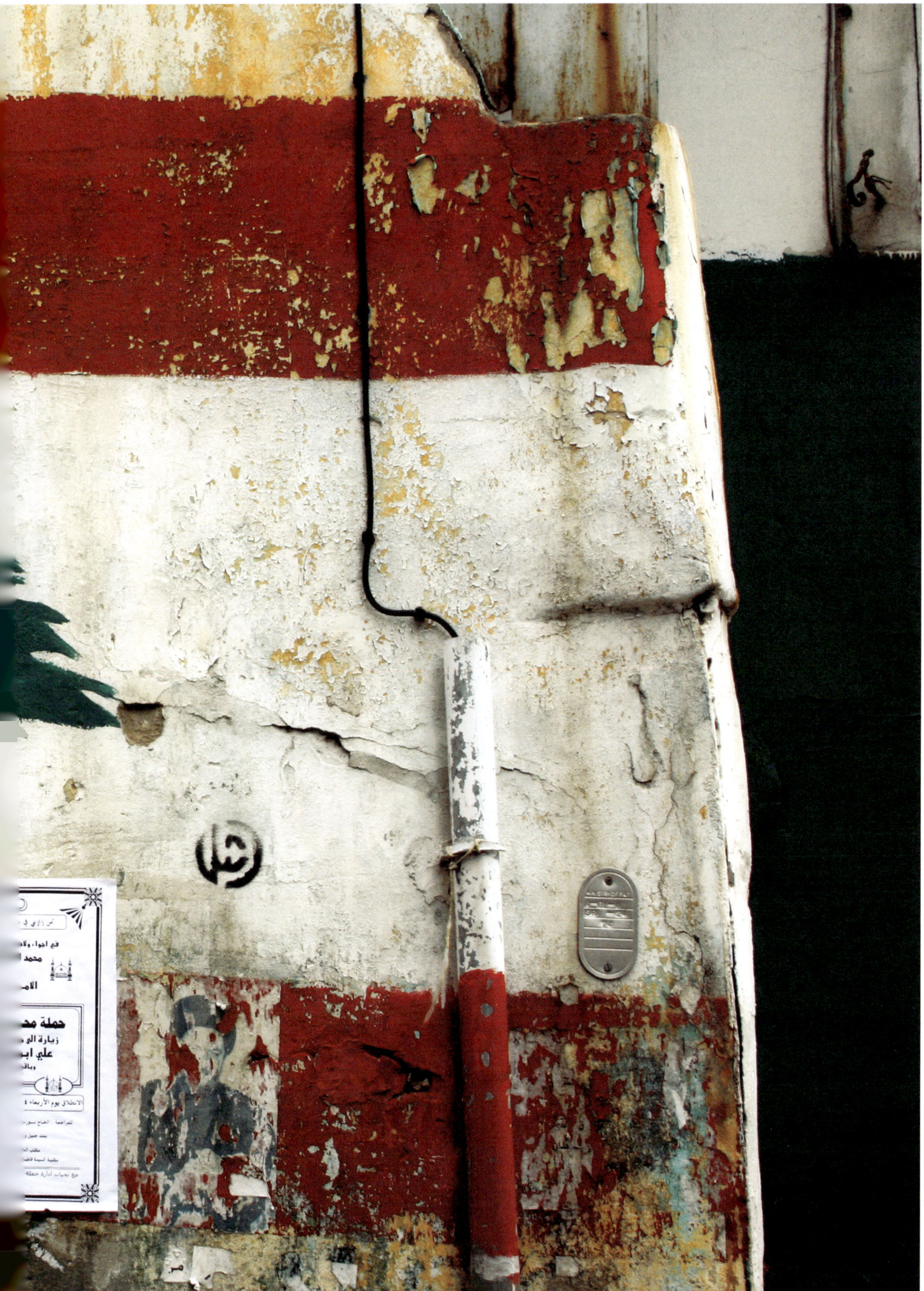

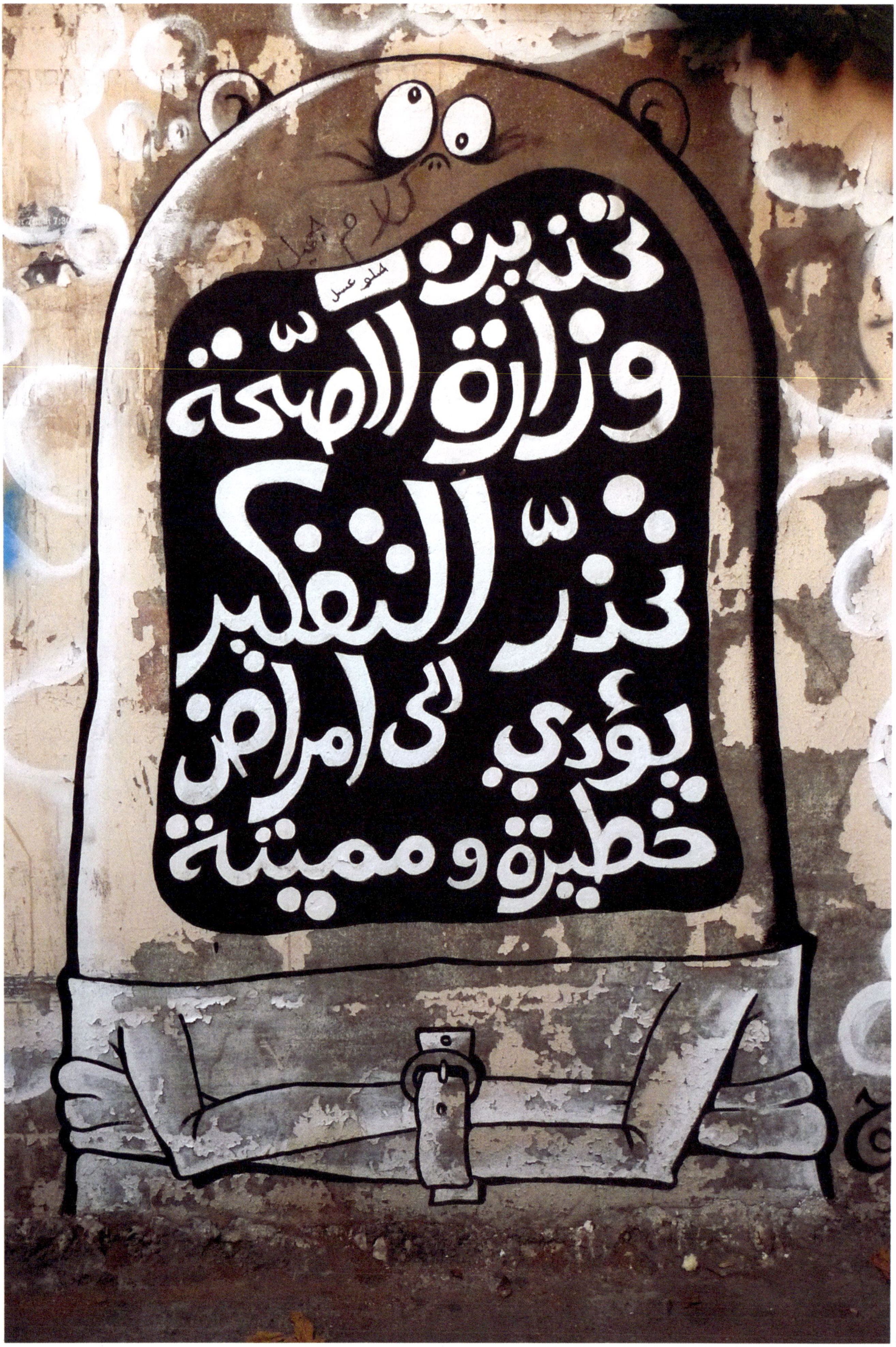

1

2·7
Beirut's Graffiti Writing & Street Art
فنون الشارع ورسوم الغرافيتي البيروتية

Pascal Zoghbi

تحذير: وزارة الصحّة تحذّر التفكير
يؤدي الى أمراض خطيرة ومميتة

1. **"Warning: the Ministry of Health warns that thinking leads to dangerous & fatal diseases", unknown artist, Hamra, Beirut, Lebanon**

2. **View of downtown Beirut from the sea bay promenade**

Due to the poor political, economic and social situation in Lebanon, graffiti is spreading and voicing the pain of the people. The pierced city walls which resisted all the bombardments of the civil war are now mostly covered with urban writings and drawings. During the last thirty years, most of the urban graffiti interventions were political and sectarian. The voices of the Lebanese people were not manifested on the streets; instead, the slogans of the political leaders covered the walls. Lebanese, Palestinian fighters and Syrian soldiers used graffiti as the main medium to spread their slogans and propaganda. Party members and supporters sprayed the political party's words and sentences as well. Each party had its own logo or icon as stencils, which they used to mark territories in Beirut. The icons created an encoded map of Beirut and towns all over Lebanon.

By the end of the 90s and the start of the new millennium, around ten years after the end of the Lebanese civil war, people started ignoring the political writings on the roads and they went unnoticed. In conjunction to that, artistic paintings were starting to emerge on the streets and gaining the curiosity and attention of the Lebanese people. The political battles in the streets transformed into a war throughout the media: in newspapers, on televisions and billboards. The fighters liberated the walls from their political slogans and parallel to that, the Lebanese graffiti and Hip Hop underground movement started to develop. Since then, Lebanese Arabic rap and Hip Hop culture has been growing and artistic graffiti is becoming increasingly present on the streets of Beirut.

When Lebanese graffiti crews started painting in Beirut, they first chose hidden walls and surfaces in old, neglected houses or factories and empty parking lots. These places were their practice grounds for experimentation and development of their skills and styles. As they became more confident of their writings and remained unrestricted by the police, they took over the walls of the main highways in Beirut. In Lebanon graffiti is not yet seen as vandalism or as a felony. Even though it is not a legal act, as long as the message of the graffiti does not imply any direct political meaning, graffiti artists are usually not bothered when spraying on walls, even in broad daylight.

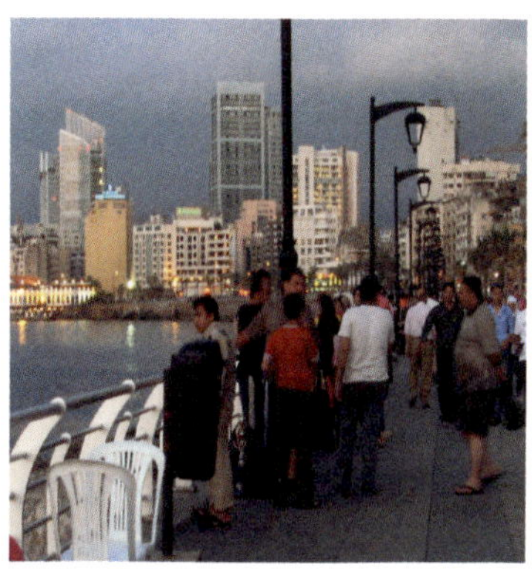

2

The graffiti scene in Beirut is still in its preliminary phase. As with most Lebanese design styles and trends, the first Lebanese graffiti was heavily influenced by Western graffiti. The tags and drawings were done in English and French instead of Arabic, and the letters had no link to Arabic calligraphy whatsoever. Among others, European graffiti artists like Prime and Fabu from France and Sens from Germany visited Beirut and influenced the

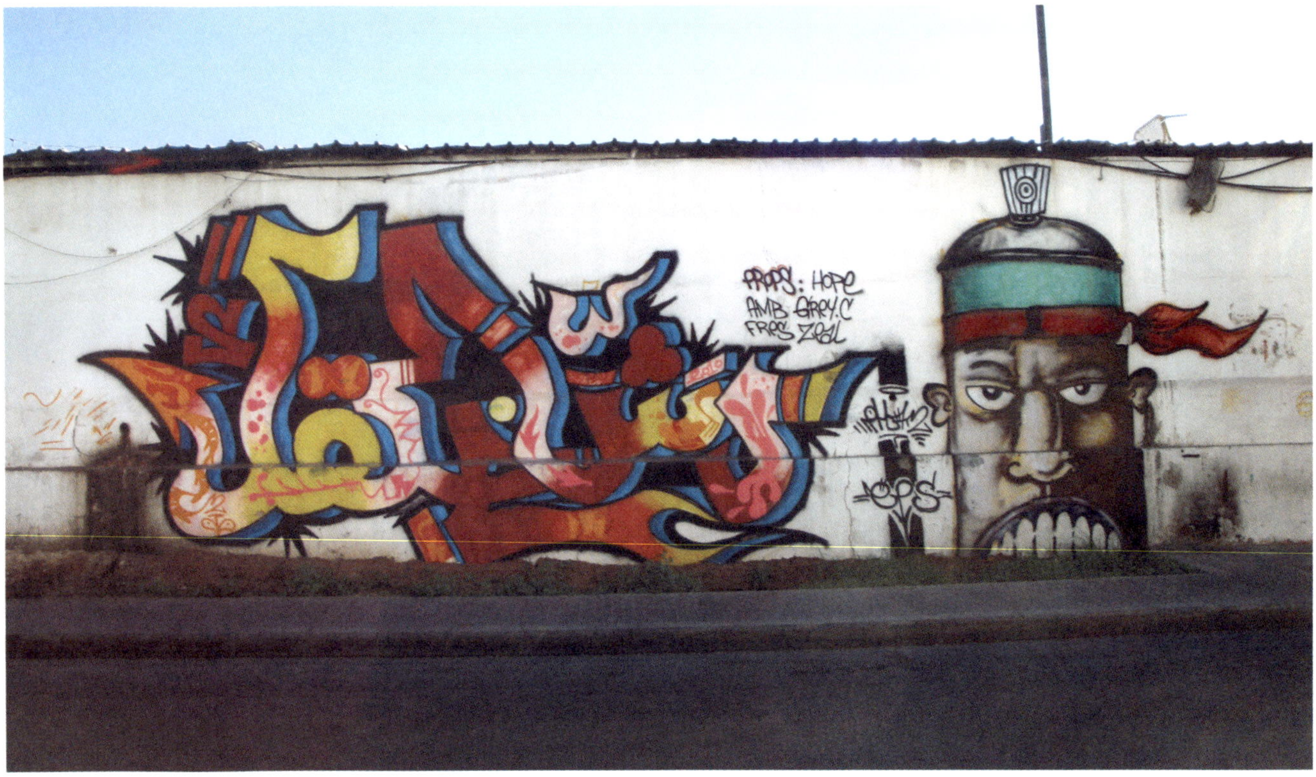

1

رشّ خلقك
1. "Spray your patience", PHAT2, EPS, FRES, etc., Flea Market, Jisr Al Wati, Greater Beirut, Lebanon

2. Mar Mikhaël an-Nahr, Beirut, Lebanon

العيون ع بيروت
3. "All eyes on Beirut", ASHEKMAN, Karantina, Beirut, Lebanon

شعب نعسان
4. "Sleepy people", ZE M3ALIM/REK, Jisr al-Basha, Greater Beirut, Lebanon

start of the Lebanese graffiti scene. Since then, several Lebanese graffiti crews have been born, such as the Red Eyed Kamikazes (REK), Ashekman, P+G Group and Katiba Khamsa (the fifth brigade). Independent artists like Fres, Phat2, RGB, EPS, Gup, Yazan, etc. are also active. Some groups and independent artists tag their names in different Western urban styles and spray stencils, while others are more concerned with socio-political issues and expressing their thoughts and fears on the dirty walls.

REK was originally founded by Fish and early members Rat and Siska. It is a growing group of artists now composed of several members. Ze M3allim (the master) and Kabrit (the matches) are among the latest young members. They often painted «٩٦١ بيروت من تحت الأرض» (961 underground), in reference to their Lebanese underground identity. Besides tagging REK on almost every wall in Beirut, they express their anger with strong Lebanese slang words like «جوعتونا» (you starved us), «مزاج بيروت» (the mood of Beirut), and the well-known phrase «بيروت إن حكت» (if Beirut could speak), echoing Saïd Akl's book title "If Lebanon could speak". They are behind the remake of the famous sentence «بيروت ما بتموت» (Beirut never dies), which was originally created by Siska and Prime before REK emerged.

Ashekman is a Lebanese Hip Hop duo composed of the twin brothers Omar and Mohamed Kabbani. Two pioneers in Lebanese Arabic graffiti, their work draws from the problems of the Lebanese people, and their writings stem from vernacular Lebanese words and are created using simplified Arabic typography. «الشارع إلنا» (the street is ours), which implies that they control the streets using their art as a weapon, «العيون ع بيروت» (all eyes on Beirut), which indicates that Beirut has become a playground for the regional powers, and their graffiti dedicated to Gaza, «غزة في قلبي» (Gaza in my heart), are some of their powerful graffiti messages. As graphic designers, the brothers decided to merge their graffiti with their passion for Hip Hop all within an Arabic context.

Katiba Khamsa is a Palestinian graffiti and Hip Hop group living in a refugee camp in Beirut. They express their frustration with the humanitarian and political situation in the Palestinian refugee camps in Lebanon, their loyalty to and love of Palestine and the ongoing Palestinian struggle. «عَمال نحرقها» (we are burning it) is one of their strongest writings. Katiba Khamasa are more active in the Arabic Hip Hop scene and they occasionally create graffiti.

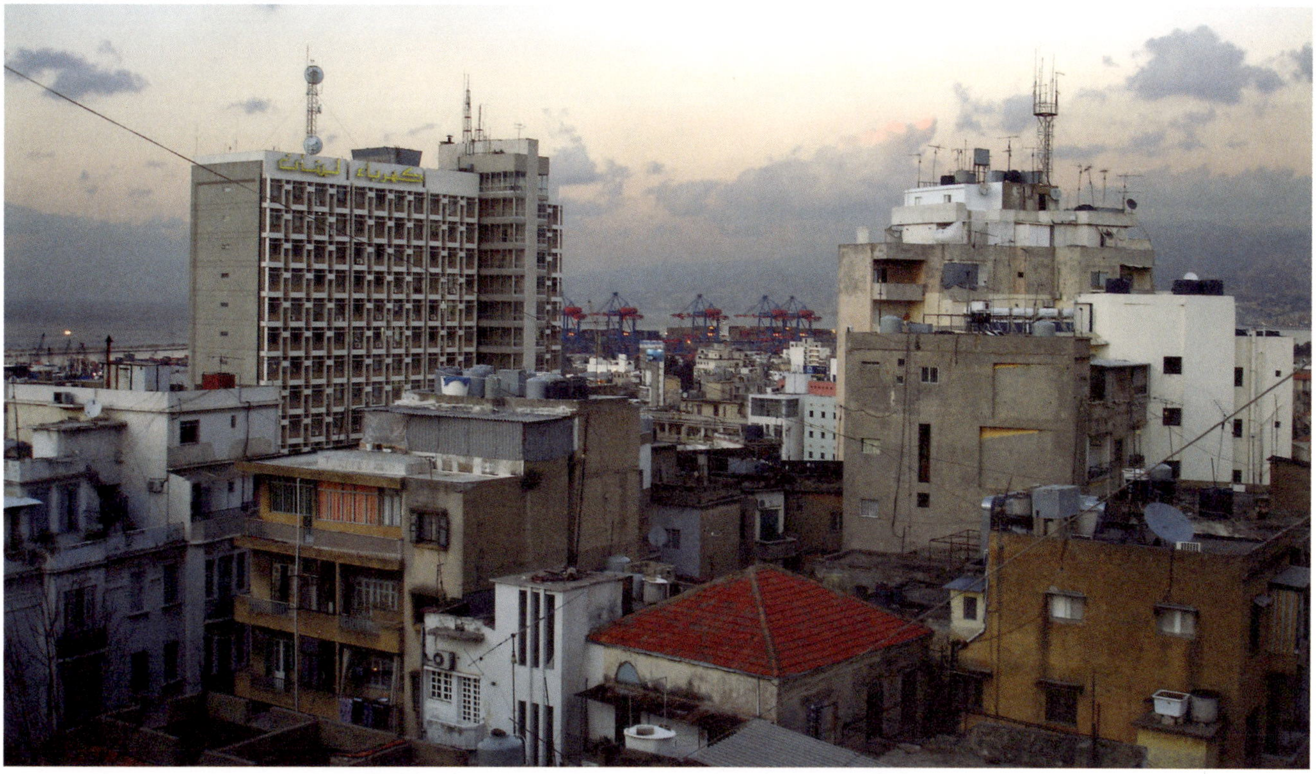

2

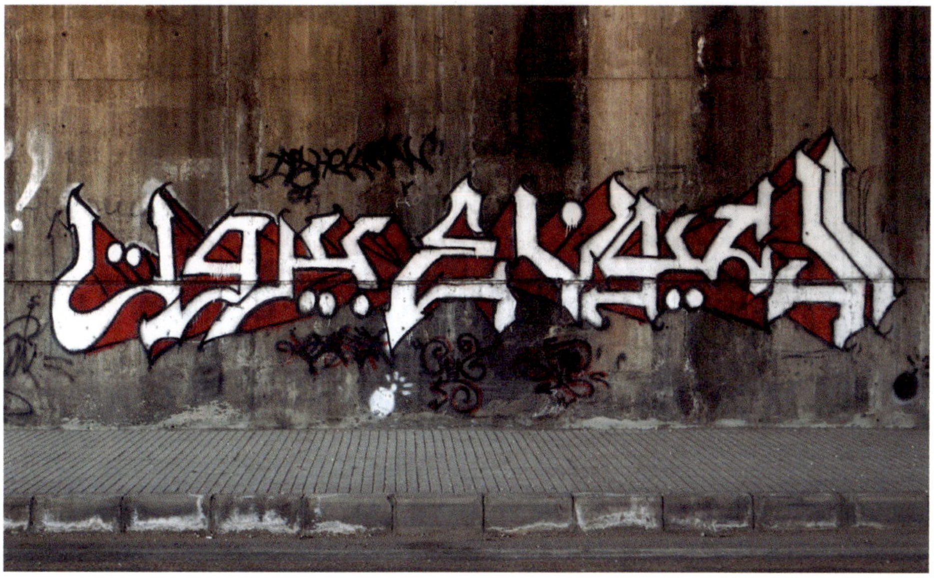

3

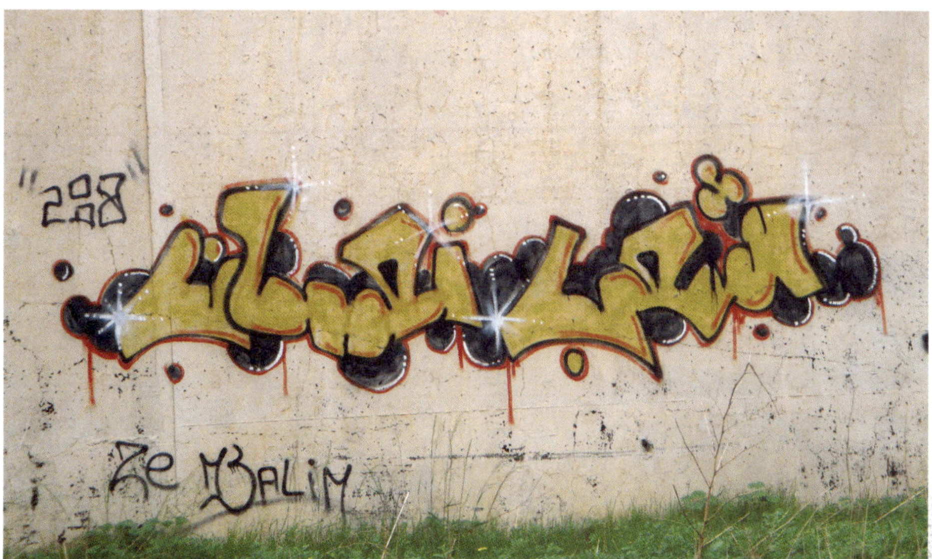

4

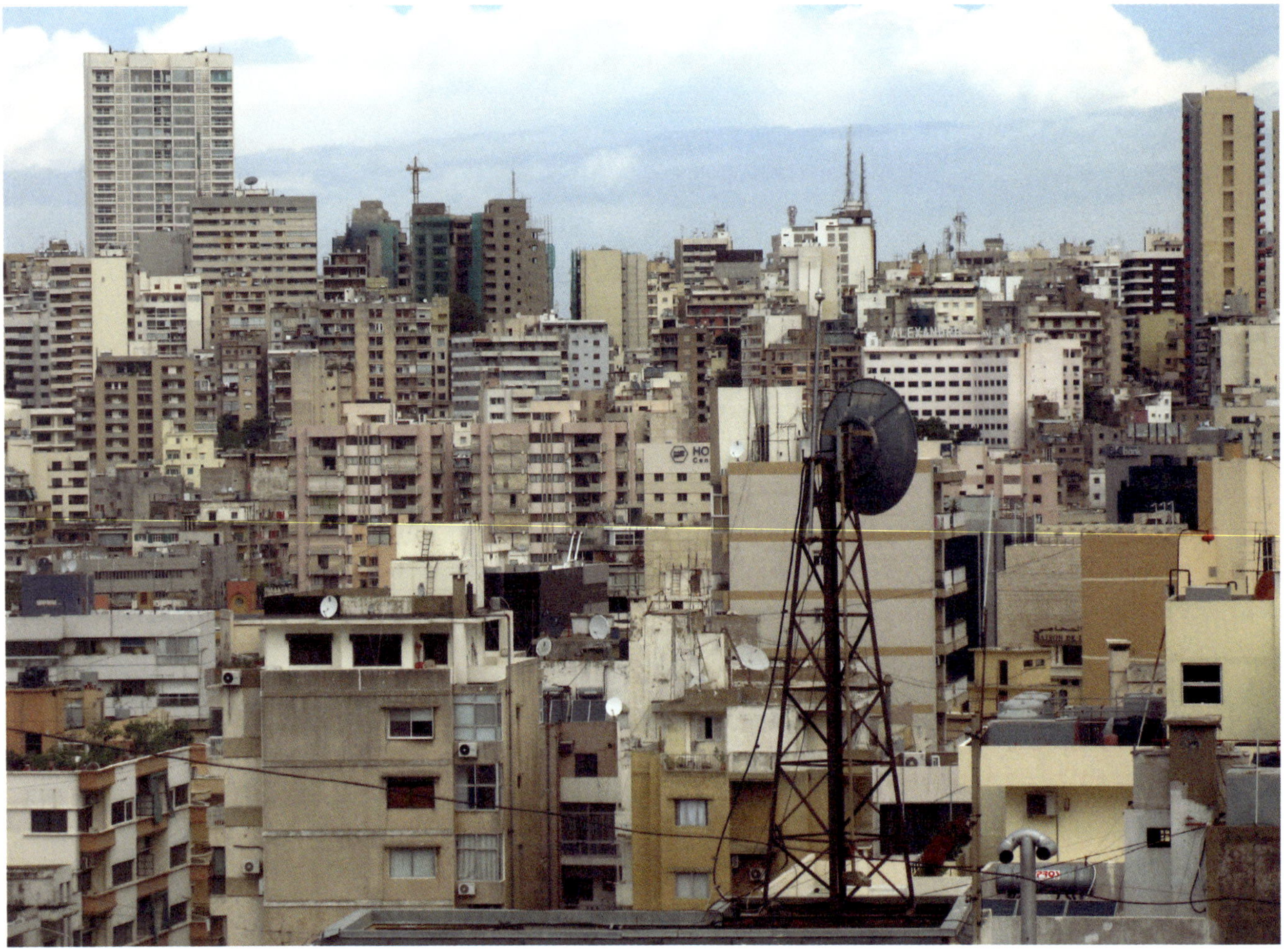

1

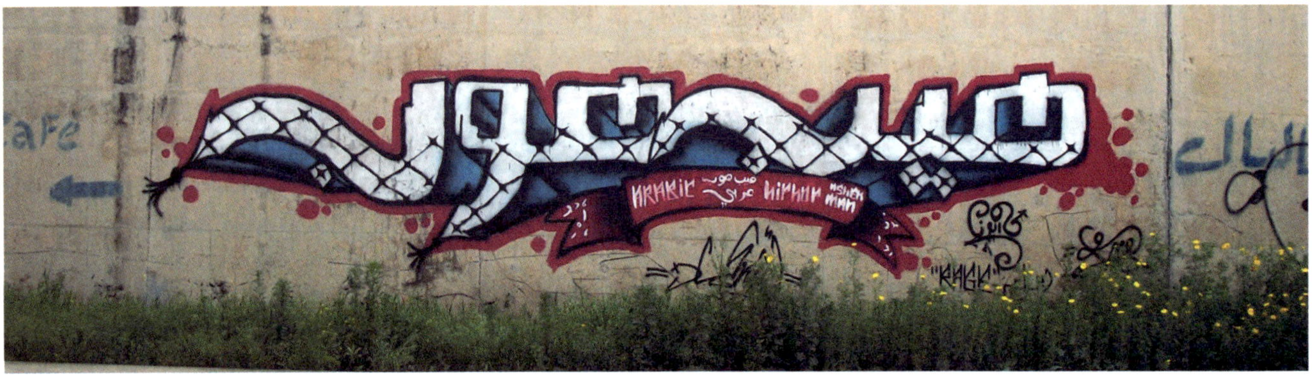

2

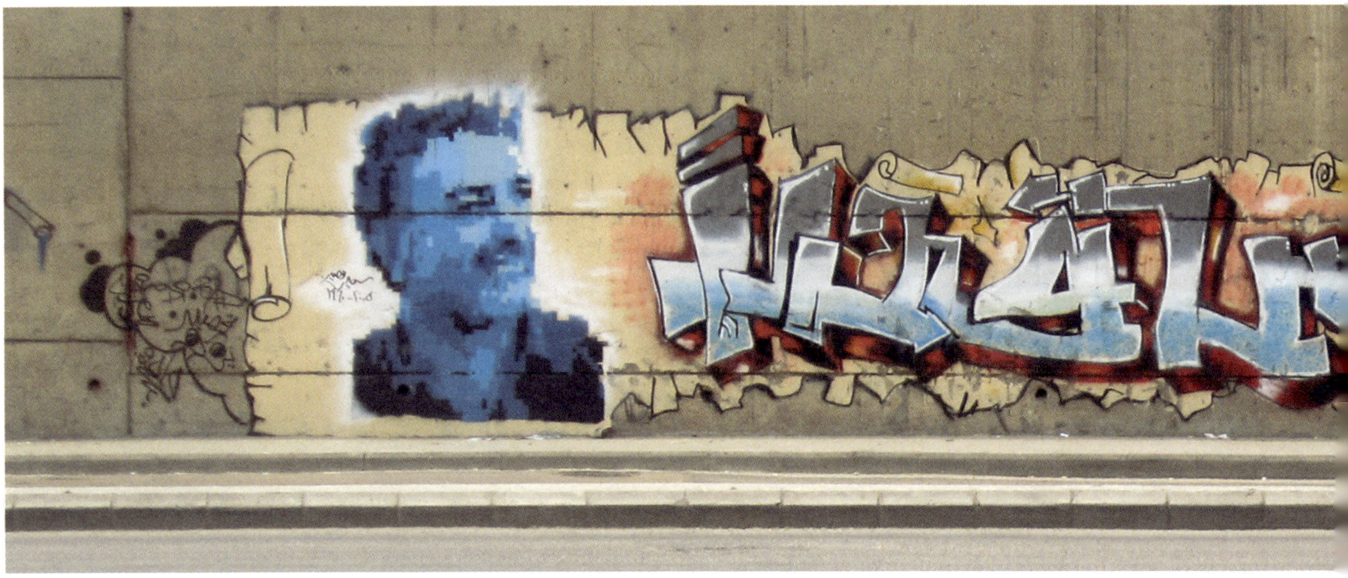

Parekour+Graffiti (P+G) was founded by Oras and friends from the Armenian community in Beirut. They emphasize a different viewpoint and express themselves while remaining distant from political connotations. They are an important asset in the underground graffiti scene in Beirut even though they are not involved in Arabic or socio-political writings.

Several graffiti workshops have taken place in Lebanon since the underground scene emerged. International and local graffiti artists are collaborating with educational and cultural organizations to create projects which encourage exchange. Some workshops involve professional and amateur graffiti artists, while others are targeted towards children in schools, humanitarian organizations, refugee camps, etc.

A five-day workshop entitled "Spray Can Art, Culture is Dialogue — Graffiti workshop for young local artists" was one of the most significant workshops given to teenagers in Tripoli. The German graffiti artist Claudia "MadC" Walde visited Lebanon and collaborated with the German Dialog Centre Tripoli and the Goethe Institute in November of 2006. The theme of the joint artwork was "Culture is dialogue".

Don "Stone" Karl, German graffiti writer and the co-author and publisher of this book, collaborated with the Goethe Institute and SoundBomb on the workshop "Bombing Beirut", for designers and professional Lebanese graffiti artists. The workshop was held at Zico House and the pieces were created on the main highway in the Karantina area of Beirut. The workshop focused on the use of Arabic script in the drawings and the development of contemporary graffiti styles.

Sens (Steffi Peichal) is a German graffiti artist who currently lives in Beirut. She is working with non-governmental organizations and did several mural projects and graffiti workshops with children inside Palestinian refugee camps throughout Lebanon.

These and other workshops have played an important role in the development of the Lebanese graffiti scene.

Graffiti is a form of street art which connects people in an urban setting. In our view, Arabic Lebanese graffiti needs more time to mature in order to achieve a strong Oriental style and to stop copying the West. More Arabic graffiti pieces are spotted nowadays in Beirut than in the late nineties, and a strong Lebanese Oriental style will unquestionably emerge in the coming years. Graffiti artists should learn to appreciate the Arabic script and calligraphic styles, and elaborate their Arabic writings consequently.

1. Ashrafieh, Beirut, Lebanon

هيب هوب
2. "Hip-Hop", ASHEKMAN, Jisr Al-Basha, Greater Beirut, Lebanon

إن الإحباط ليس قدراً
3. "Defeat is not destiny" beside Samir Kassir's portrait, YAZAN, Karantina, Beirut, Lebanon

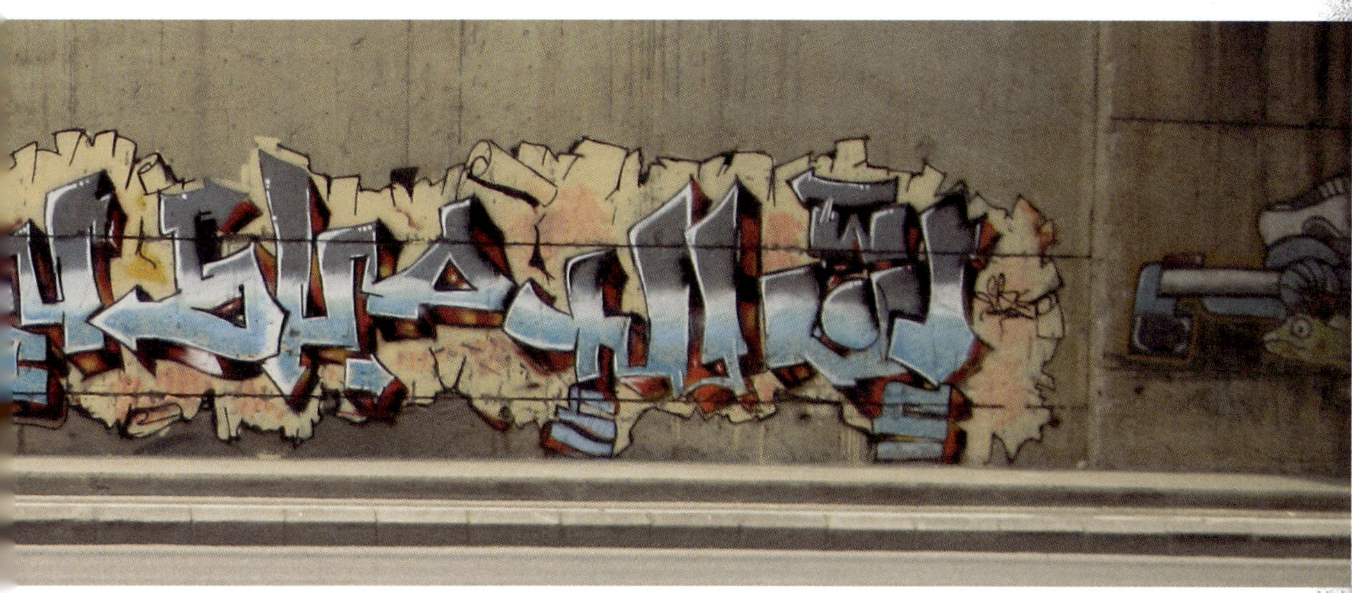

3

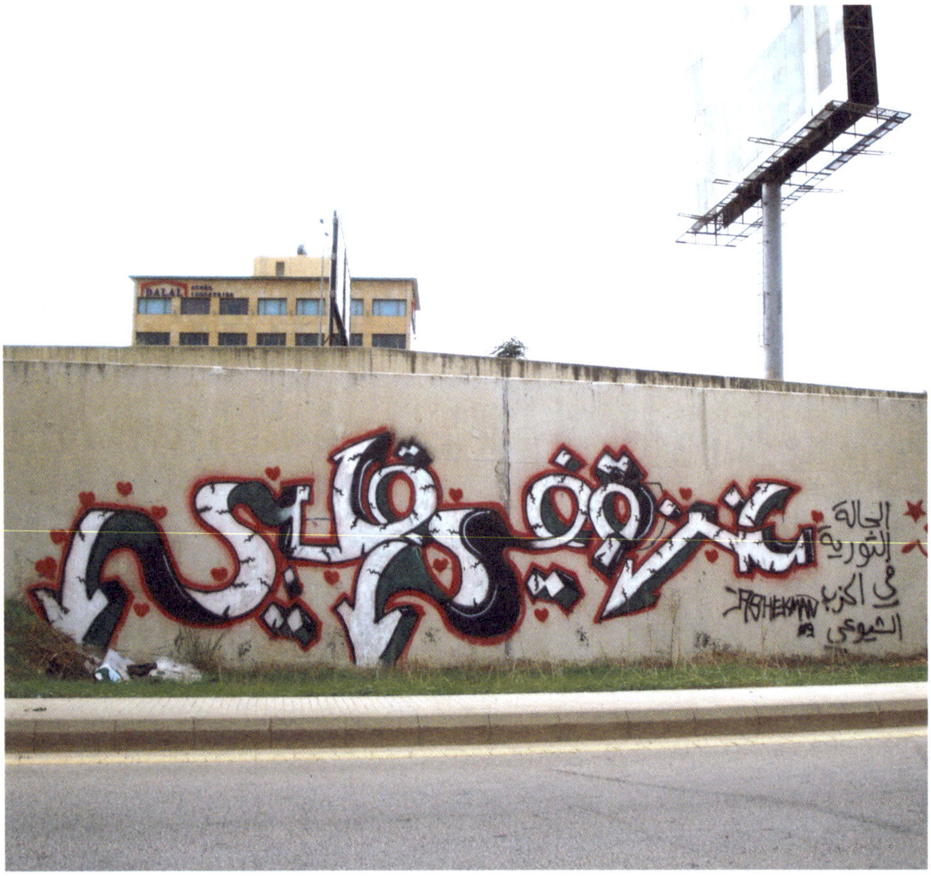

1

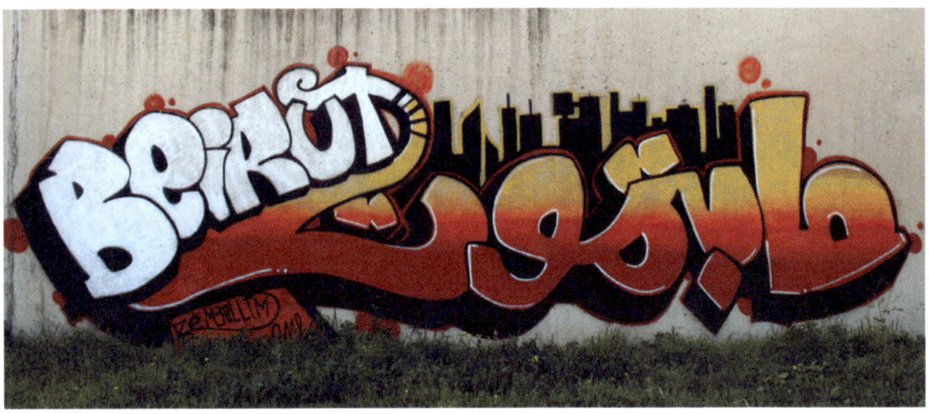

2

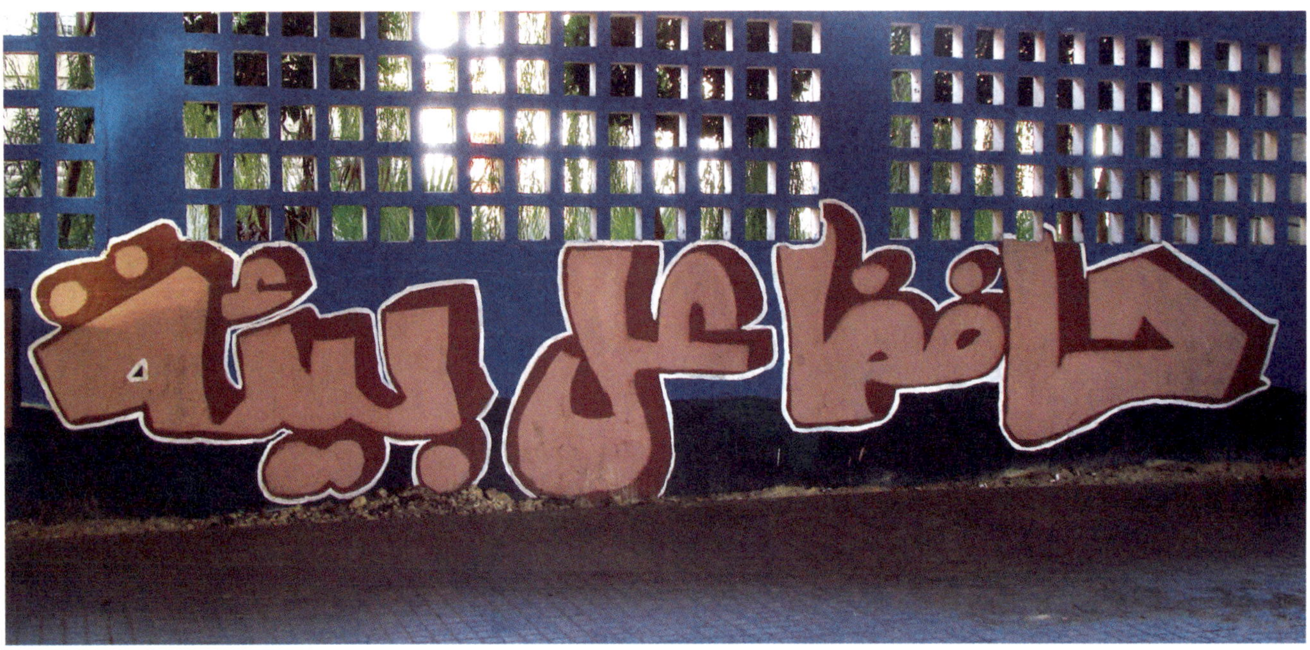

3

غزة في قلبي
1. “Gaza in my heart”, ASHEKMAN, Jisr al-Basha, Greater Beirut, Lebanon

بيروت ما بتموت
2. “Beirut never dies”, ZE M3ALEM/REK, Jisr al-Basha, Greater Beirut, Lebanon

حافظ عل بيئة
3. “Protect the environment”, unknown artist, Bourj Hammoud, Lebanon

بيروت ٩٦١ تحت الأرض
4. “Beirut 961 Underground”, REK, Gemayzeh, Beirut, Lebanon

فن شارع
5. “Street Art”, ASKEKMAN, Karantina, Beirut, Lebanon

شارعنا واحد
6. “Our street is one”, PAC, KOUSSA, SAAB, etc., Jisr al-Basha, Greater Beirut, Lebanon

إهانة حرفية
7. “Literal Offense”, ASHEKMAN, Jisr Al-Basha, Greater Beirut, Lebanon

أجمل بلد
8. “The most beautiful country”, ZE M3ALEM, Karantina, Beirut, Lebanon

بيروت
9. “Beirut”, KABRIT, Karantina, Beirut, Lebanon

جوّعتونا
10. “You starved us”, REK, Karantina, Beirut, Lebanon

أنا بحلم
11. “I dream”, ZE M3ALEM, Jisr al-Wati, Greater Beirut, Lebanon

عمال نحرقها
12. “We are burning it”, KATIBA KHAMSA, Karantina, Beirut, Lebanon

من هو العربي
13. “Who is the Arab”, PASCAL ZOGHBI, Karantina, Beirut, Lebanon

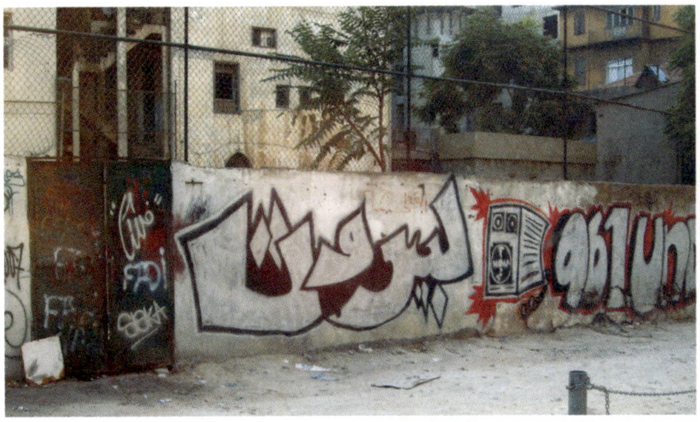
4

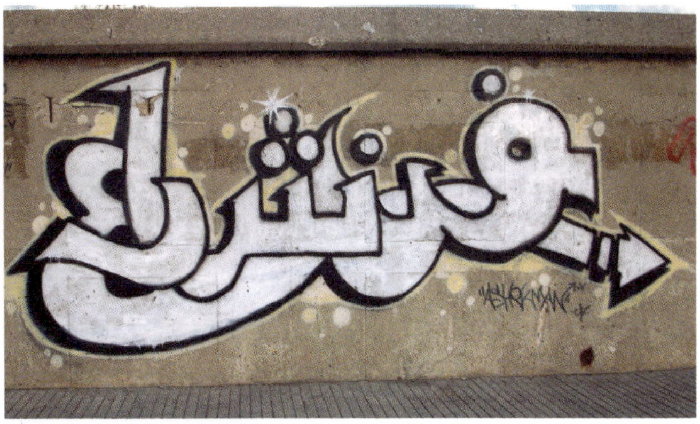
5

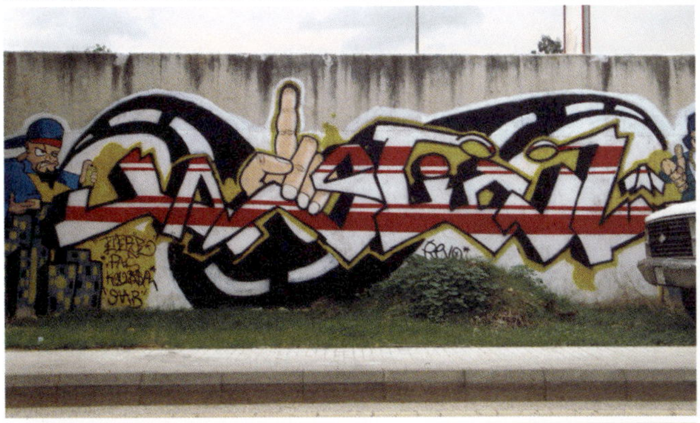
6

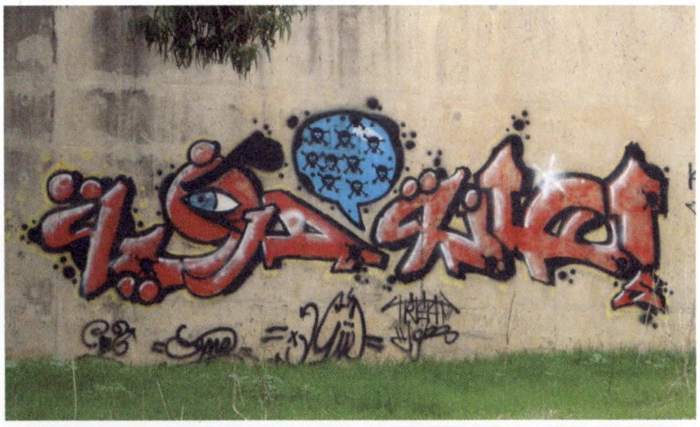
7

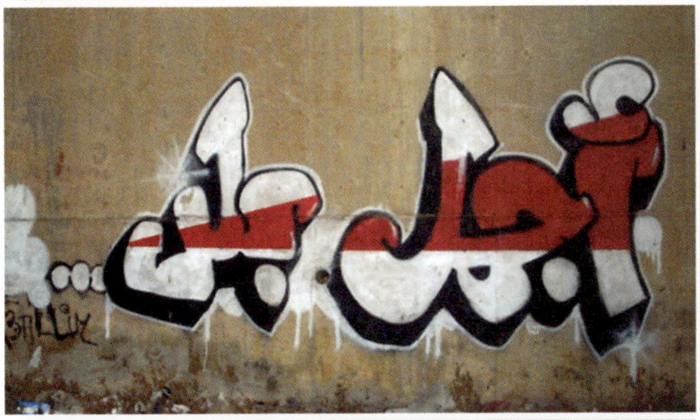
8

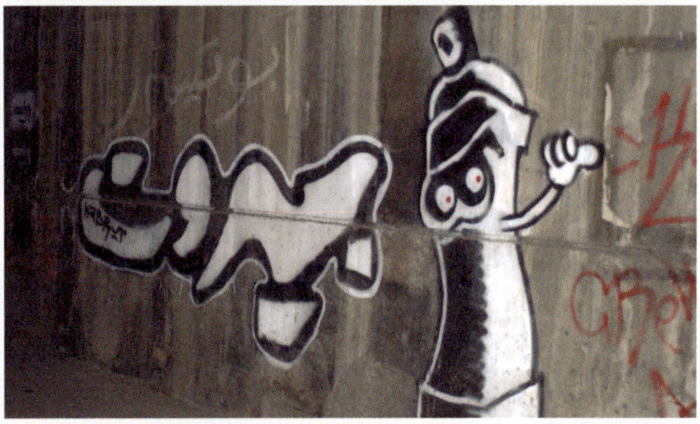
9

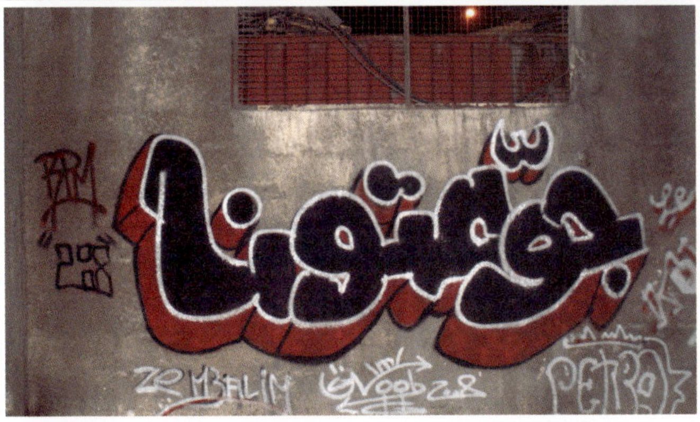
10

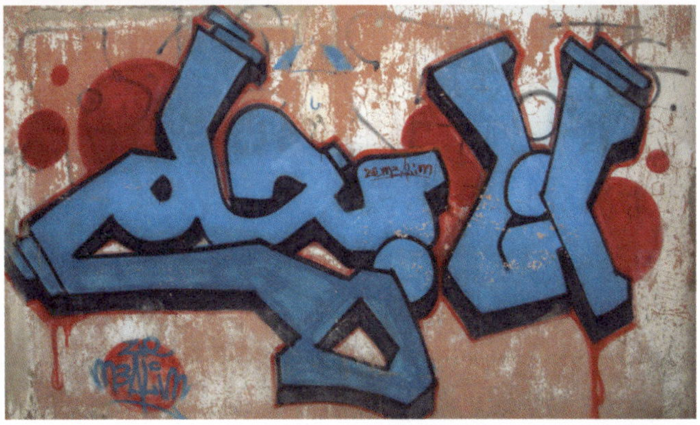
11

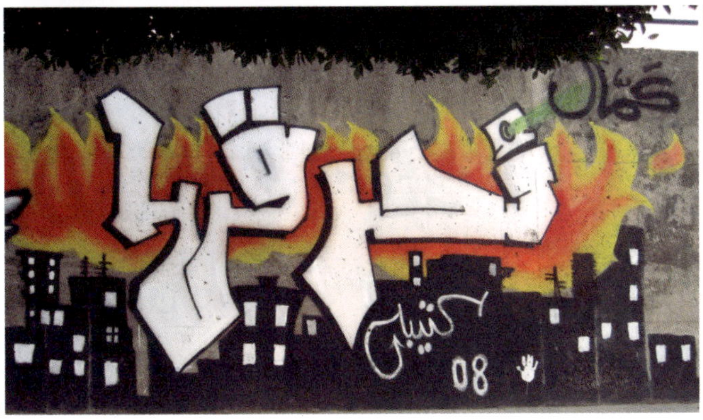
12

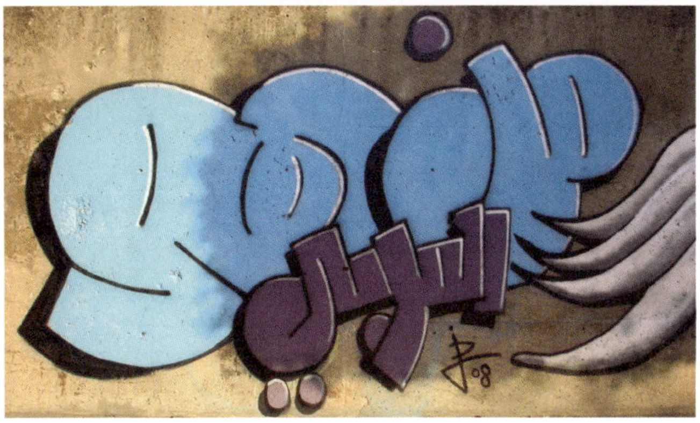
13

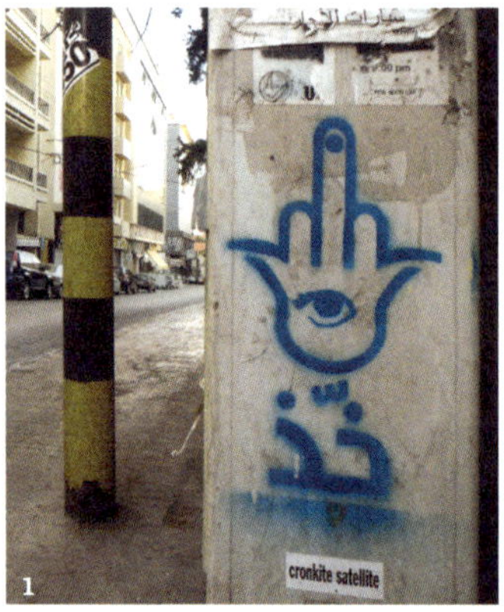

1

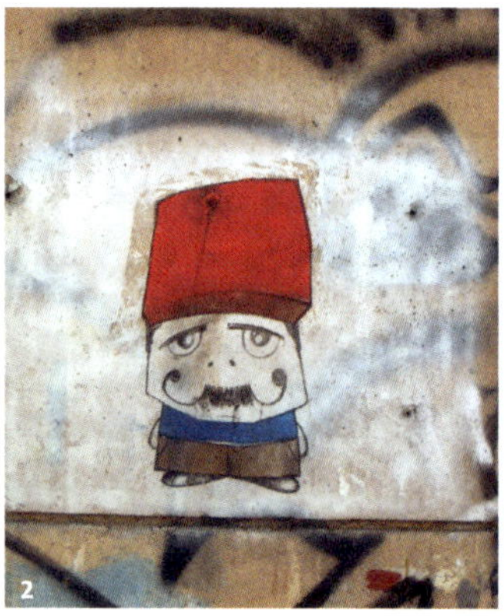
2

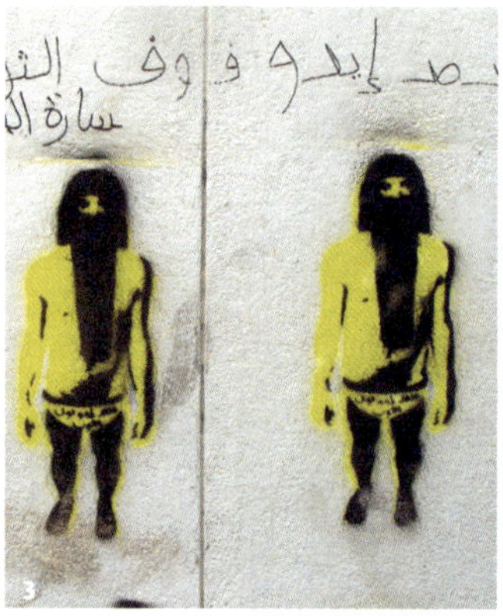
3

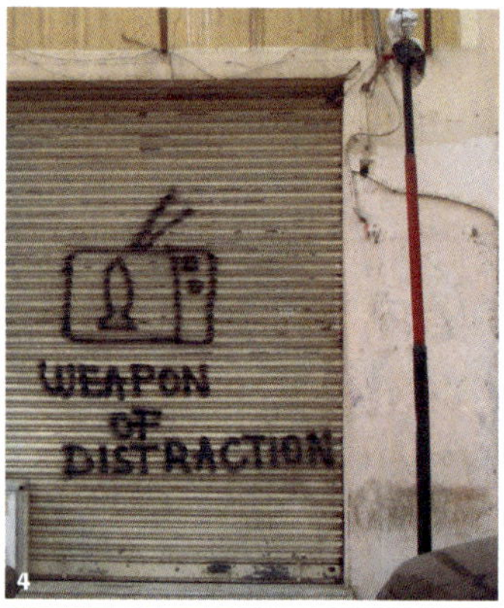

4

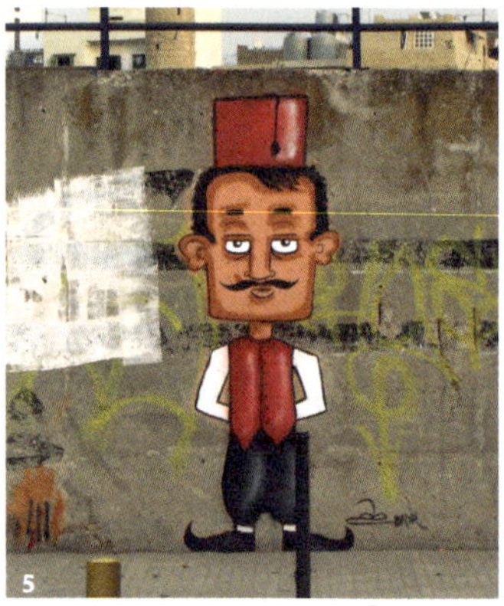
5

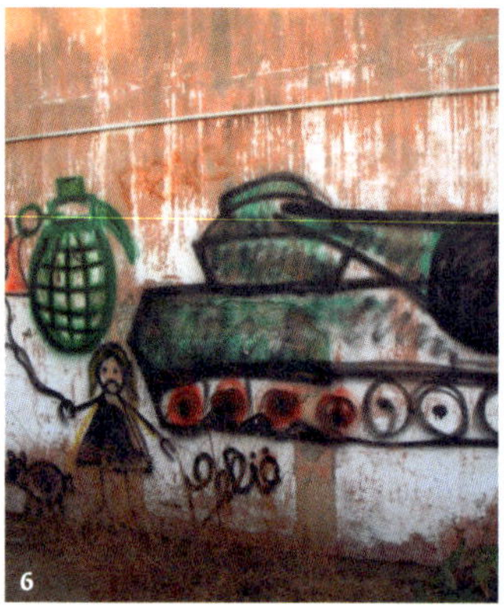
6

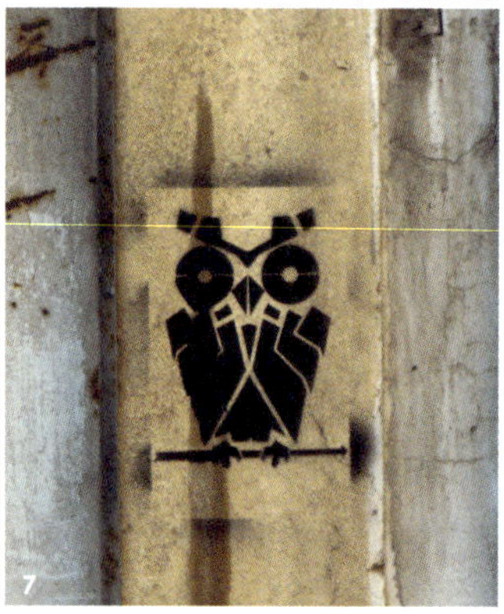
7

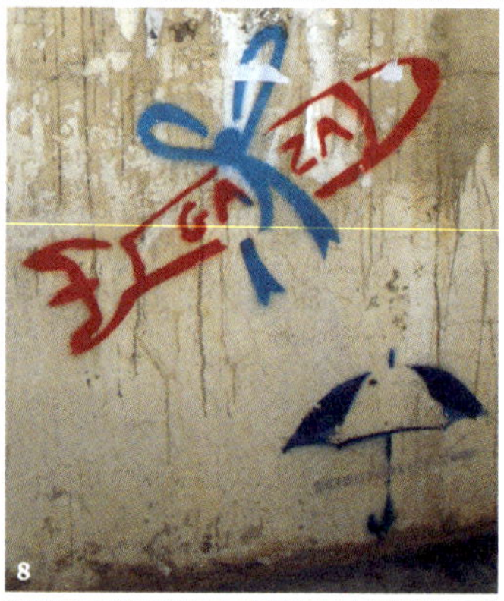
8

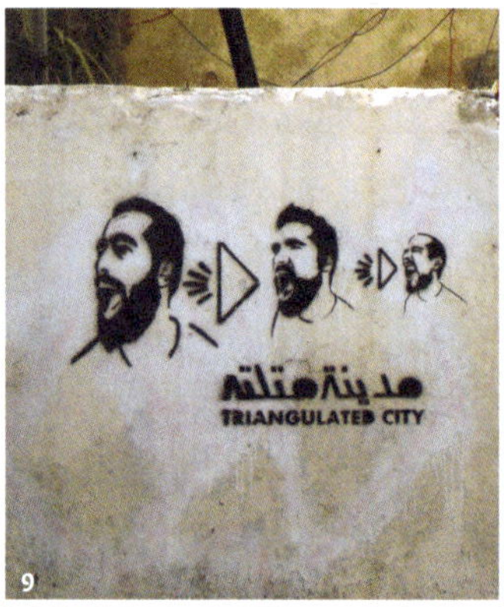

9

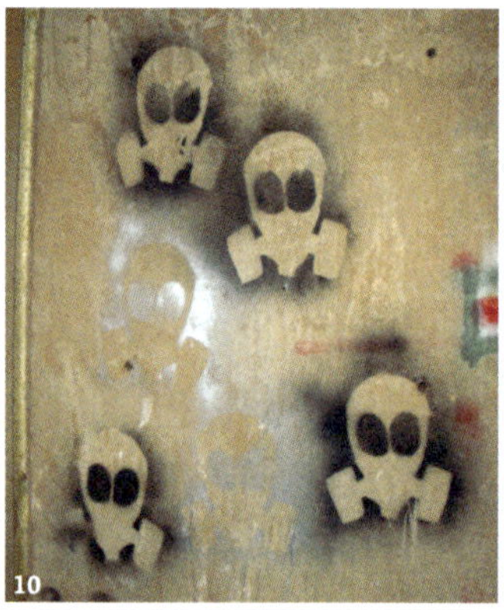
10

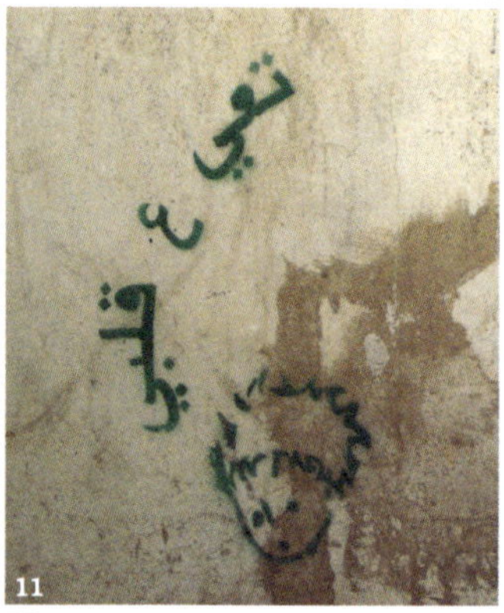
11

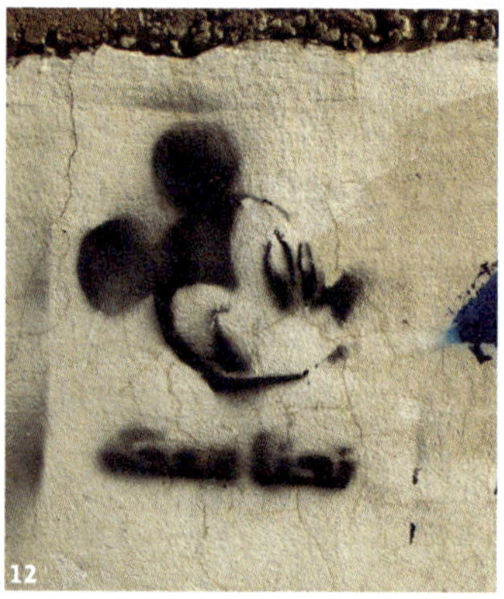
12

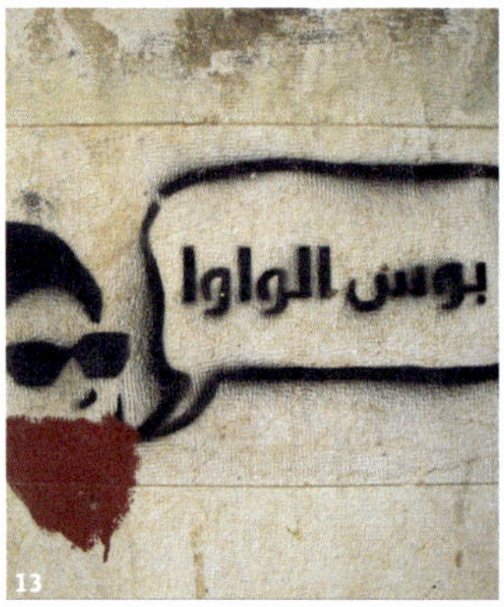

13

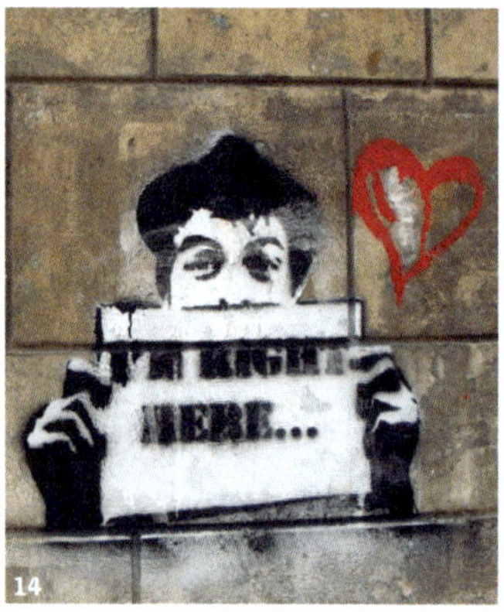
14

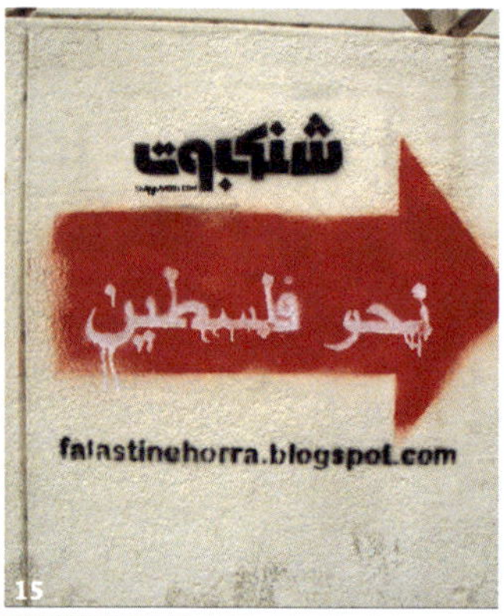

15

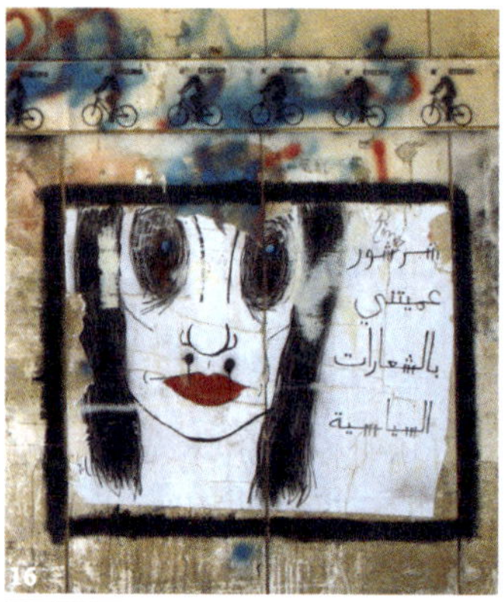
16

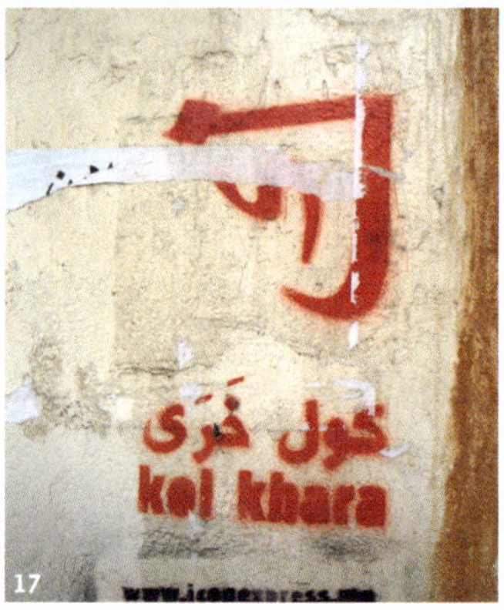

17

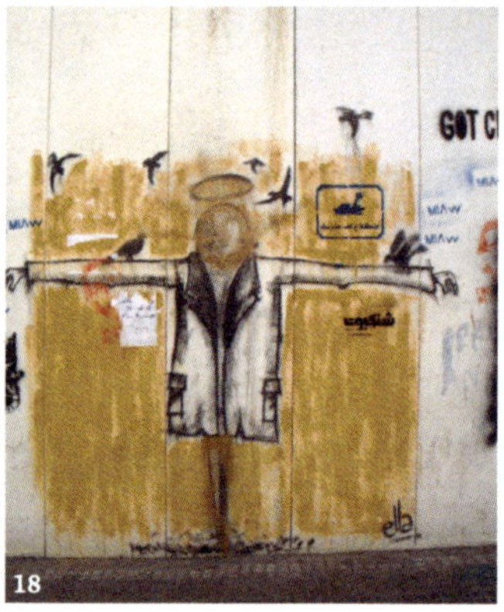
18

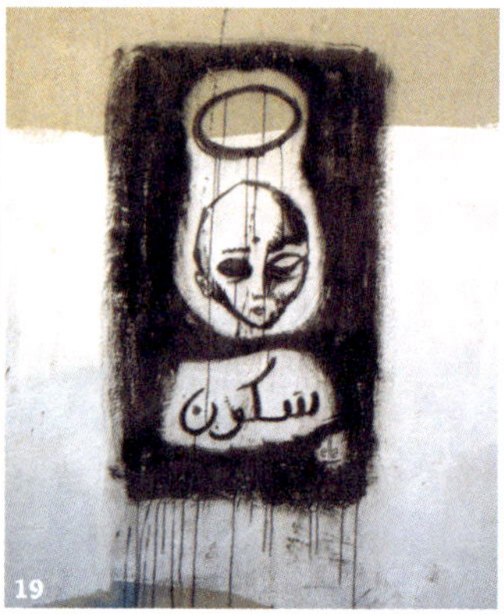
19

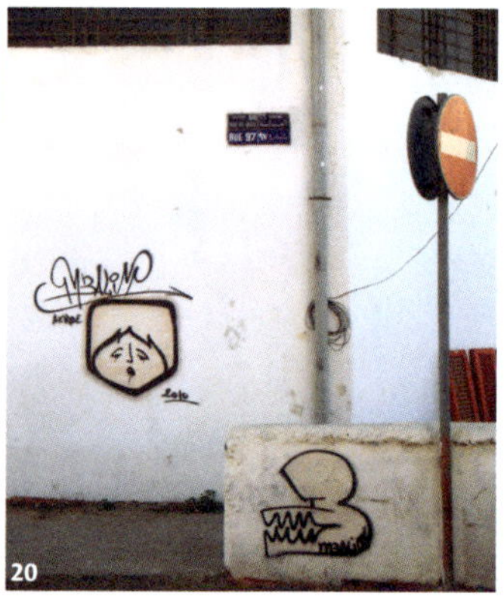
20

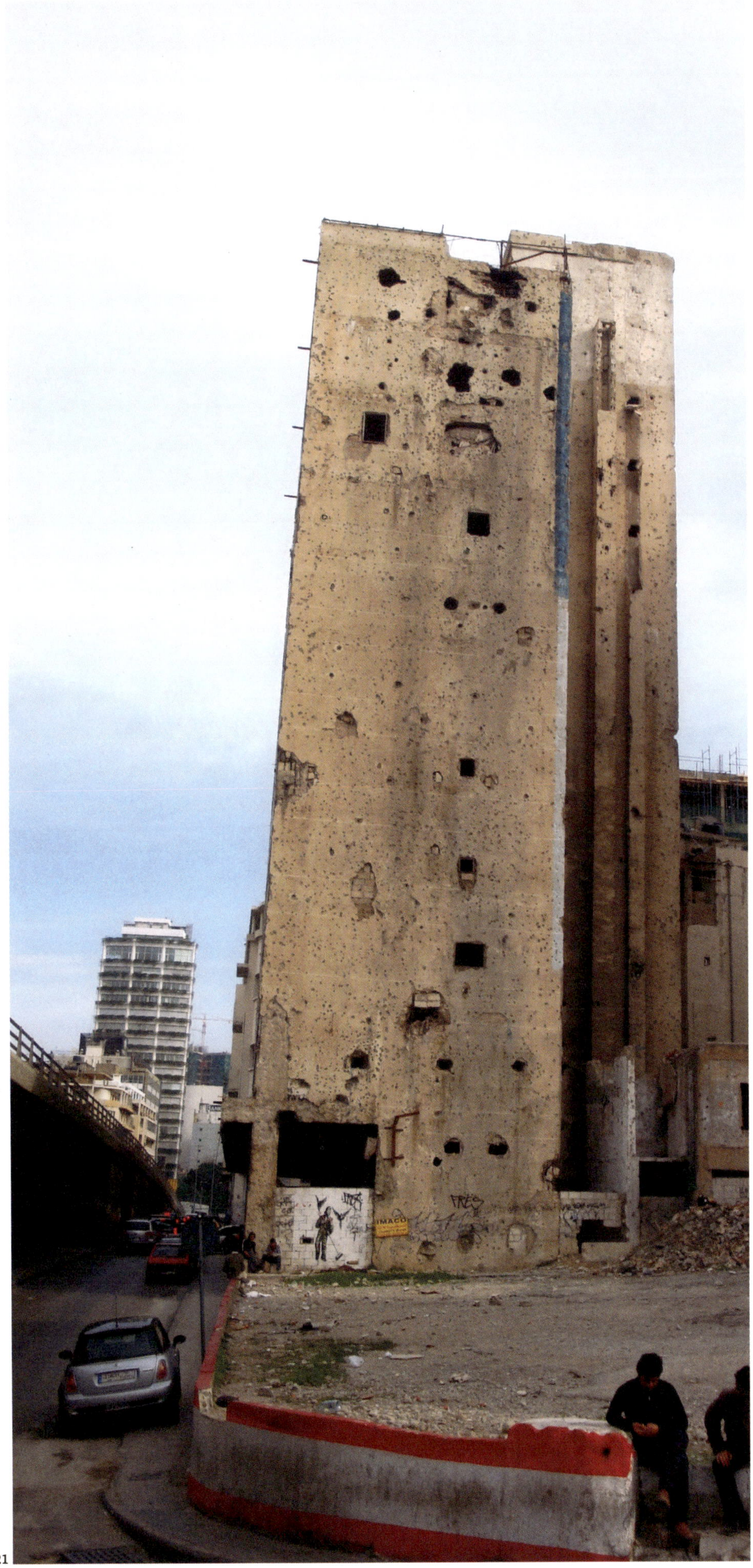

21

خُذ
1. “Take That”, Hamra, Beirut, Lebanon

أبو الزلُف
2. Traditional Lebanese man, DAVID HABSHI, Karantina, Beirut, Lebanon

مدمد إيدو فوق الثوب
3. “His hand is sneaking on the underwear”, Bliss Street, Beirut, Lebanon

4. “Weapon of distraction”, Gemayzeh, Beirut, Lebanon

5. Traditional Lebanese man, Karantina, Beirut, Lebanon

6. Little girl crying under a grenade and next to a tank, Jisr al-Wati, Beirut, Lebanon

7. Owl, ACOUSMATIK SYSTEM, Hamra, Beirut, Lebanon

8. “Gaza Bomb Gift”, Hamra, Beirut, Lebanon

مدينة متلته
9. “Triangulated City”, Hamra, Beirut, Lebanon

10. “Gas masks”, Hamra, Beirut, Lebanon

تعي ع قلبي
11. “Come to my heart”, Hamra, Beirut, Lebanon

نحنا معك
12. “We are with you”, Hamra, Beirut, Lebanon

بوس الواوا
13. “Kiss out the pain”, title of a controversial, silly erotic song & the great Arab singer Oum Koulthoum with brown pubic hair over his mouth, Hamra, Beirut, Lebanon

14. “I'm right here”, Bliss Street, Beirut, Lebanon

نحو فلسطين
15. “Towards Palestine”, Hamra, Beirut, Lebanon

شرشور عميتني بالشعارات السياسية
16. “Honeybunch you blinded me with your political slogans”, Bliss Street, Beirut, Lebanon

كول خرى
17. “Eat Shit”, KAISS AL KAISSY, Bliss Street, Beirut, Lebanon

18. “Angel Scarecrow”, ELLA, Bliss Street, Beirut, Lebanon

سكون
19. “Silence”, ELLA, Jisr al-Wati, Greater Beirut, Lebanon

20. “Sad Boy”, ZE M3ALEM, Jisr al-Wati, Beirut, Lebanon

21. Worker sweeping bullets, Monot, Beirut, Lebanon

Following pages 90 & 91:

مكان عام
“Public Space / Espace Publique [sic]”, Beirut, Lebanon

PUBLI
عام
ESPACE

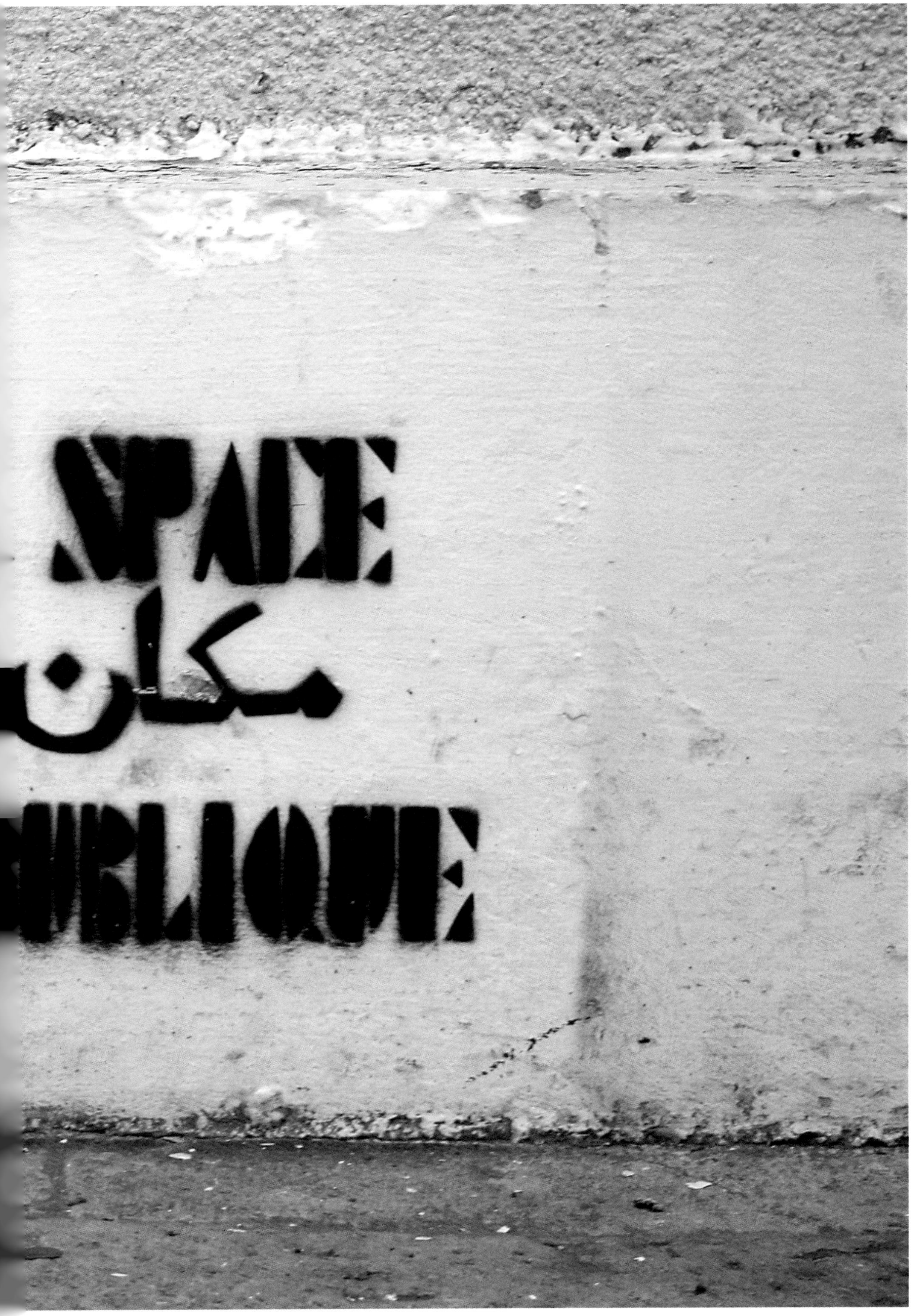
SPACE
مكان
UBLIQUE

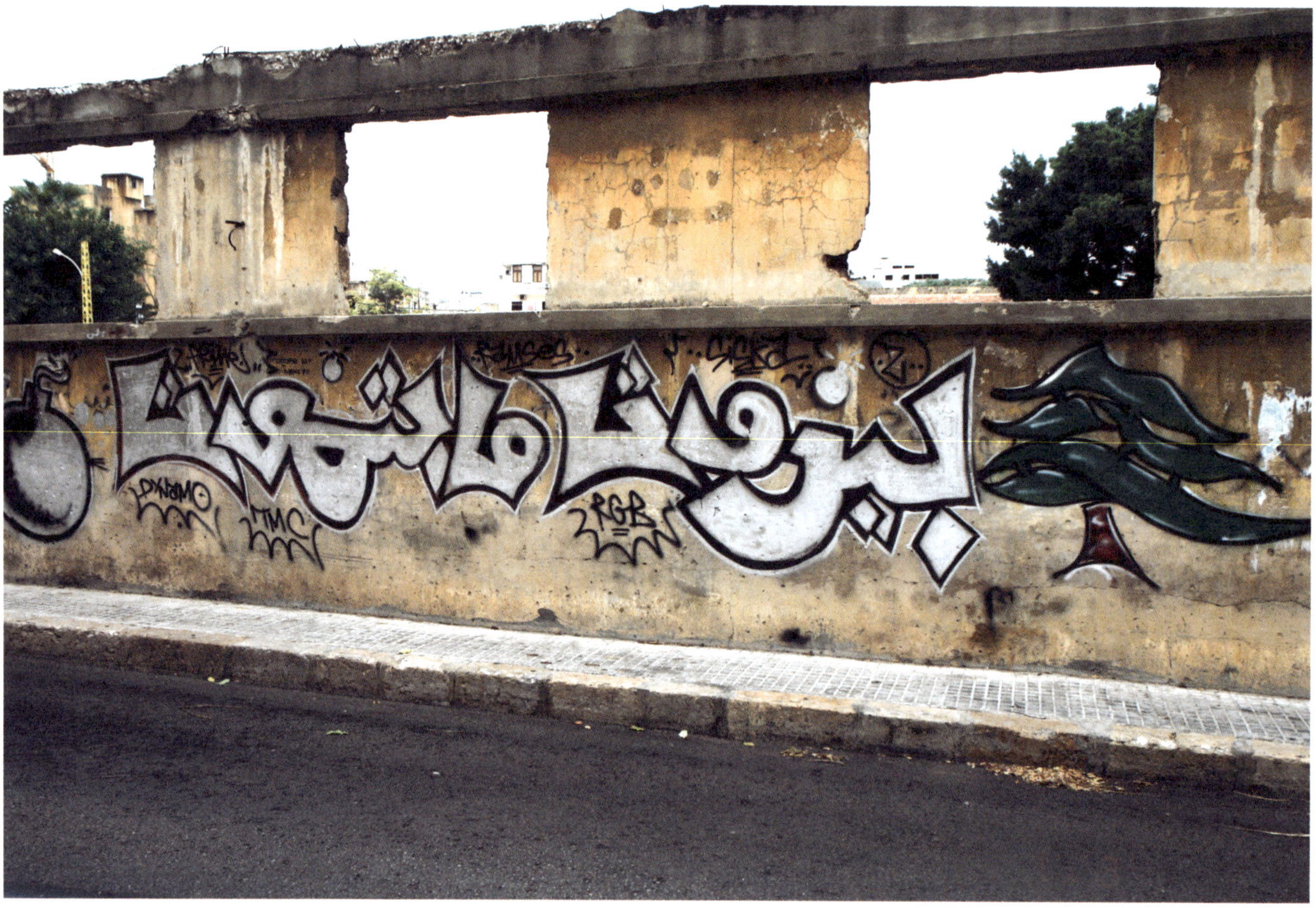

1

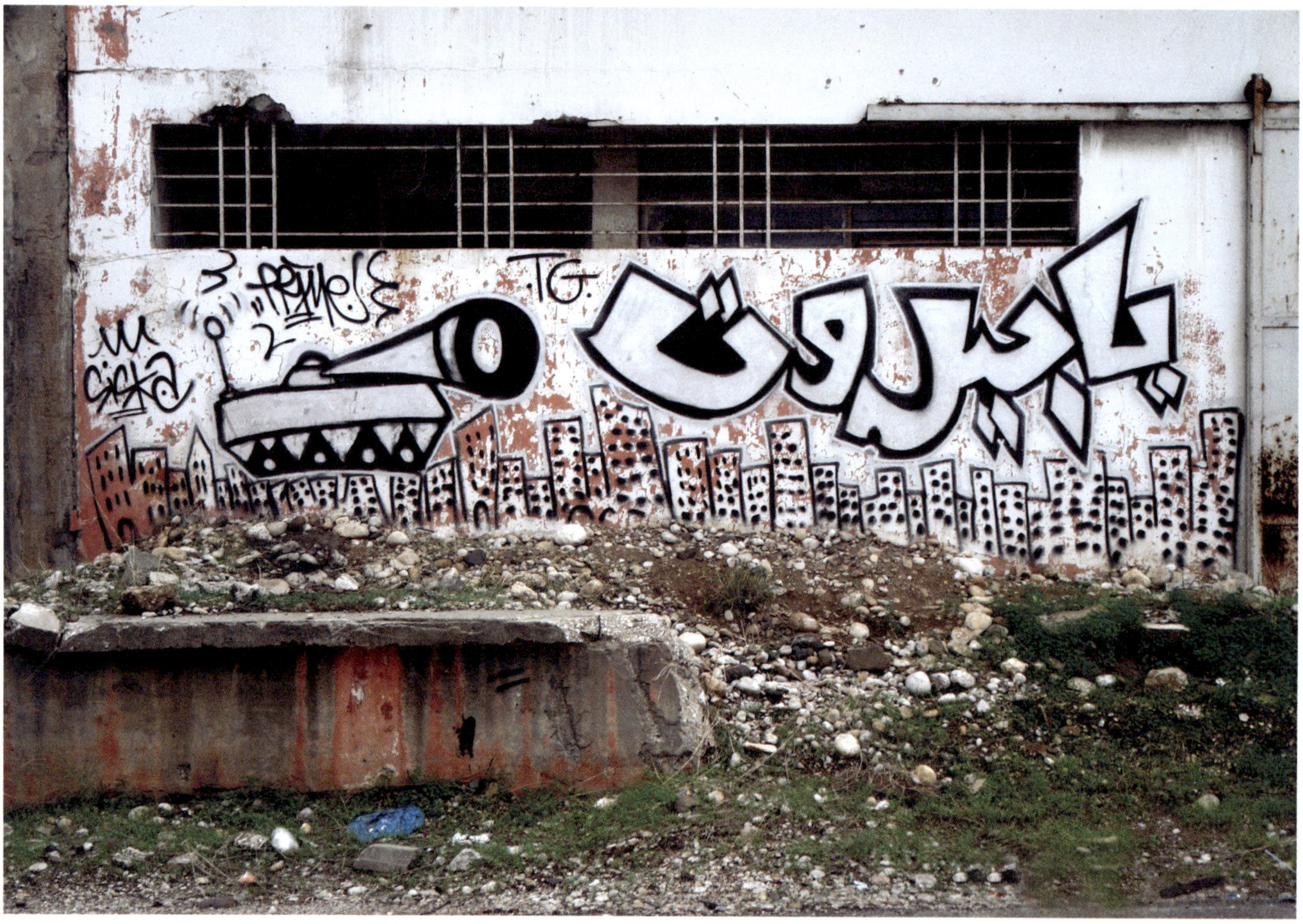

2

2·8
Beirut Never Dies
بيروت ما بتموت

Siska

بيروت ما بتموت
1. **"Beirut never dies", SISKA & PRIME, Gemeyzeh, Beirut, Lebanon**

يا بيروت
2. **"O Beirut", SISKA & PRIME, Gemeyzeh, Beirut, Lebanon**

Beirut is an Oriental city but it has an Occidental, Western feel to it. Towards the end of the 90s, the Lebanese Hip Hop scene was born, and artists were rapping their lyrics in Lebanese. In terms of Latin lettered graffiti, Fish and the REK crew represent the first generation of writers. When they started out in the late 90s they were called BW, which stands for Beirut Warriors. Later I joined them, but at the time I was part of «قطاع بيروت» (Sector Beirut). We were the first Hip Hop group to use Arabic in rap in Lebanon. This is how the whole interest in Arabic graffiti started. There was really no such thing as an Arabic graffiti scene here. What existed all over the city walls though were names of lovers, local heroes, political messages and stencils.

In the summer of 2006 during the last Israeli war on Lebanon, Beirut was empty, gray, and desperate. The citizens were sad, there was a strong will to express what they saw but they felt stuck. So together with the French graffiti artist Prime, who was a resident of Beirut at the time and represented the TG crew, I started painting in Arabic letters. I was doing the writing and he was doing the coloring. It was a combination of two completely different styles. The outcome of the different graffiti pieces we wrote was a series of messages written for the city of Beirut and its inhabitants using the same means that political messages used to use. Usually, political messages and signs were meant to divide the city into different territories. Our idea was to unify the message and the territory — one message for all, one city for all. But this time we wrote in big letters using chrome and black.

All the messages were centered around the word "Beirut" to provoke an immediate reaction among citizens in a time where people were thirsty for a smile of motivation. We first wrote «بيروت ما بتموت» (Beirut never dies) on a wall in the city center in Monot. This area used to be notorious for fighting during the civil war since it was close to the green line, the front line that divided the Muslim west and Christian east of Beirut—but it later became a popular party place with a number of bars. Being in the heart of Monot, the wall we used was the wall of a parking lot that was full of bullet holes. This graffiti was sprayed during the Israeli night shift bombings of the southern suburbs of Beirut in July 2006. I remember the image of the metal doors of the shops bouncing each time a bomb hit the city.

Despite all of that I really tried to relate to Beirut with the style of writing and not only copy a European or American style. I wanted to find the font of our city and carefully place the messages in the right spots around the city, which has suffered such a long history of being marked by different groups and interests.

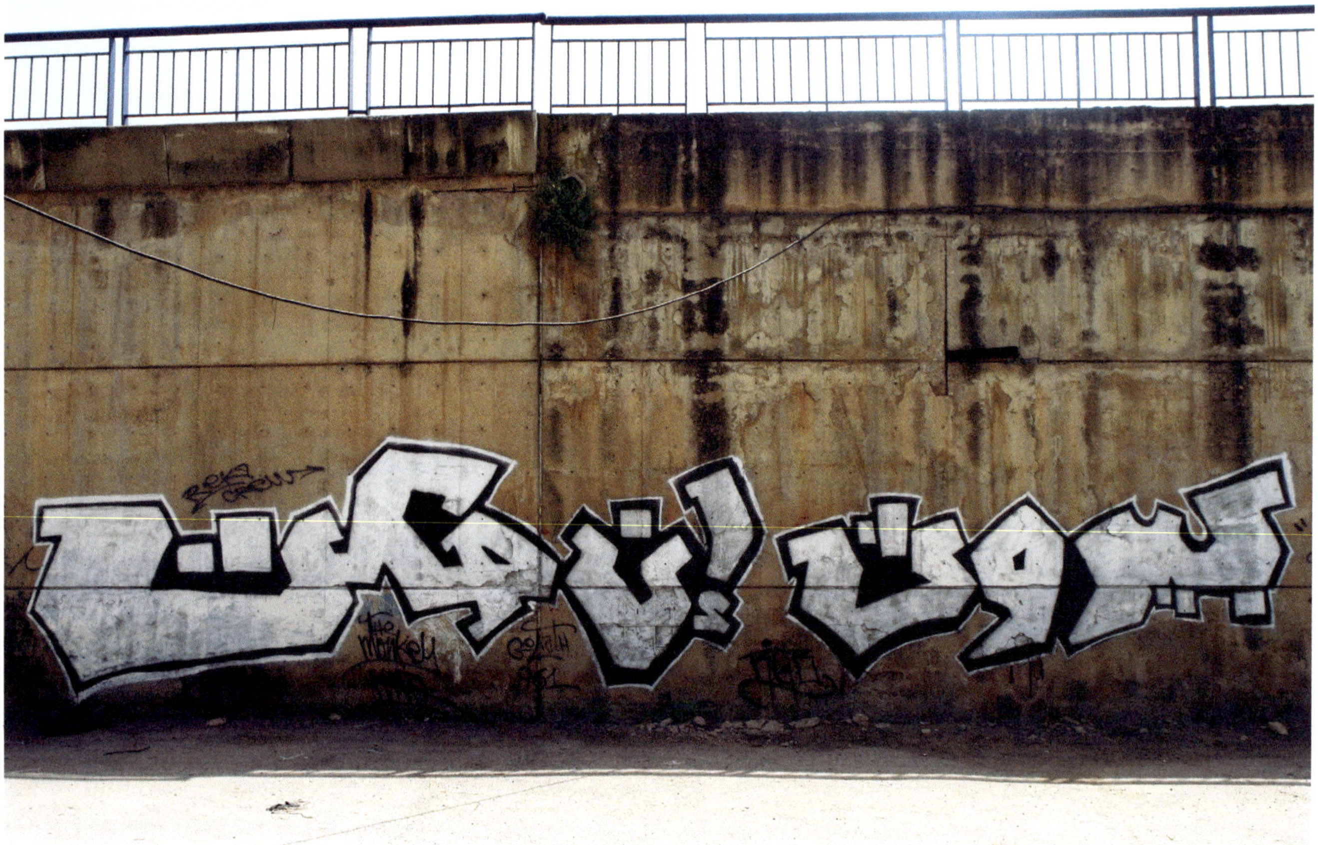

1

بيروت إن حكت
1. “If Beirut could speak”, SISKA / REK, Karantina, Beirut, Lebanon

2. Beirut, 2007

Since 2005, a series of mysterious car bombings targeting high-ranking politicians, security officials and journalists has haunted Lebanon. I felt that we were pushed to react. Even though the message did not speak about the specific incident, it was a way to not slip into the mode where you stay home, don't move and switch your brain off, which happened to most of the city whenever a bomb exploded. After an explosion people did not leave the house for a day or two until life got back to normal again, which meant the streets were empty and we were able to spray freely.

Towards the end of 2007 I had already written six different messages, like «بيروت عيب» (Beirut shame), «لي بتموت» (for Beirut) and «بيروت إن حكت» (if Beirut could speak) together with Fish, the most prominent and oldest Lebanese graffiti artist. “Beyrout in Hakat” was sprayed on a big gray bridge wall in the area of Karantina, next to the river of Beirut. Karantina offers a lot of empty space. It is an industrial area, very gray, and full of concrete bridges that lead up to the north-south highways and those which connect Beirut with Damascus in the east. Located next to the port of Beirut, it has an intense history from being an Armenian refugee camp in the 1920s, and later on a Muslim island in a Christian controlled neighborhood mainly inhabited by Palestinian refugees. It experienced massacres during the civil war and is now home to slaughterhouses and factories along the river of Beirut.

To me the area was always my favorite place to start spreading graffiti in Beirut. People seemed to care little about us spraying, but the visibility was very high since everyone passes by in cars, like a sort of gallery. One year after writing the first graffiti piece there, graffiti started appearing next to it and, as if a virus had started, within a few months the whole area was painted with graffiti by younger people, a lot of them using Beirut in their writings too, such as “eyes on Beirut” in an Arabic font. People signed, wrote messages like “don't eat chocolate, eat fruits” and lots of them were done by Armenians from the neighboring area of Bourj Hammoud.

The graffiti «بيروت ما بتموت» (Beirut never dies) was the first Arabic graffiti piece of its genre in Beirut, it became somewhat of a hero due to the exposure it got. Its picture appeared in many different articles and local newspapers and was part of many TV and on-line reports. The slogan itself was copied many times, cultural festivals were named after it, it was transformed into propaganda for the 2007 parliamentary by-elections and went on big billboards all over the city under the signature of one specific political party. Then a series of postcards appeared with the graffiti on them and were sold in a big music store in downtown Beirut. Shortly after that, a Lebanese fashion designer named Sarah Beydoun used it on one of her handbags as a motif. Later, the slogan was sprayed once more by a group of graffiti artists in a different area of Beirut using another more Western style with vivid colors. And I even found someone who had it tattooed on her arm.

In 2009 I was invited by 98weeks (an art initiative from Beirut) to take part in the "Subvision" exhibition in Hamburg. Artists from all over the globe were asked to make interventions on shipping containers that belonged to the port of Hamburg. Hafencity is just another one of these big real estate development projects, a skyscraper ghost city, and containers are usually used to connect the world as a part of globalization. In Beirut, though, during the civil war they were standing on roads as a wall to separate east and west along the green line. My contribution was a graffiti piece that said «هامبورغور ما بتموت» (Hamburger never dies) sprayed in chrome and black as an ironic homage to the famous "Beirut never dies" and the famous "Hamburger". On a second container I wrote graffiti quotes from Beirut that I had collected in the streets. Some dated back to the civil war, others were from lovers in the 80s, other ones were recent writings; all joined together on one wall. Poetic messages were placed next to political beliefs and nonsense sayings: "Ciel Bleu nuit Blanche" (Blue sky white night), "Fuck the Arabs", «هذه ڤيتنام الجديدة» (this is the new Vietnam), "My Full Moon" and «أبو علي مرَّ من هنا» (Abou aali passed by here).

• SISKA
is a visual artist and filmmaker from Beirut currently based in Berlin. He has worked in the underground Hip Hop scene as part of the Lebanese Hip Hop crew Kitaa Bey-Route and wrote a series of graffiti messages in Beirut. As part of the 98weeks art collective he took part in many exhibitions like the "No soul for sale" (Tate Modern London) or "Subvision" (Port of Hamburg) and his films have been screened at festivals internationally.

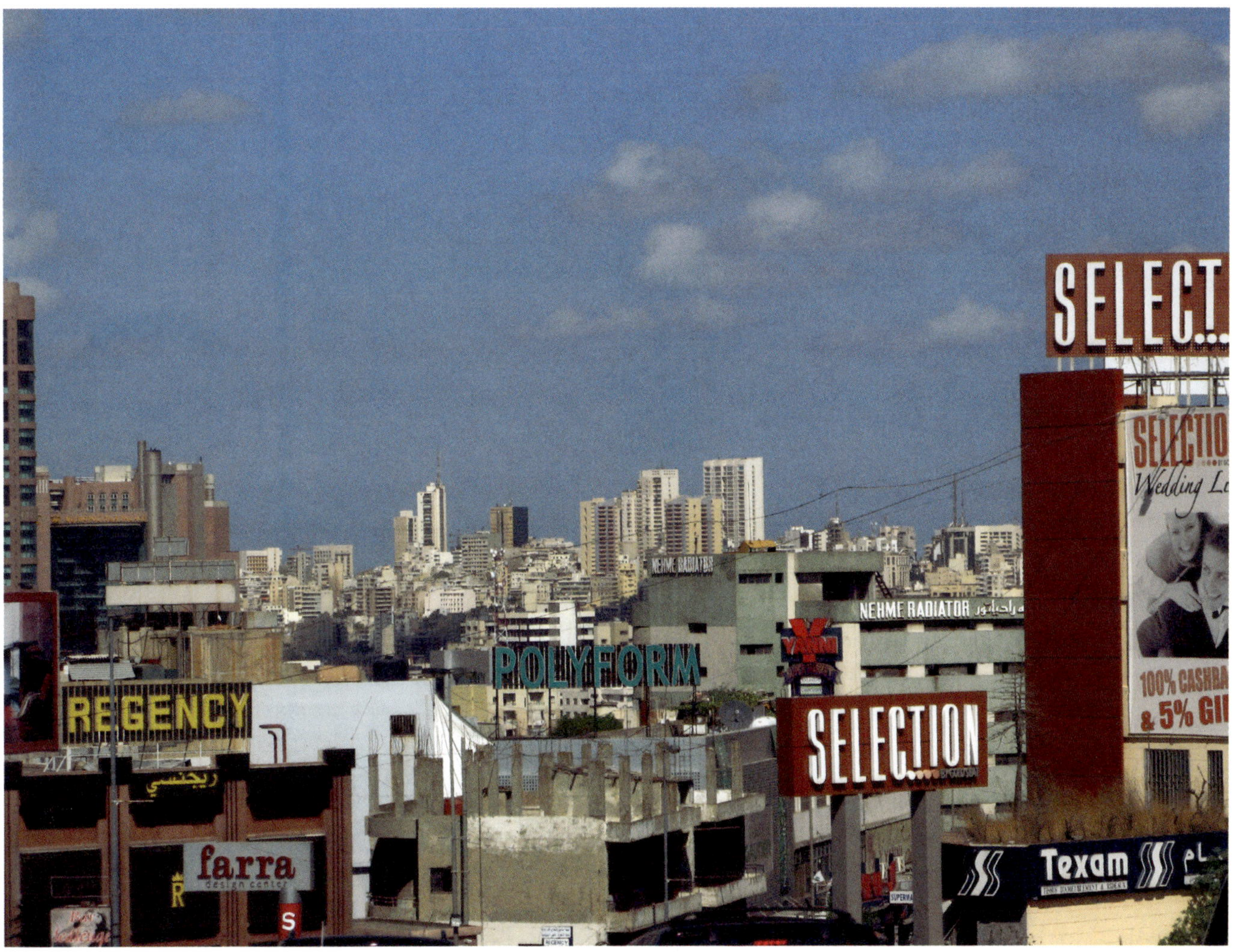

2

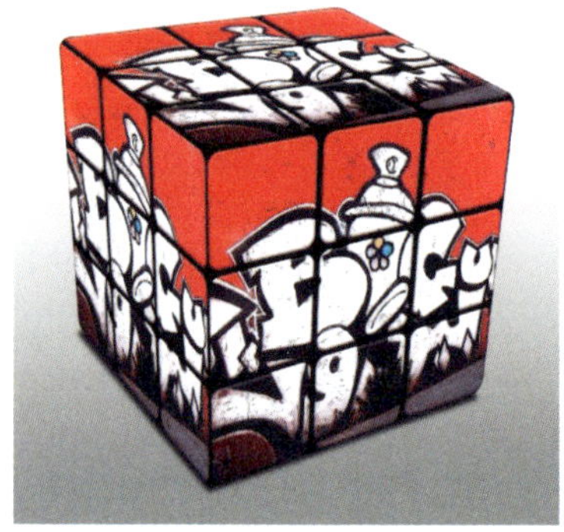

1

1. “Big Up Beirut”, Rubik’s cube, Beirut, Lebanon

2. “Beirut never dies” clutch bag, Sarah’s Bag, Beirut, Lebanon

3. “Beirut never dies” clutch bag, Sarah’s Bag, Beirut, Lebanon

4. “Beirut never dies” tattoo

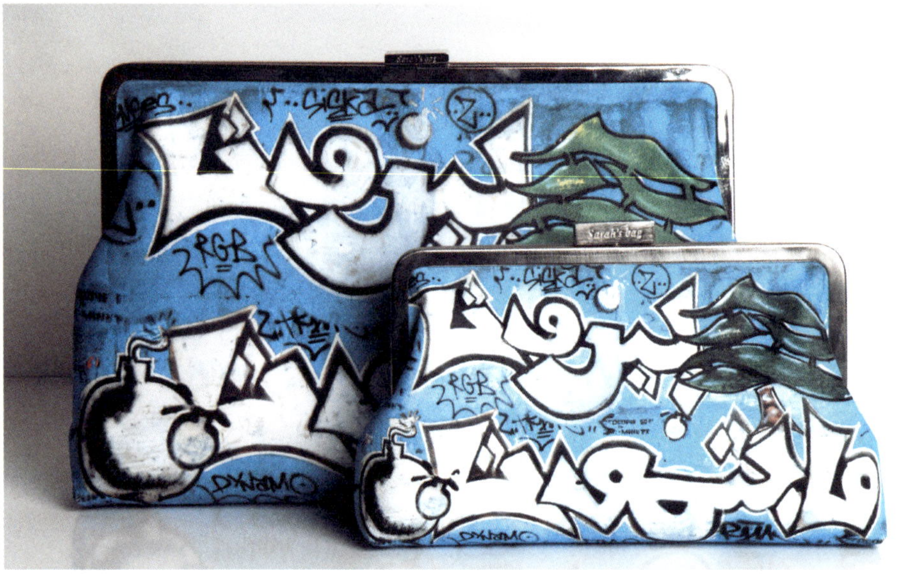

2

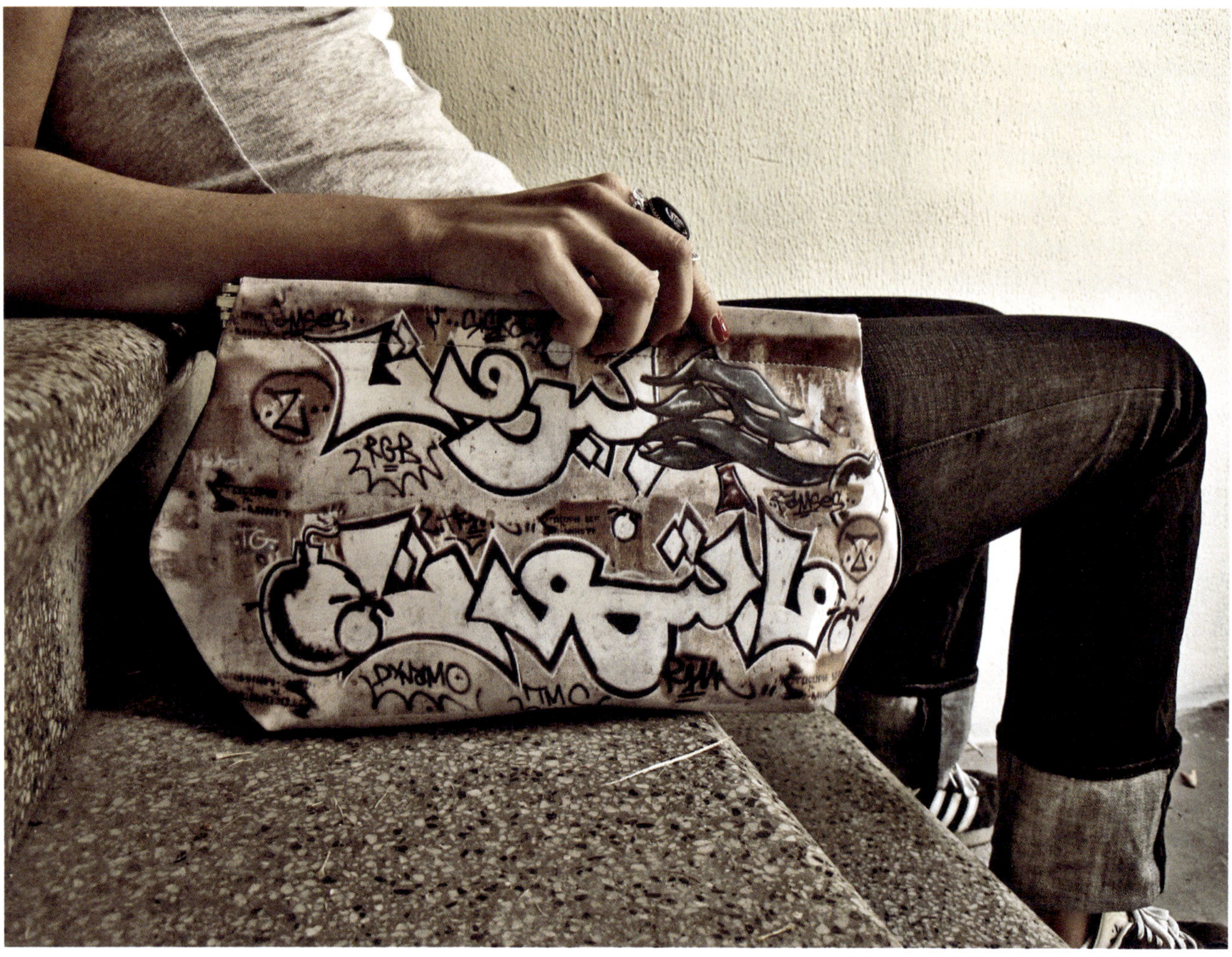

3

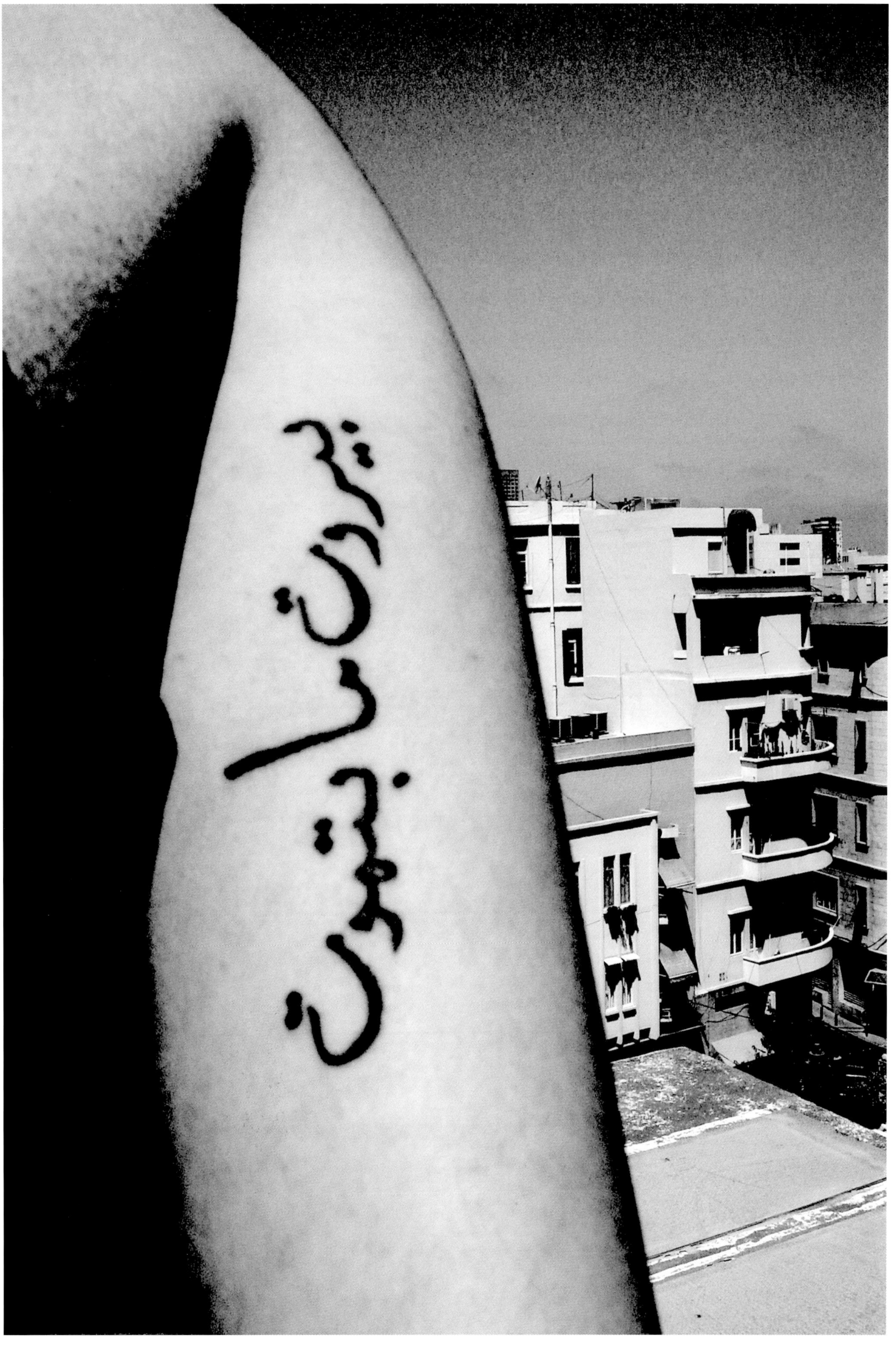

4

Artists

eL Seed
Hest1
Julien Breton aka Kaalam
L'Atlas
Sair 4 aka Puya Bagheri
Native & ZenTwO
Sun7 aka Jonas Bournat
Sadhu
Monsieur Cana aka Askar
Zepha aka Vincent Abadie Hafez
LightGraff
Blouzaat
Mohammed Ali / Aerosol Arabic

3.

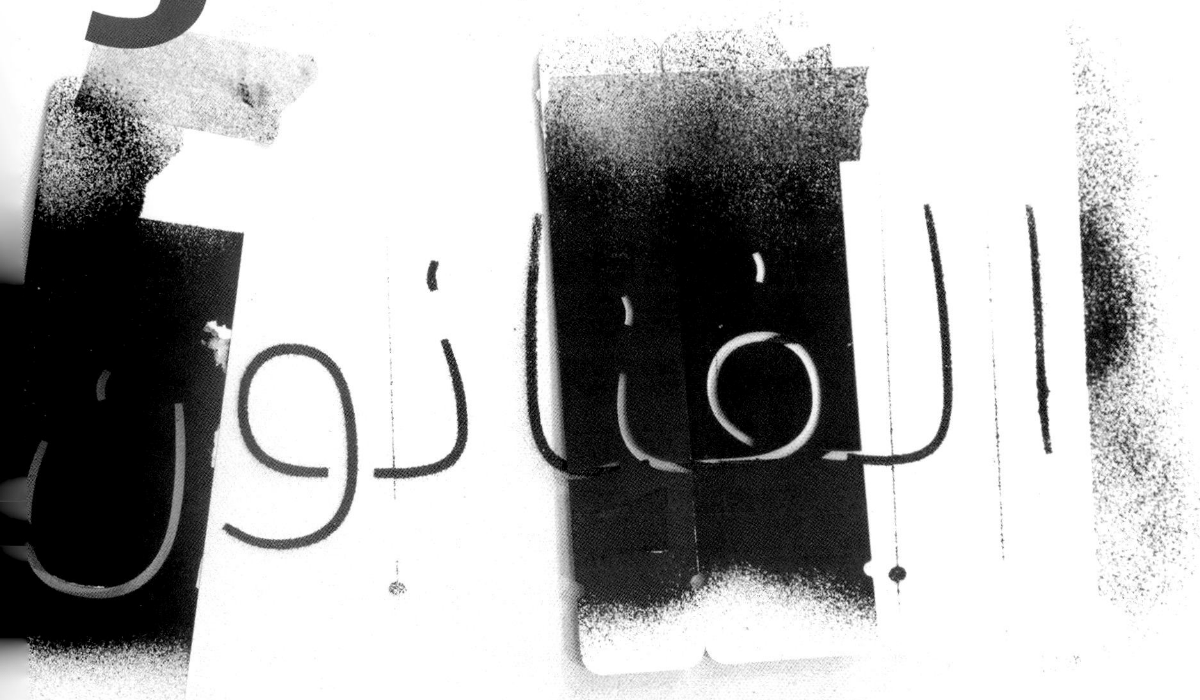

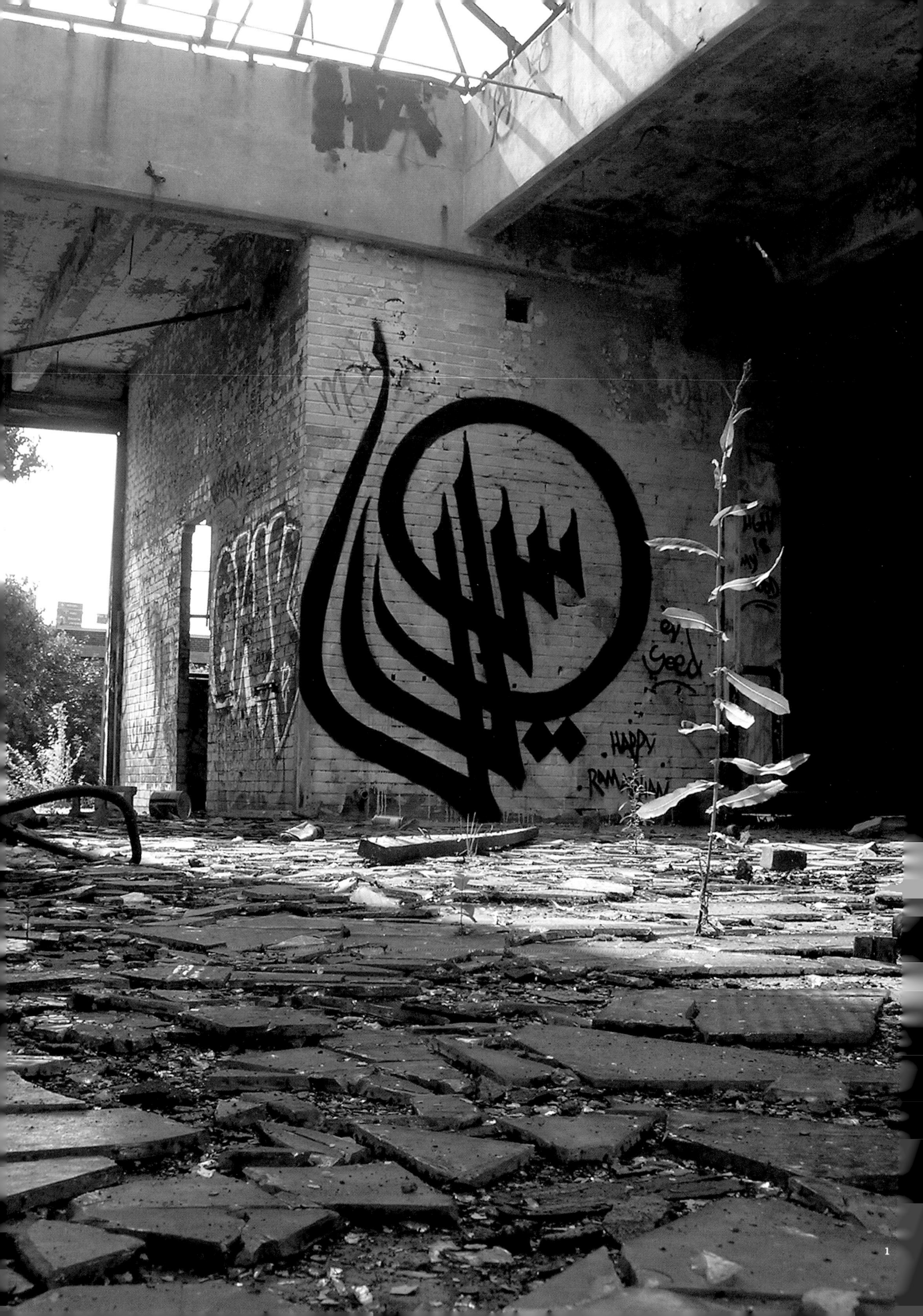
HAPPY

3·1
eL Seed
السيد

Born 1981 in Paris
Lives in Montréal, Canada

الغابة الحضرية
1. "Urban Jungle", EL SEED, Montréal, 2008

افتح الباب
2. "Open the door", EL SEED, Montréal, 2008

eL Seed began adorning the walls of Paris with his graffiti in 1998. A few years later in 2004, he decided to learn calligraphy, but due to lack of available professors he resorted to studying on his own. After moving to North America, eL Seed widened his repertoire. Meeting Hest1, he was inspired to combine his love for graffiti with his love for calligraphy, and began to paint using Arabic script. Thus, his particular style of Arabic graffiti was born.

eL Seed perceives Arabic calligraphy as a tangible expression of his search for identity. Throughout his work, myriad paths intersect and mirror the multiple sources of inspiration which nourish his art. Emanating from this confusion is an amalgam of harmony and balance.

His work is a mixture of street art and Arabic calligraphy, through which he endeavors to bridge cultural divides caused by fictitious dichotomies. eL Seed no longer tags his name on walls. He has decided to adopt a proverbial tradition in which the name disappears and only the message remains. Therefore, rather than searching for what distinguishes him from others, eL Seed searches for what unites him and others. His art is a link, an arm outstretched.

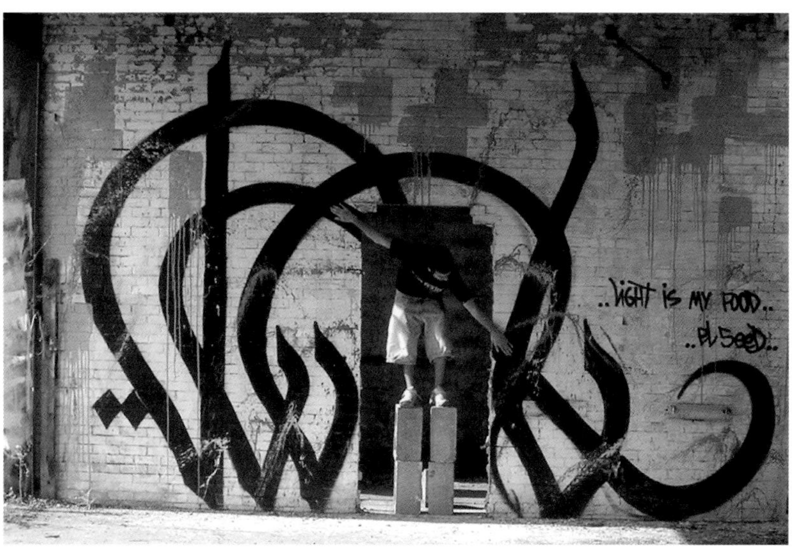

2

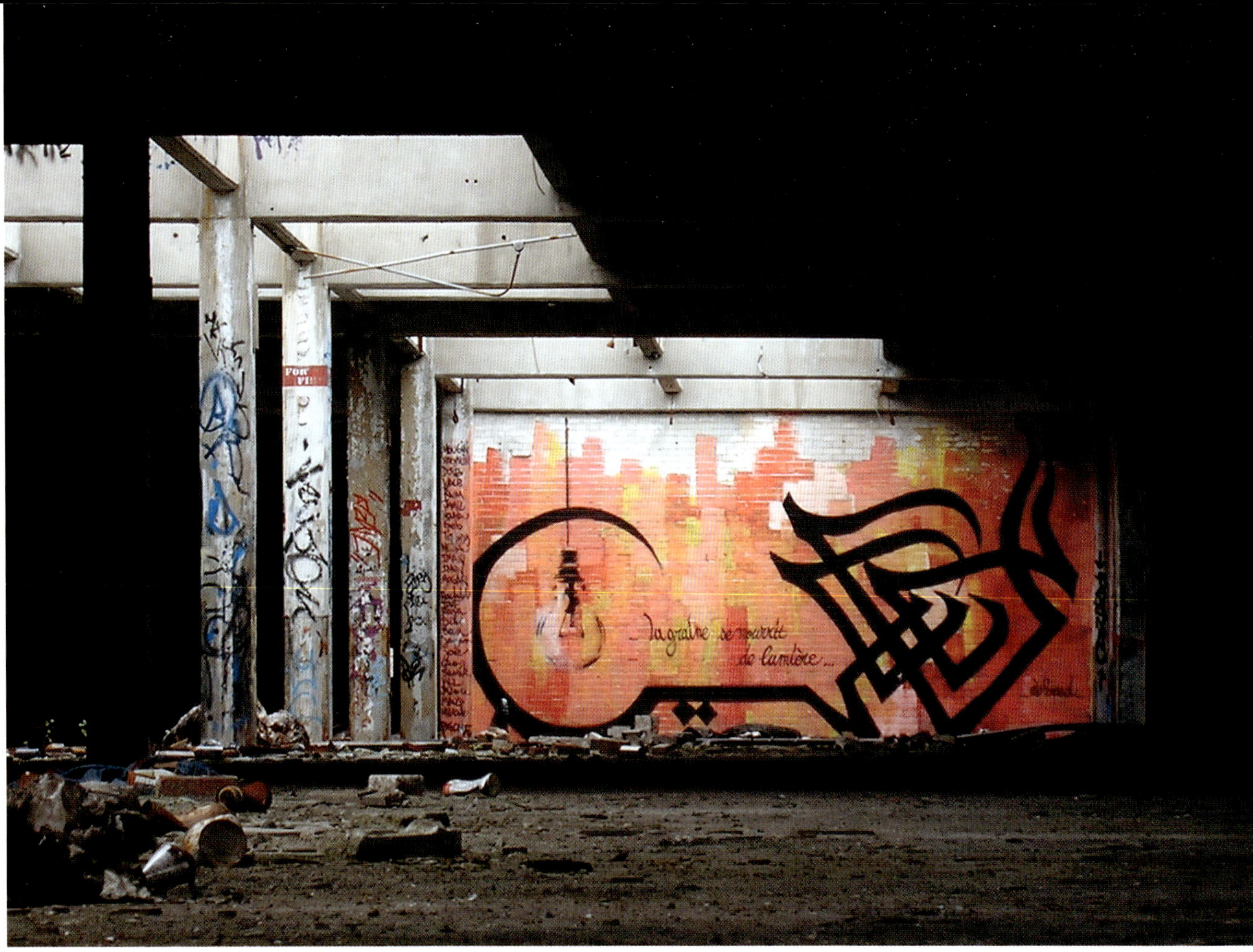
... la graine se nourrit
de lumière ...

1

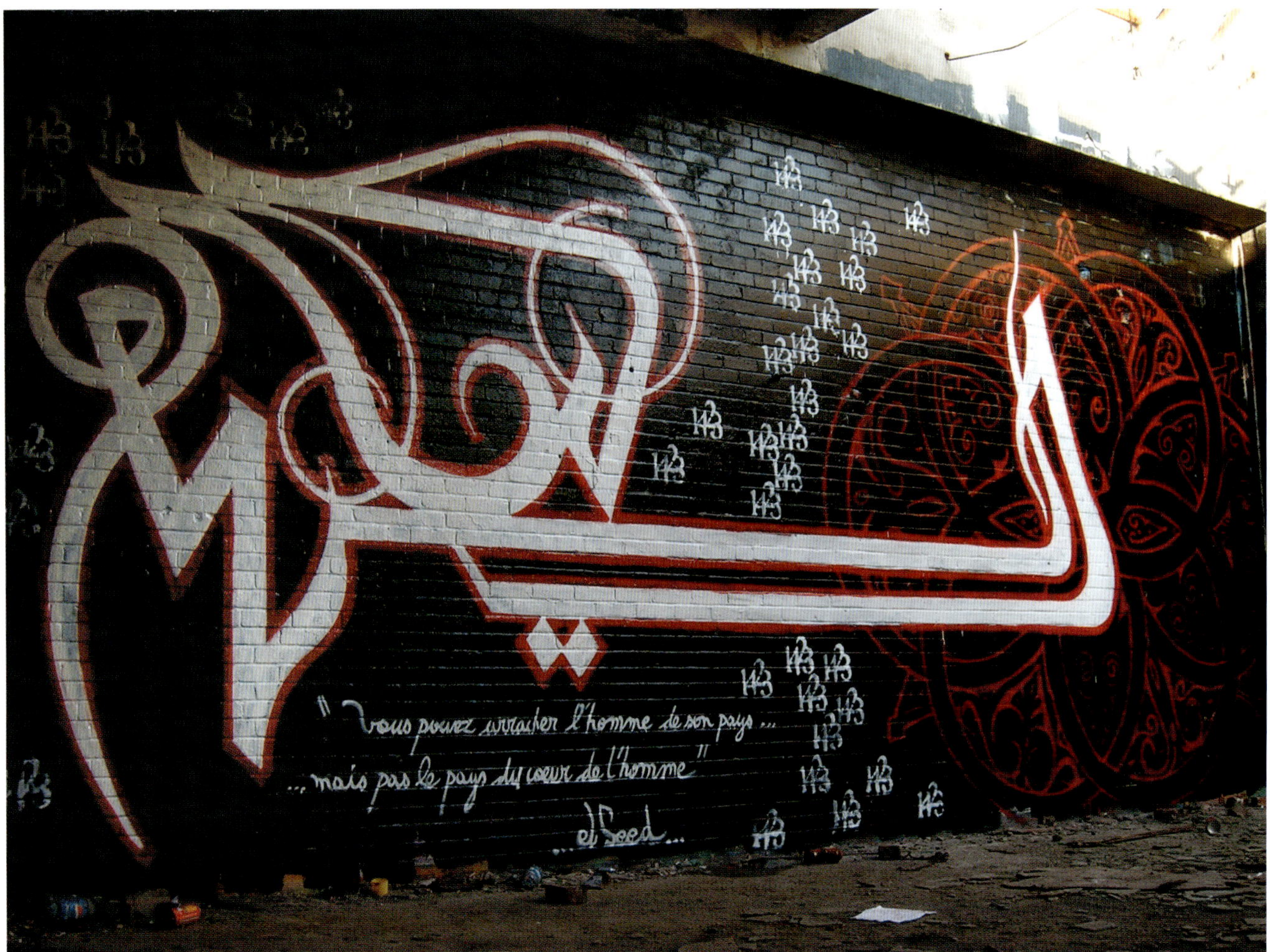
" Vous pouvez arracher l'homme de son pays ...
... mais pas le pays du coeur de l'homme "
... el Seed ...

2

3 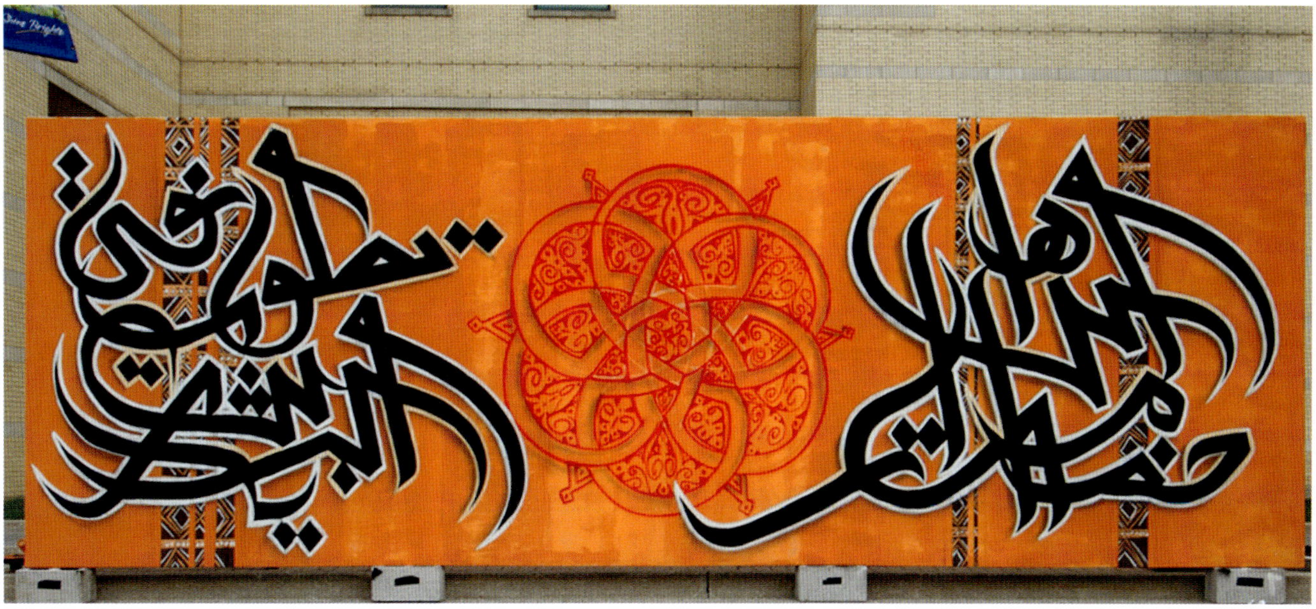

النور
1. **"The Light", EL SEED, Montréal, 2008**

فنون البلد
2. **"Bled Art", EL SEED, Montréal, 2008**

اسهام الحضارات في تطور البشرية
3. **"Civilization", EL SEED, Toronto, 2010**

• ARABIC GRAFFITI: A QUEST FOR IDENTITY
eL Seed

The letters I use in each Arabic graffiti composition represent the journey through which I have formed my identity, both as an individual and an artist. The multiplicity of identities which make up the fabric of each person are reflected in each letter. Sometimes bold and cutting, sometimes soft and complacent, they weave together and intersect to create the meaning of a word. Navigating identities is often a difficult process, as these are both consciously and unconsciously created, and often imposed on us. The late Edward Said pioneered a form of critical understanding of identity which deconstructed the Orientalist gaze emanating from colonizing entities. An essential part of reclaiming an identity strewn with foreign prejudices and assumptions begins with self-reflection. One of my goals is to try to reconcile different aspects of my specific 'identity crisis' through Arabic graffiti. I hope that others are able to relate to this and to extract from it their own situational analysis and, from this, to deconstruct the world in which their particular identities are embedded.

The art I produce strays from classical forms of Arabic calligraphy and is therefore often deemed illegitimate; much like graffiti has been deemed an illegitimate form of art equated with vandalism. This tension is also present in my hyphenated identity, as despite my being born and raised in France, I am not considered actually French. The irony of course is that this perception is then internalized, meaning that even I do not perceive myself as completely French, but rather French with strong North African roots which I want to keep alive. Thus, the art I create becomes a reflection of my social reality.

Many influential actors within the mainstream media work with specific agendas to support the proliferation of stereotypes, which make for entertaining news. The past few decades have witnessed the demonization of Arab, Persian, and other Eastern peoples, as well as Muslims, who the media present as subhuman and one-dimensional. Developing from the traditions of neocolonialism, Arab and Muslim voices are stifled by dominating stereotypes which are often unconsciously absorbed. The creation of art, especially highly visible street art, takes back this voice through authentic expressions of identity and culture. Due to this, Arabic graffiti takes on an important role in re-affirming the presence of a strong, albeit struggling, identity independent of domineering outside influences.

My particular approach to Arabic graffiti is a response to the globalization of 'Western' culture, which has insidiously invaded most parts of the globe. Serving to homogenize an

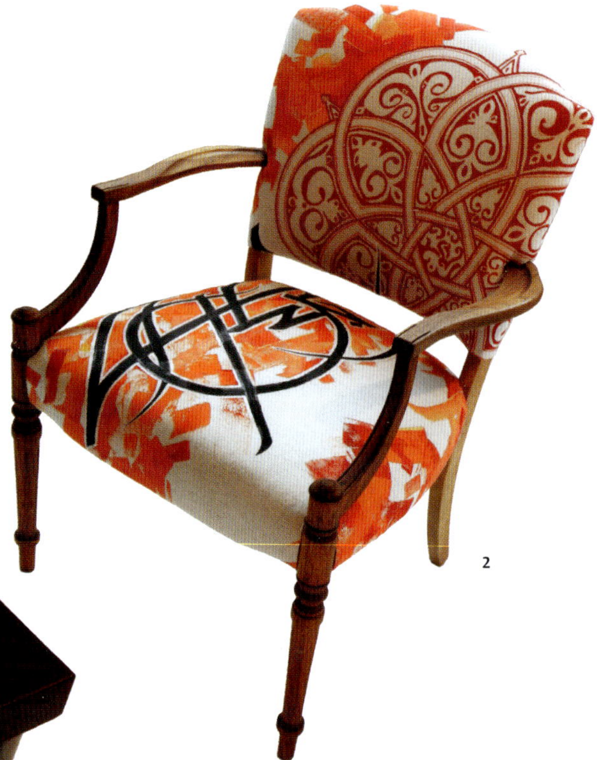

2

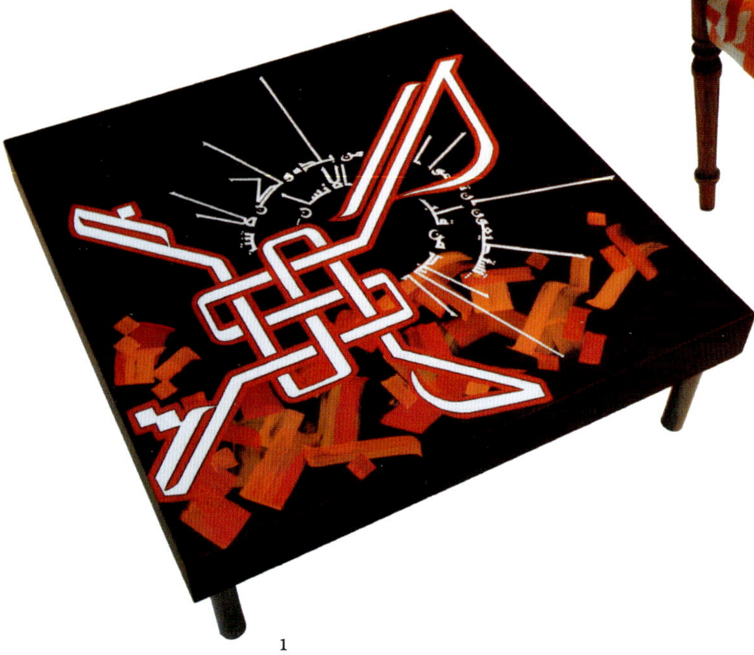

1

بلدي
1. “My country”, EL SEED, table, acrylic paint, 80 × 80 cm, 2009

اجلس
2. “Have a seat”, EL SEED, chair, acrylic on canvas, 2009

ثقافة
3. “Crossed culture”, EL SEED, spray paint on canvas, 3 pieces 120 × 30 cm, 2010

أنا عربي
4. "I am Arab", EL SEED, acrylic on canvas, 160 × 70 cm, 2010

هويتي
5. “My identity”, EL SEED, spray paint and acrylic on canvas, 160 × 100 cm, 2010

أحتاج تاريخي
6. “I need my history” (Pieces of Identity), EL SEED, spray paint and acrylic on wood, 100 × 70 cm, 2010

otherwise diverse world, it has effectively shut up and shut down expressions of difference. Because of this, it has been my conscious choice to paint solely in classical Arabic, although I do drop an occasional phrase in English or French. This is a statement against the particularly hegemonic role of language and the part it inevitably plays in spreading the globalized monoculture. Furthermore, Arabic graffiti serves to carry the traditions of Arabic and Islamic art whilst stepping outside the box of traditionalism. Much like a young adolescent searching for an authentic voice in order to step out from under the shadow of his or her parents, Arabic graffiti is struggling to affirm a new generation of identities which are amalgams of modern and traditional paradigms. Extrapolating the difference between tradition and traditionalism, I personally try to nurture the religious and cultural traditions of my heritage while composing them alongside my modern realities. As an artist, I believe it is my duty to be culture creative and find methods through which to keep my heritage alive.

The proverbial traditions which inspire and shape Arabic graffiti stem from the fundamental principles of Islam. This becomes all the more important when the message aims to raise awareness about sensitive issues and bring about a higher level of consciousness. In my view, artists have a social responsibility to push boundaries, question the status quo and encourage critical reflection. Furthermore, the artist has a responsibility to live the message he or she is transmitting, as it is an Islamic principle in and of itself. Communitarian art, in which one does not tag a name but rather a shared message, means a certain denial of ownership. I do not write my name, and therefore I do not claim territory when I paint, but rather I offer something back. The wall becomes the primary medium through which one communicates with others and the dimension of community is thus brought to the fore because the mural is offered freely to the public. Due to this, the piece no longer belongs to me, but to the community in which it was conceived. Nourished by Islamic values, art emanating from Islamic communities must therefore carry some notion of brotherhood and sisterhood, free of the negative competition which so often defines our lives today.

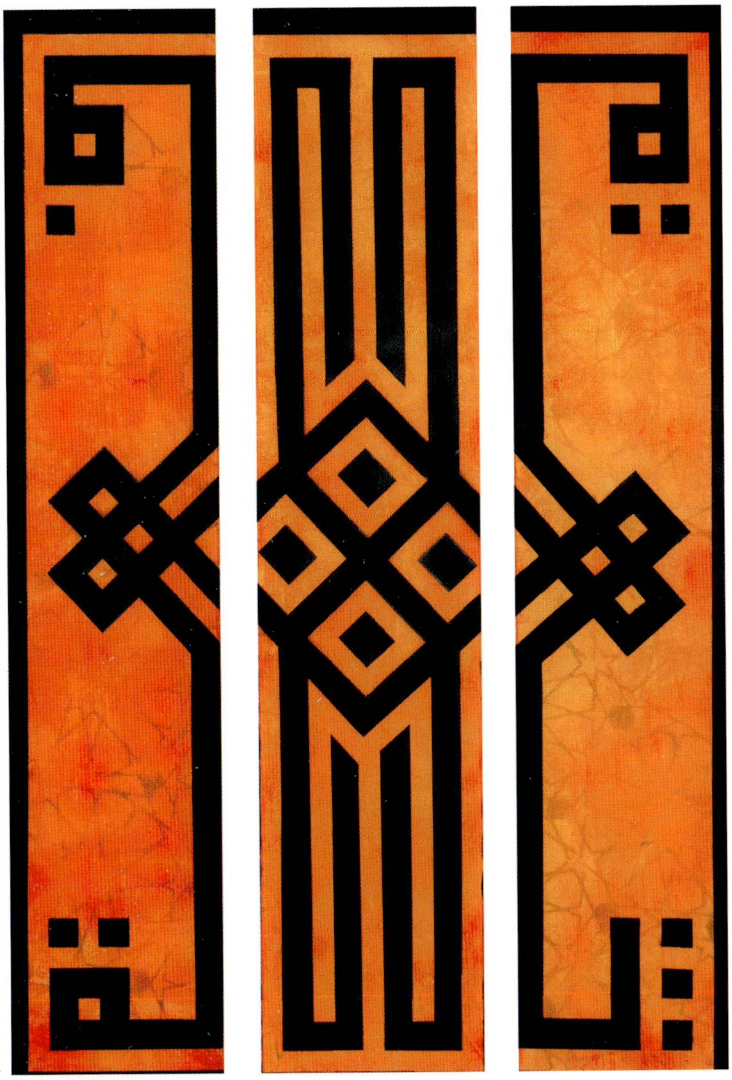

3

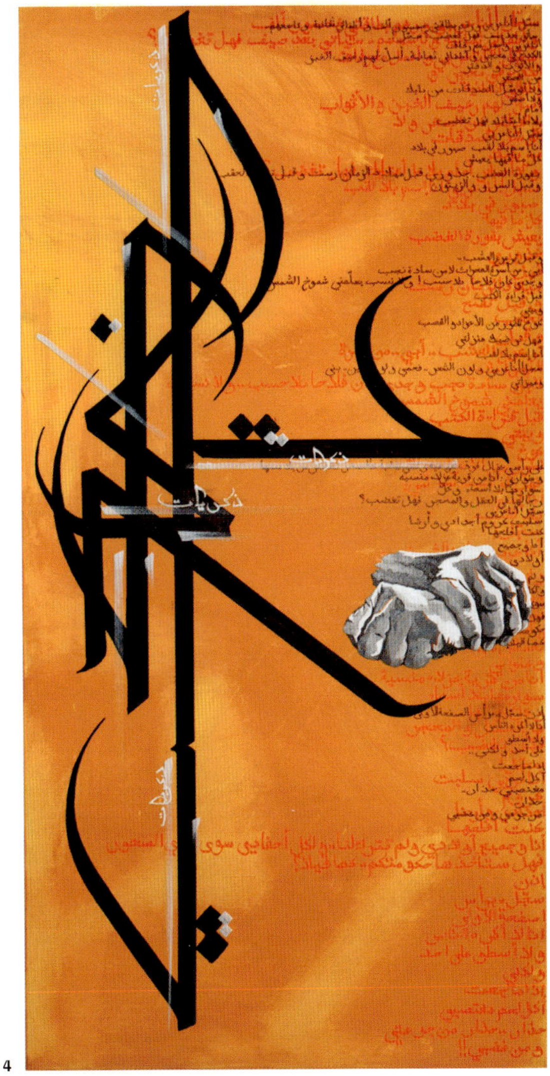

4

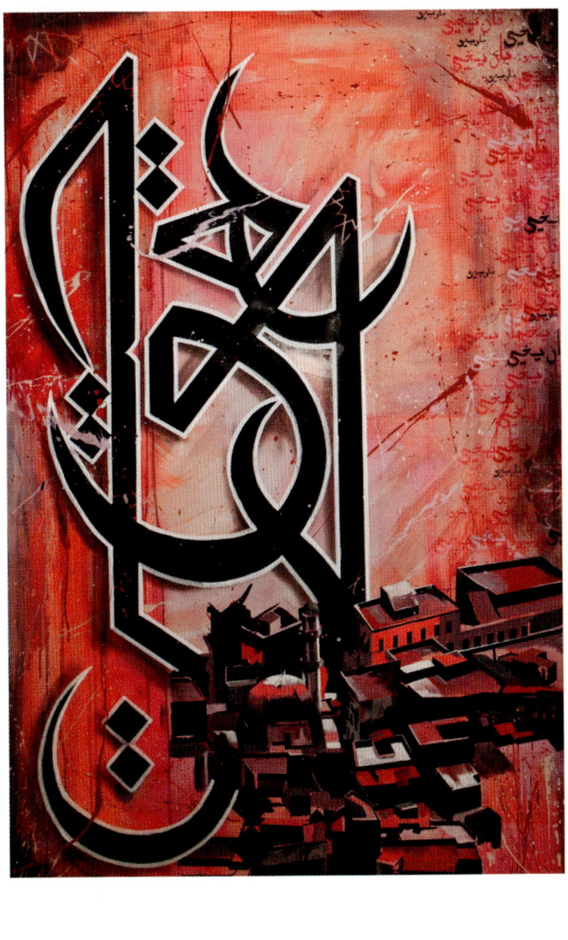

5

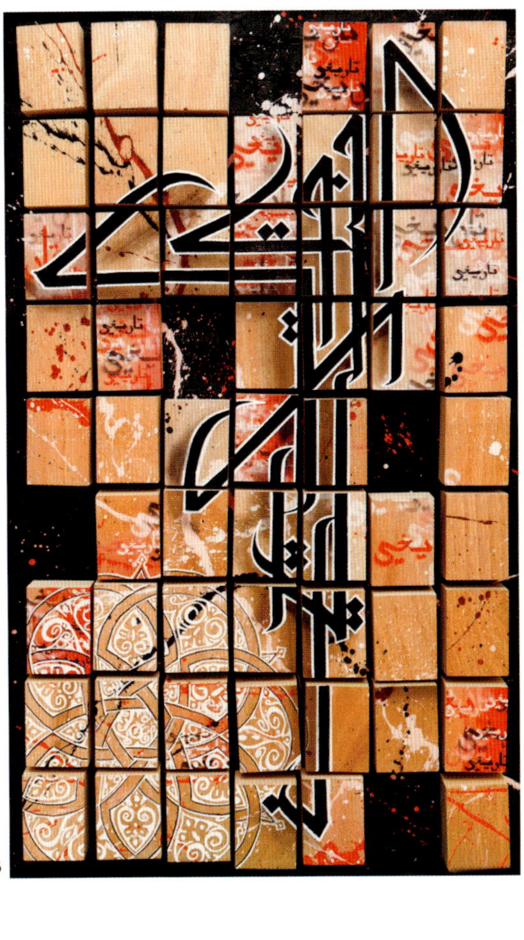

6

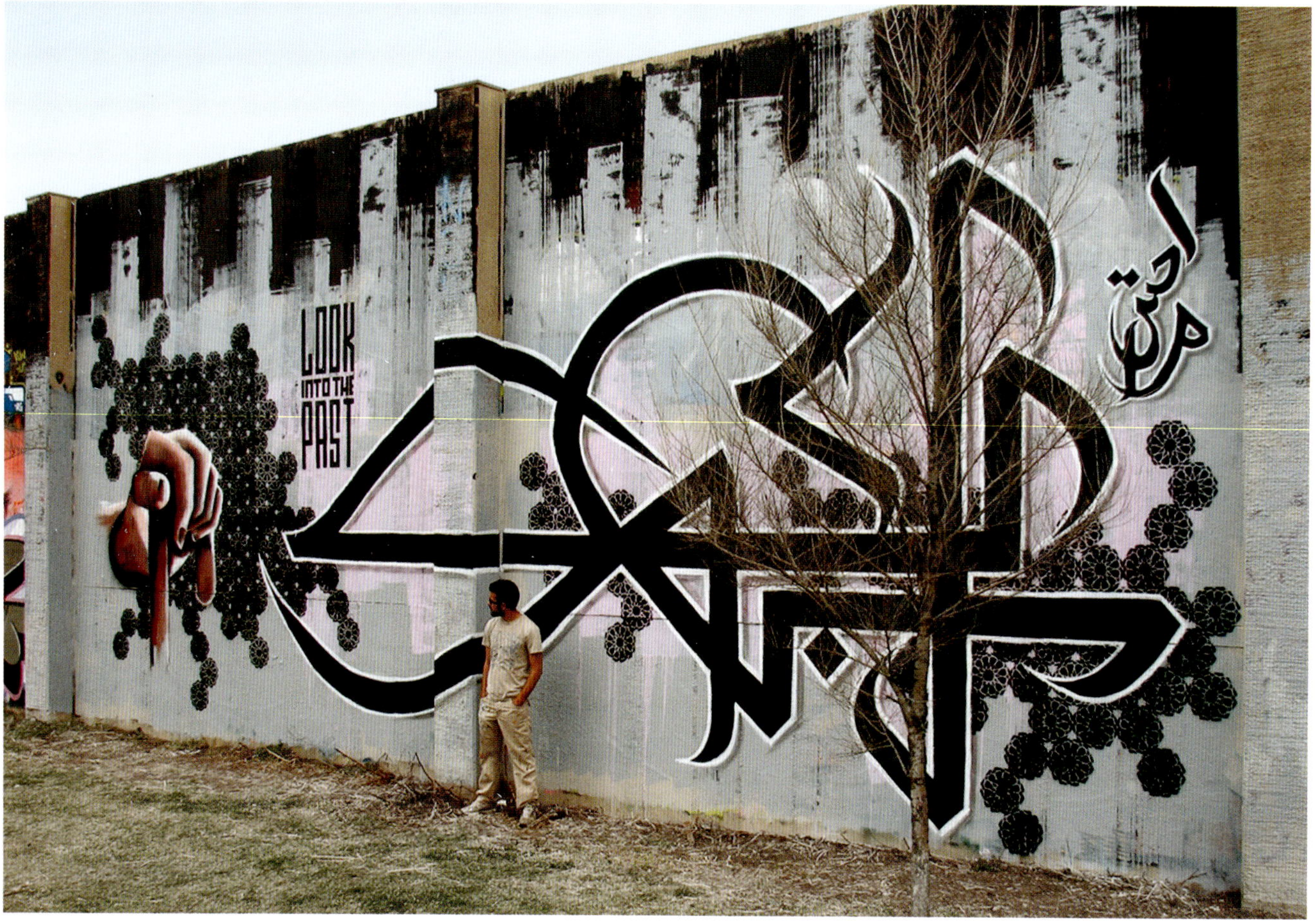

1

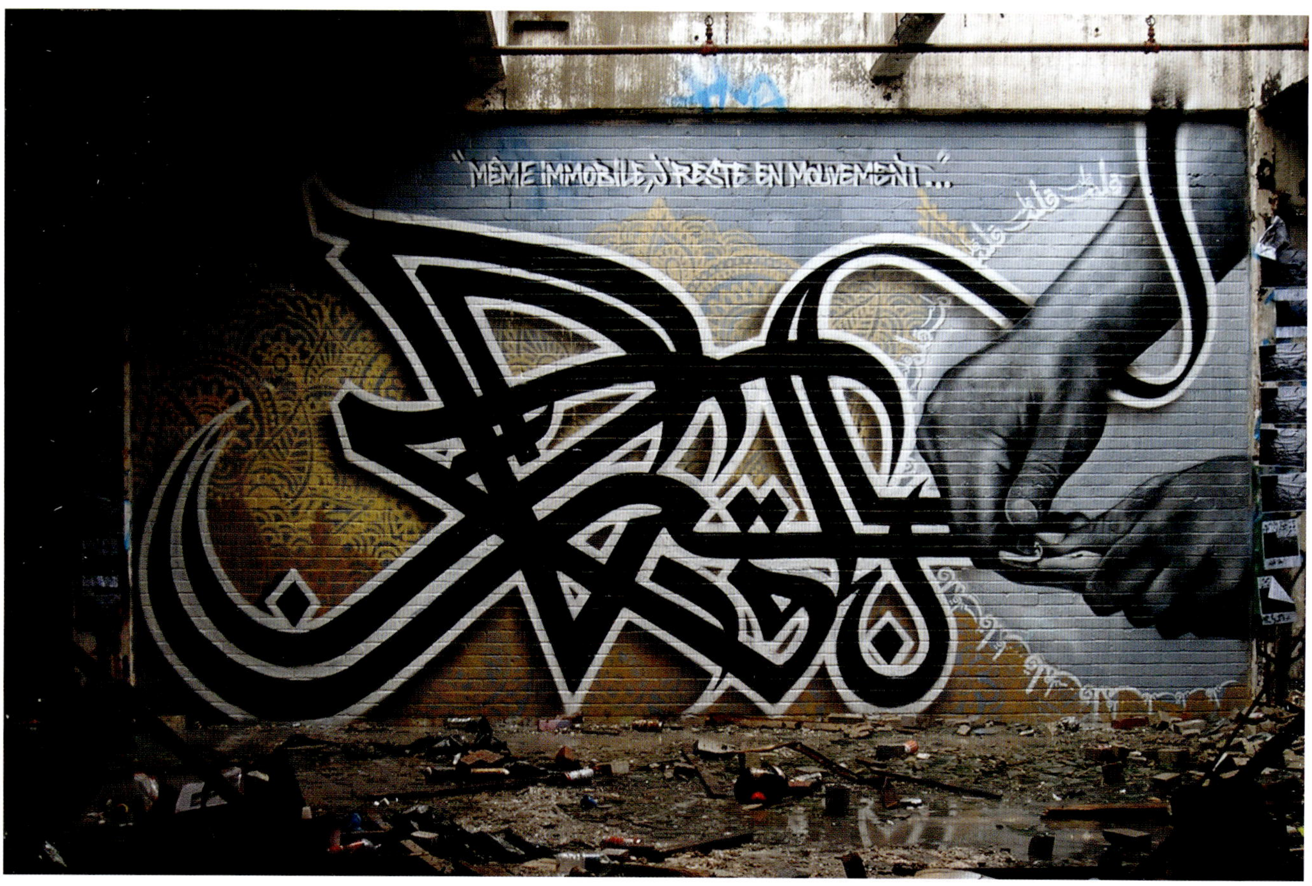

2

• THE PROVERBIAL TRADITION
eL Seed

On the Arabian Peninsula, before the advent of Islam, a large village named Okaz situated near Mecca was known in the region as the rendezvous for jousting poets. Each year, these linguistically shrewd men would meet at a commercial and artistic fair where they would engage in a competition of eloquence and poetic flare. It is reported that following these battles of wits, the victorious poems were embroidered onto textiles, which would then be suspended from the walls of the Kaaba. Thus their name, "Mu'allaqat" (suspended poems). It is said that several thousand poems once adorned the walls of the Kaaba. Since the revelation of Islam, only seven poems remained on the sacred walls and it was these poems that gave classical Arabic some of its rules and structures. The Mu'allaqat tell the story of anonymous men belonging to the proverbial tradition who thus influenced the future by simply, yet eloquently, retelling the events of their everyday lives. In the spirit of the Mu'allaqat, my art retells my time and my social reality, and endeavors to influence the future.

A proverb is usually defined as a wise saying or precept which can be understood as atemporal or universal. For me, there is nothing more malleable than a proverb, not in its formulation but rather in its meaning. A proverb expresses the truth of an experience and these experiences are as varied as the human race. In light of this, I permit myself to interpret the proverbial tradition as an invitation to universal self-questioning and self-reflection. Proverbs not only create bridges between people who recognize themselves in a specific collective imagination, but they also weave connections between the trivial reality from which they issue and different forms of metaphysical understandings.

The contemporary artist finds in his or her message the limits of ones own language. Classical Arabic is my chosen contextual instrument since it is, in my opinion, one of the least discriminatory languages in current usage. Even those who do not read Arabic script can derive an idea of its meaning from the curves and forms of the words. It is this dual nature within calligraphy that attracted and inspired me. As I create Arabic graffiti, I write, and therefore I say and express in words, but at the same time, I draw, and therefore I say and express in images.

The aesthetic and the style of an artistic piece intervene in the transmission of a message and can be as influential as the title or the message itself. I would qualify my graffiti pieces as proverbial in the sense that aesthetically they represent the deeper message put forward. Through this, I hope that the emotion is born within viewers even before they venture to discover the meaning of the calligraphy. In my artwork, the initial visual impression must give a clue to the meaning of the word or phrase and should awaken the curiosity of the spectator. I manipulate each letter with specific attention in order to amplify the message.

To bring coherence to my discourse, I decided to no longer sign my murals. This in my opinion would be a perversion of my message. One can only hope to truly touch the world as an anonymous contributor as part of the proverbial tradition; anything else would amount to a kind of egocentrism which ultimately drowns out the essential message.

احترام الكبار
1. "Respect our elders", EL SEED, Montréal, 2010

توازن
2. "Balance", HEST1 & EL SEED, Montréal, 2008

Following pages 108 & 109:

إلهام
"Inspiration", HEST1 & EL SEED, Montréal, 2008

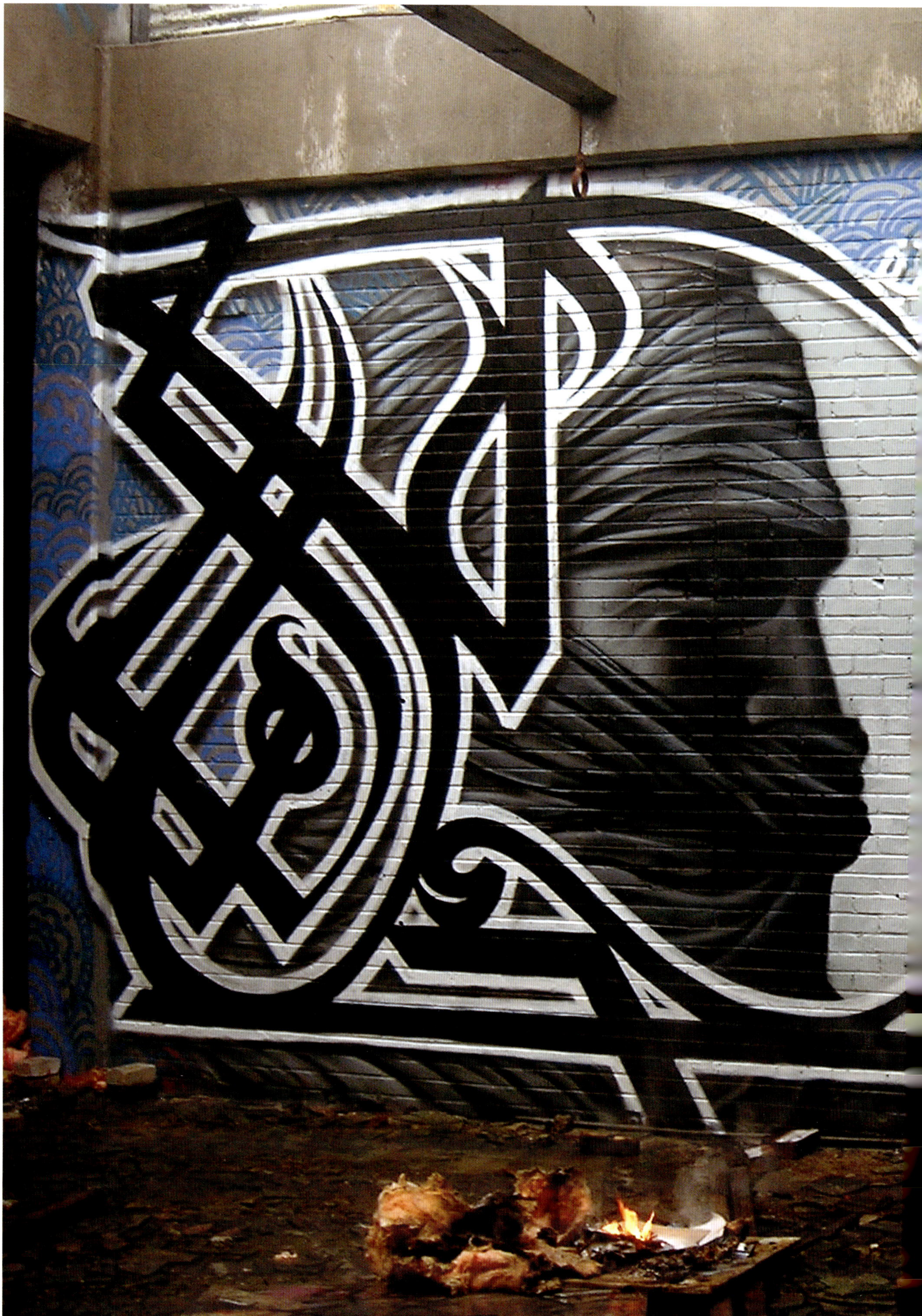

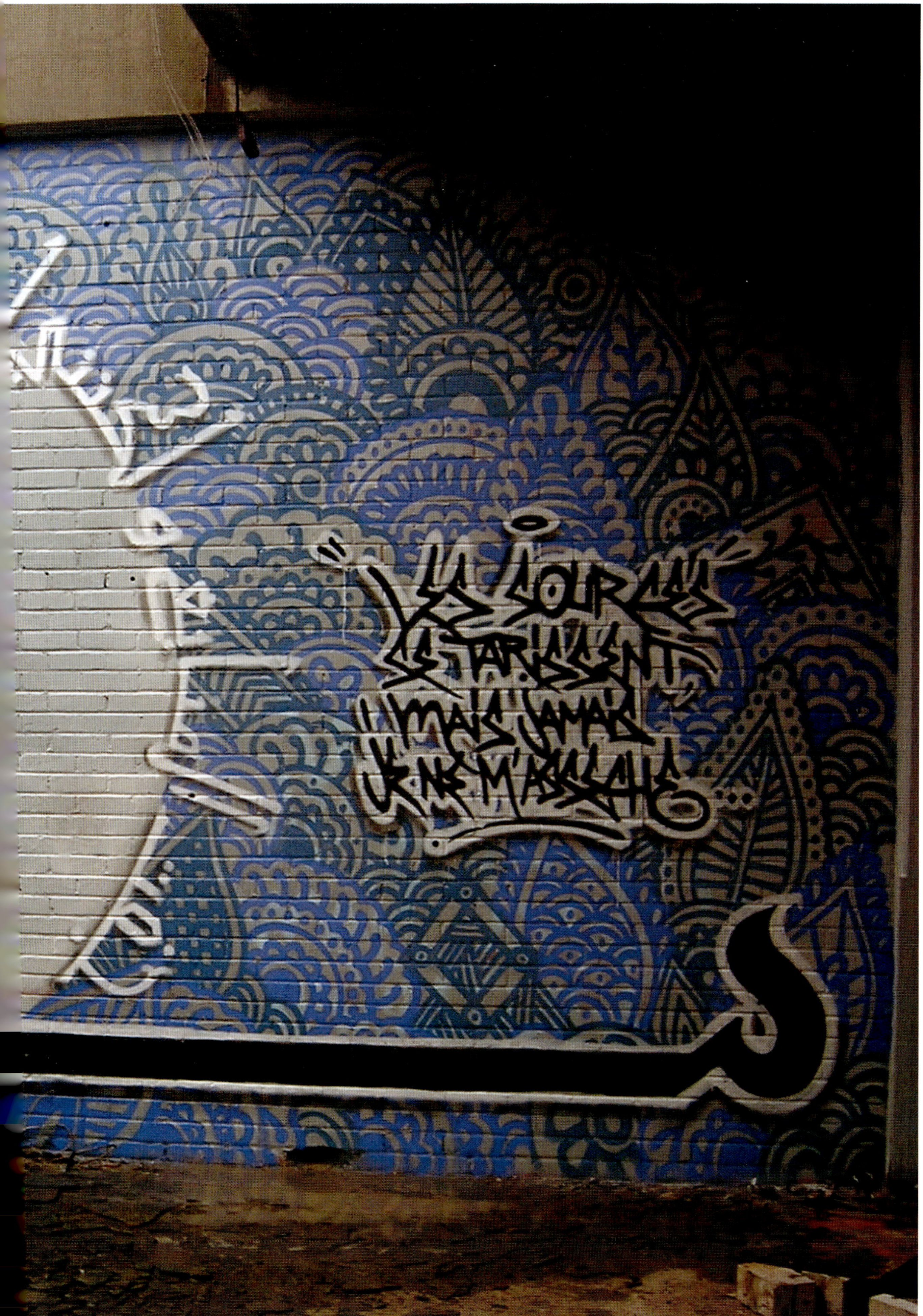
LES SOURCES SE TARISSENT MAIS JAMAIS JE NE M'ASSÈCHE...

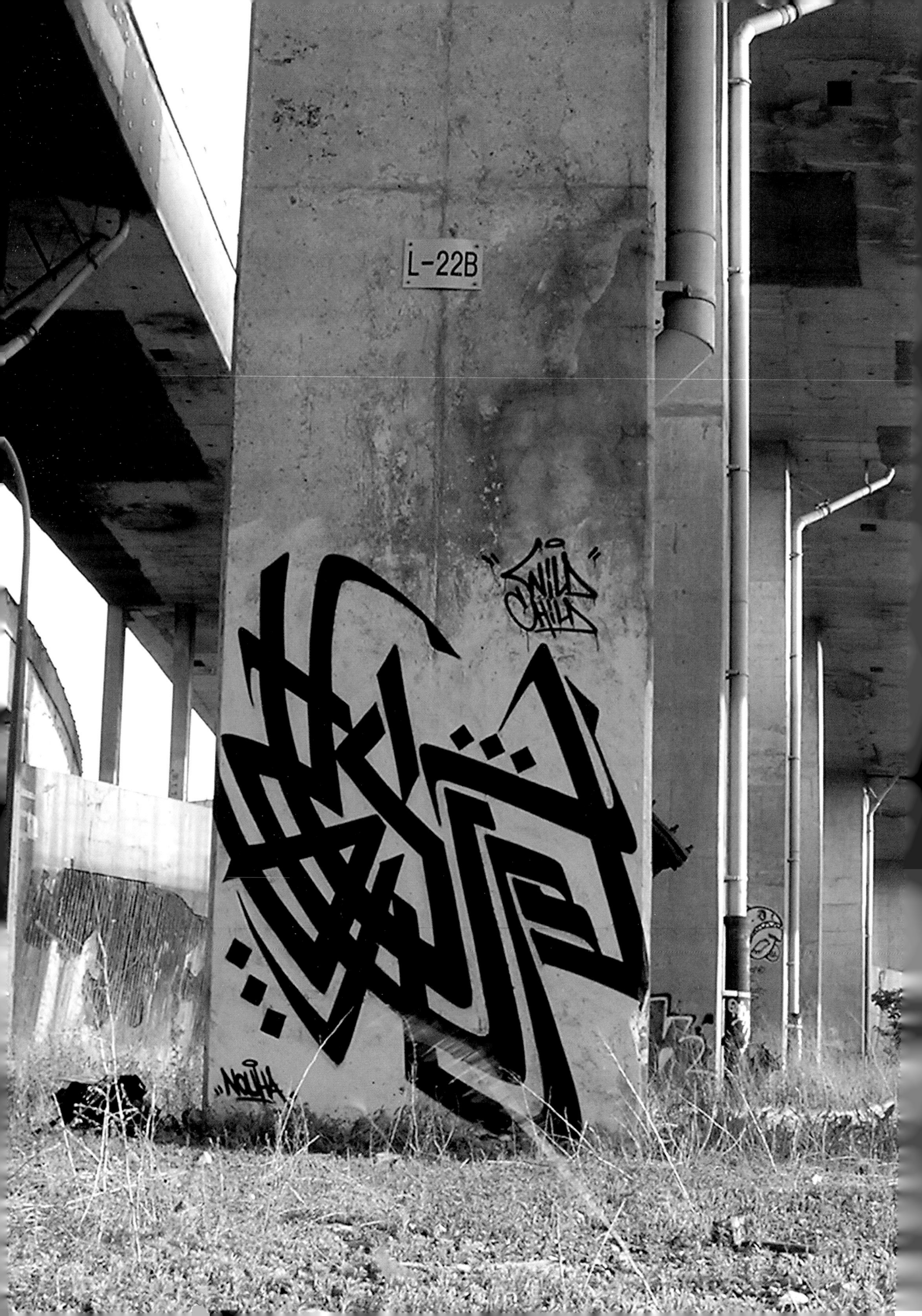
L-22B
NOUHA

3·2
Hest1

هيست ١

Born 1976 in Paris
Lives in Bali, Indonesia

1. "Hest1", HEST1, Turcot, Montréal, 2007

"Why am I as I am? To understand that of any person, his whole life from birth onwards must be reviewed. All of our experiences fuse into our personality. Everything that has ever happened to us is an ingredient."
Malcolm X

I grew up surrounded by a multitude of people of different nationalities, religions and backgrounds, and all of this had a real influence on who I am today. My quest for knowledge, understanding, consciousness and truth brought me to a lot of places, and I found myself along the way. If I was inspired to study and use Arabic calligraphy to a certain extent, it is only a reflection of what I learn and experiment with.

Born and raised in one of the working class districts of Paris, as a young boy I witnessed the birth of the Parisian graffiti movement. Erupting beneath the windows of every high-rise building, the advent of graffiti in my community soon began to consume every aspect of my life. Since then, my hands have constantly been covered with droplets of paint, the ink mixing with my blood. Not a single day has gone by on which I haven't felt the desire to feed my deeply entrenched addiction to graffiti. Countless scraps of paper, walls and other surfaces fell prey to my need to write, paint and express. This daily exercise has helped me to channel my emotions, to release my anger and my joy, and it has also helped to nurture a strong work ethic which allows me to push my own limits and overcome those hurdles which happen to stand in my way.

Life experiences and chance encounters have molded the manner in which I work and have undeniably formed the channel through which my art flows. Many people have helped me along my personal and artistic quest. I strive to live up to those artists, such as Hoctes (old school writer from Paris), who have carried graffiti to new heights, while at the same time staying true to my own style of expression. I endeavor to make art which leaves behind the glitter of fame, artistic pride, and territorial attitudes of 'ownership'. I simply try my best to live in the moment, to feel alive through the act of creating, and to share my experiences with humility, in order to leave (God willing) a scratch on the surface of the graffiti world and a fleeting memory of one person's earthly experience.

1

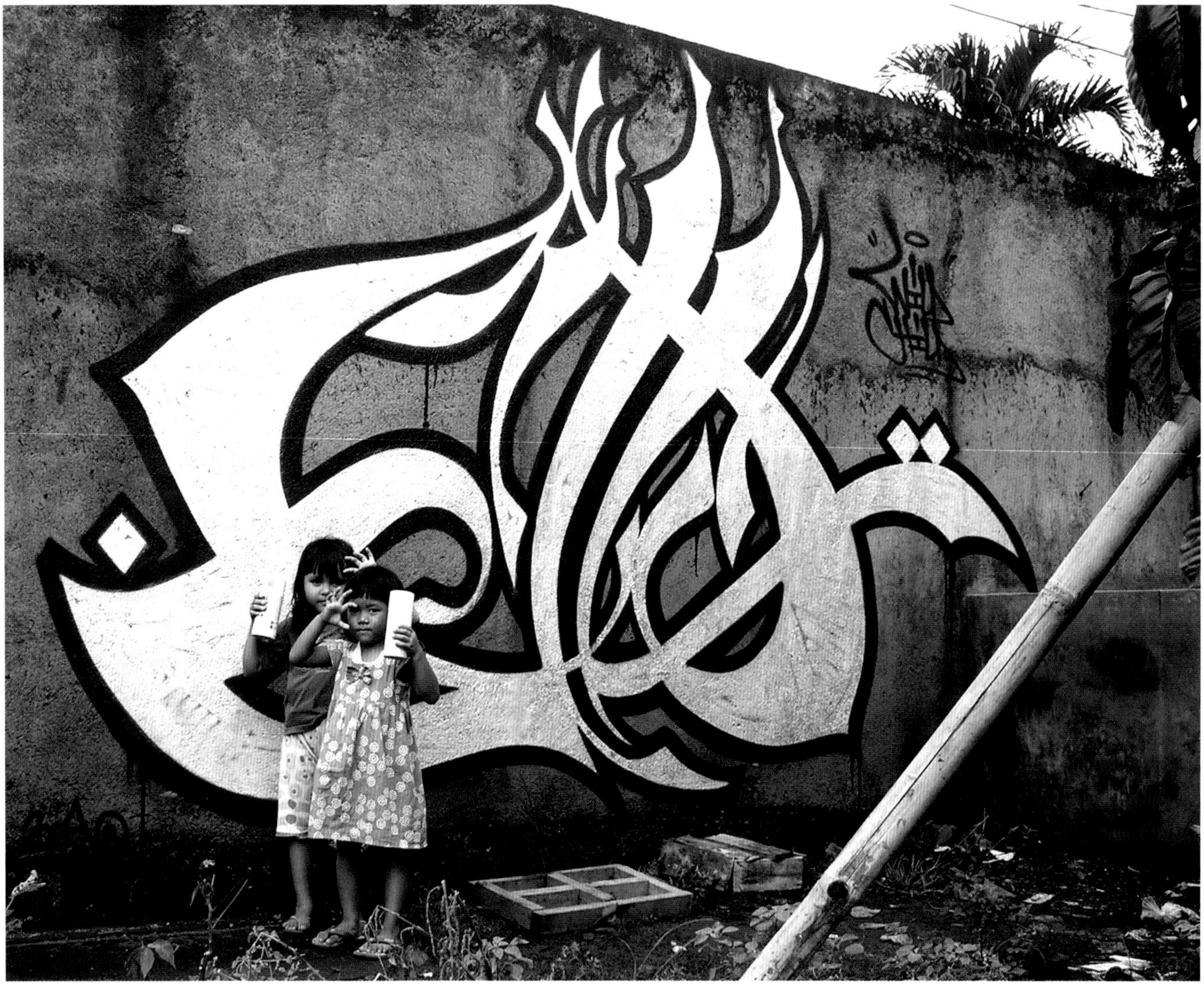

1

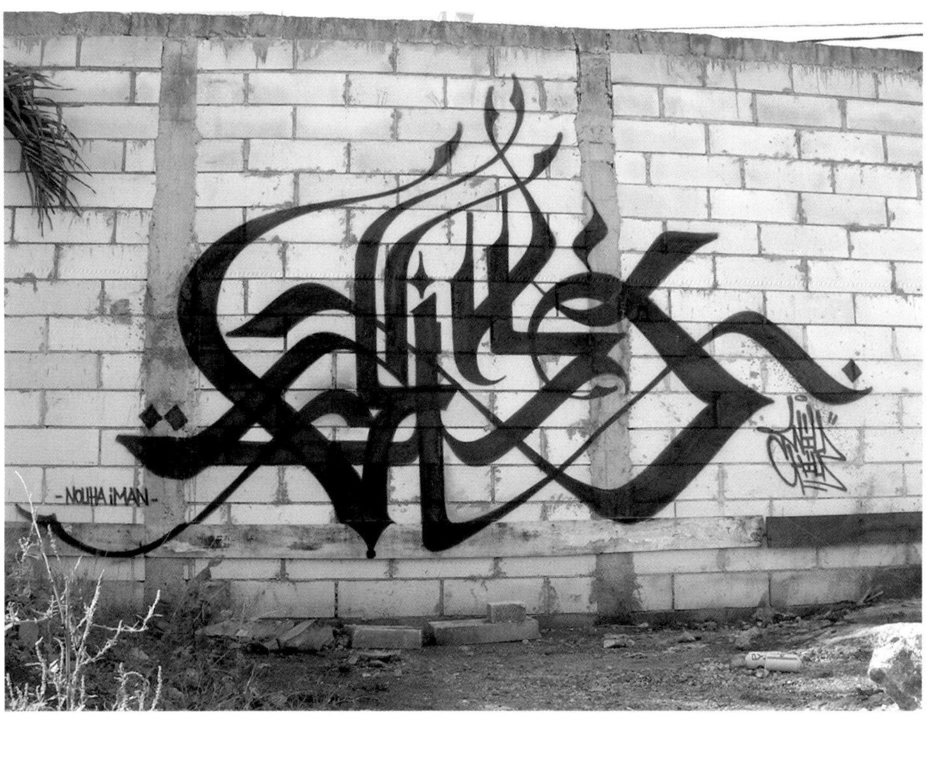

2

1./2./3."Wild Child", HEST1, Jakarta, Indonesia, 2009

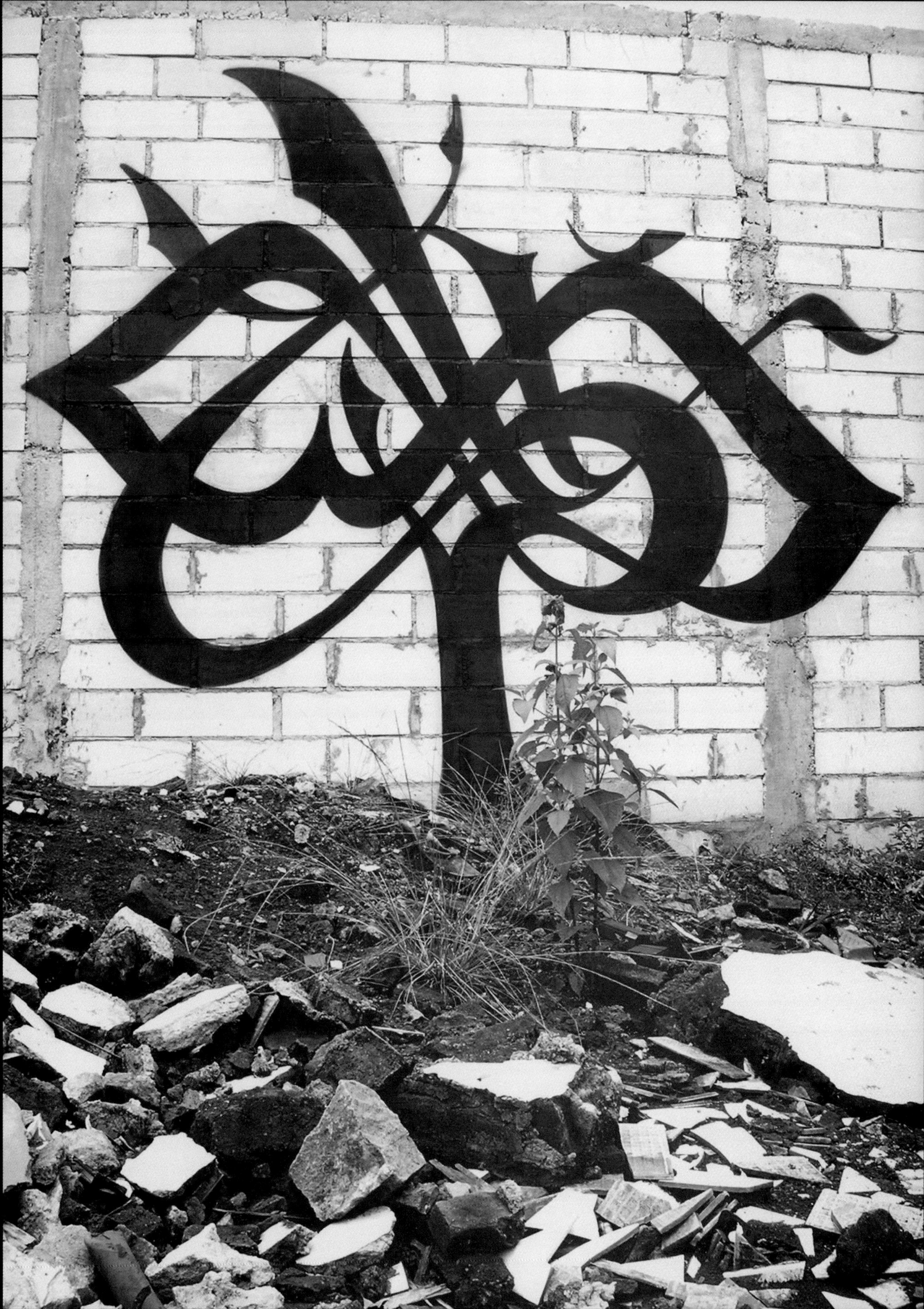

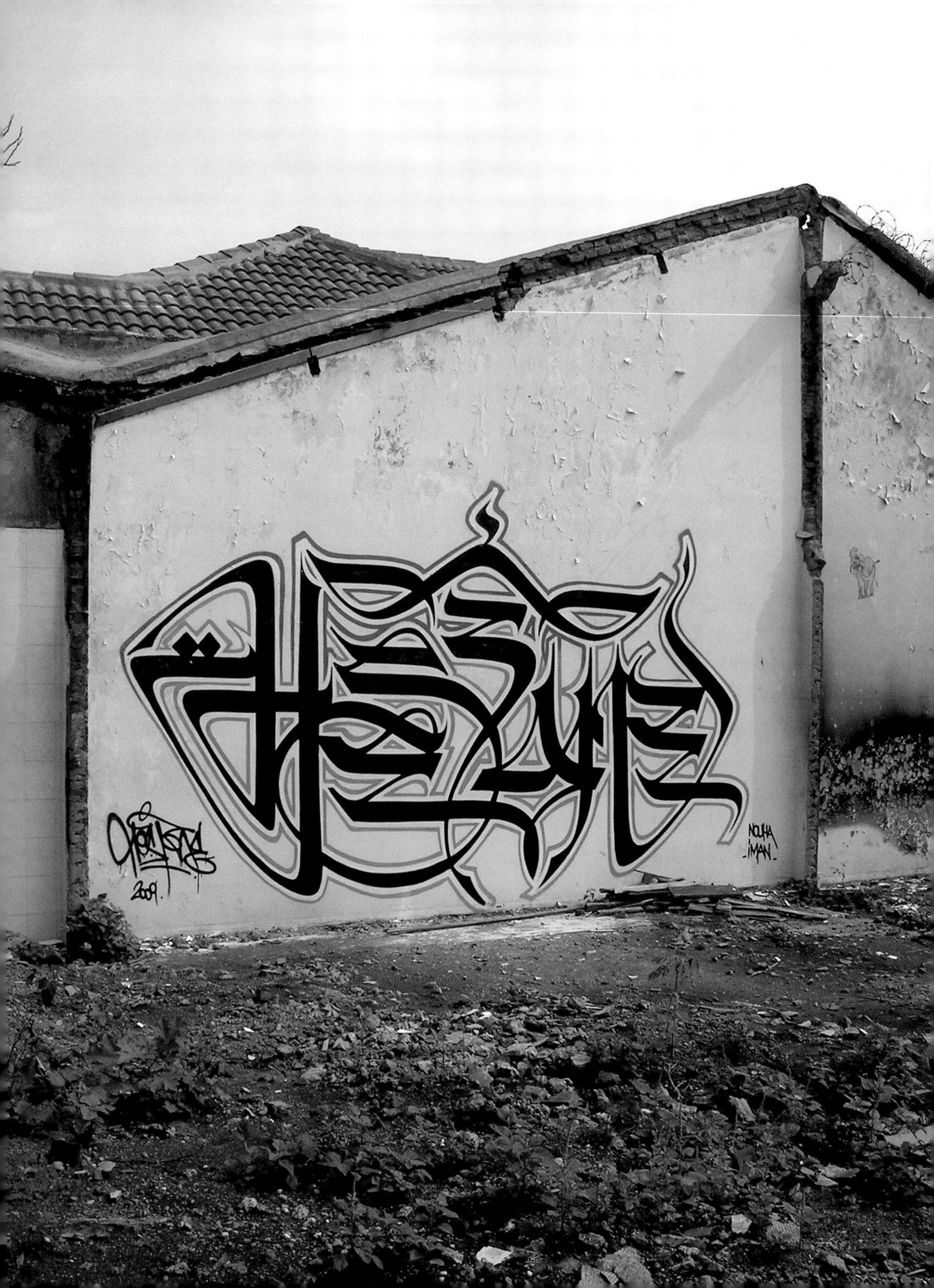
2009.
NOUHA
IMAN

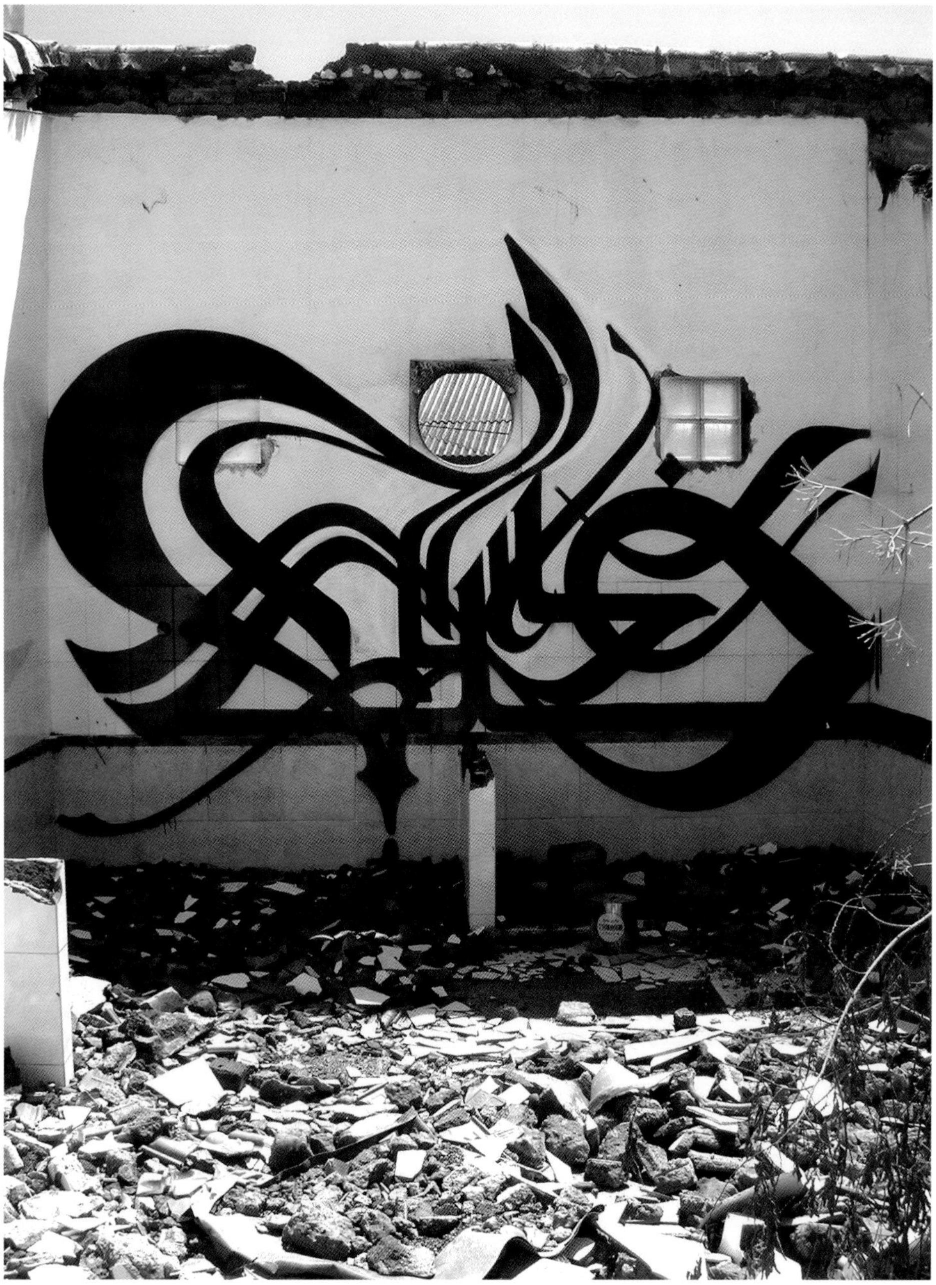

2

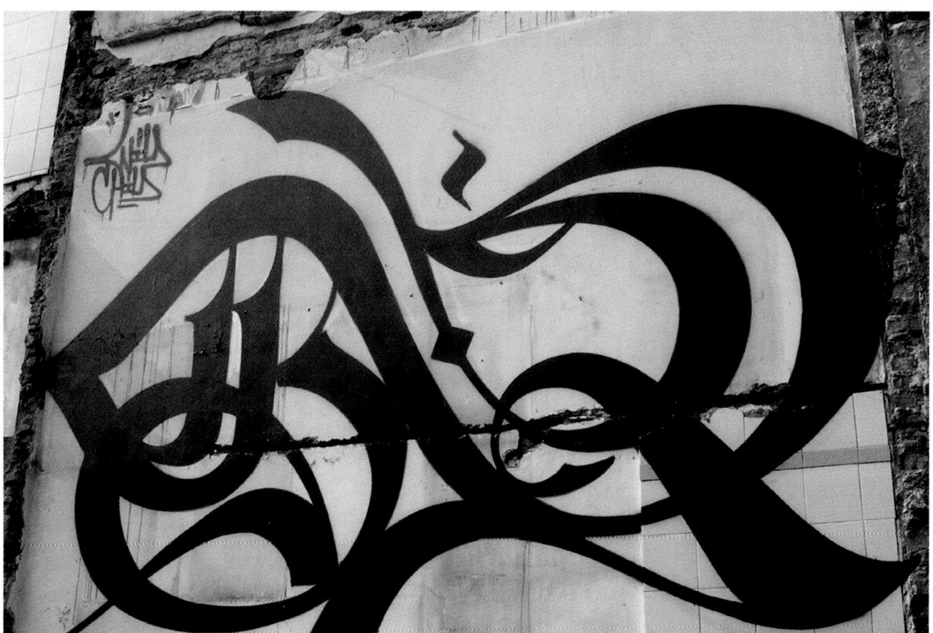

3

1. "Hest One", HEST1, Jakarta, Indonesia, 2009

2. "Wild Child", HEST1, Jakarta, Indonesia, 2010

3. "Wild Child", HEST1, Jakarta, Indonesia, 2009

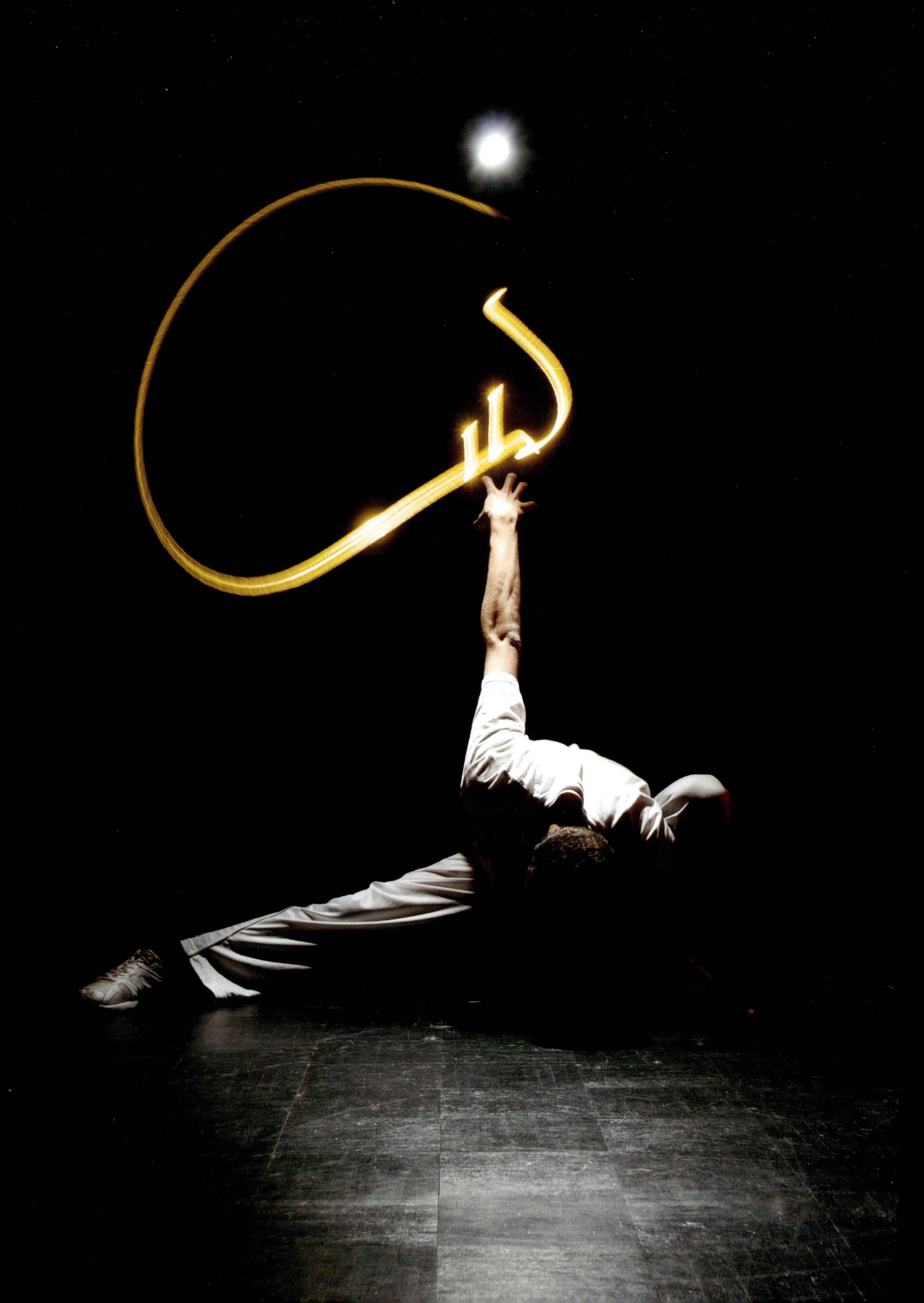

3·3
Julien Breton aka Kaalam
جوليان بروتون المعروف بكلام

Born 1979 in Nantes, France

Kaalam grew up in a multicultural environment with friends of diverse backgrounds, including Portuguese, Moroccan, Algerian, Tunisian and Turkish. Graffiti was his first approach to the art of writing, and its aim of deconstruction of lettering and reclaiming public space especially motivated him.

His debut in calligraphy came after his discovery of Hassan Massoudy and Lassaad Metoui. He began to translate Arabic styles into the Latin alphabet, greatly inspired by their work. They have been the inspiration for this quest for beauty ever since. He aims to build a bridge between Arabic and Latin culture. In his writings, he uses phrases of philosophers and Hip Hop. He creates each piece with the desire to transcend the meaning of the phrase, to create energy, a singular aestheticism, a balanced and languorous form which differs from the traditional writing and the arbitrary order of letters.

When he discovered the "lightgraff" process, he started to experiment with a new way of creating. He discovered a form of expression that is marked by body language, calligraphy and choreography. The possibility to "write in space", to work calligraphy according to the background perspective, colors and history gives him the will to explore this new form of pictorial expression. Ink becomes light, paper becomes photography. All landscape and architecture is a pretext to be marked by them, to play with them, to write calligraphy on them and immortalize this meeting between writing and photography.

1. Lucien Pacault, Compagnie Cortex, abstract light calligraphy without digital manipulation, JULIEN BRETON, 2010

1

السكوت

1. "The Silence", poem by Kyle J. Currathers, JULIEN BRETON, 2010

2. "De 2 choses Lune, l'autre est le Soleil", French wordplay by Jacques Prevert, JULIEN BRETON, 2006

3. Abstract Calligraphy, JULIEN BRETON, 2010

الفن

4. "il n'y a en art ni passé, ni futur, l'art qui n'est pas dans le présent ne sera jamais" — (To me there is no past or future in art. If a work of art does not live in the present, it must not be considered at all), quote by Pablo Picasso, JULIEN BRETON, 2007

1

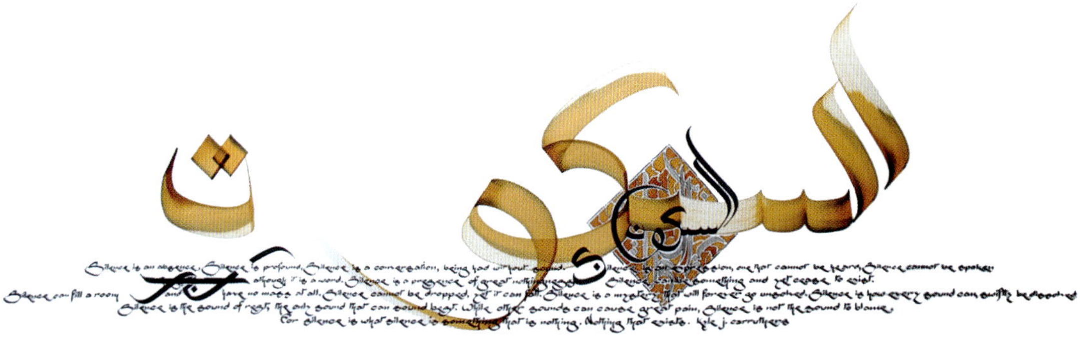

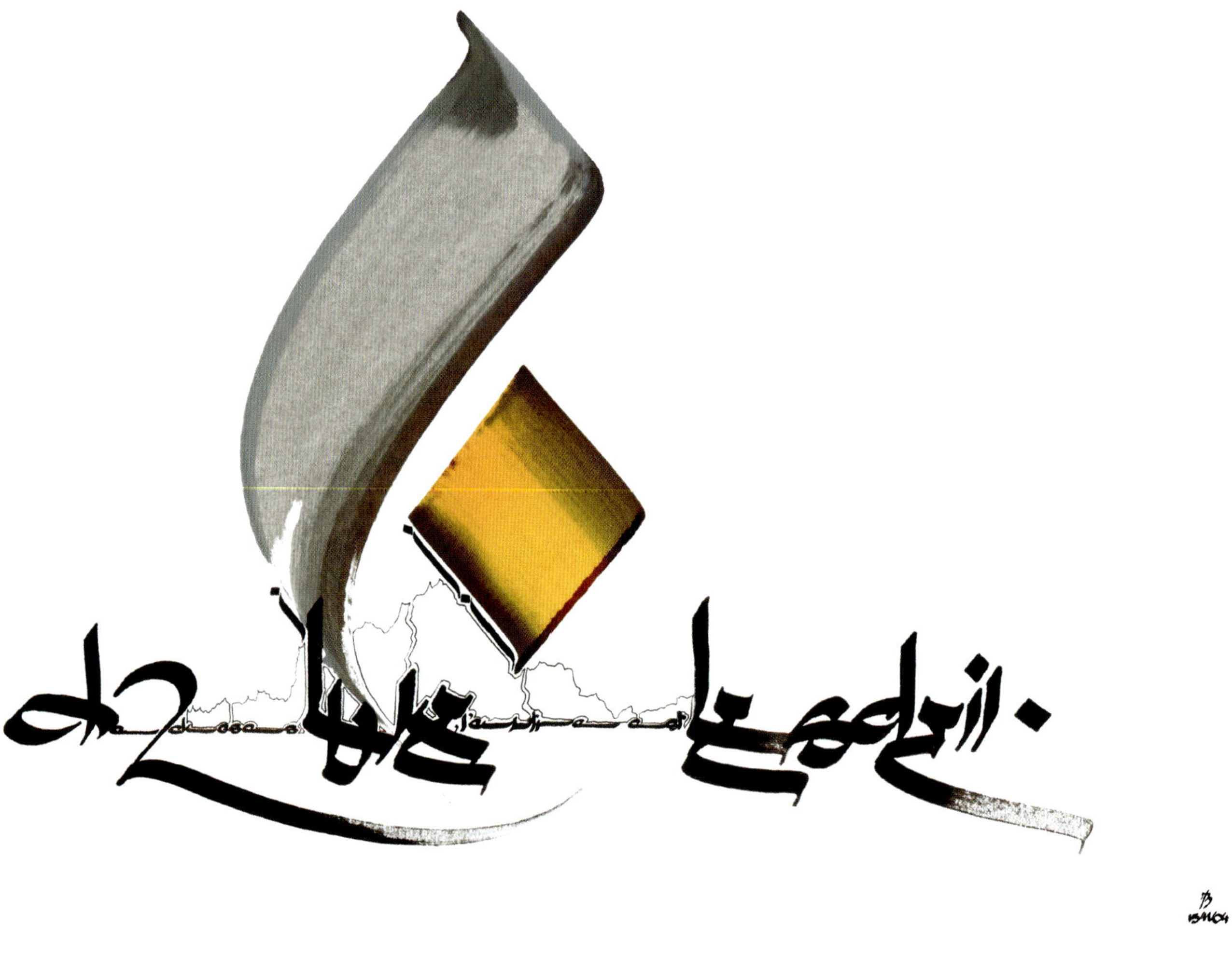

2

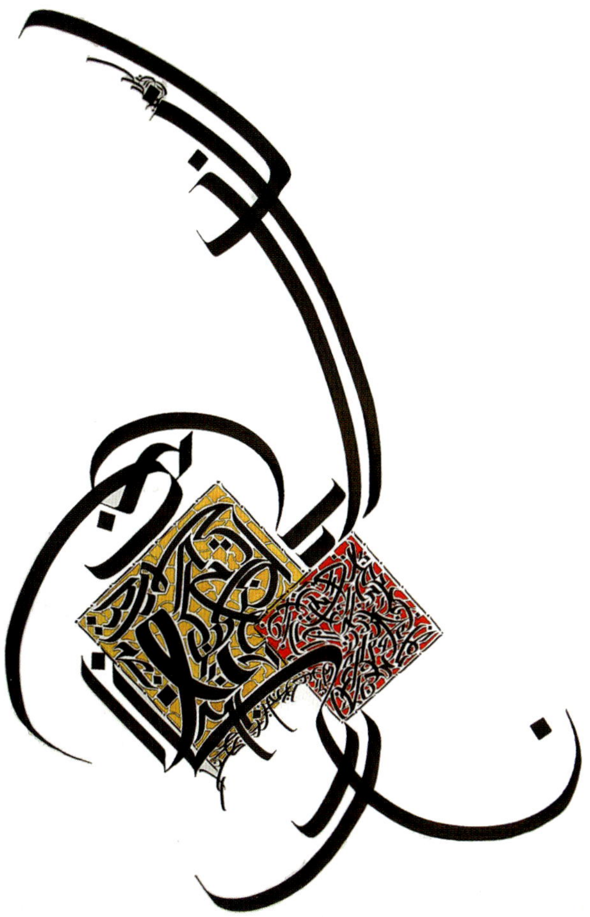

3

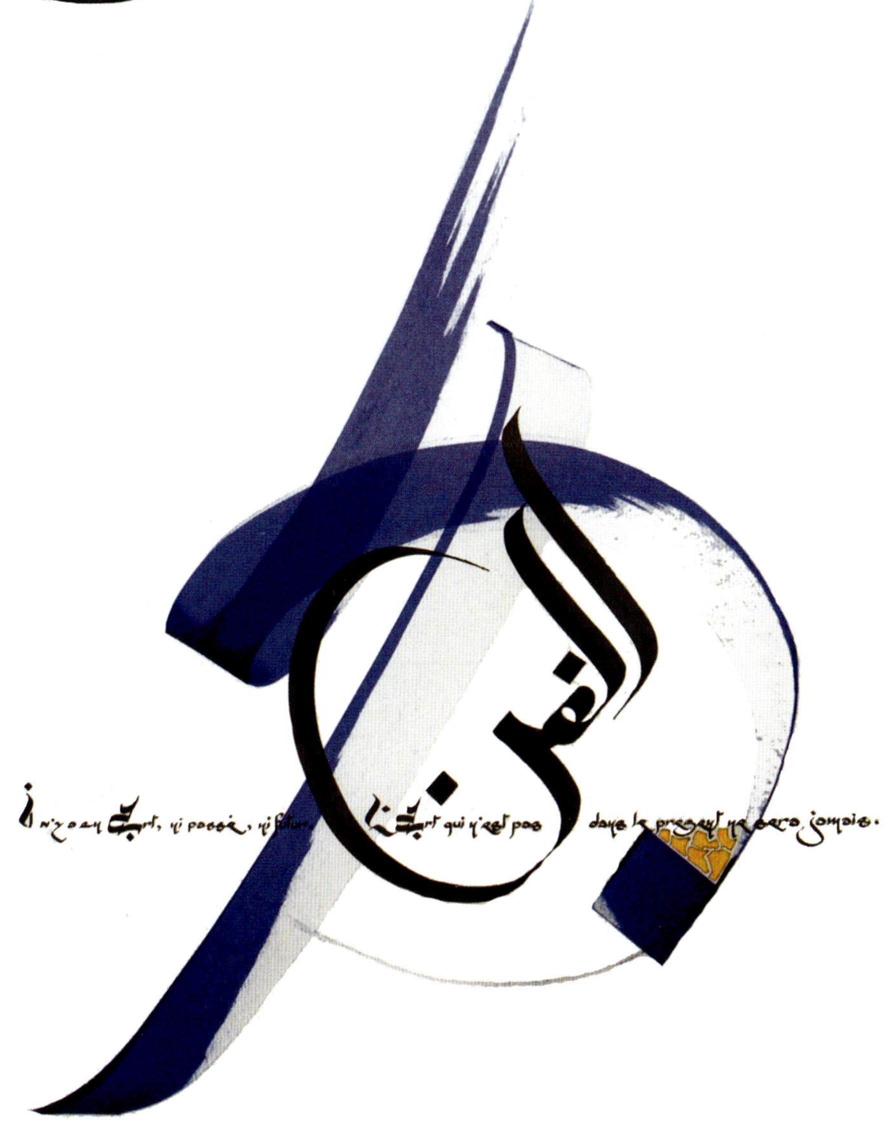
Il n'y a en l'art, ni passé, ni futur. L'art qui n'est pas dans le présent ne sera jamais.

4

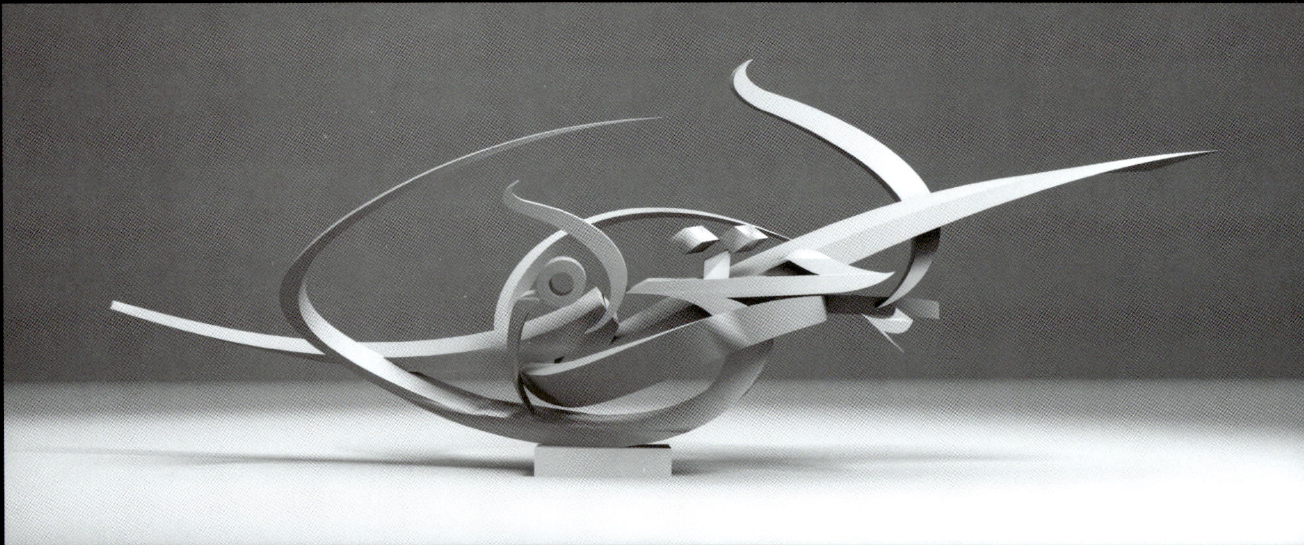

1

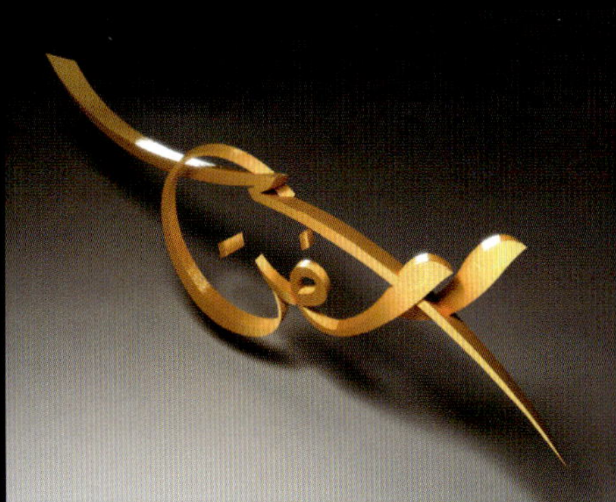

2

إحترام
1. “Respect”, Arabic 3-D calligraphy, JULIEN BRETON, 2010

الفن
2. “Art”, Arabic 3-D calligraphy, model by Graffiti Technica, JULIEN BRETON, 2010

3. Kaalam vs Graffiti Technica, 3-D model by Graffiti Technica, graffititechnica.com, JULIEN BRETON, 2010

4. “Y sincerely believes”, JULIEN BRETON, abstract light calligraphy without digital manipulation, Le Cellier, 2009

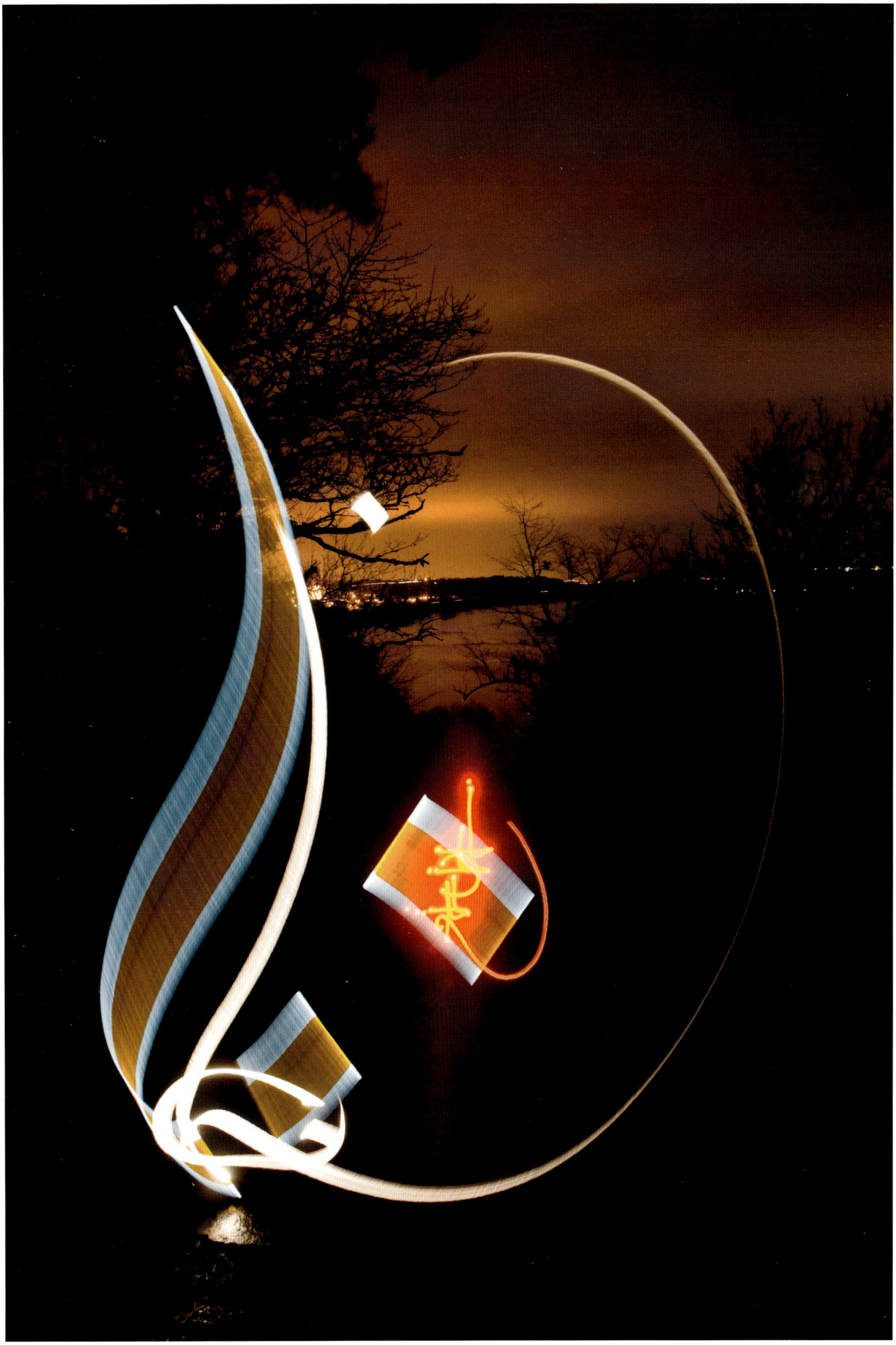

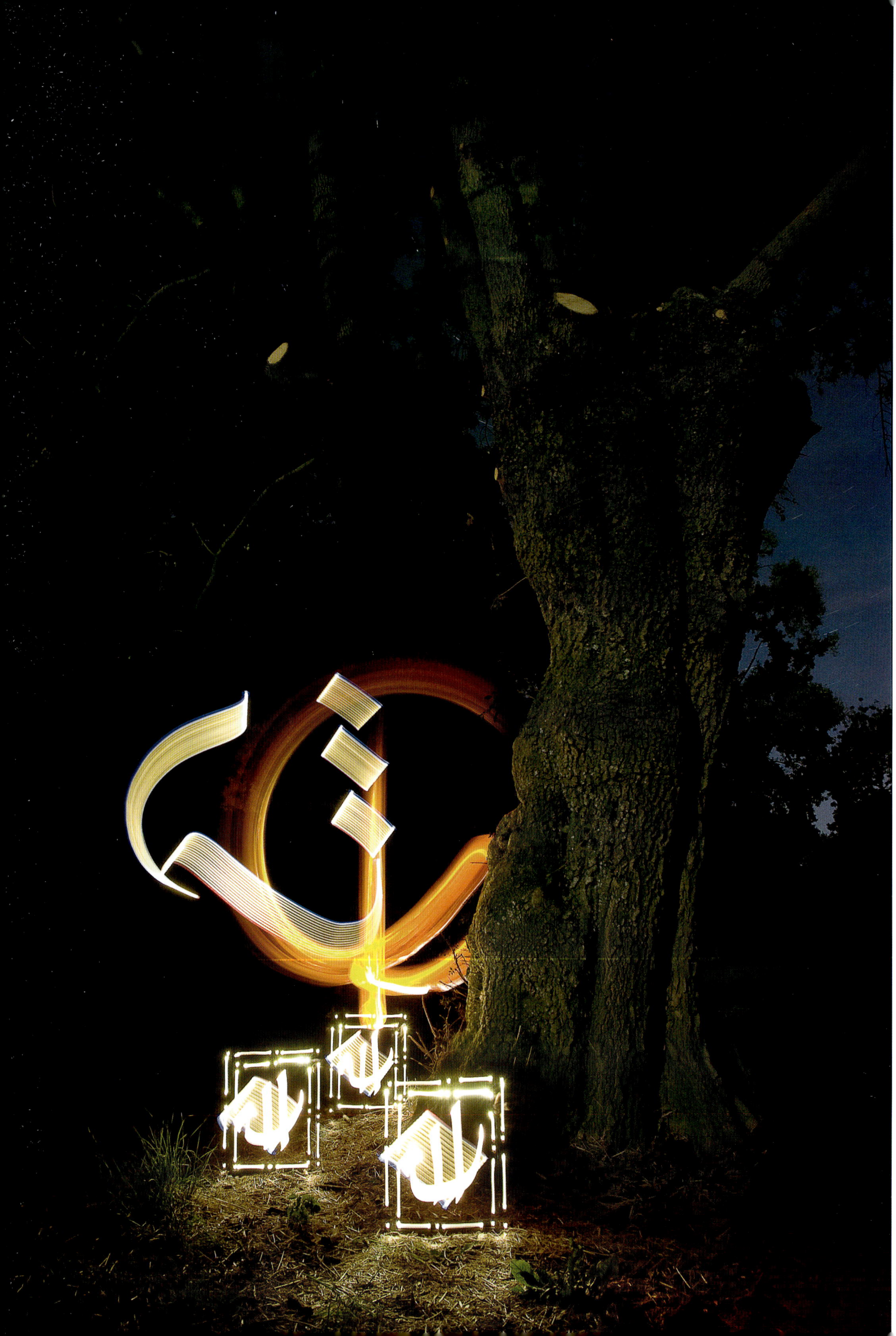

1

2
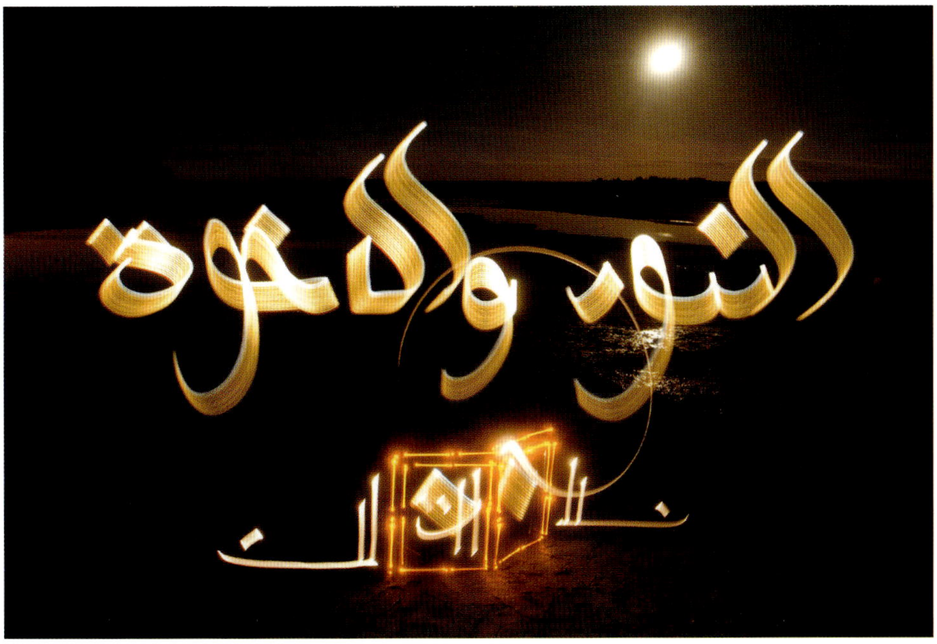

1. "When man no longer has room for nature, perhaps nature will no longer have room for man." Stephan Edberg, abstract calligraphy, JULIEN BRETON, Ile Neuve, France, 2009

النور والأخوّة

2. "Light and brotherhood", JULIEN BRETON, Arabic calligraphy, Benodet, France, 2009

3. "Poetry", JULIEN BRETON, Light calligraphy without digital manipulation, Pol'n, Nantes, France, 2007

3
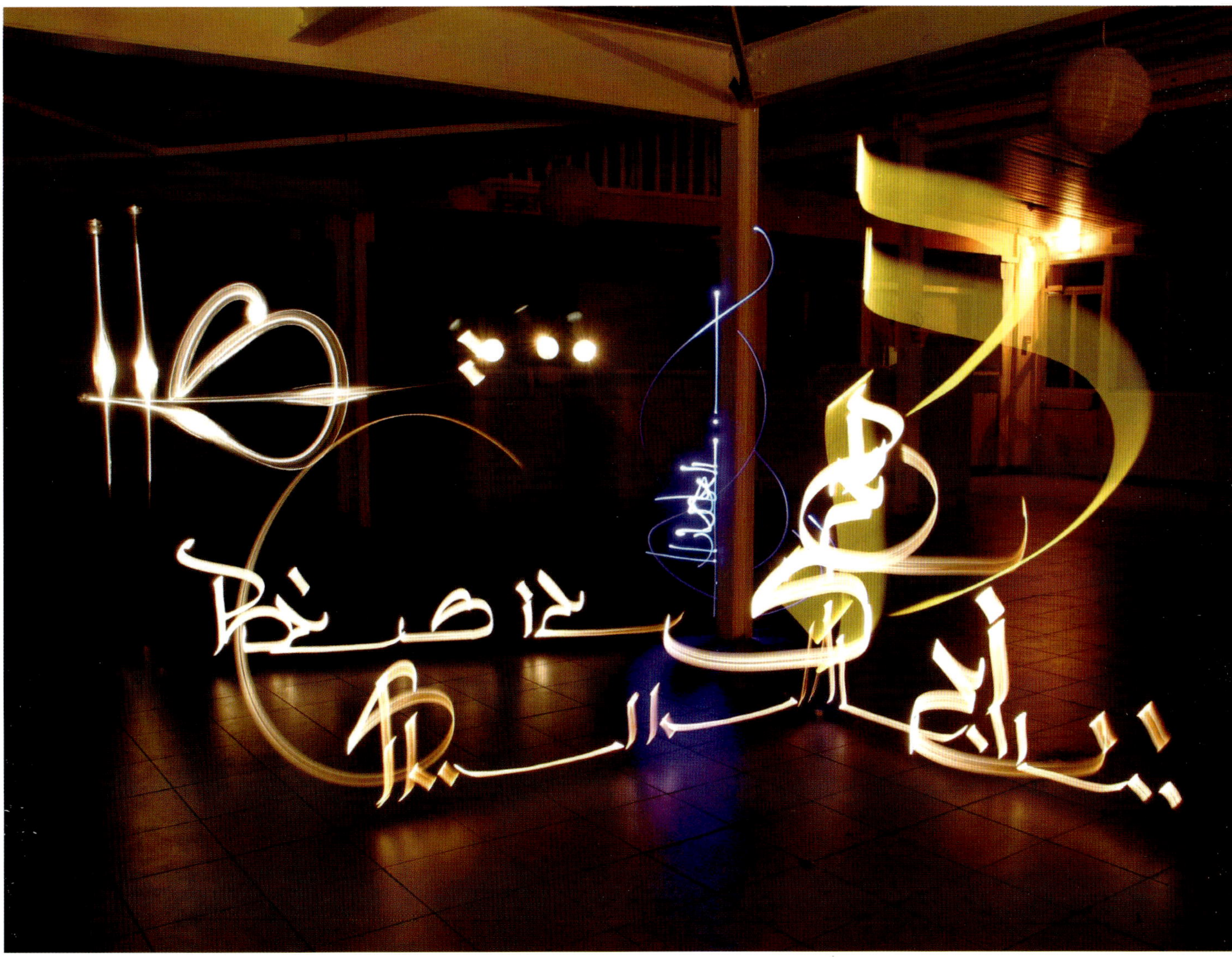

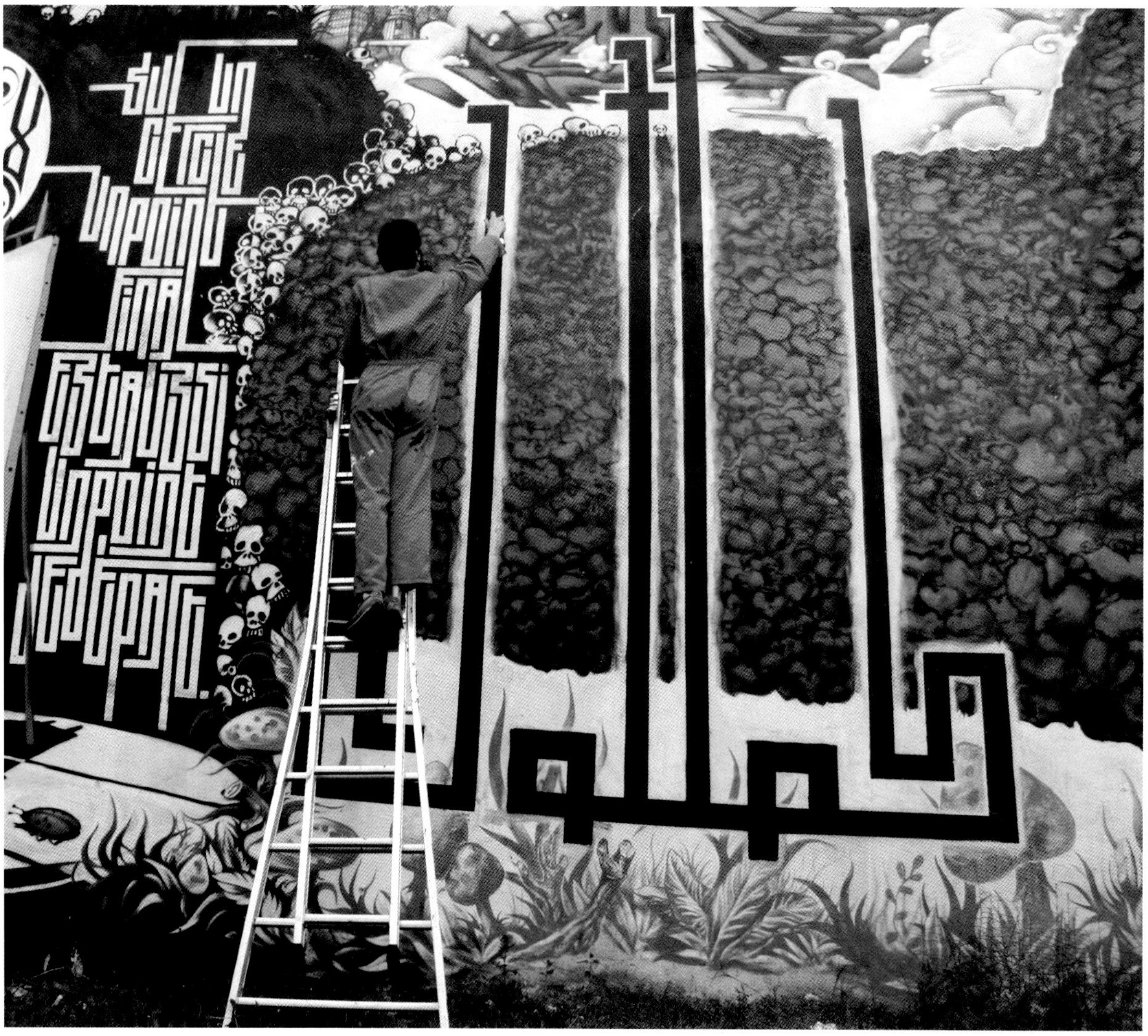

1

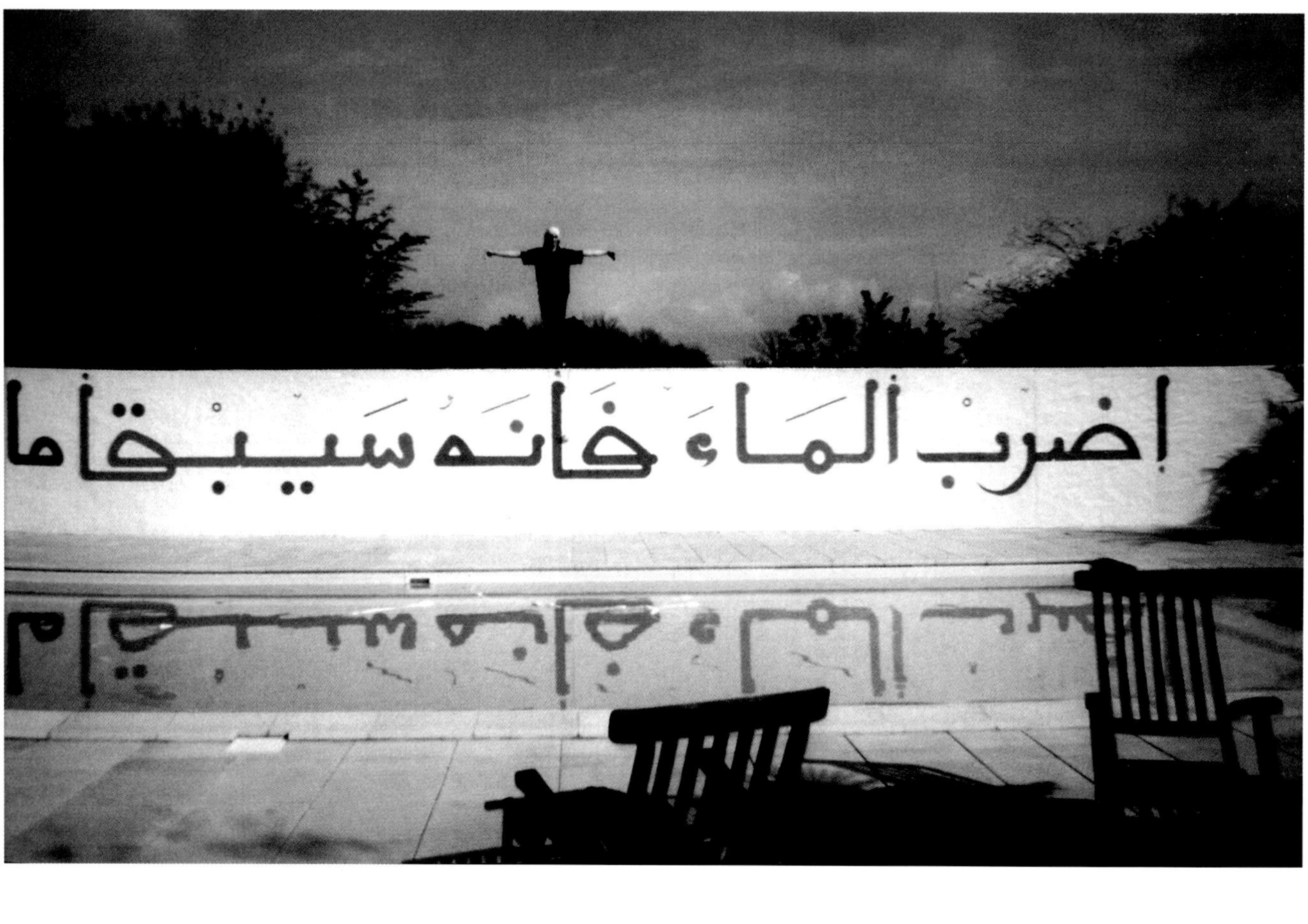

2

3·4
L'ATLAS
الأطلس

Born 1978 in France

L'ATLAS started to write graffiti in the 90s. Fascinated with the line and the craft of writing, he went to study traditional Arabic calligraphy in Morocco, Egypt and Syria. He takes special interest in the Kufic script, whose geometric shapes he transposes and encodes into the Latin alphabet, creating a unique typography.

He has also worked in the cinema industry, learning the techniques of montage, and has directed a few documentaries. Becoming stronger with experience and without stopping his interventions in the street, he is developing a pictorial universe in which each letter is considered as a shape, and each shape as a letter. Little by little, the city itself appears to him loaded with signs which he collects with a special printing technique in an almost abstract trail. He lives and works in Belleville, Paris.

1. "On a circle, a final point is also a begining point" (Heraclitus), L'ATLAS, La Forge, Paris 2004

إضرب الماء فانه سيبقا (كذا) ماء
2. "Beat water, it is still water", L'ATLAS, Swimming pool of Gerard Lanvin, La Beaule, 2003

3. "Love is not a Game", L'ATLAS vs. SUN7, Portait of Inna Modja, La Forge, Paris, 2009

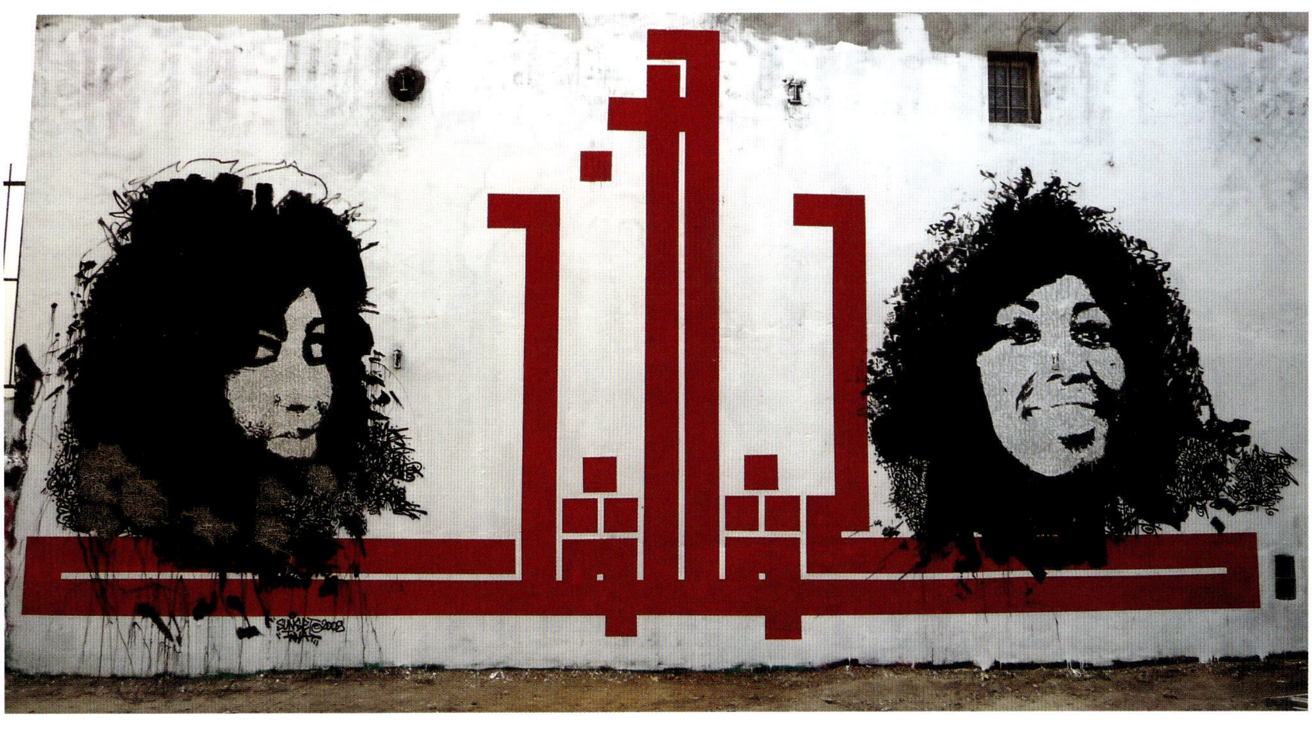

3

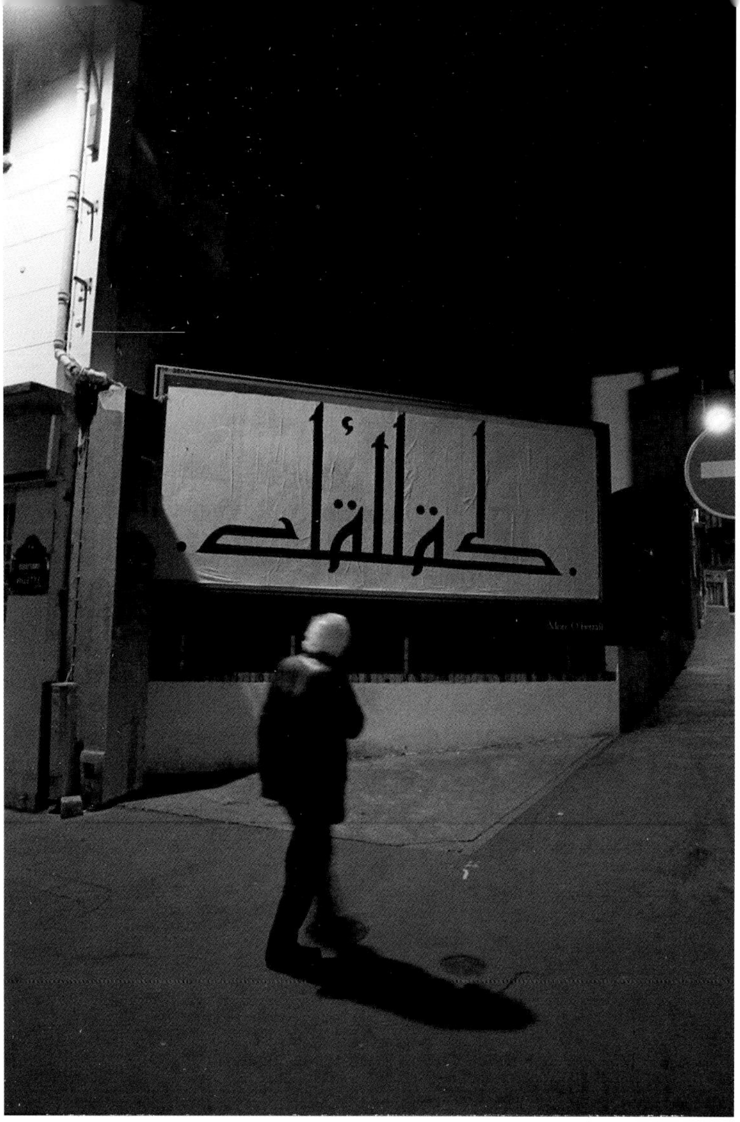

1

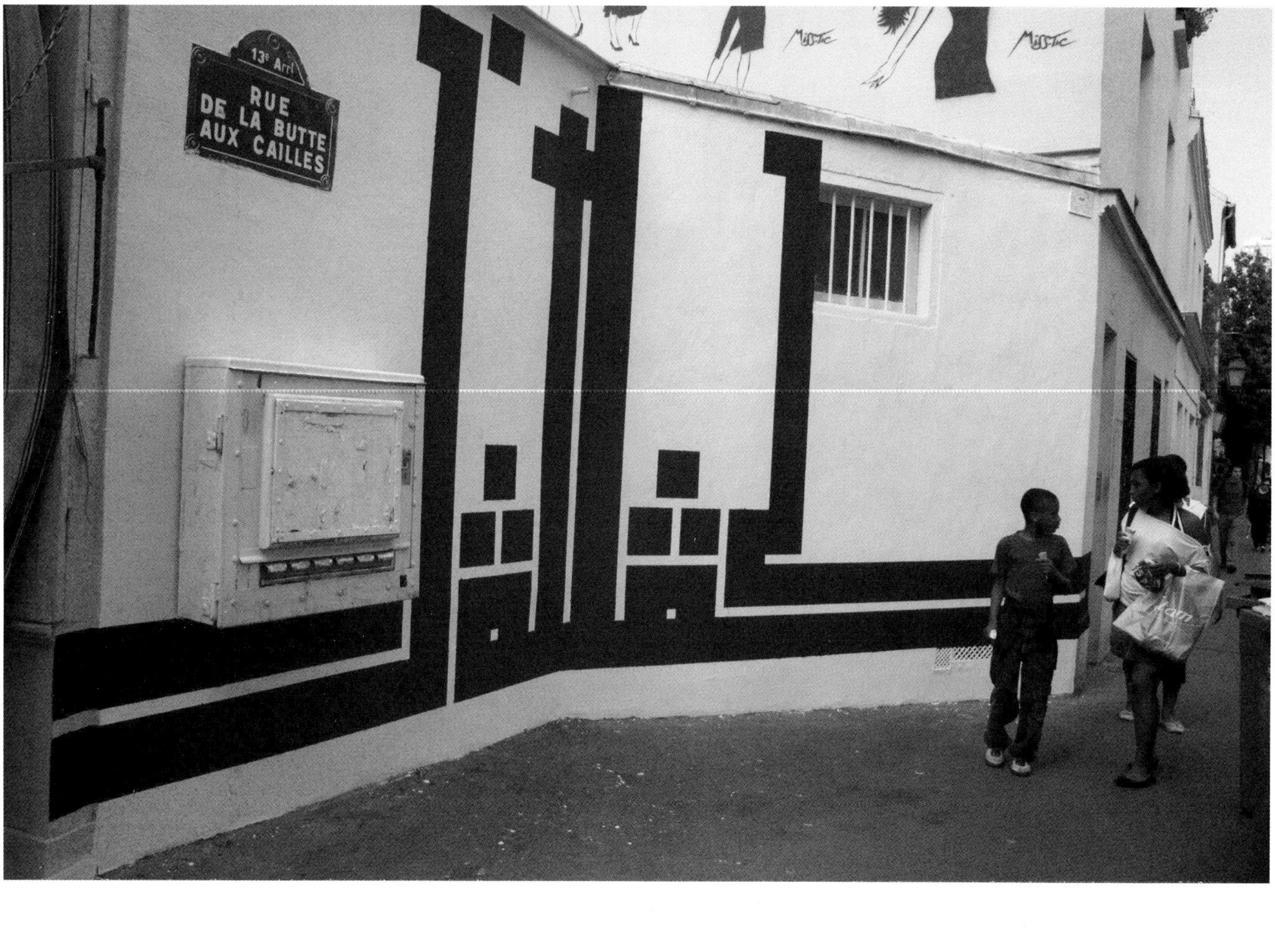

2

1. L'ATLAS, paste up on advertising billboard, Blvd. de la villette, Paris 2004

2. L'ATLAS, painting on wall, Butte aux cailles, Paris 2006

3. L'ATLAS in action, Rue st Maur, Paris, 2005

Following pages 128 & 129:

L'ATLAS, Yogyakarta, Indonesia, 2005

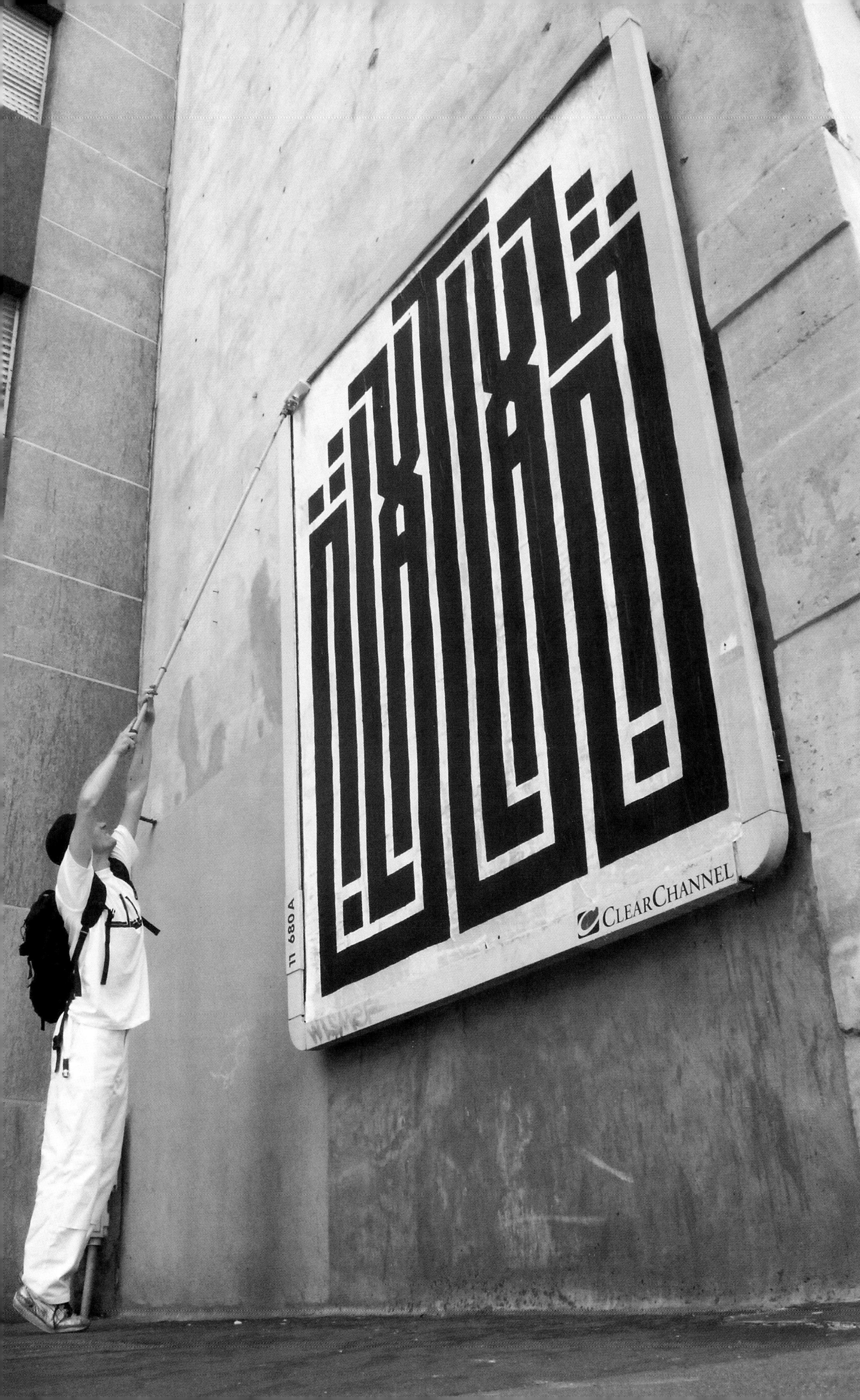

3

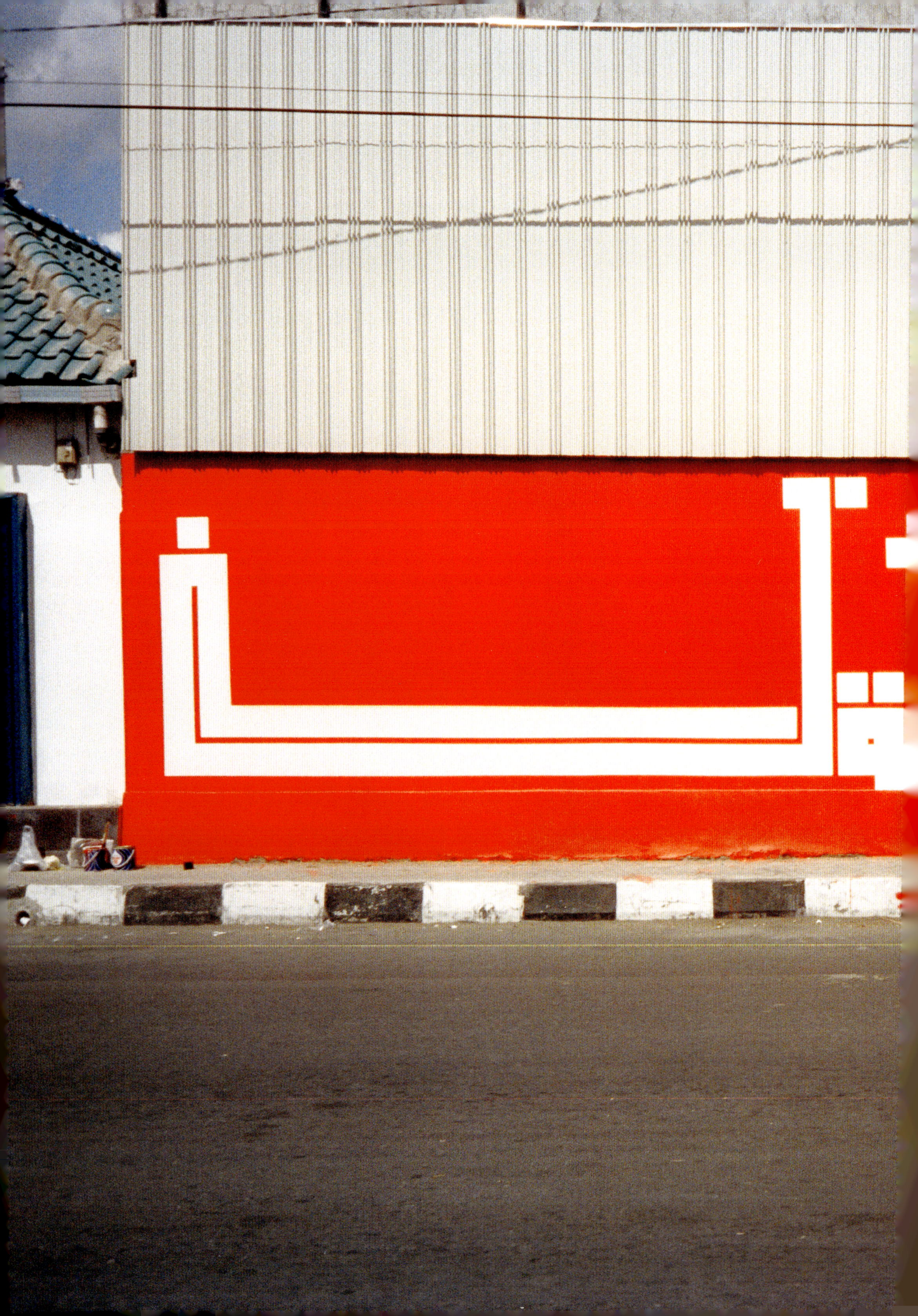

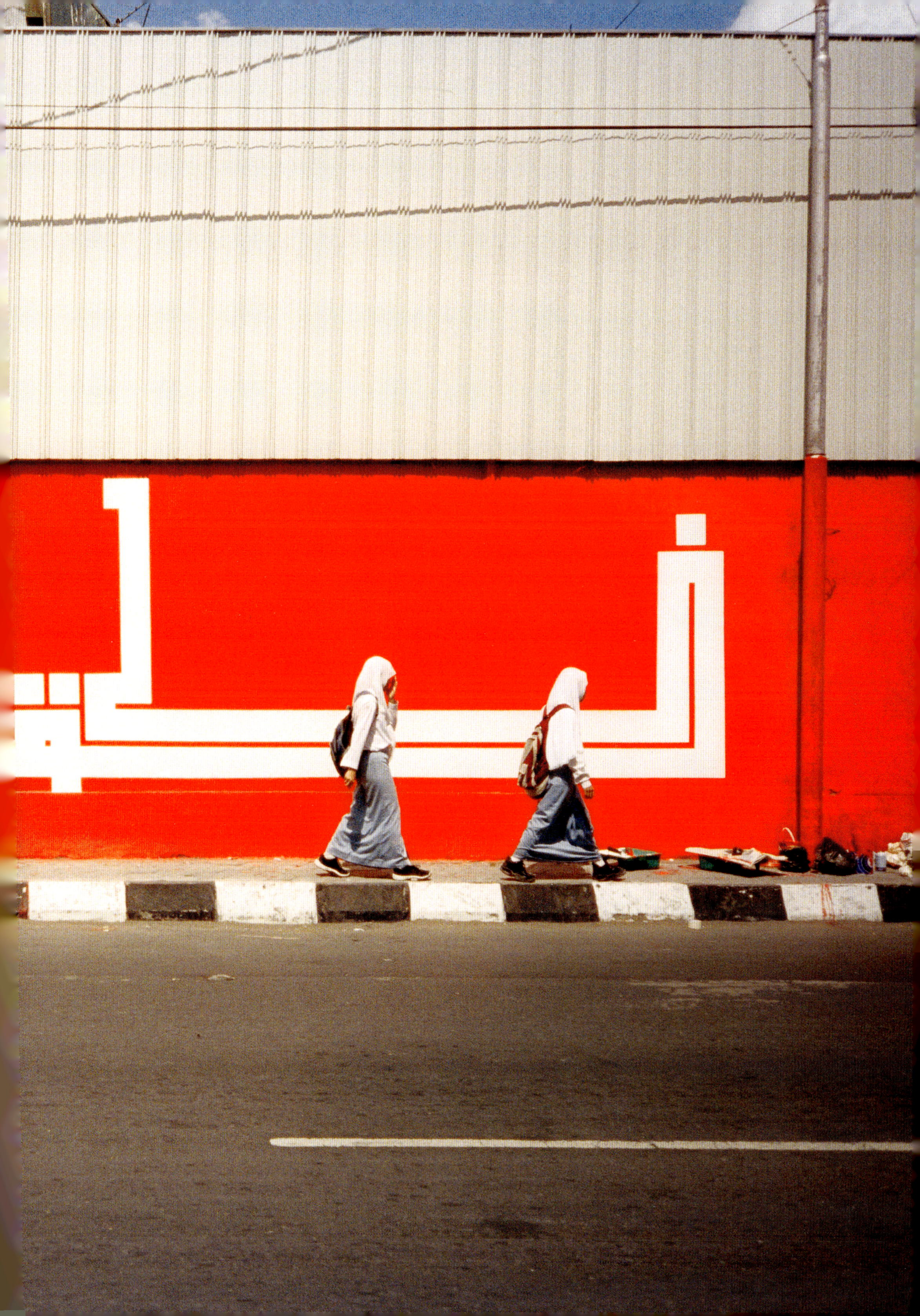

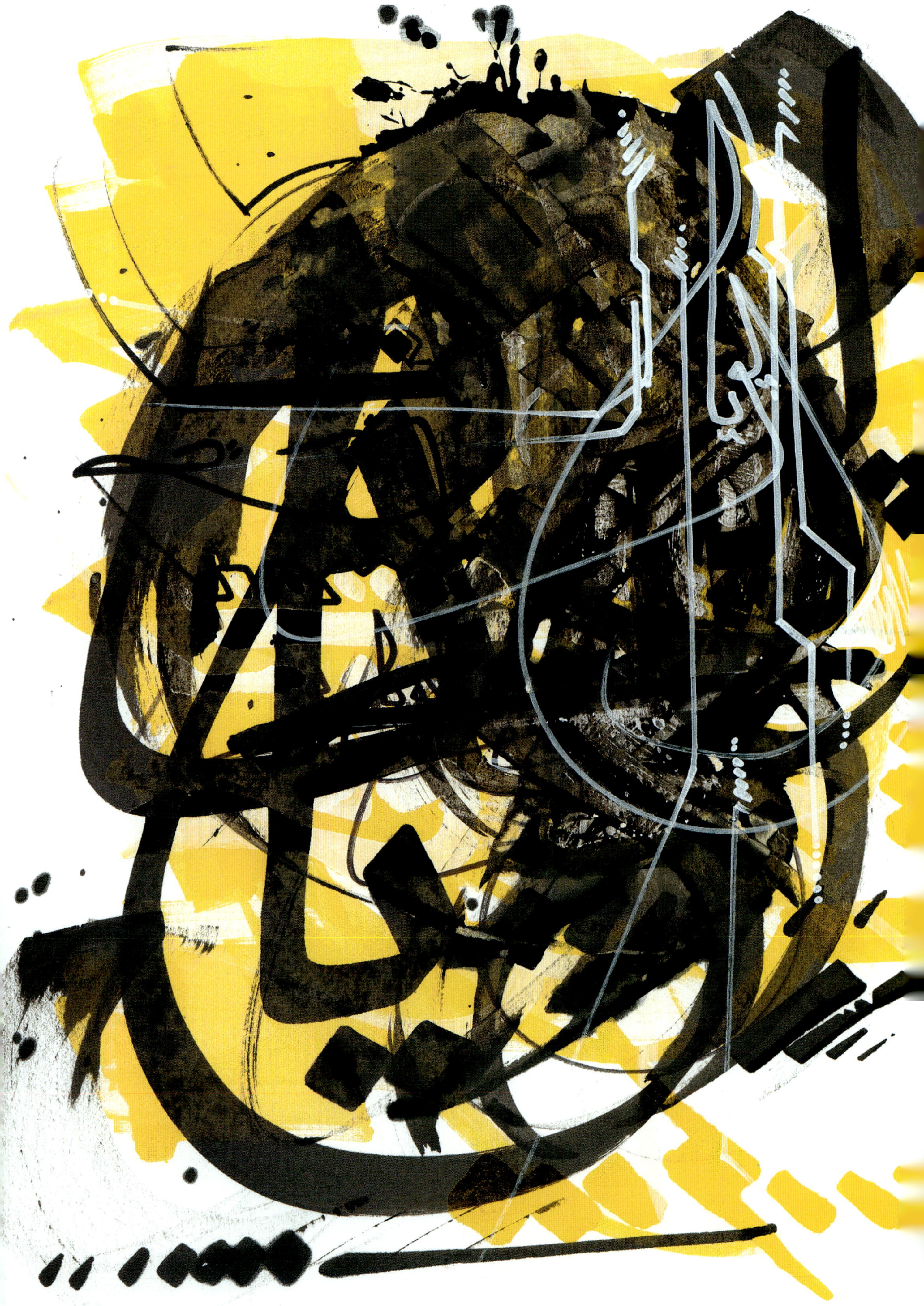

3·5
Sair 4 aka Puya Bagheri
سير ٤ المعروف
بيويا باقري

Born 1980 in Tehran, Iran
Lives in Cologne, Germany

Sair 4's family fled from political persecution in Iran in 1987. His whole life was shaped politically through this background as well as by his parents. Expulsion and escape made the search for his identity very important, but also very difficult for him.

Growing up in a workers' satellite town of Cologne, he had to visit a German school. But his parents were determined to have him learn about his heritage. Not only did they want him to speak his native tongue, but also to be able to read and write Persian texts. Thus he was sent to an Iranian school every day after finishing his German school. It took him a while to appreciate the fact that he actually had to go to school twice, but today he says it was "worth its weight in gold". He learned to write and read Arabic script and in this way came in contact with Persian poetry. Two hours of the school were spent reading poems

پویا
1. "Puya", SAIR 4, mixed media on paper, 21 x 30 cm, 2004

2. Freestyle, SAIR 4, mixed media on wall, 2005

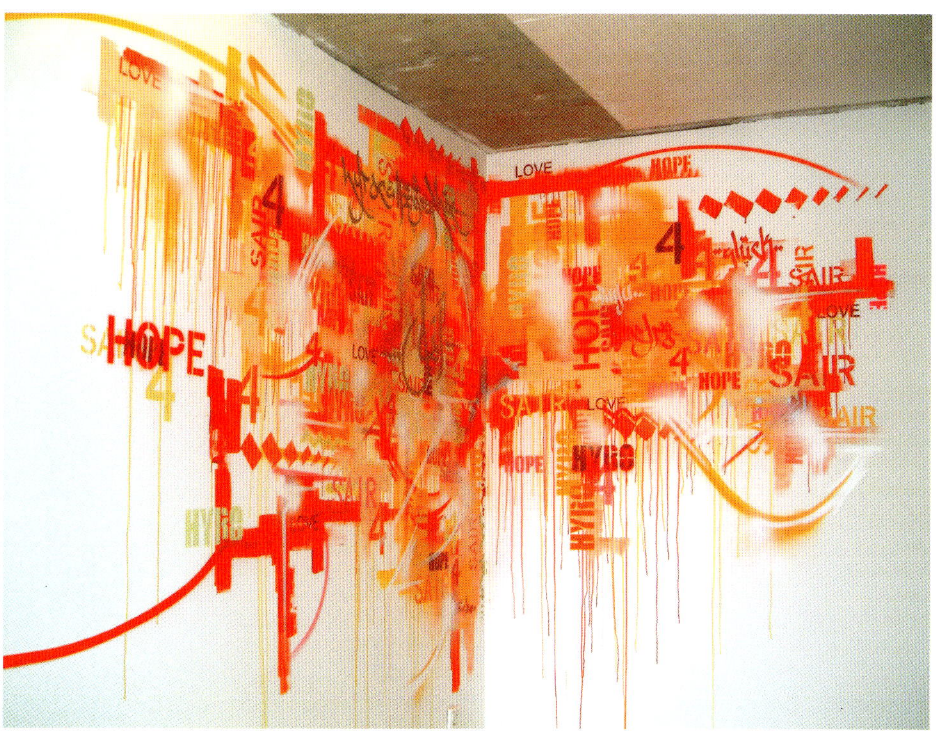

2

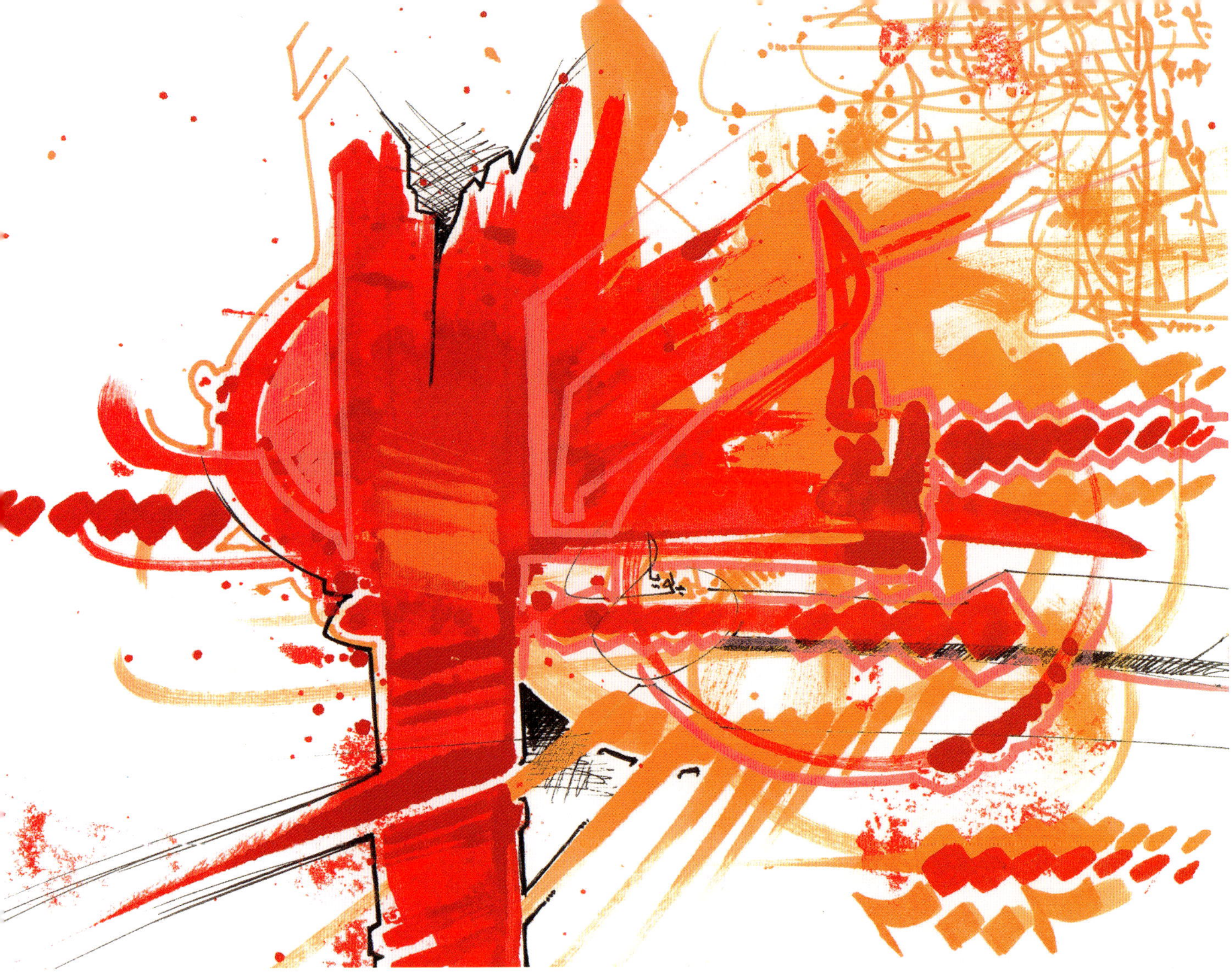

1

with a great teacher, as he remembers. She always showed her pupils beautiful calligraphies alongside the poems.

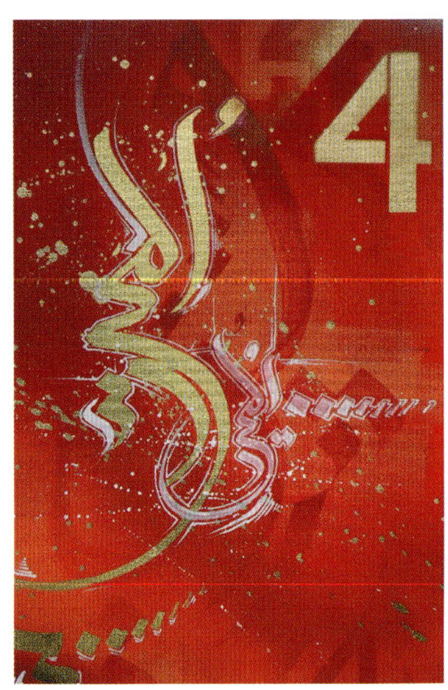

2

In 1995, he started writing graffiti as Sair 4 and he became a member of the ALME crew. He went the classical way and his New York-style graffiti, of which he soon became a master, was done in Latin letters. While doing various commissioned pieces of art, he became more and more interested in large-scale murals in public spaces. But he also began to work on canvases. According to him, he aims to put on the canvas the things that he yearns for. “I long for Iran”, he says, “but also for the New York flavor and graffiti writing.”

In 2001 Sair 4 started to work with Persian calligraphy, teaching himself from books. Seeing two veins of Arabic calligraphy, religion and poetry, he explains that — especially in Iranian culture — calligraphy is omnipresent in poetry. The richness of contemporary works from Persia inspired him and he fused his style writing with classical calligraphy. It was a way for him as an artist to deal with his own identity and explore new paths. The results are his unique “Hyrocalligraphix”.

Graffiti writing as an international movement always leads a graffiti artist to learn about and deal with different cultures. On this voyage, Sair 4 found calligraphy as a way of contemplating his own culture.

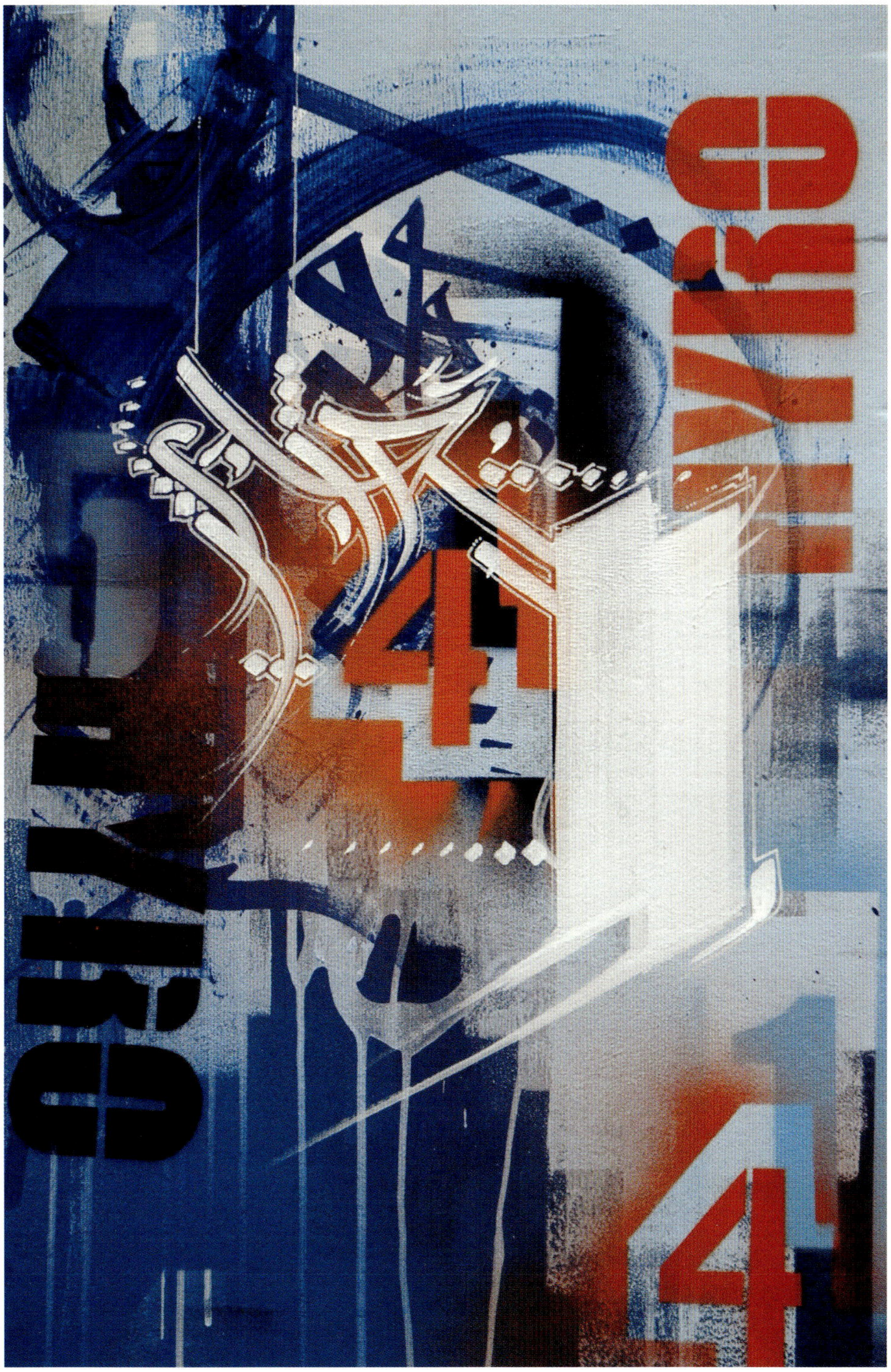

3

پویا
1. "Puya", SAIR 4, mixed media on paper, 21 × 30 cm, 2004

أمید
2. "Hope", SAIR 4, mixed media on canvas, detail, 80 × 80 cm, 2005

پویا
3. "Sair 4 & Puya", SAIR 4, mixed media on canvas, 90 × 45 cm, 2004

پویا
4. "Puya XXL" SAIR 4, mixed media on canvas, 180 × 120 cm, 2005

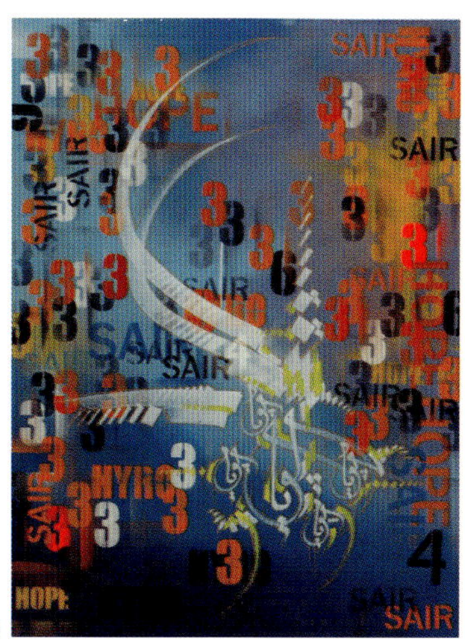

4

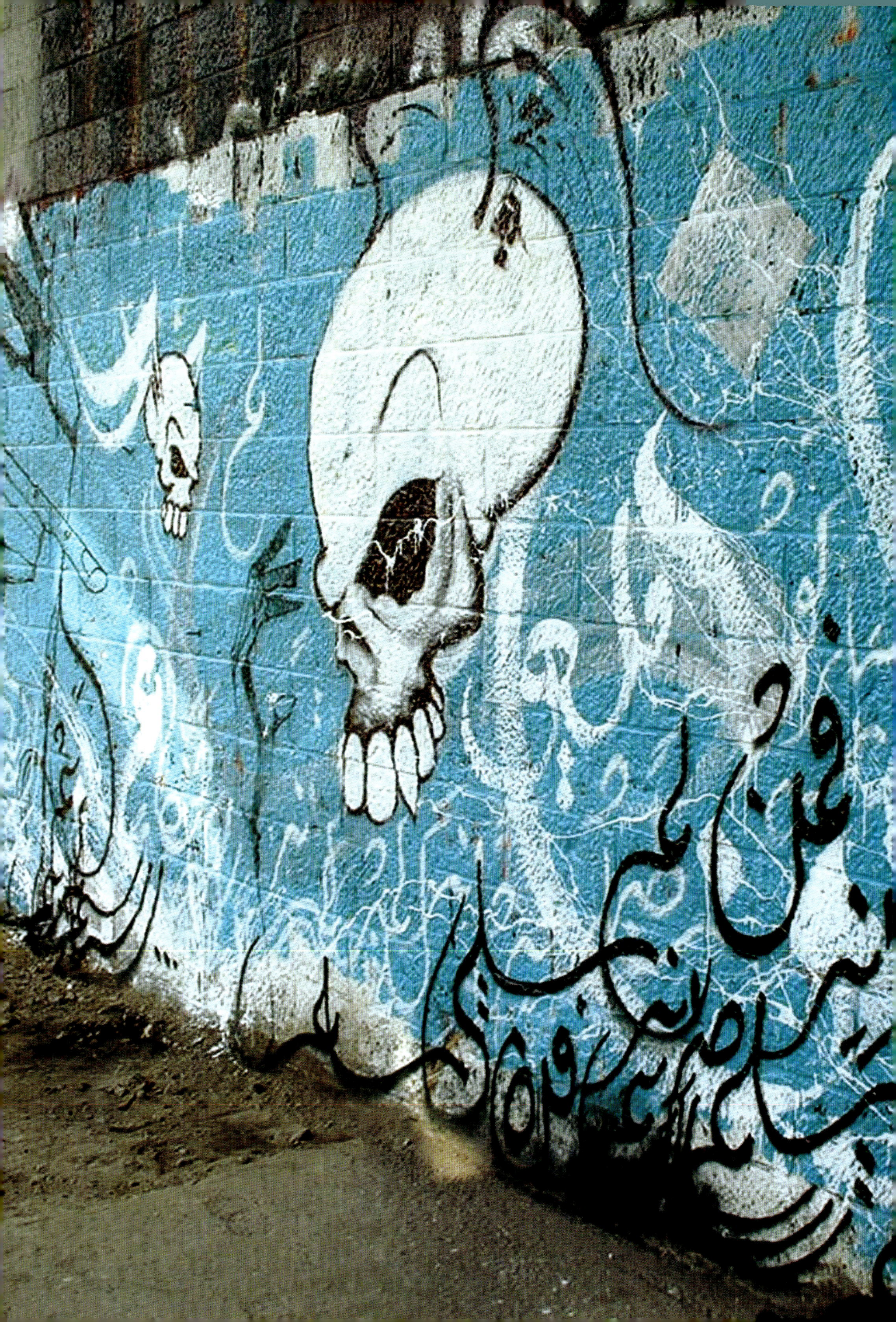

3·6
Native & ZenTwO
نايتيف وزين تو

Native and ZenTwO are two artists that hail from similar cosmopolitan backgrounds, and they work together as a collective on various calligraphic illustrations, canvases and murals. They have a radical approach to Arabic calligraphy. While being well aware of thousands of years of tradition, they like to ignore and tear down its strict rules. For them, this is not only a necessity to adjust calligraphy to the energy and speed of graffiti writing, but also a way to first rip apart and then re-organize their own complex identities.

1. **"Dead flies don't wear no flags", NATIVE & ZENTWO, St Denis, 2007**

Native Maqari, born in 1980 in Nigeria, lives in Paris, France. "I am from Nigeria and Brooklyn NYC and a few other places. I have been drawing and painting from as far back as I can remember and have been painting walls for half that time. I'm still trying to figure out what my biography has to do with all that. However, I can talk about my work as far as painting in the streets goes for the last thirteen years. I see it more as an expression forged by a life in big cities and exposure to the multitude of their faces than it is a representation of a movement. I travel to live and interact with these cities in order to gain access to their daily grind. It is sort of an attempt to absorb and filter it through a personal medium. My approach to actual painting was influenced by my immediate surroundings over the years, the streets of mega-urban cities that pulse daily with the movement of a million people perpetually hustling to adjust to modern urbanity."

ZenTwO, born in 1981 in Munich, Germany, lives in Paris, France. Half Austrian and half French, ZenTwO was raised between the Middle East and Europe. This unlikely mixture led to the development of a particular style in which he combines calligraphy, illustration, and spontaneous dynamic paint drips. His work leans towards the raw and finds expression in the uneven, in an attempt to access, engage, and integrate rough emotions, feelings of depression, and a destabilizing aesthetic. ZenTwO currently works in Belleville, Paris.

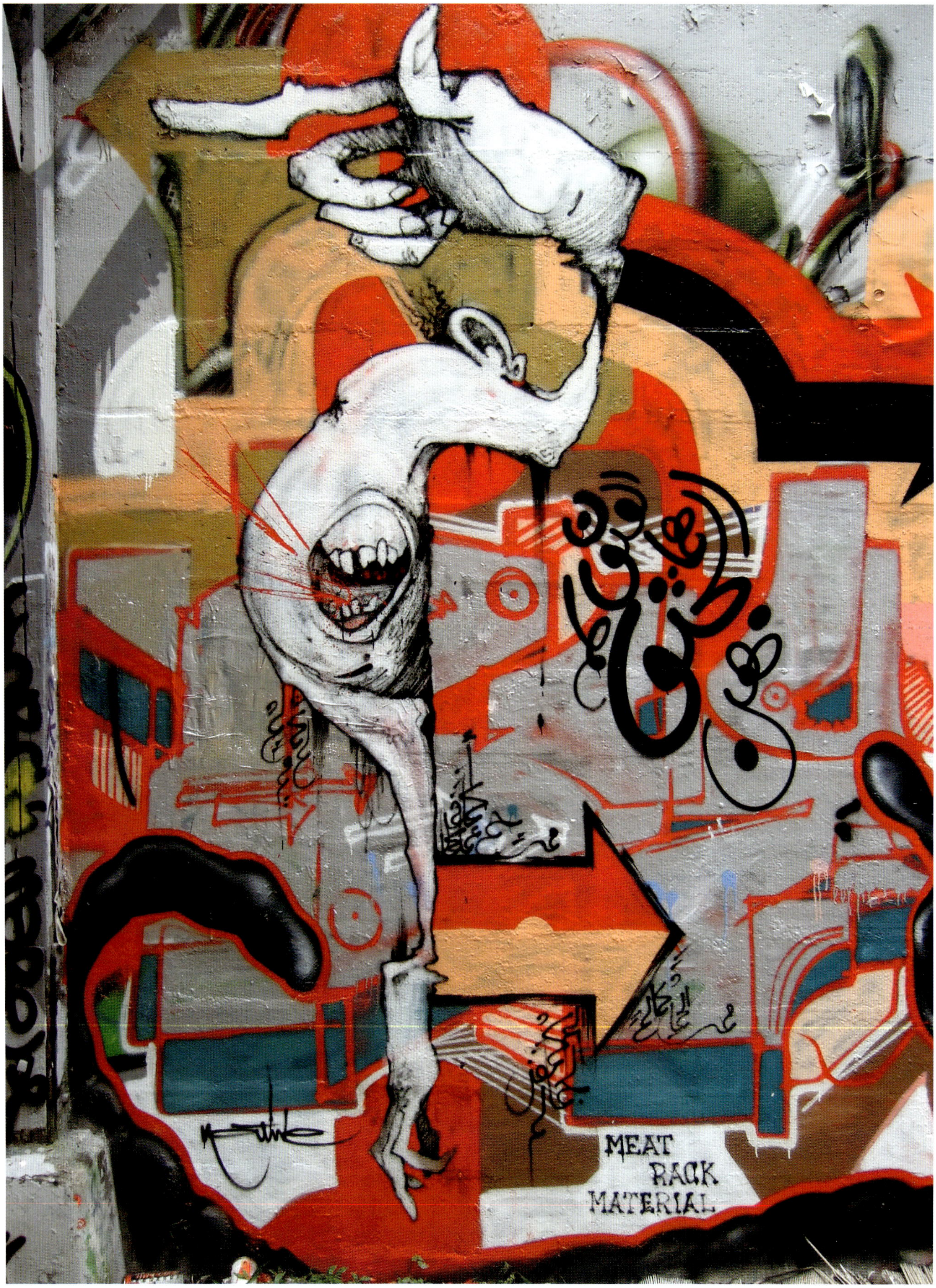

1

1./2. NATIVE, Luger, LaForge, Belleville 2

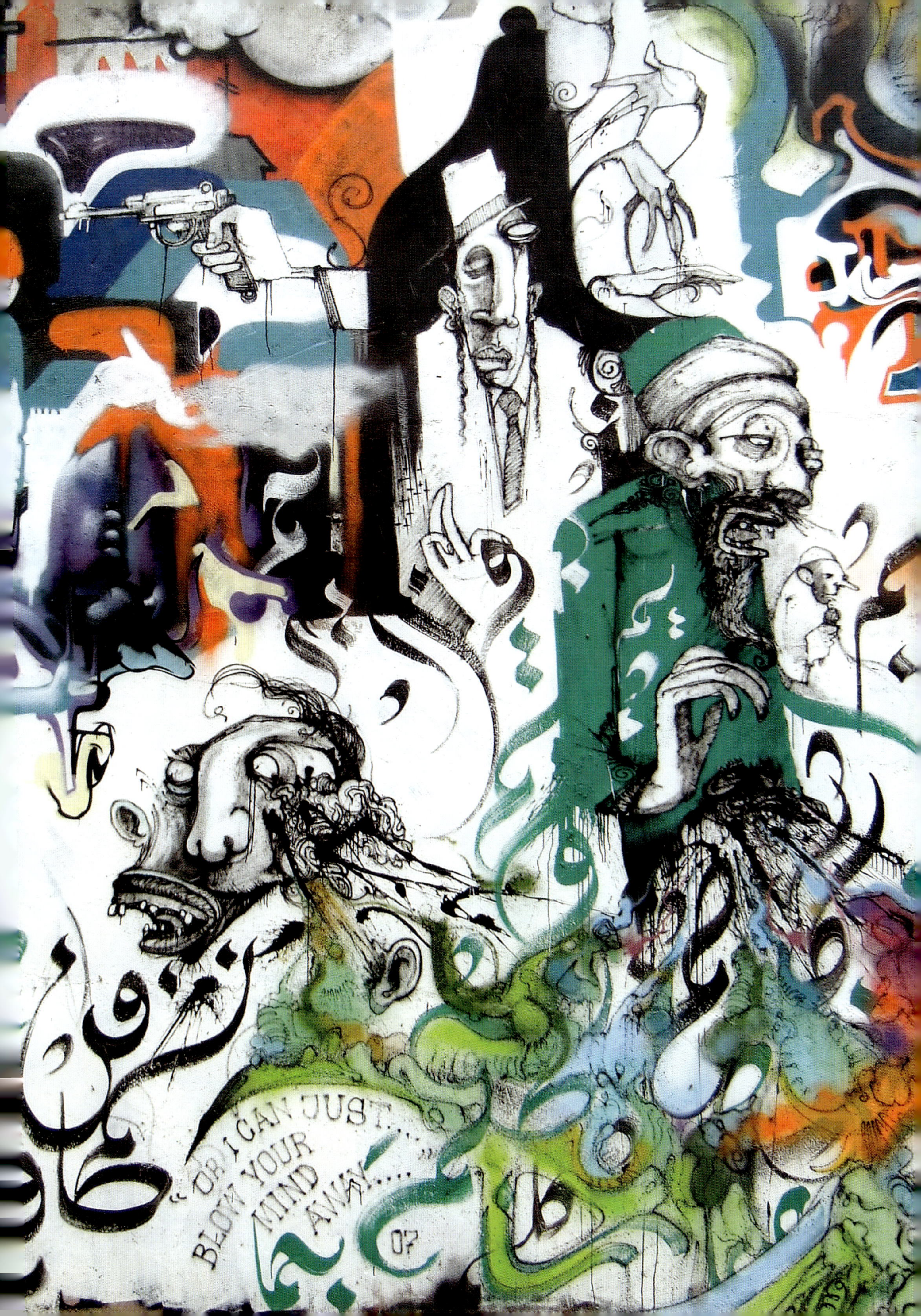
"OR I CAN JUST....
BLOW YOUR
MIND
AWAY...."
07

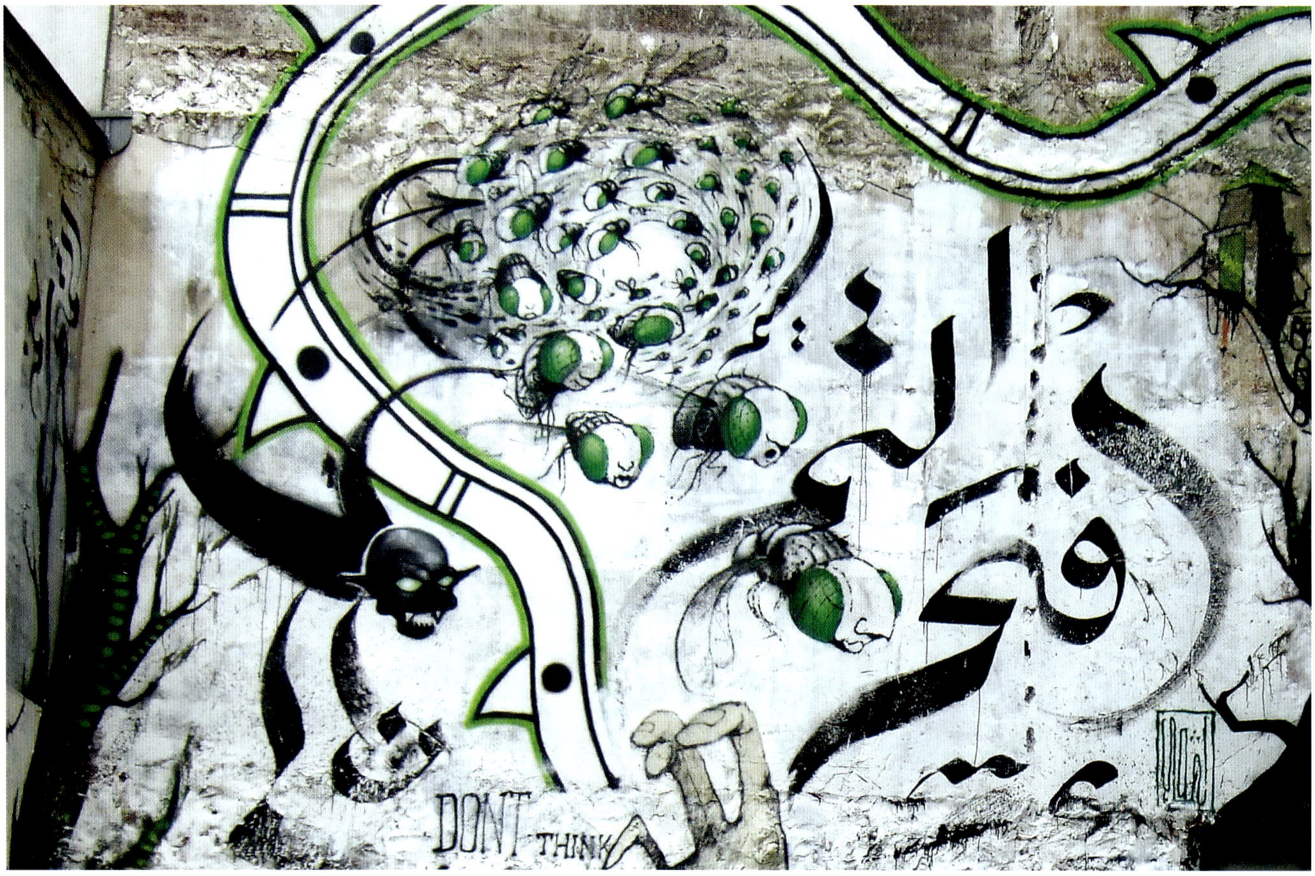

1

• CALLIGRAPHY, ELASTIK STYLE
Native & ZenTwO

We had two opposite introductions to Arabic calligraphy. One of us has an academic background and the other one is self-taught. But our point of view on calligraphy is the same.

Arabic calligraphy is supposed to be used with a lot of rules to keep your style clear and readable. We learned to use the alphabet to tag things in the streets and trains and not to write essays, so when we got into calligraphy this approach made us face certain issues. We use Arabic letters to make them fit our personal sensations. We don't care about hypothetical boundaries, which are there to corner ones creation.

This approach to calligraphy becomes something athletic, where the body plays a key role. I find this is a very natural evolution when one compares the atmosphere in which we paint today with the one in which most of the traditional rules or styles were created. We paint in pandemonious urban cities, in streets that are pulsing with millions of people hustling daily. Our spontaneous approach to calligraphy becomes a plastic representation of this daily chaos.

We started working together on letters mixed with illustrations. Step by step these two major components morphed into each other — we draw and paint like we use calligraphy and the other way around. Each stroke, each drip is definitive, and the dynamic, the expression and the composition are the main focus. We both use this approach very differently but in the end the atmosphere generated is quite similar. Our recent works involve fewer words than they used to but the strokes, the textures and the dynamic of the calligraphy compositions are more present than before.

Our calligraphy is ELASTIK.

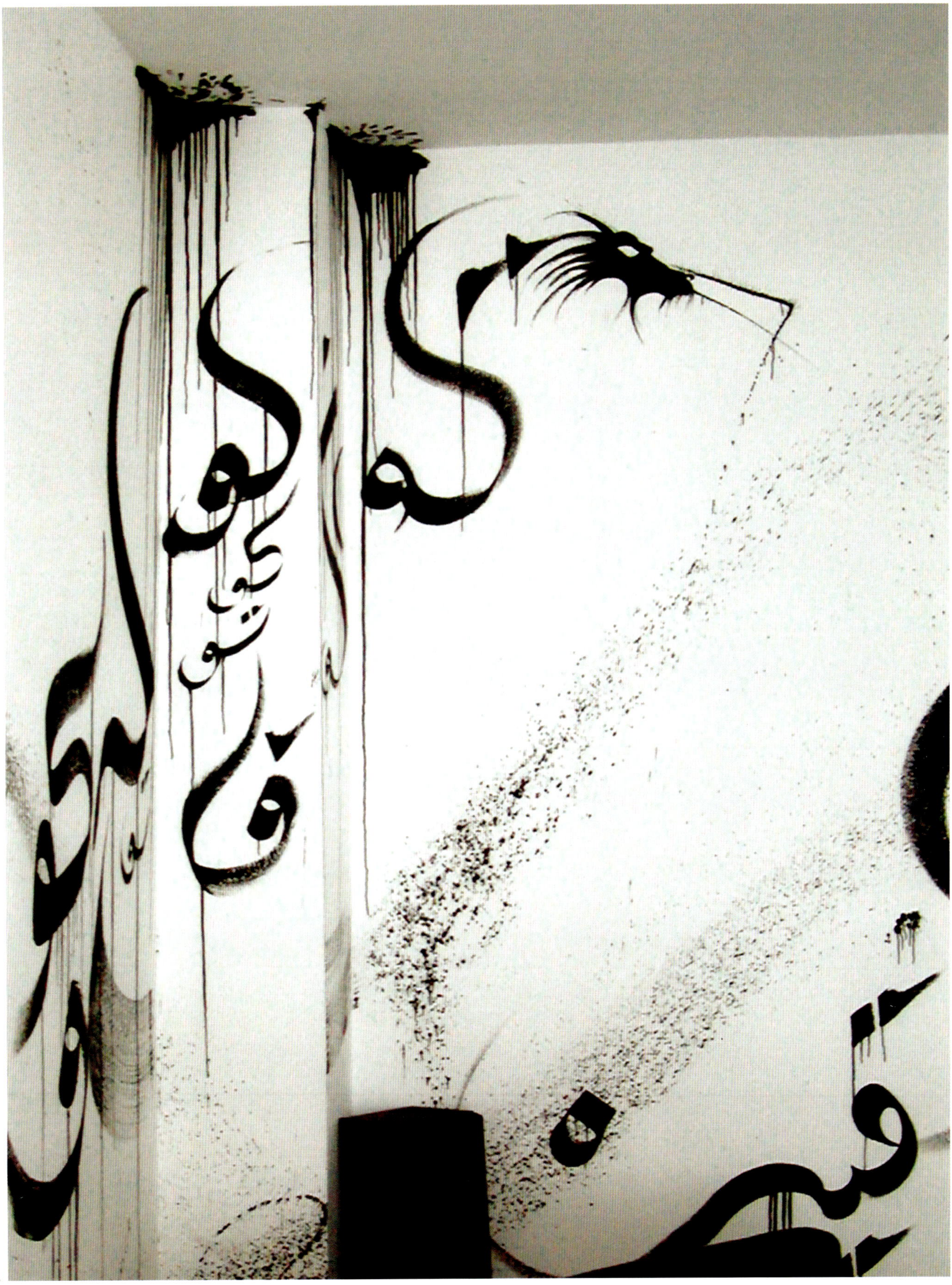

2

1. "Dead flies don't wear no flags", NATIVE & ZENTWO, Arabic Graffiti, La Forge, Belleville, 2007

2. "Vato Loco", ZENTWO, Arabic Graffiti, private collection, Frankfurt

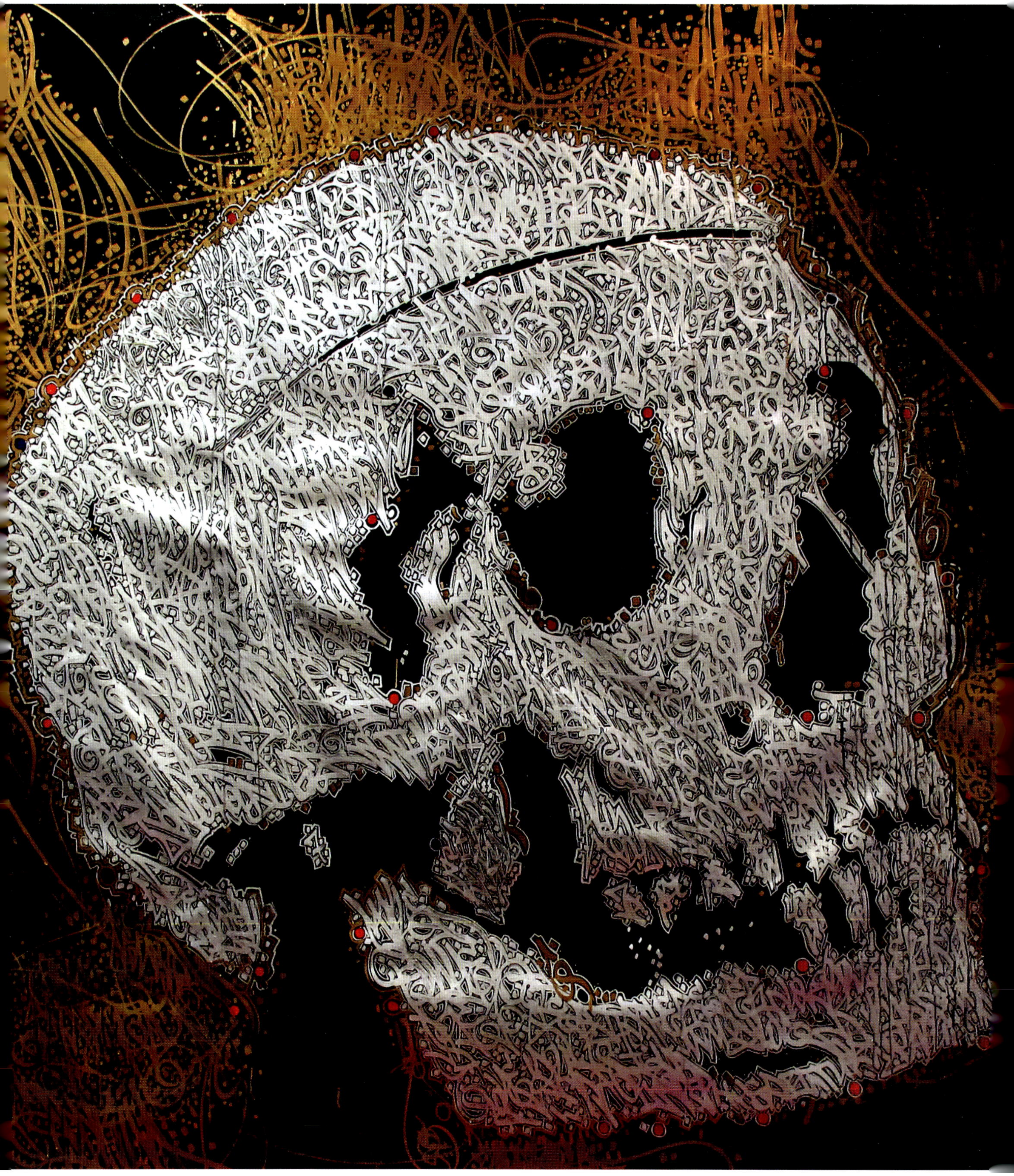

3·7

Sun7 aka Jonas Bournat

سان٧ المعروف
بجوناس بورنا

Born in 1977 in Paris, France

Sun7 (pronounced 'sunset') is obviously a child of word and image, poetry and color, art and street. In the early 1990s, he discovered New York tag culture. Spray can in hand, he took on the skin of walls in Paris and New York, and moved on to performances and installations, not only in Paris, Lyon and Marseille, but also in Shanghai, Hong Kong, Jakarta, and lately Marrakesh. He then started using canvases, signs and metal plaques. His register became permeated by multiple new influences: action painting, Arabic calligraphy, Latino gang graffiti and tattoos. But words and calligraphy remained dominant — a mesh of words, a lace of letters, most often indecipherable but through which, together, he made portraits and self-portraits. Obvious portraits and coded texts create a subtle play of appearance/disappearance, in which everything related to calligraphy, glyphs and ideograms becomes as unreal as can be, nurturing a sense of mystery.

1. "Silver Diary Skull" (Jacques Bournat RIP), writings of important moments and elements in his father's life, SUN7, mixed media on canvas, 200 × 200 cm, 2010

2. "Emilie", SUN7, ink on steel, detail of 200 × 100 cm, Espace Culturel Louis Vuitton, Paris, 2009

Following pages:

1. "Inna Modja", SUN7, written portrait, mixed media on canvas, 116 × 146 cm, L'Agence, Paris, 2009

2. "Tamesloht", SUN7, Copper & Brass, detail of 200 × 50 cm, Marrakesh, 2009

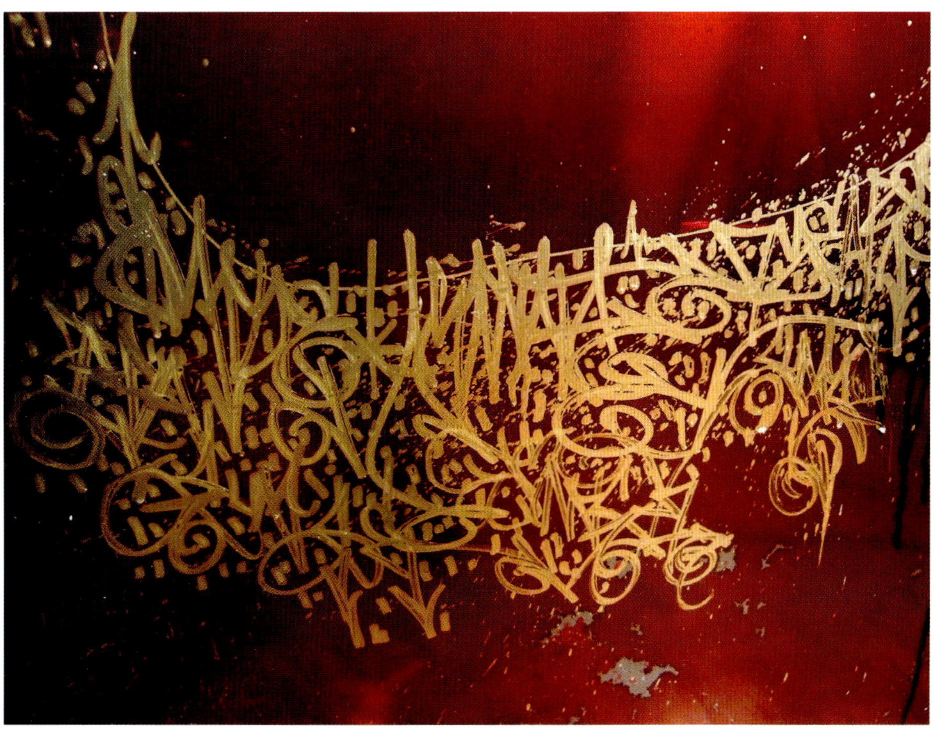

2

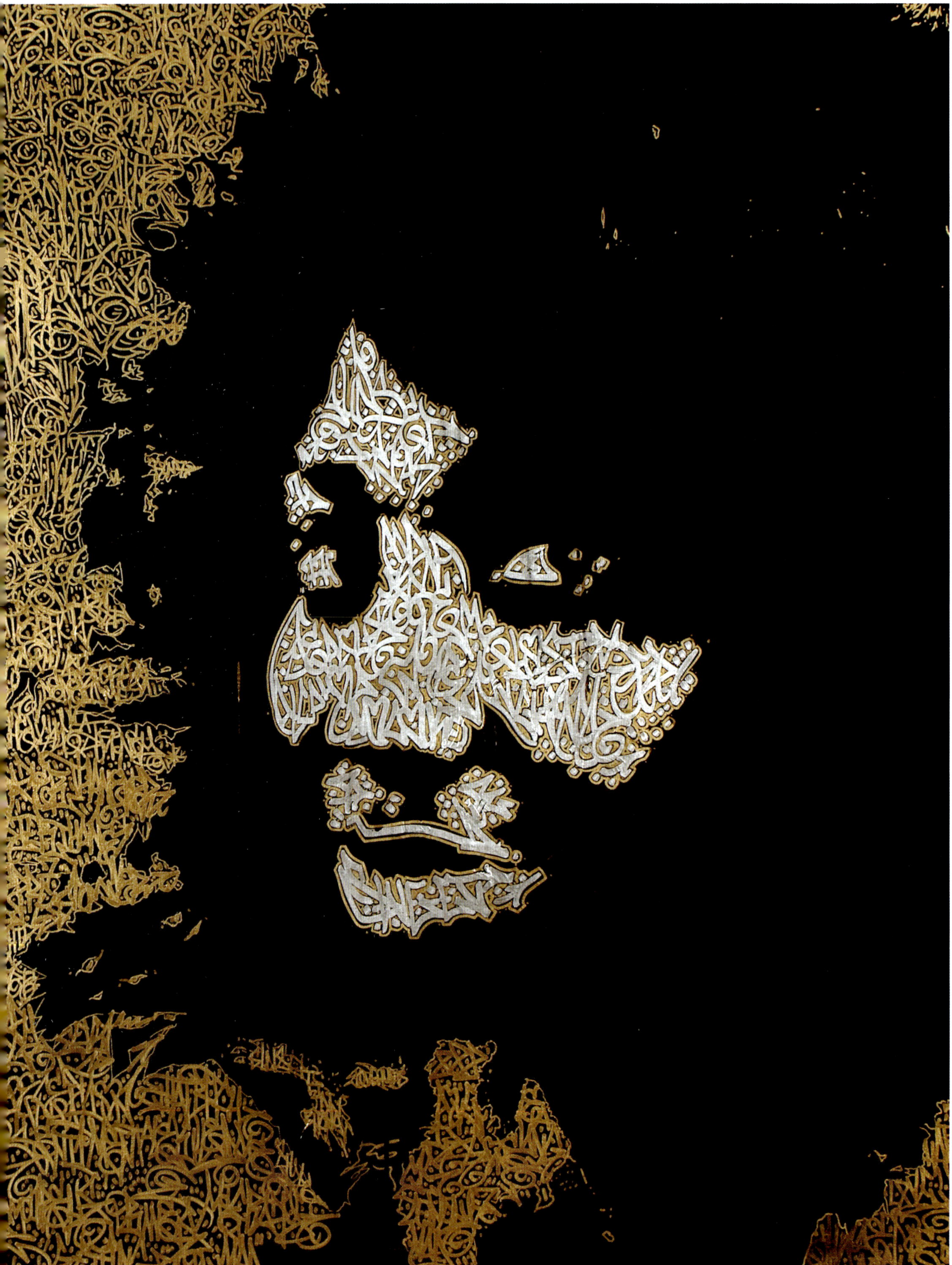

1

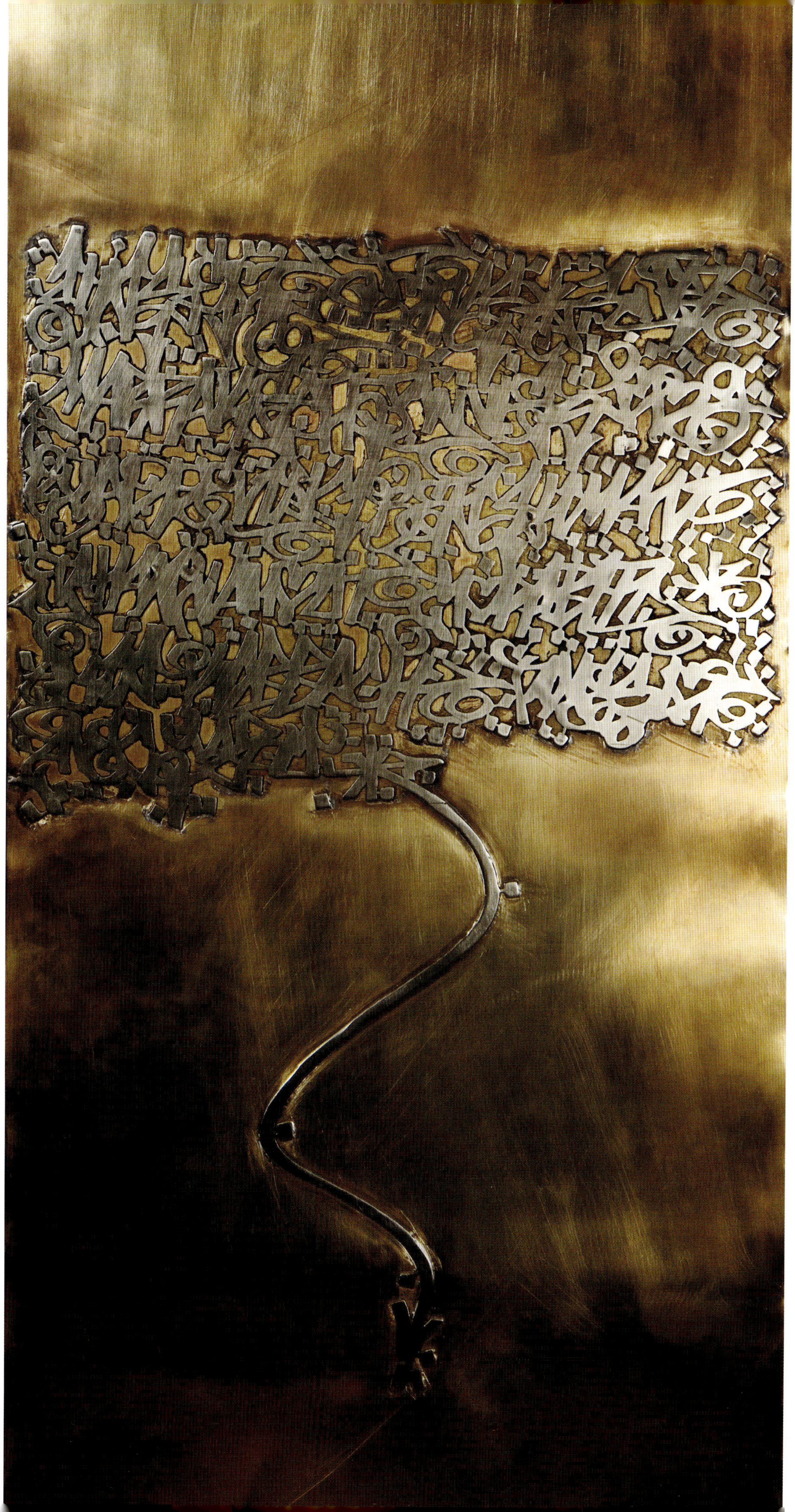
2

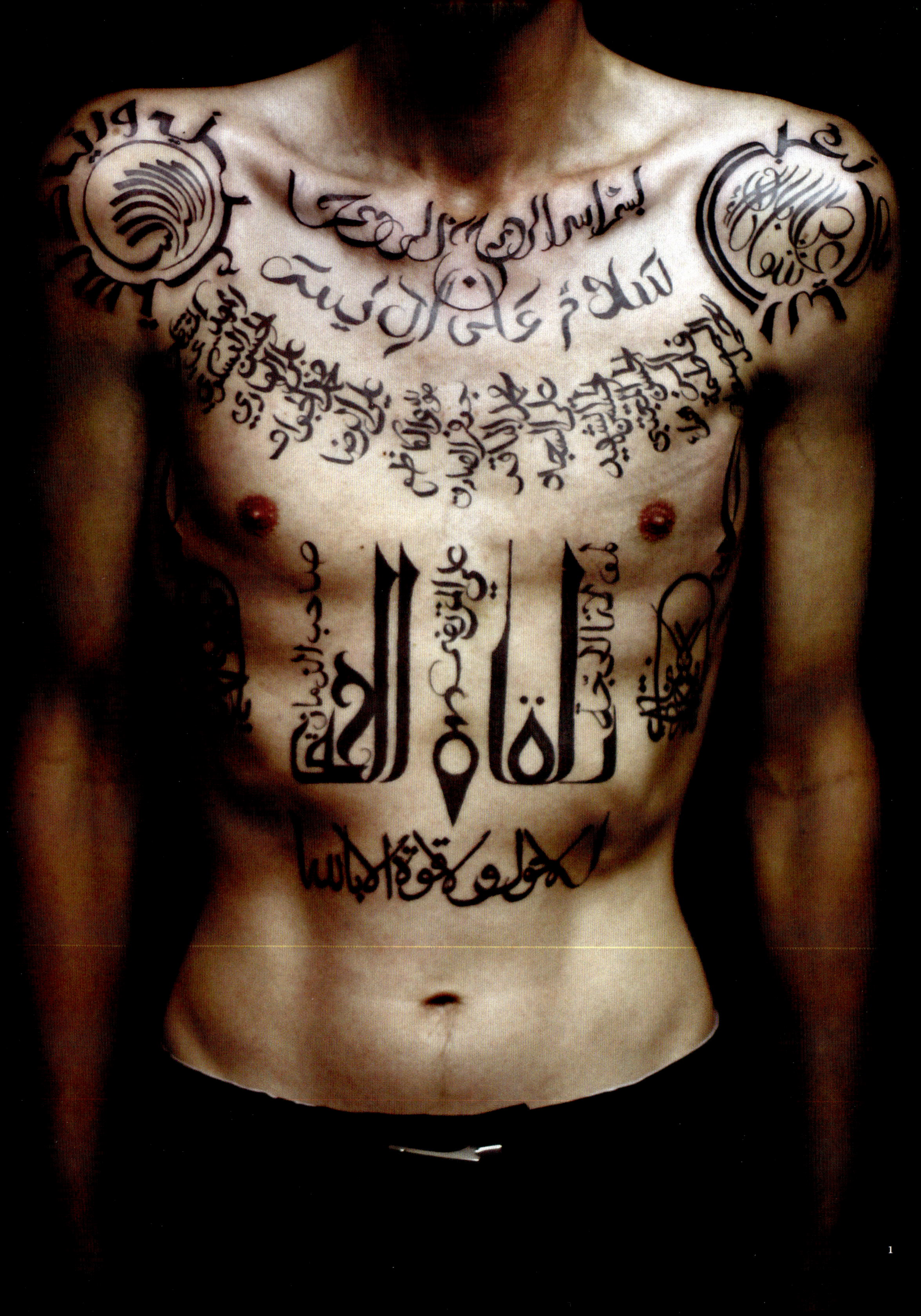
بسم الله الرحمن الرحيم
لا حول ولا قوة الا بالله

3·8

Sadhu

سادو

Born 1976 in Perpignan, France
Lives in Paris

After studying at École des Beaux-Arts nine years ago, during which his classical aspirations and aesthetic were shaped by his education, Sadhu began creating stencils and calligraphy. His work is influenced by Art Deco, Mucha, the Secessionists (who refute differences between art and craftsmanship) and by his own creativity. Upon his arrival in Paris in 2002, he began to develop a higher level of technical complexity and used polychromy. Around this time he started to use arabesque styles in his work.

He takes pleasure in art, as he does in photography, graphic design and film, and these are the art forms most central to his work. Among other things, lately he has concentrated on combining painted stencils and handwritten calligraphy. His graffiti, graphic design, tattoos and video work have been featured in exhibitions and books internationally, and he has also done artwork for bands such as Green Day. He is also a member of the OldSerb-Club crew, whose images subvert classic political propaganda.

Sadhu had the opportunity in 2007 to learn tattooing from Roberto Dardini at Art Corpus (Paris), an established, creative studio that houses many other great artists. Since 2008, he has dedicated most of his time to two passions: stenciling and tattooing.

1. Islamic prayers, SADHU, tattoo, model: Haydar, 2010

2. "Sadhu", arabesque calligraphy, ink on paper, 2004

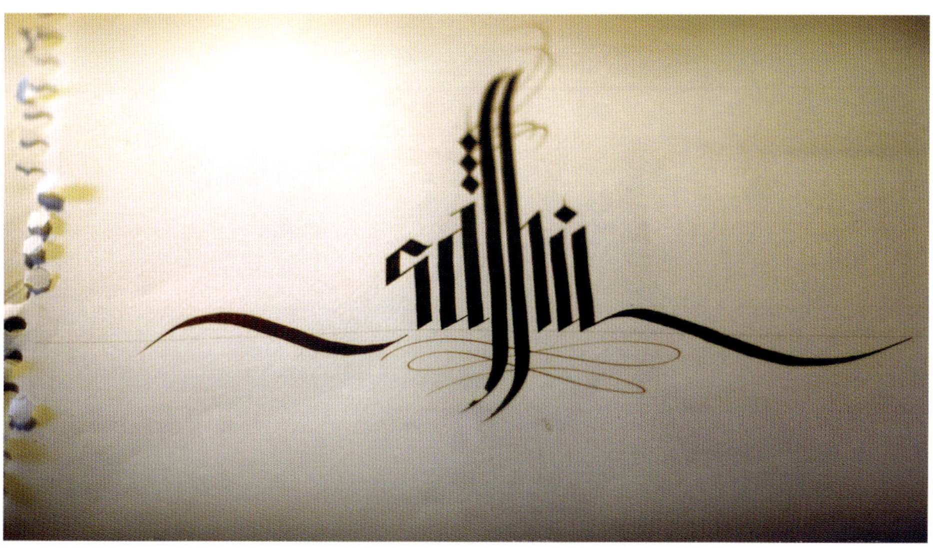

2

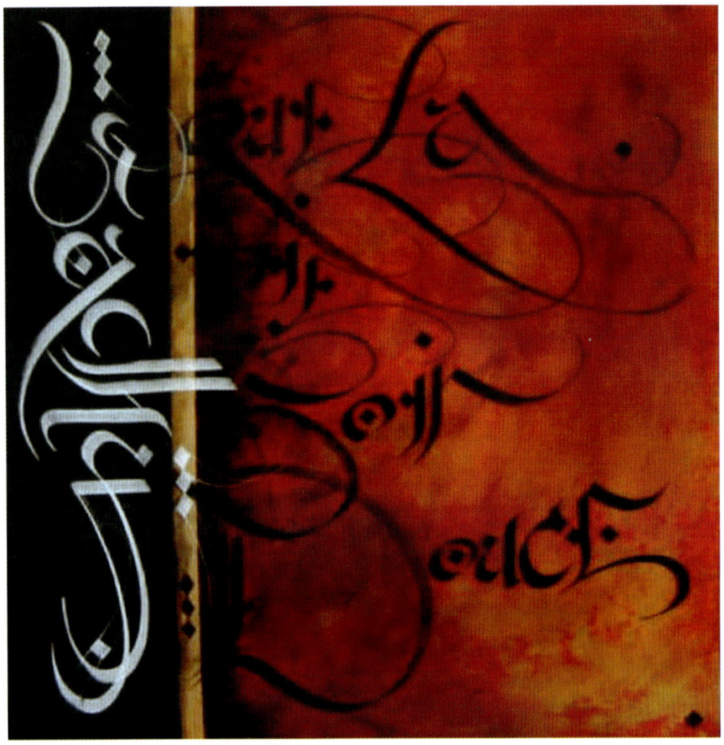

1

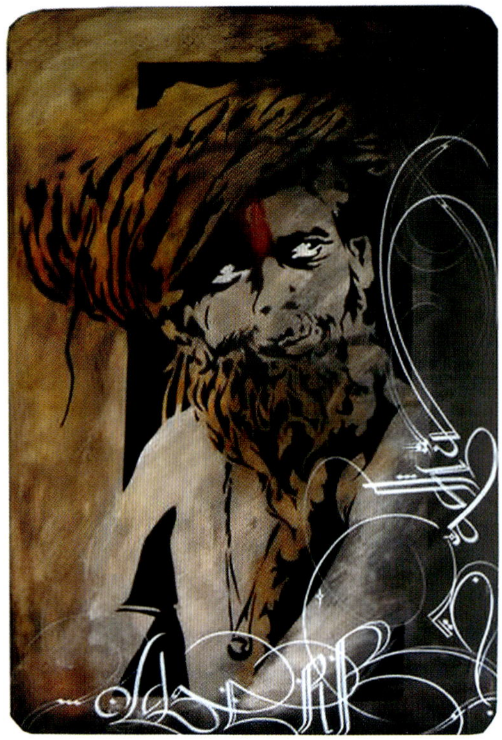

2

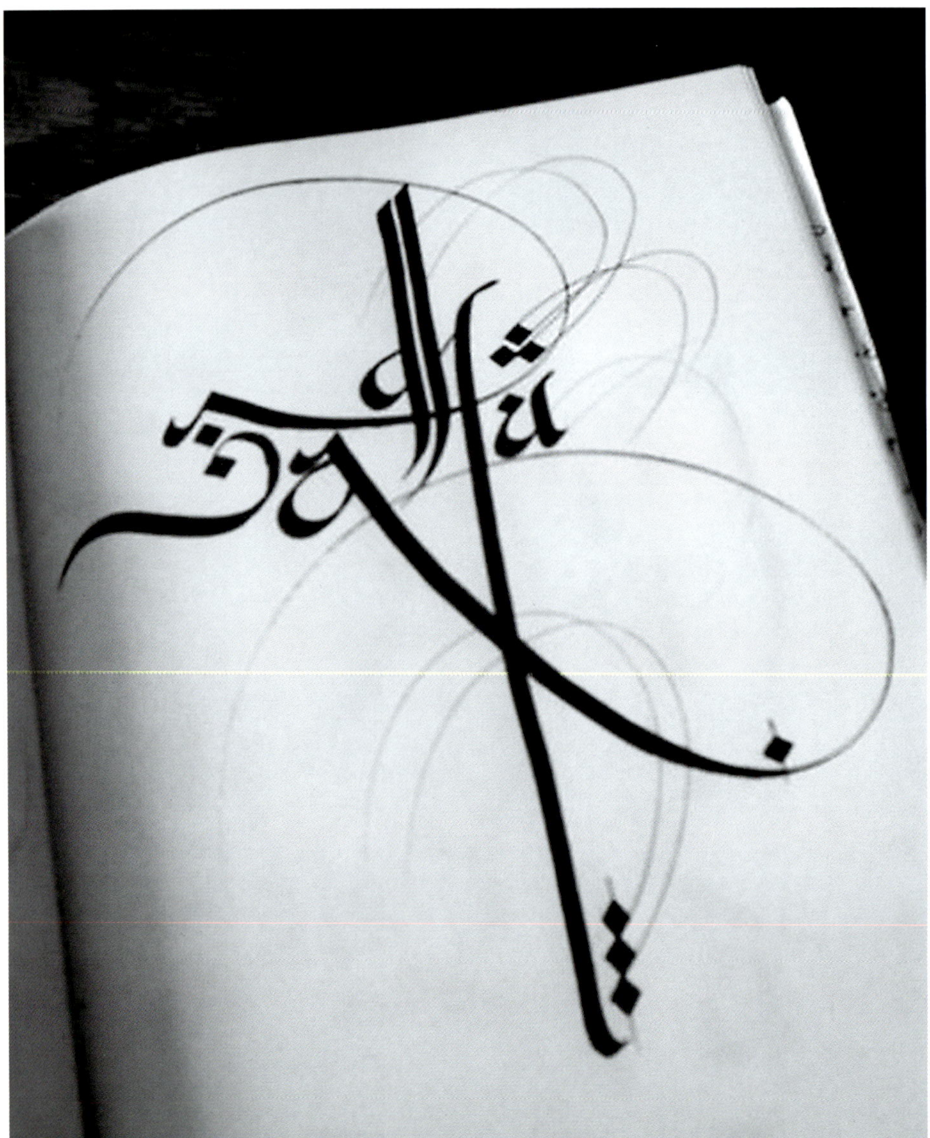

3

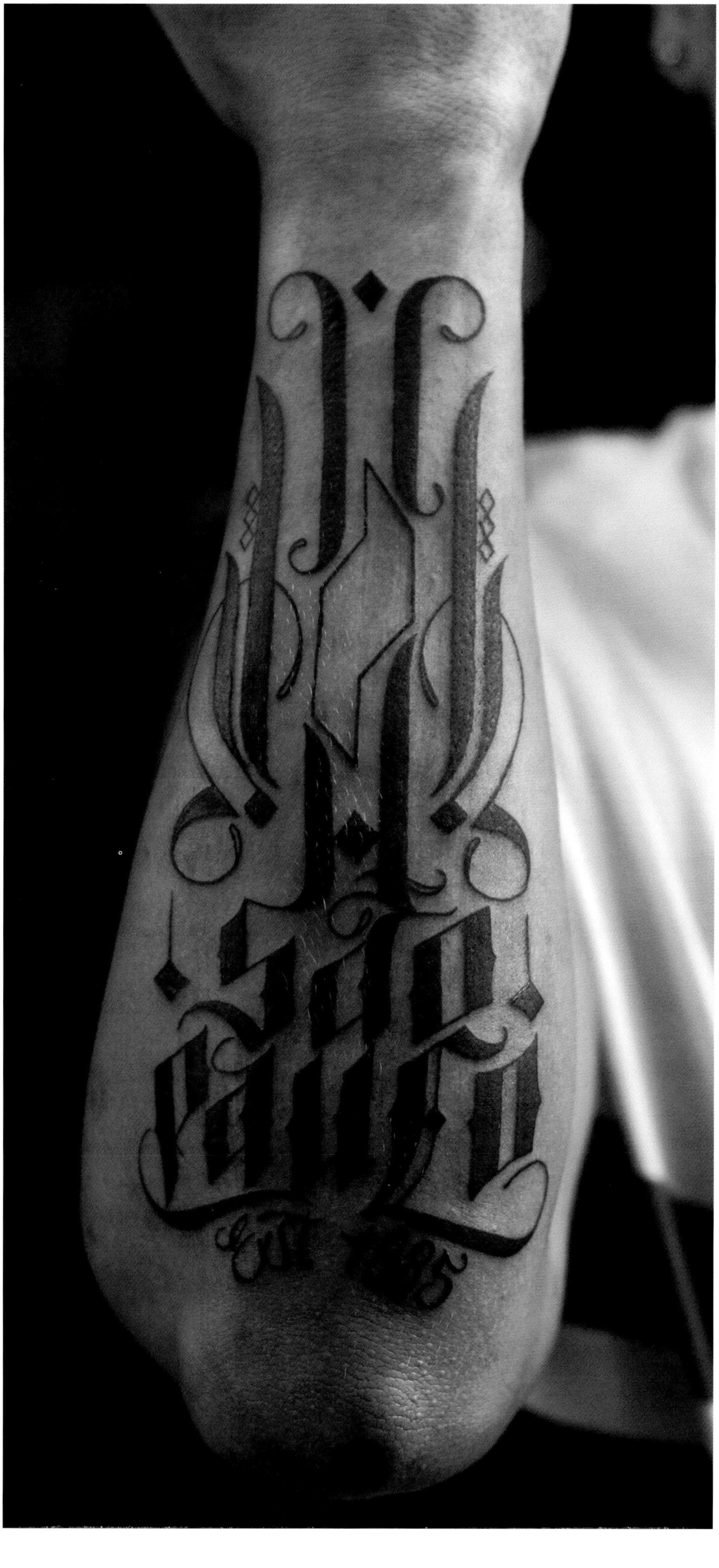

4

1. SADHU, ink, acrylic spray & marker, 80 × 80 cm, 2003

2. “Sadhu Turban”, ink, acrylic spray & marker on wood board, 2003

3. “Sadhu”, arabesque calligraphy, ink on paper, 2003

4. “Sao Paulo”, SADHU, tattoo, model: Mario, 2010

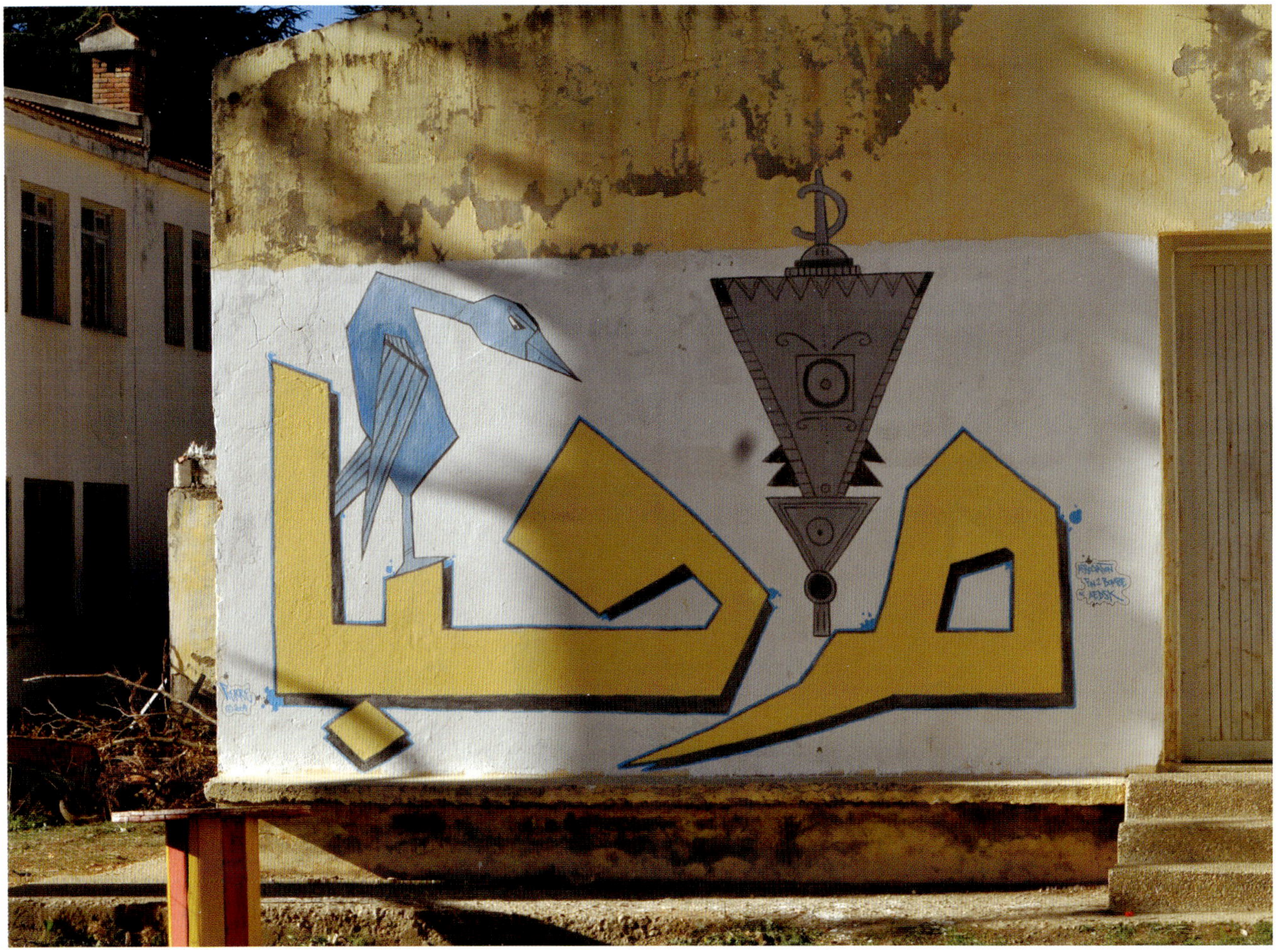

1

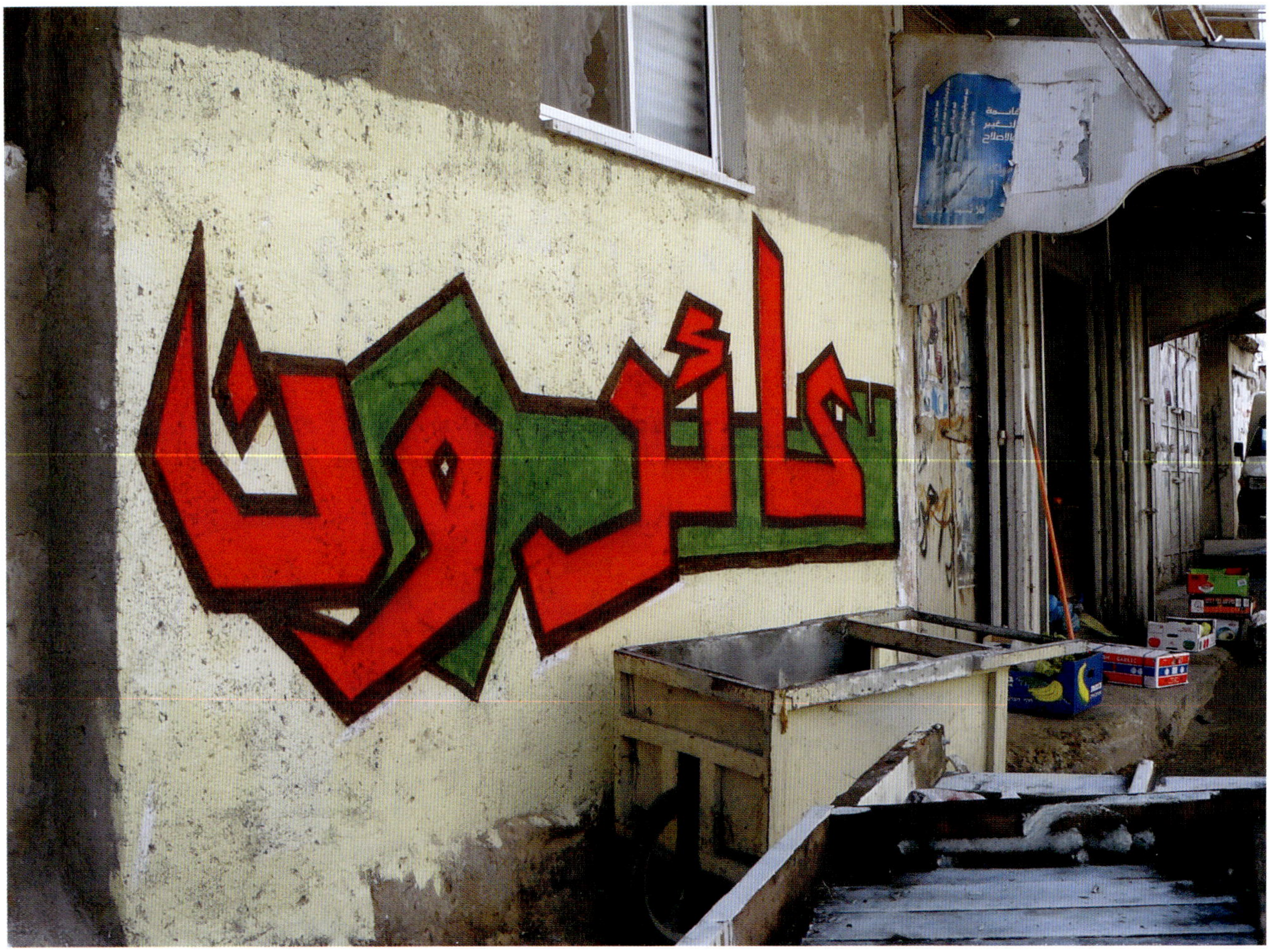

2

3·9
Monsieur Cana aka Askar
أستاذ كانا المعروف بعسكر

Born 1980 in France

مرحبا
1. "Welcome", MONSIEUR CANA, Ketama, Morocco, 2009

عائدون
2. "We will return", MONSIEUR CANA, Al Amari refugee camp, Ramallah, 2009

My alias, Askar (soldier), was given to me by Palestinian friends from the Al Amari refugee camp in Ramallah who noticed the murals I had painted in the Askar refugee camp on the outskirts of Nablus. Not wanting to impose my name or messages onto them in a foreign language, I chose instead to write words and phrases in Arabic letters. This work in Palestine allowed me to combine my passion for writing letters, painting and the commitment to a cause.

The first time I went to an Arab country, Morocco, I saw shop signs and immediately recognized the link that connected me to Arabic calligraphy. While I use straight lines in my drawings and lettering, I use curves in my graffiti writing. I found them again in Arabic calligraphy in abundant forms, including curved and stylized shapes. When I write in Arabic I write with the same flexibility and accuracy as when I do a graffiti piece. To create good calligraphy, whether in Arabic or graffiti writing, you should be focused and know your lines to get a good result.

I was raised as a grandson of Polish and Spanish immigrants in Denain, an industrial city and the poorest town in France in 2010. In 1991, writing messages on walls caught my interest and I decided to start tagging. I needed color in this gray city. In the early 90s, France was politically hardened with social problems resulting from unemployment and immigration. In order to convey messages through graffiti while fighting for a cause, I created the ALP crew in 1994 (Against Le Pen, the leader of the French National Front). In those years my career as a vandal really started to take off, focusing on graffiti writing with markers and scratching in the streets and on train lines. Soon, graffiti writing was omnipresent in my life. In 2001 I got caught in the act. The police had been looking for me for a very long time. But I was still able to continue painting in the streets, to give free art to the people and get messages across. Having no other artistic training than what I had learned in the street, I became interested in art history and found some aspects of my approach in folk art, calligraphy and primitive art. I turned my graffiti into masks and faces, keeping my sense of straight lines and symmetry.

I managed to balance artistic practice with professional work with kids. In 2002, friends and I created the NGO Fin 2 Bombe, which aims to give all people access to art. We work in France, Morocco and Chad, as well as with Palestinian refugees in Palestine, Lebanon and Jordan. We're trying to get people to invest in and improve their neighborhoods by making murals and art workshops.

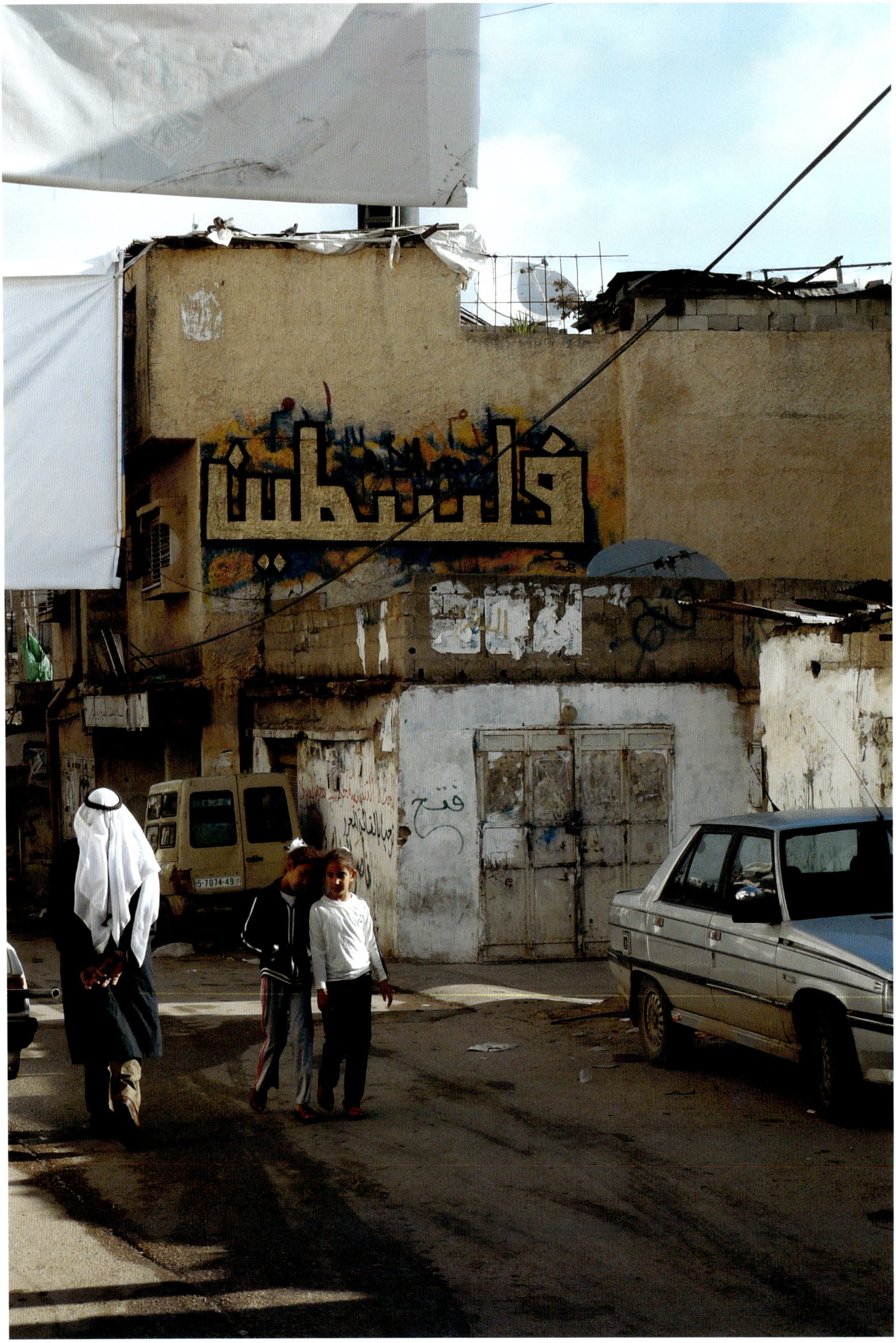

1

I was really attracted by Palestinian graffiti, its slogans, messages and words. This was my kind of graffiti: the street as a medium to convey ideas. Since 2005, I have worked with children and residents, painting colorful and uplifting messages in the streets of the refugee camps with them. We did not change the course of this conflict but for a while we changed the gray life of these camps.

I am not a political activist, I protest with colors, and my commitment ends there. I want to allow children to be able to express themselves and help their streets. But when I returned to Palestine for the seventh time in April 2010, invited by the French Cultural Centre in Ramallah to do an exhibition and to continue my workshops in the Al Amari refugee camp, the Israeli authorities refused my entry without explanation. They put a red stamp in my passport and I'm no longer permitted to enter Israel and therefore Palestine. This situation is very hard on me, I miss my friends but I'm waiting patiently.

فلسطين

1. "Palestine", MONSIEUR CANA: "In 2008 I wanted to paint this wall in Al Amari, it is central and clear (unlike where the streets are very narrow). So I painted 'Palestine' over some graffiti which was already there. That evening a friend told me that one day Israeli soldiers arrived, and forced a man at gunpoint to paint 'Salam' (peace) many times on the roof, the wall that I had just painted. Camp residents had never erased it to remember this story. I did not know what to say and I immediately felt remorse. Then they said: 'Don't worry Askar, a page turns, everybody is happy, Shukran (thanks).'"

فلسطين

2. "Palestine", MONSIEUR CANA, Askar refugee camp, Nablus, Palestine 2007

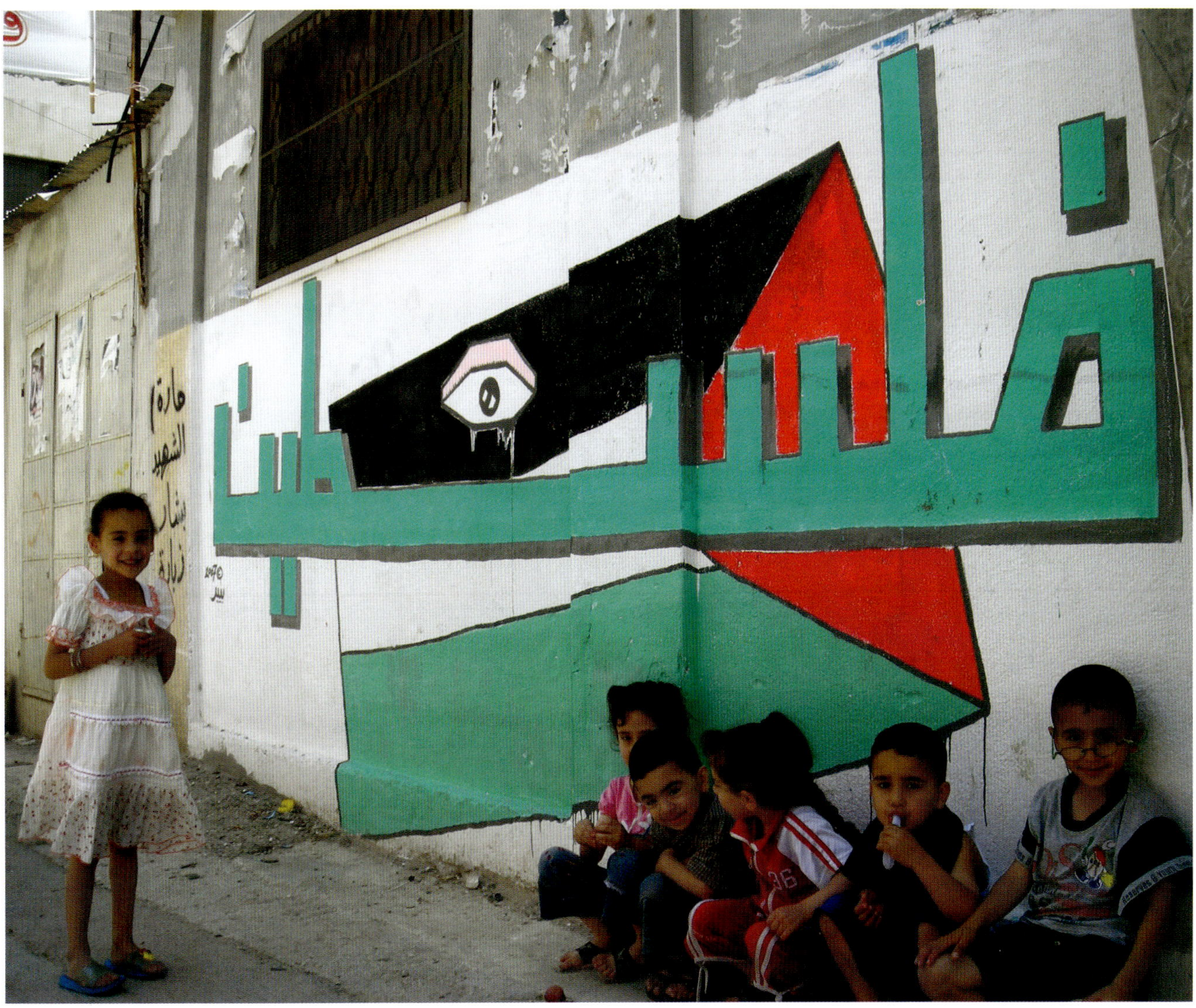

2

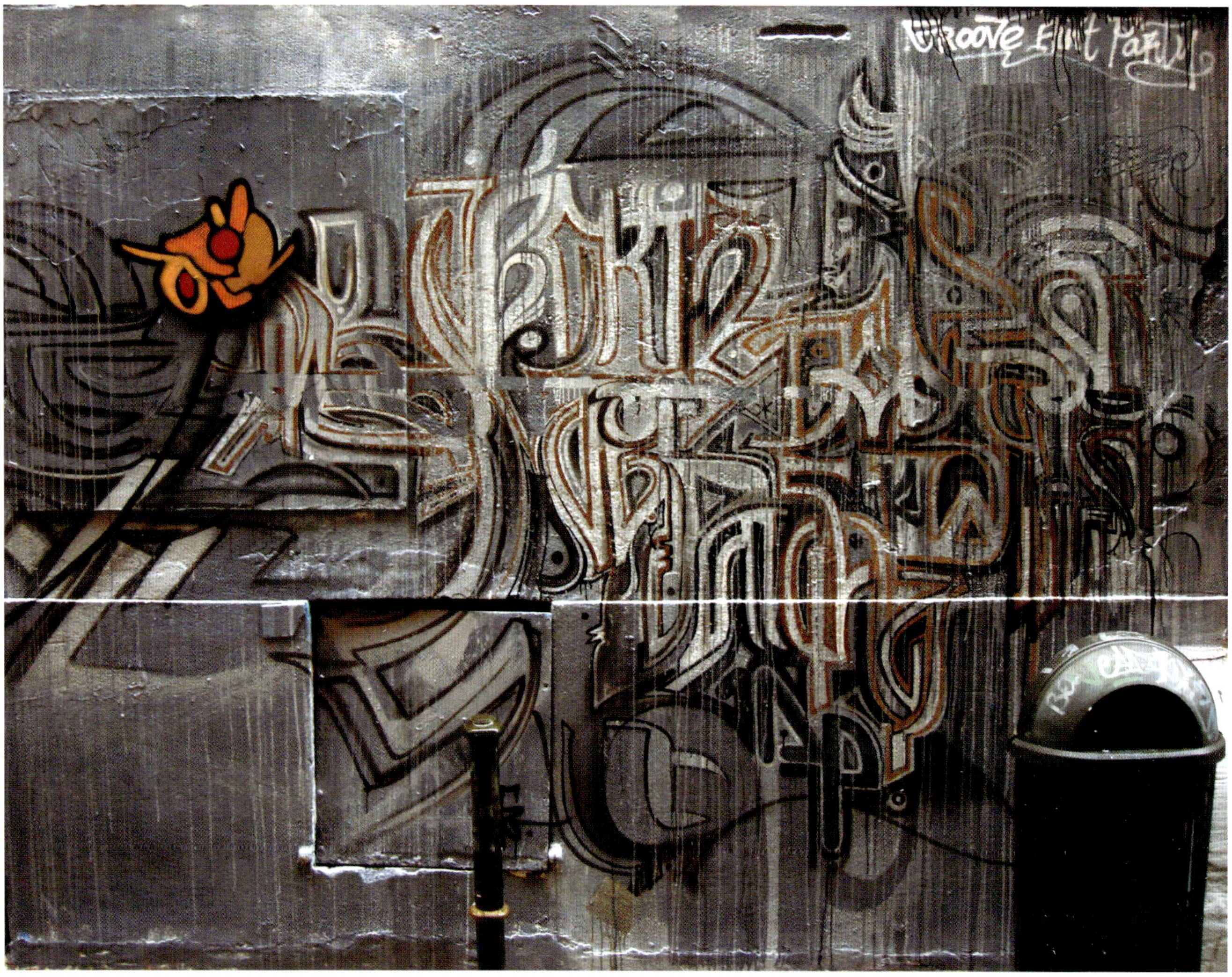

1

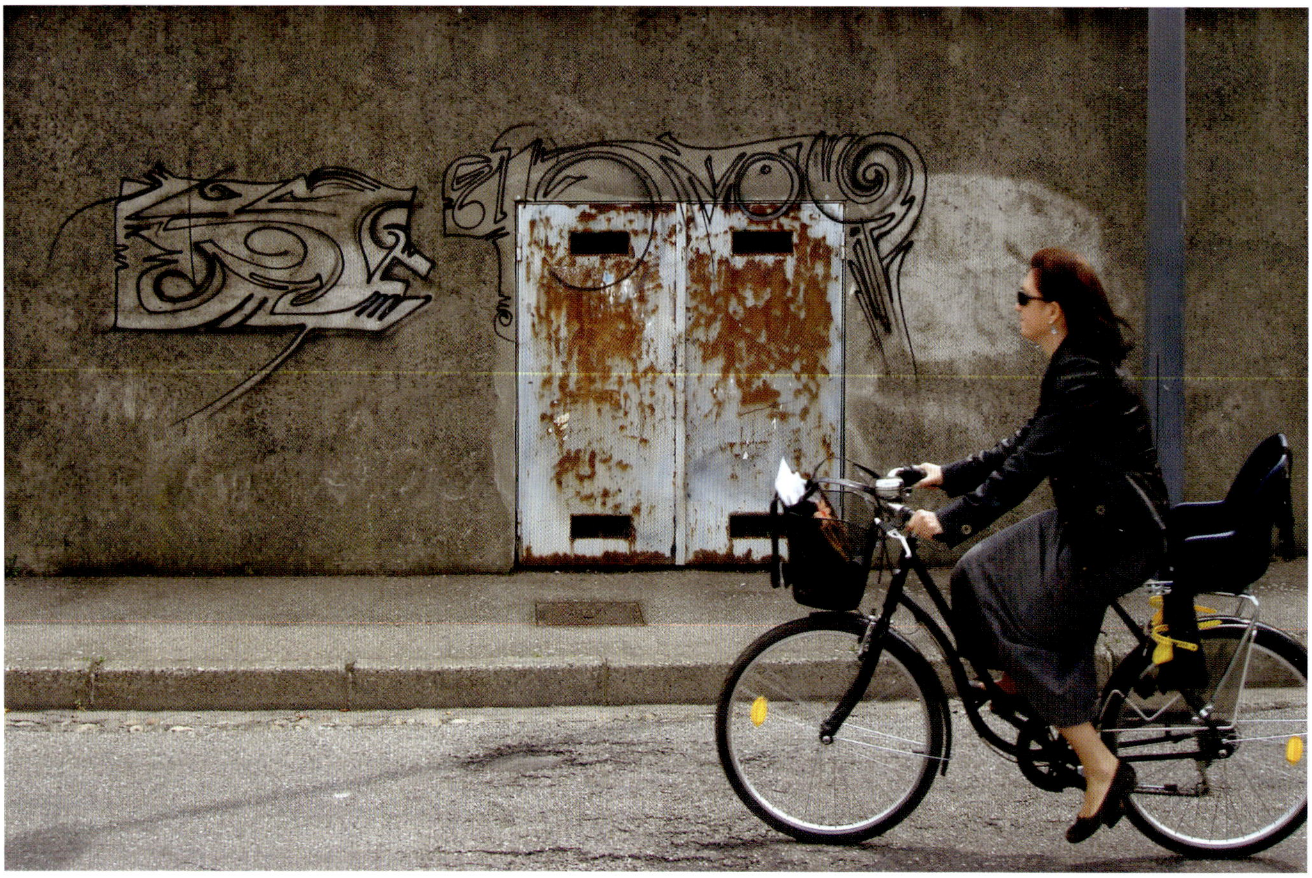

2

3·10
Zepha aka Vincent Abadie Hafez

زيفا المعروف
بمنصور عبادي حافظ

Born in 1977 in France

Cosmopolitan, the work of Zepha is the result of a crossbreeding of several cultures. It was in a Parisian suburb in 1989 that he started to impose his name and that of his crew and it has not stopped since. He appropriates public space and disrupts visual habits: a graphic utopian fight undertaken against a system guided by a savage man-eating liberalism and its 'enfant terrible': advertising.

Parallel to his graffiti writing, Zepha developed a graphic and visual language based on movement, in which many elements intersect: the influence of the craftsmanship of ancient civilizations, calligraphy, the immediacy of the movement 'Figuration Libre', the spontaneity of 'Lyrical Abstraction', and finally the risk-taking of random graffiti.

Arabic calligraphy strongly influences his work through his training by the Moroccan calligrapher Abdelatif Mustad and the discovery of the work of the Sudanese Ahmed Abdel Aal. With Kufic style and the lively Diwani style, he has rediscovered the workings of composition, balance of letters and movement appropriated by graffiti. A unique graphic vocabulary takes shape, showing a balance of instinct and thought-out composition, with the research of the letter as a basis. What is Latin or Arabic gets distorted, diverted, connected, mixed and accumulated, leading to a form of dreamlike and labyrinthine writing. Contrasts, oppositions and complementarity enrich the production of pieces produced in multiple formats. Worn out by time, they are bearers of memory, the result of questioning a world which seems to forget the very principles of its own existence.

1. "Groove ain't Party", ZEPHA, Rue du Coq Dinde, Toulouse, France, 2009

2. "Kärcher tracking", ZEPHA, Paris France, 2008

3. "Etre captif la n'est pas la question, le tout est de ne pas se rendre" (Being captive this is not the problem, it is all about not suffering) quote by Nazim Hikmet, ZEPHA, France, 2010

3
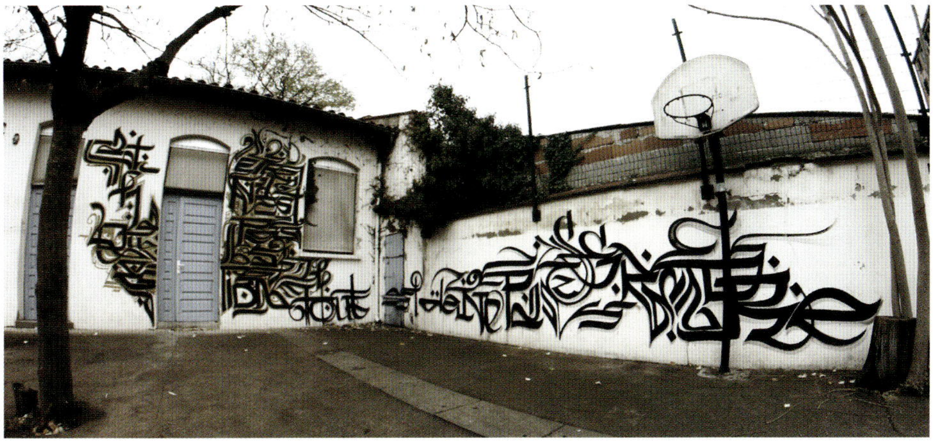

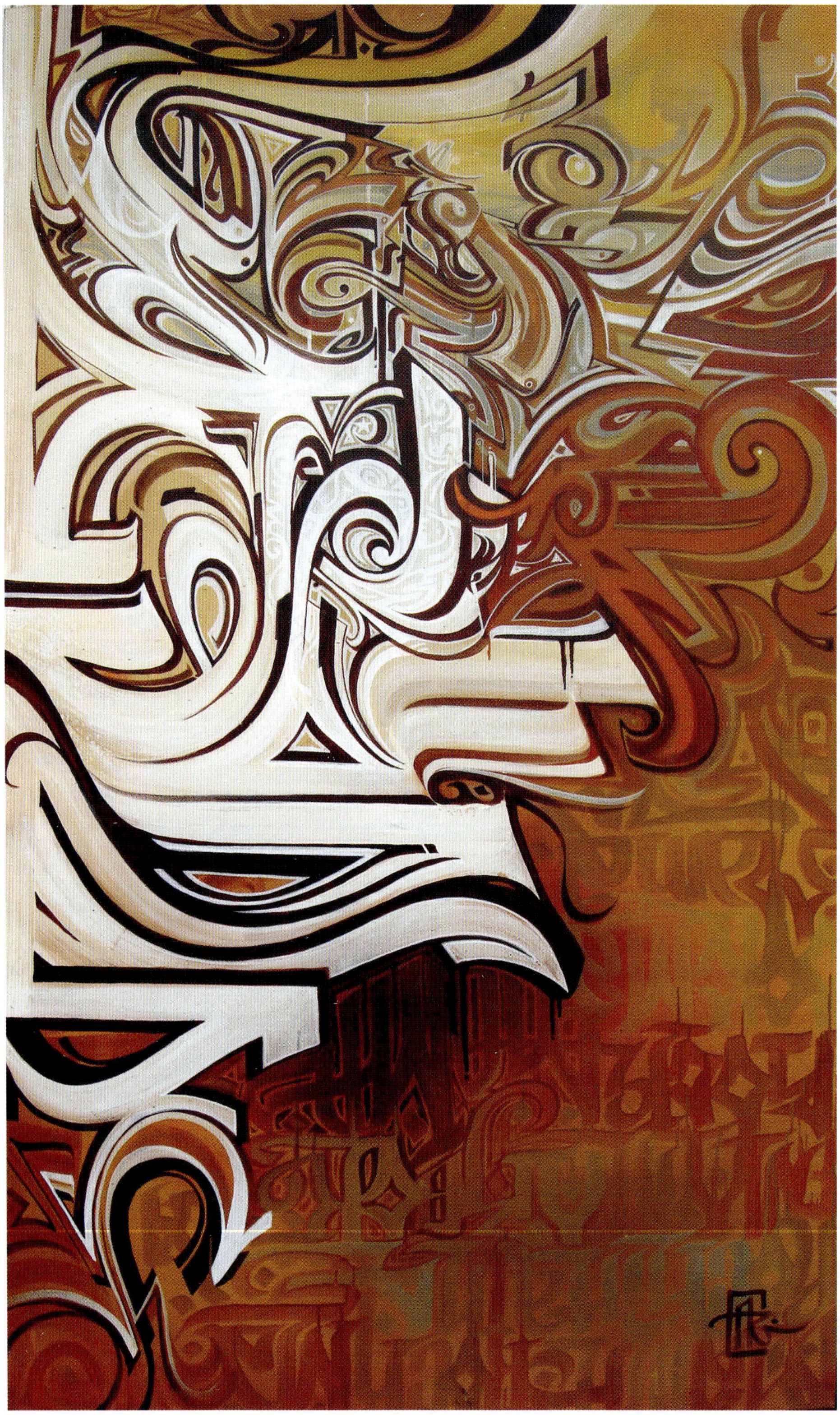

1

1. “Mama Rock”, ZEPHA, mixed media on canvas, 162 × 97 cm, 2009

2./3. "Insect dub" ZEPHA, silk-screen on paper, 50 × 30 cm, 2010

4. “La différence”, ZEPHA, mixed media on paper, 80 × 50 cm, 2008

5. “La reine & l'oiseau”, ZEPHA, mixed media on paper, 80 × 50 cm, 2008

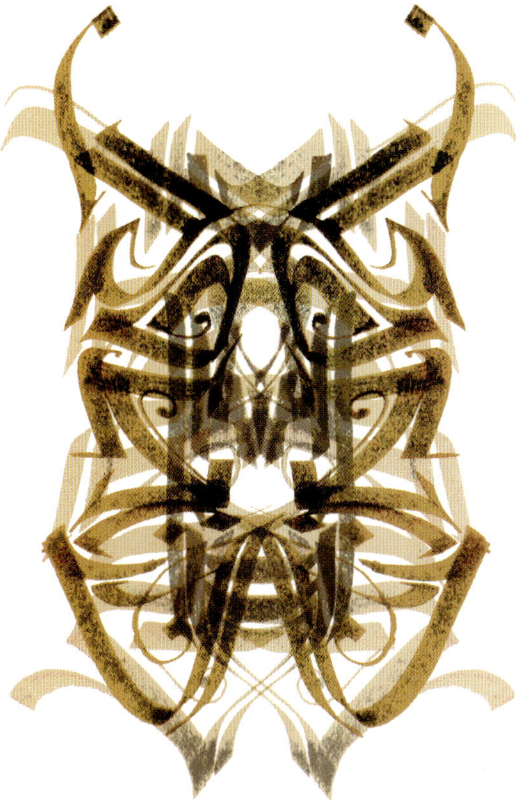

2

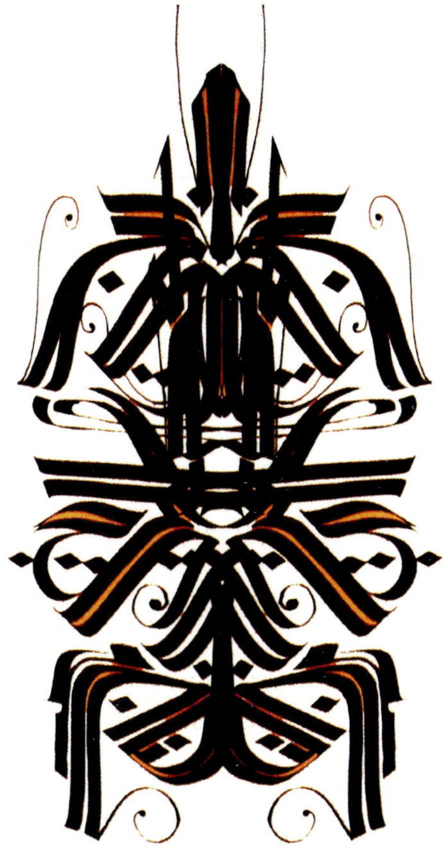

3

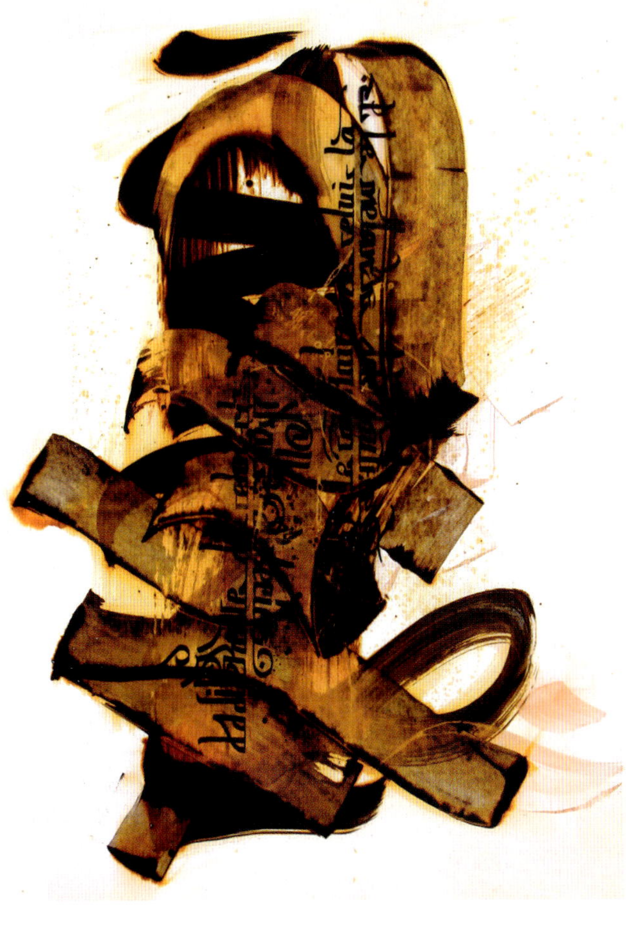

4

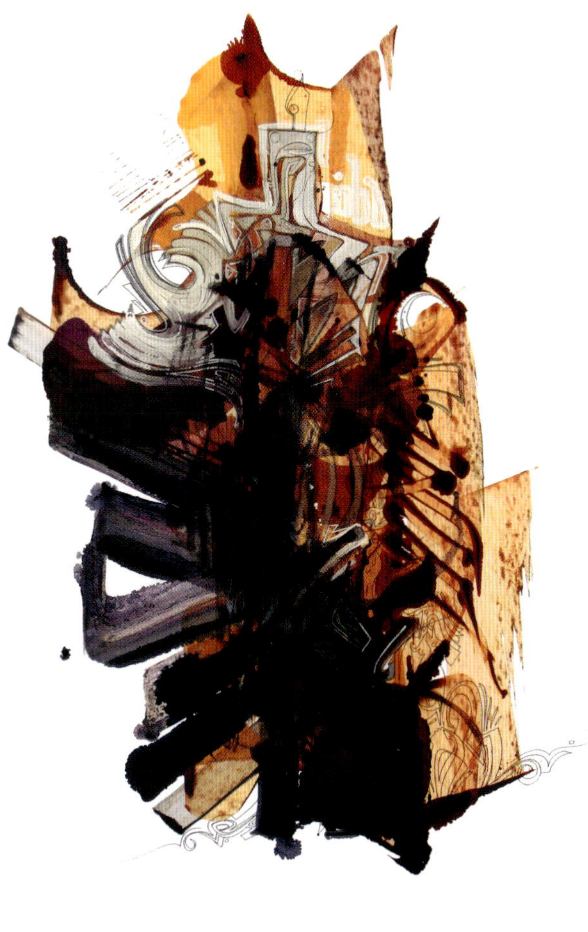

5

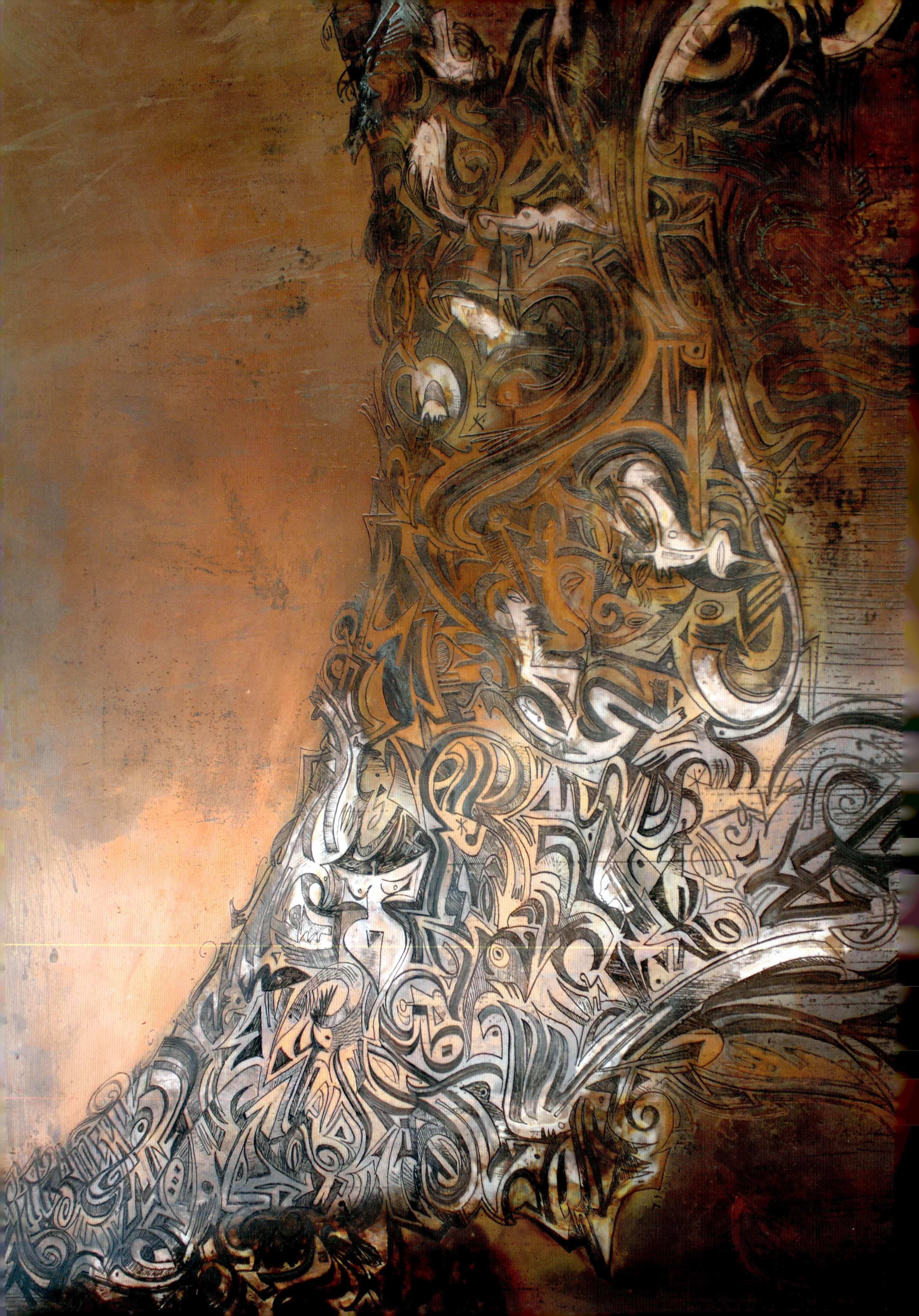

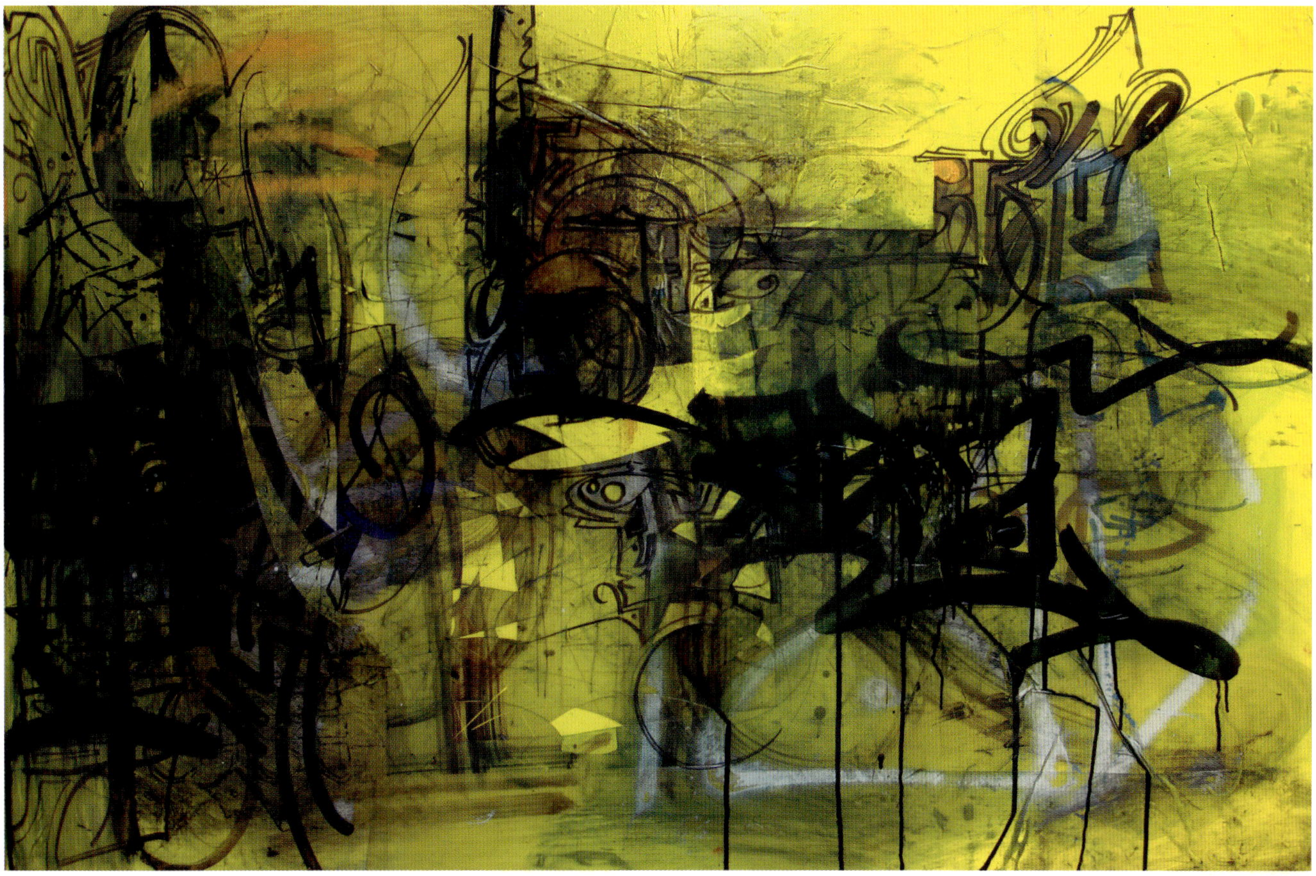

2

1. "Alpha & Omega", ZEPHA, etching on copper, 100 × 80 cm, 2009

2. "RER nostalgic", ZEPHA, mixed media, 90 × 120 cm, 2010

3. "Earth, wind and fire", ZEPHA silk-screen on paper, 25 × 35 cm, 2010

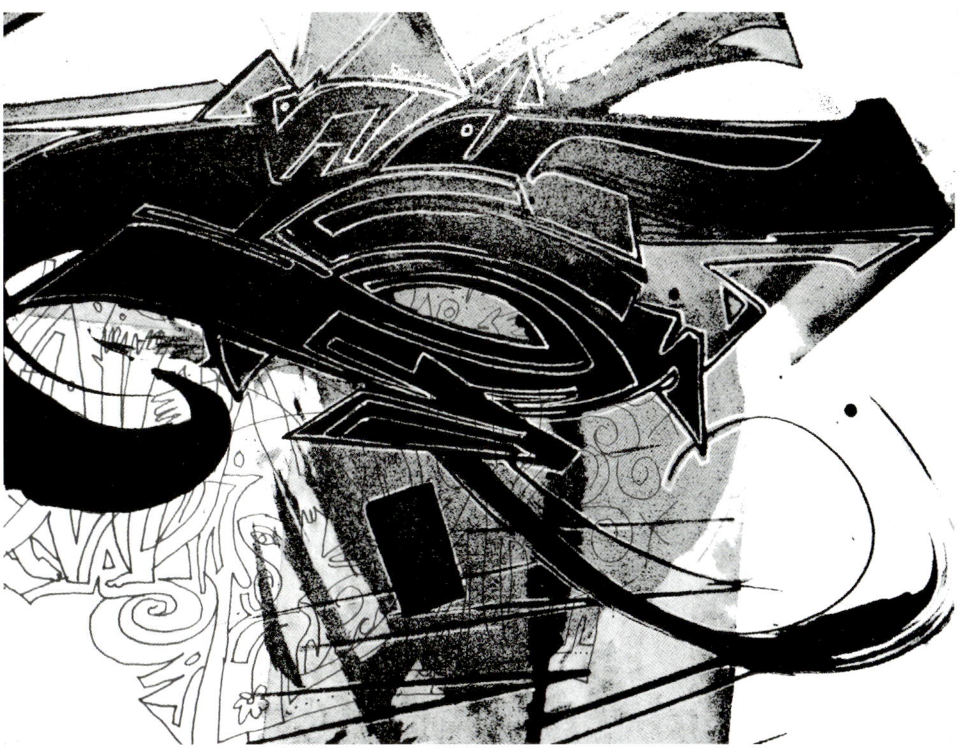

3

1

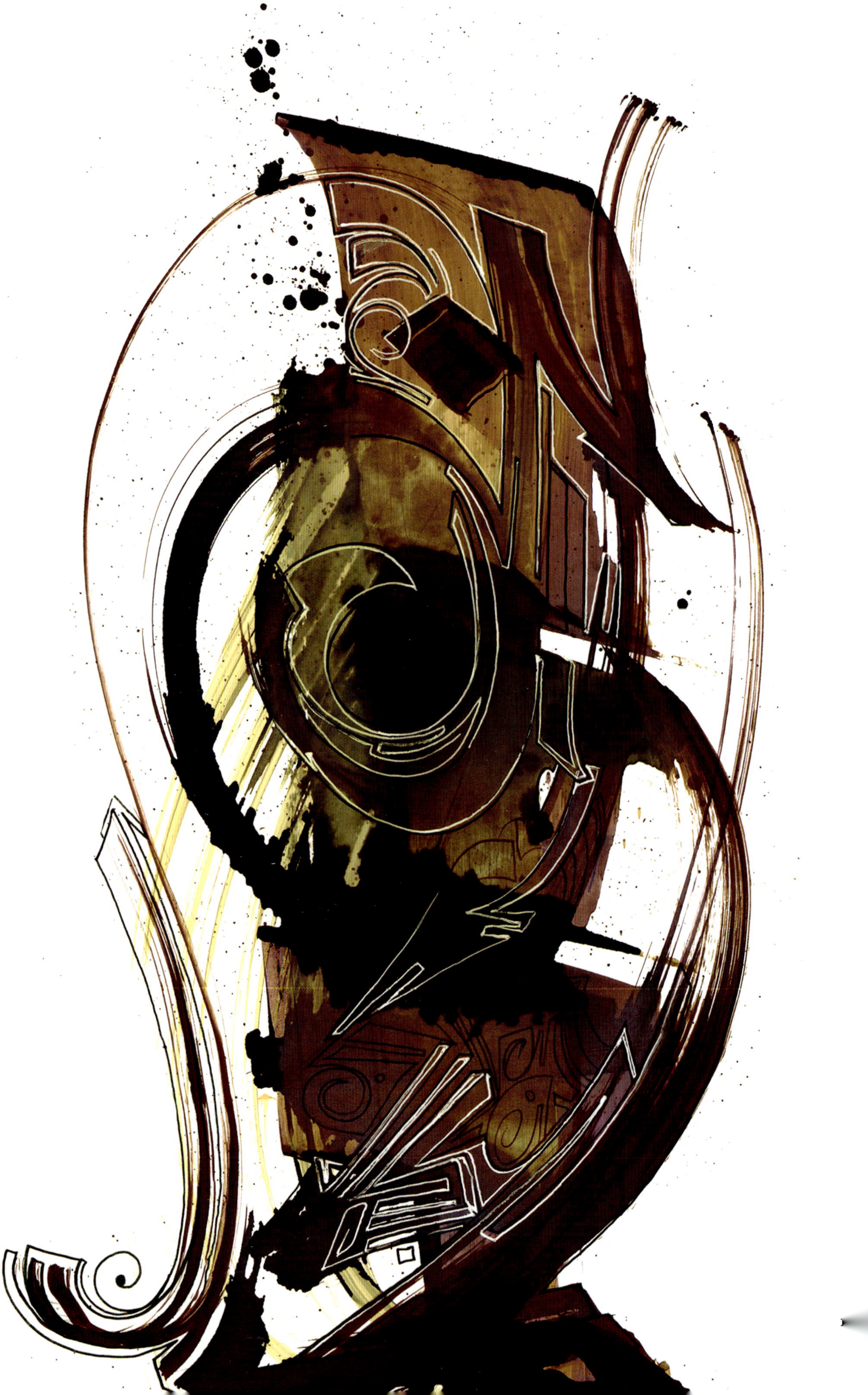

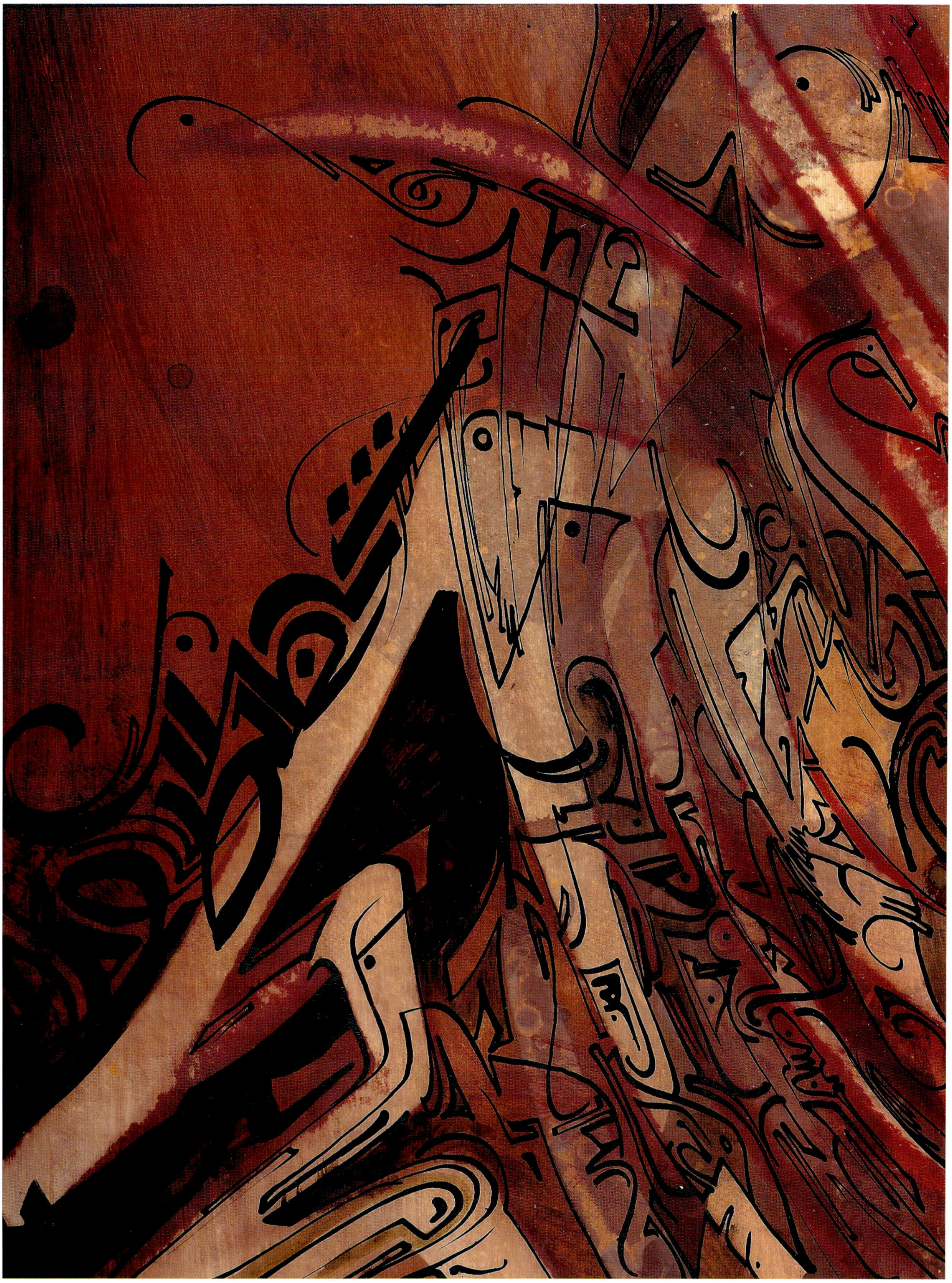

2

1. "Spiral Tribe", ZEPHA, mixed media on paper, 20×30 cm, 2008

2. "Crowned", ZEPHA, mixed media on paper, 15×20 cm, 2010

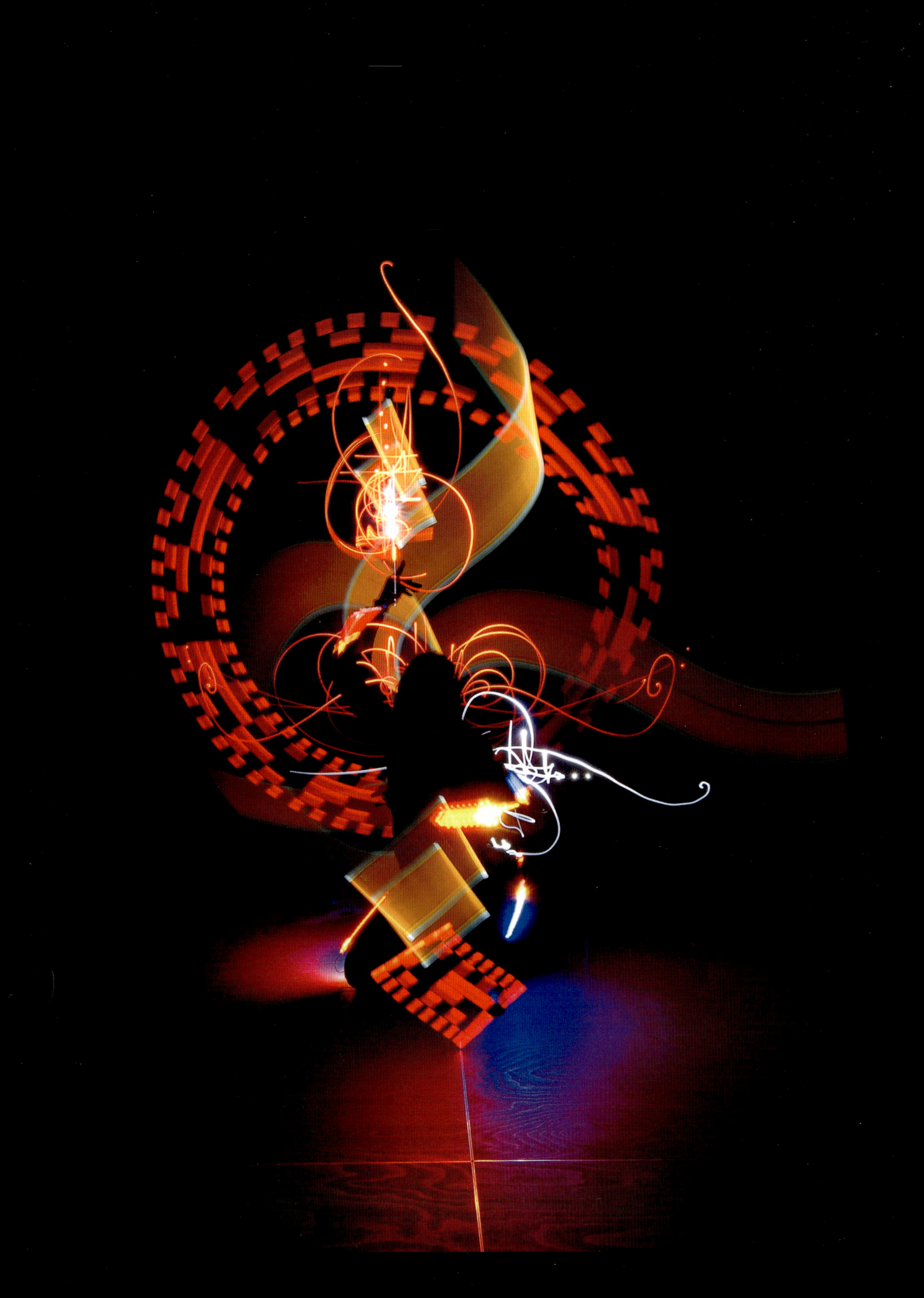

3·11
LightGraff
لايت غراف

The LightGraff collective takes the definition of the word 'photography' literally: to draw or to write (graphé) with light (photo). Only the camera is used to set the lines of light which are created with LEDs, neon lighting, laser beams, torches etc. They are combined with all kinds of filters and masks in order to get the desired results. These photos are taken at night, 'in situ', without any computer retouching.

Brusk (Light Writer), born 1976 in Lyon, France.
Coming from graffiti, I am very sensitive to Arabic calligraphy and it has become a huge source of inspiration. It's very demanding and needs a great deal of work, trials, research and rigor. It requires a lot of know-how concerning the purity of the forms. There is an inflexible balance in its composition, and its simplicity is difficult to obtain. There is a clear relationship between the calligraphy, graffiti and lightgraff in the body movements as much as in the final result (letter balancing, space and solid management, dynamism, repetition, purity).

Brusk's work has revolved around graffiti for more than fifteen years. He has explored many different areas of creativity using various media (walls, canvases, computer graphics, pieces of cloth, installations etc.) and has broadened this wide horizon even more with the new discipline of lightgraff.

Guillaume J. Plisson (Photographer), born in Lyon, France.
Guillaume is the co-founder of the photographer collective "Libre arbitre". He collaborates with both the French and international press, with some companies, institutions, news and advertising agencies. At the same time, he carries on artistic research, called "LightGraff", with calligraphers and graffiti artists. "LightGraff" has been the theme of several shows and performances, and he published the book "Lightgraff" in 2007, which helped him to let the calligraphers Hassan Massoudy and Julien Breton discover this research. Now, he continues to work with Brusk in the LightGraff collective, which unites various skills with the aim of making this artistic research evolve.

Olivar Premier (Light Tool Designer), born in the 20th century.
He creates the programmable tools for the collective with his interdisciplinary technical expertise.

1

1. LIGHTGRAFF, abstract arabesque calligraphy, Lyon, France, 2005

Following pages 162 & 163:

LIGHTGRAFF, abstract arabesque calligraphy, Caldeira du Bromo, Java, Indonesia, 2009

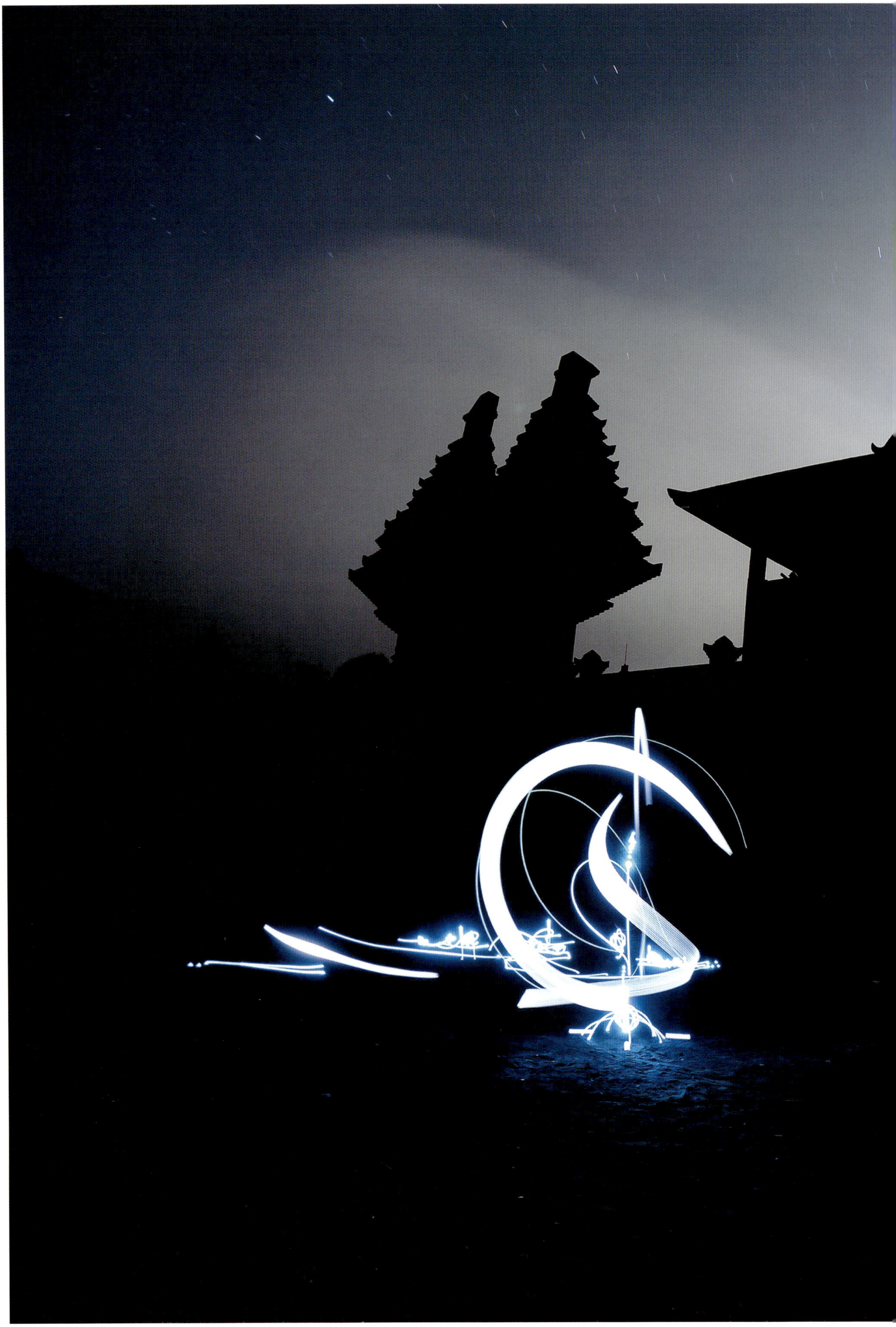

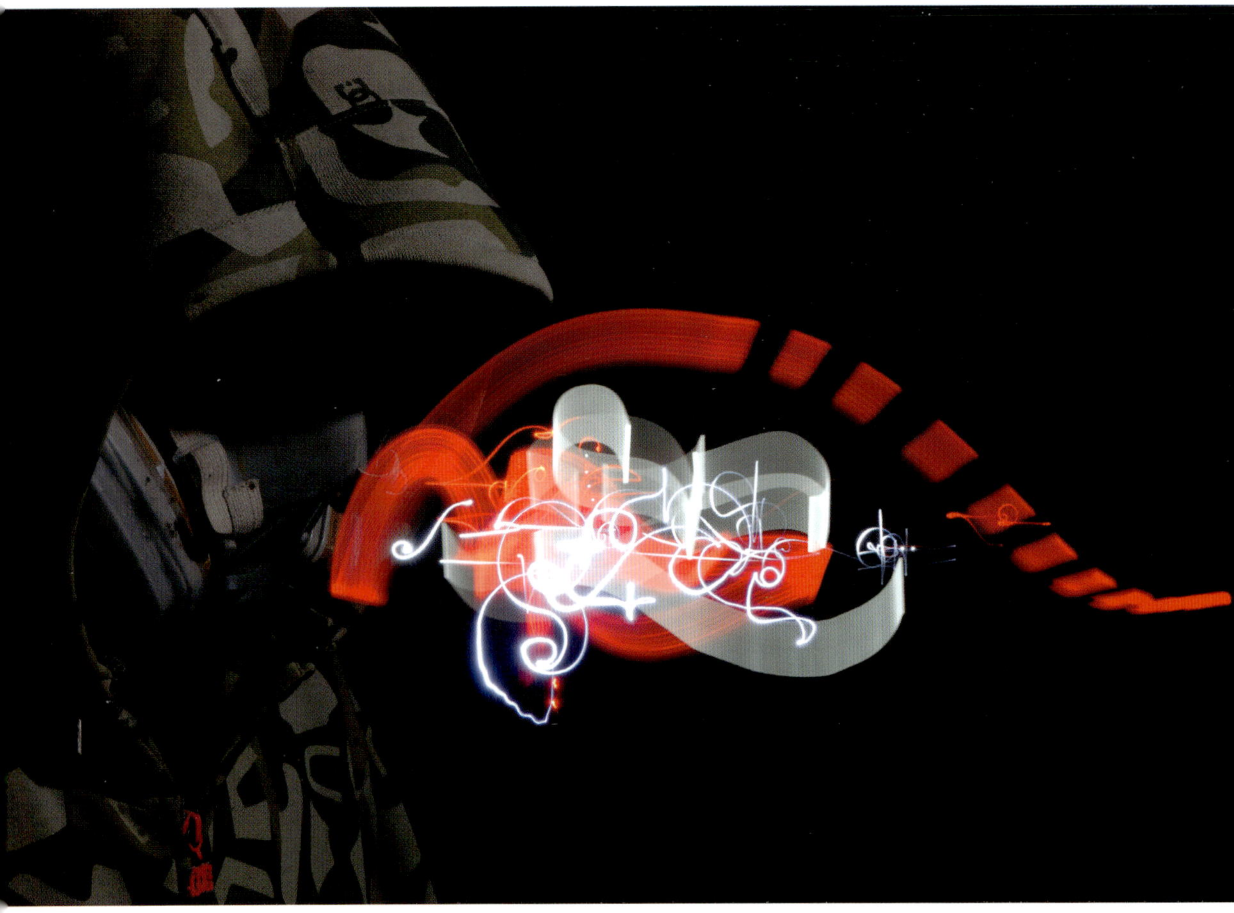

1

• **LIGHTGRAFF**
Brusk

Lightgraff is one of those mediums that uses contemporary technologies and allows us to reflect on what Picasso and Man Ray already experimented with: the relationship between light and image. Indeed, the digital medium and the materials we use comfort us in our discipline. A complex discipline, lightgraff is actually a sort of alchemy, a balance that results from two different but complementary practices: photography and 'light drawing'. The ray of light, a 'magical' tool imperceptible to the naked eye in motion, is impossible to decipher and very complex to handle.

Lightgraff rests on an ability to manage a 3-D space with depth, with landmarks such as body movement and what surrounds it. It is a discipline in itself. It requires an in-depth mastery of photography, detailed technical drawing, space management, and all of this with an added sense of freedom. Everything is based on a time exposure from thirty seconds to thirty minutes — which allows one to project a certain choreography reflected in a series of precise movements. Just like a spray can or brush, light has its own codes and characteristics, and of course its depiction is very adaptable. From its style to its thickness, from its intensity to its color, everything is adjustable.

It is with and through this wide range of graphical possibilities that we start looking for new places, new conquests that will challenge us and give us something to react to. Originating from graffiti, it is very valuable to leave a trace this way during our visit, in more or less atypical places. Once the photographer has set up and exposure time is agreed, we 'take possession' of the space. It's about telling a story, letting others experience that exact moment of the photograph, with all the emotions felt during the lapse of time between the beginning and end of the shot.

1. LIGHTGRAFF, abstract arabesque calligraphy, Lyon, France, 2008

2. LIGHTGRAFF, abstract arabesque calligraphy, Aix-en-provence, France, 2009

3. LIGHTGRAFF, abstract arabesque calligraphy, Lyon, France, 2009

Following pages 162 & 163:

LIGHTGRAFF, abstract arabesque calligraphy, Tanah Lot, Bali, Indonesia, 2009

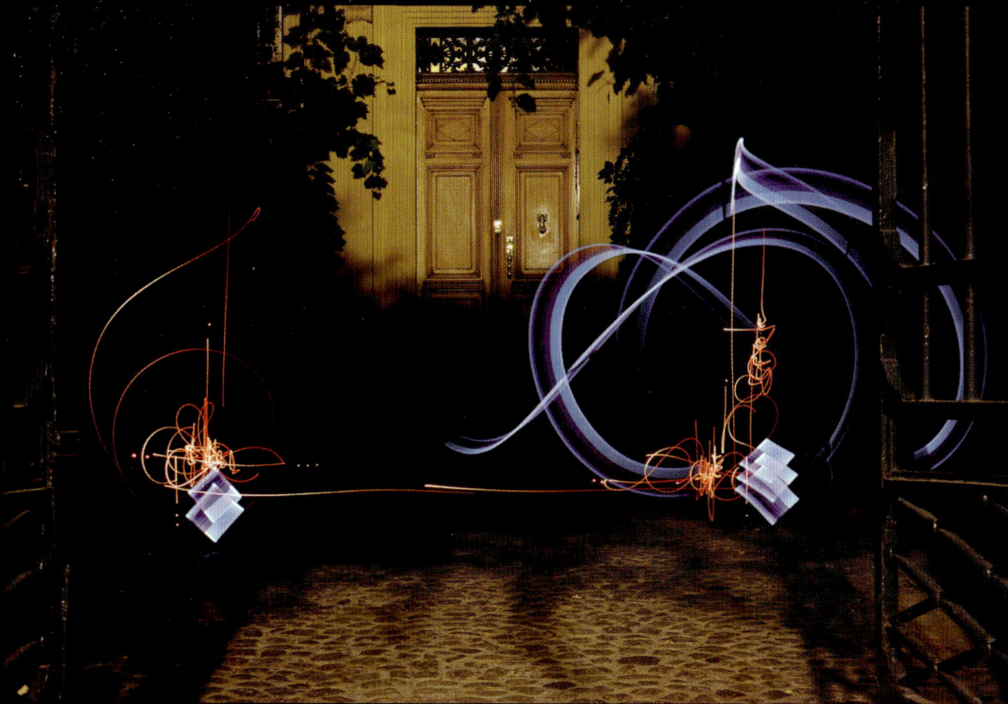

2

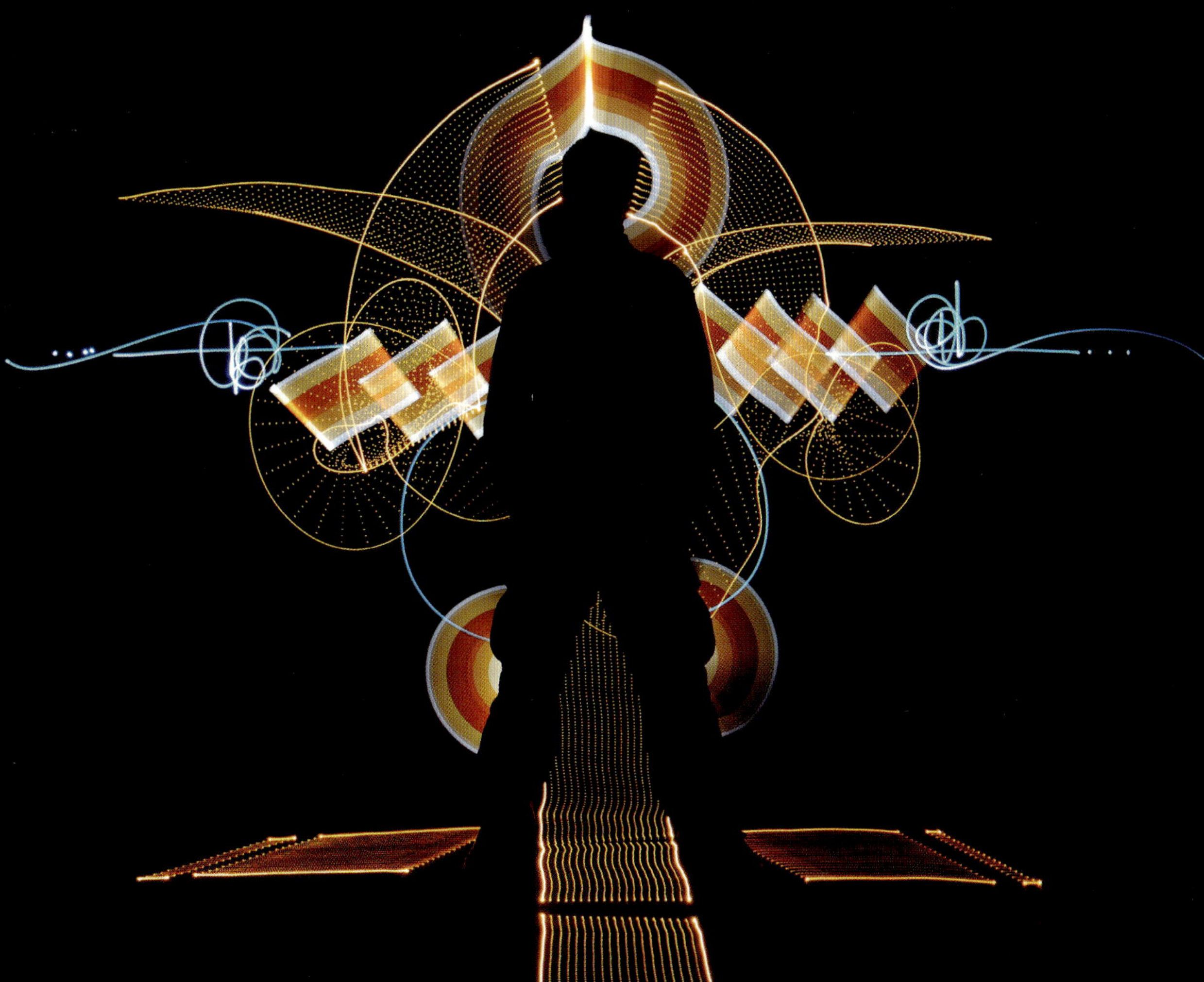

3

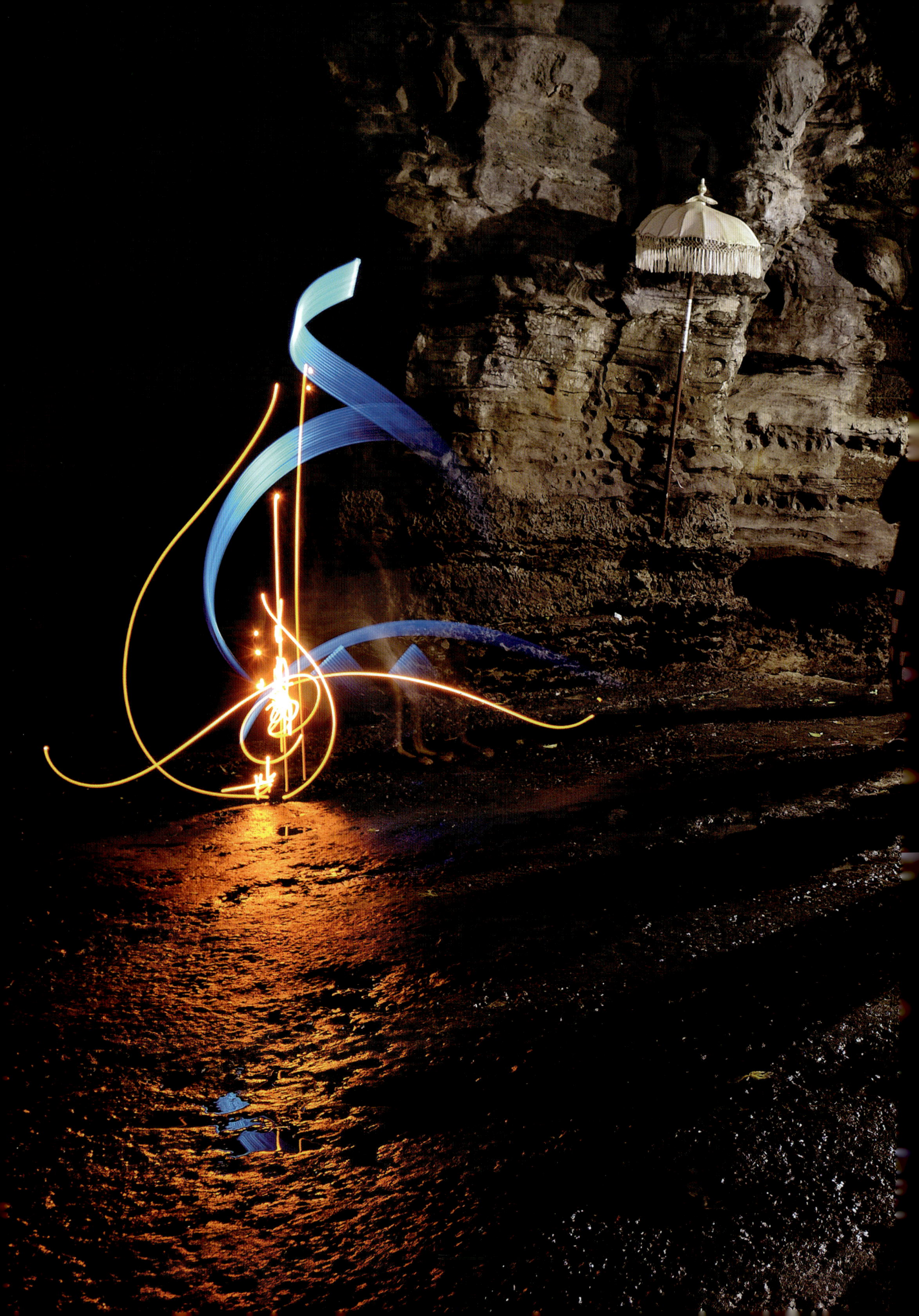

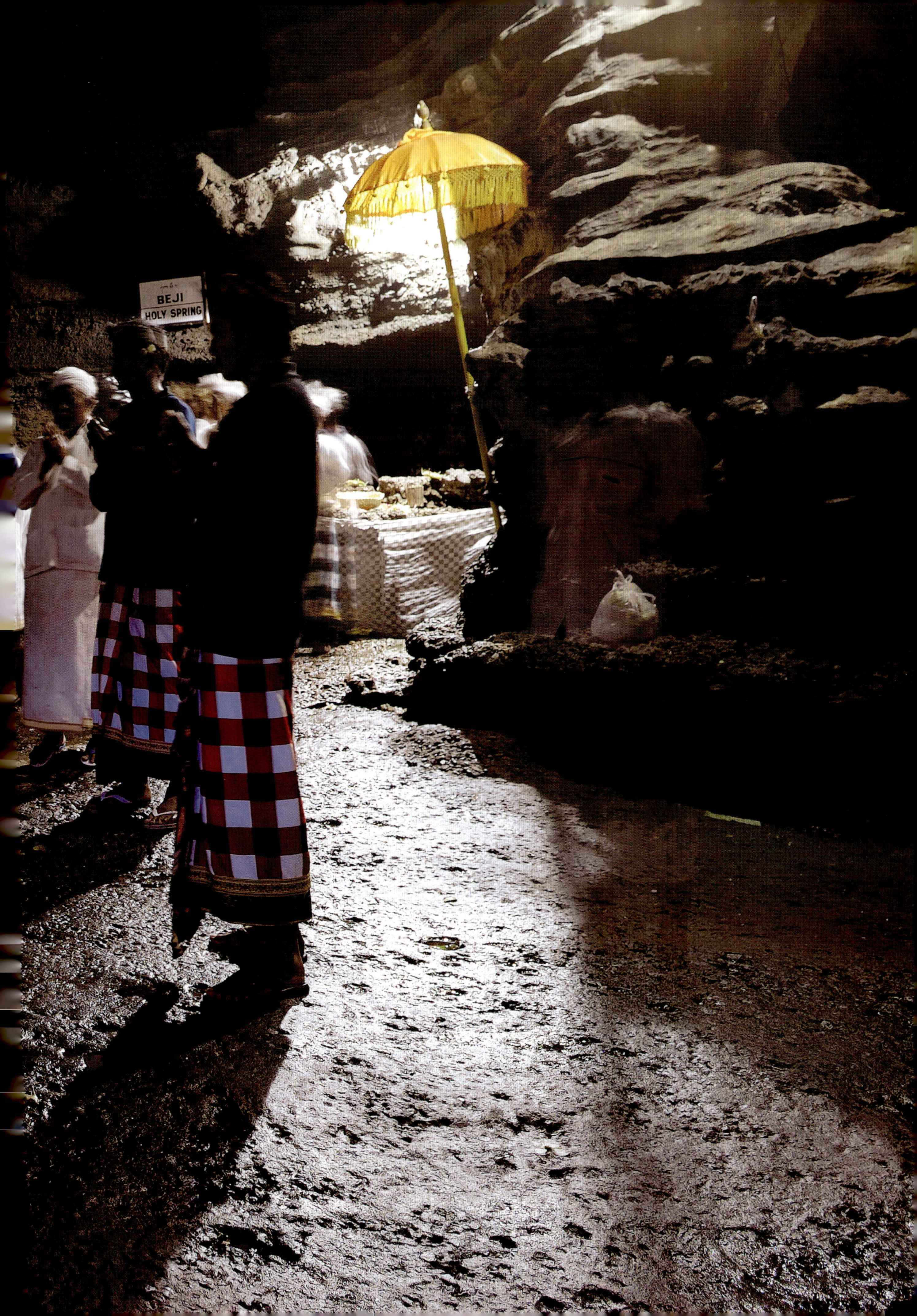
BEJI
HOLY SPRING

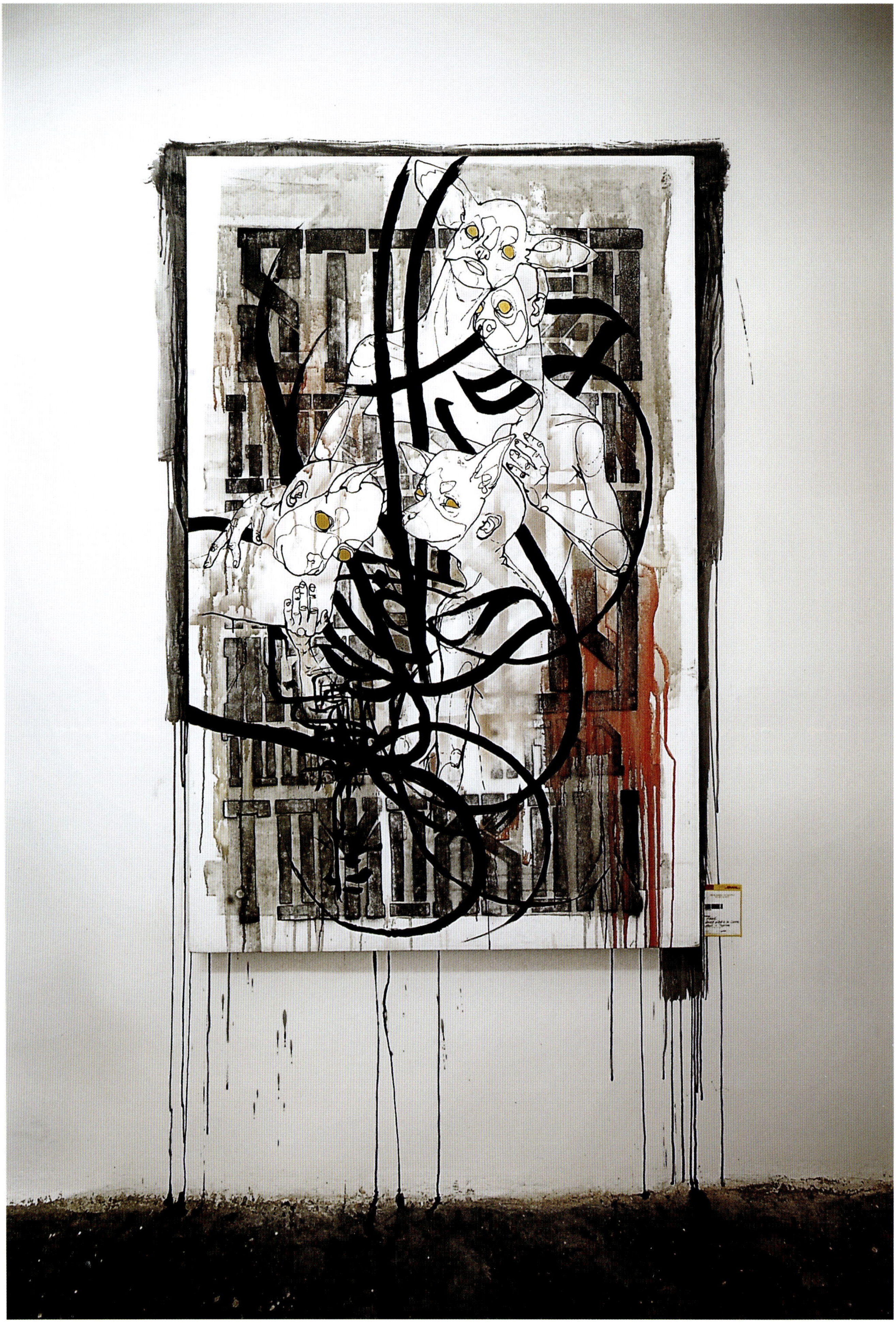

1

3·12
Blouzaat
بلوزات

Blouzaat is a cross-cultural, cross-media project, started by a group of artists from Jordan and Germany. Their frustration with the utter lack of an urban art scene in Amman provoked them to contemplate an alternative artistic culture through which artists can experiment freely and share experiences, exploring urban art and design through canvas, walls, silk-screen, clothing, and books. Their aim is not only to explore the artistic scene in the area, but also to introduce urban art by tapping into culture, music, and any other form of self-expression, building a new kind of creative community.

Ahmad Sabbagh, born 1980 in Amman, Jordan. Ahmad Sabbagh studied graphic design at the Applied Science University and graduated in 2002. After training for five years with the artists Ahmad Shawish and Husni Abu Krayyem, Sabbagh created Blouzaat. Experimenting with Arabic typography, Sabbagh aims to introduce a new visual language as well as facilitate the positioning of Arabic typography in an art form, working on "a style that is different than the common practices of calligraphy and Arabic type".

Typism aka Michael Schinköthe, born in 1978 in Germany. Typsim started experimenting with street art in 2004 after he met Akut. To merge different techniques such as conventional graphic design, silk-screen printing and urban techniques is his passion. He studied visual communication at the Bauhaus University in Weimar, Germany. Attracted by the experimental promise of the urban scene and identity of Amman, Typsim moved to Jordan in 2005 and became art director of Blouzaat.

Akut aka Falk Lehmann, born in 1977 in Germany. In 1999 Akut, Case, Tasso and Rusk formed the graffiti crew Maclaim. In 2004 Akut and Hera merged to become Herakut and the duo developed a unique and world renowned style. Akut studied visual communication at the Bauhaus University in Weimar, Germany. It is there that Typism and Akut joined to work out different ideas. In 2007 Typism and Akut went to Jordan to start up Blouzaat.

1. Typism & Akut, Arabic calligraphy by Hussein Al-Azaat, mixed media on canvas, 160 × 90 cm, Khuraif exhibition, Weimar, Germany, 2008

خُريف

2. "Storytelling", TYPISM, mixed media on canvas, 60 × 60 cm, Khuraif exhibition, Weimar, Germany, 2008

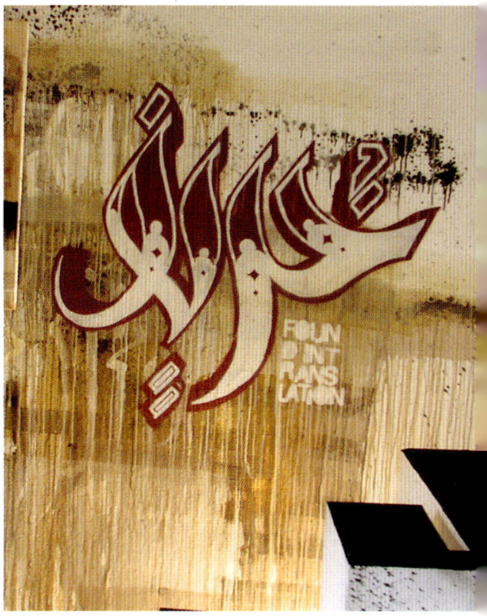

2

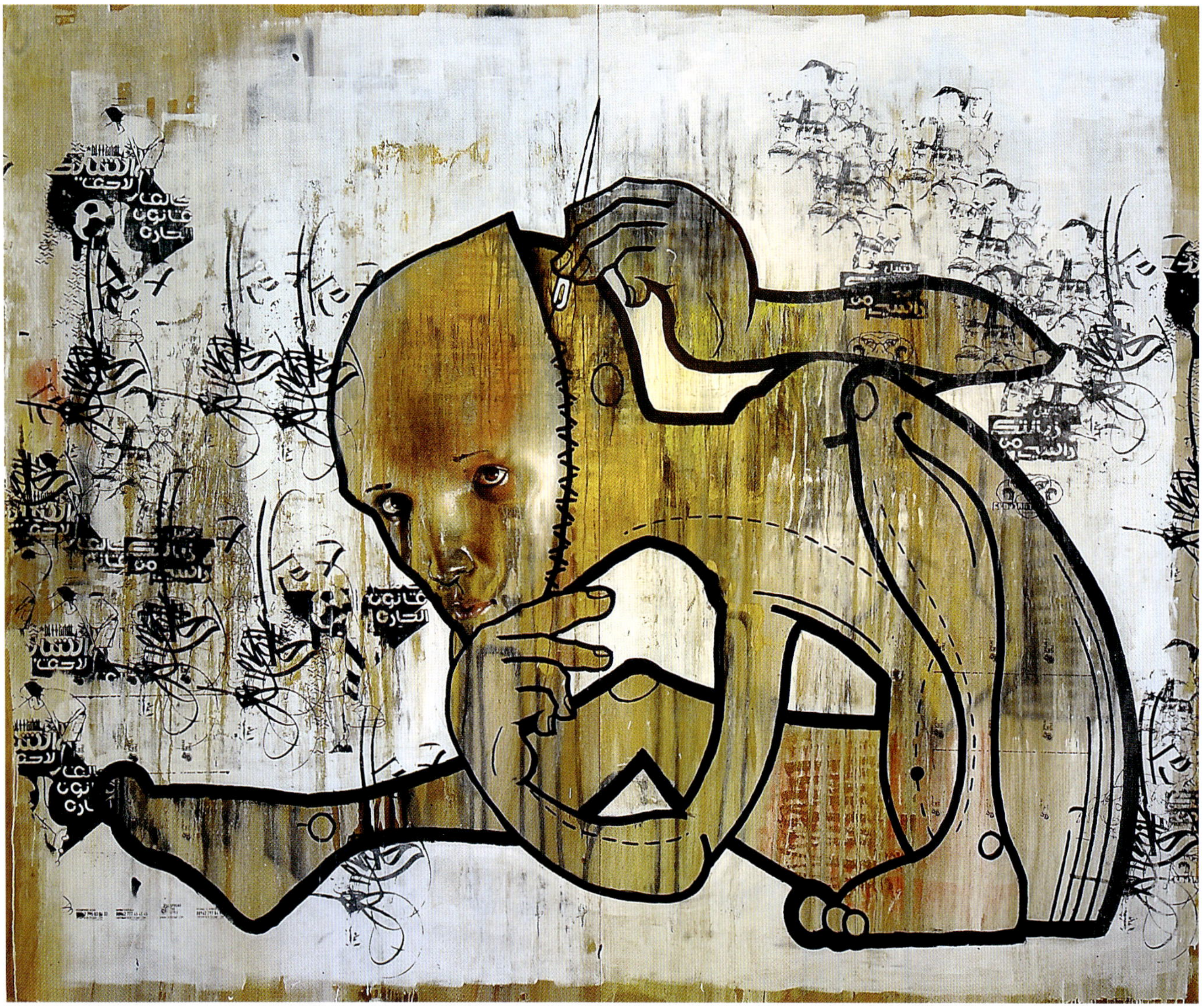

1

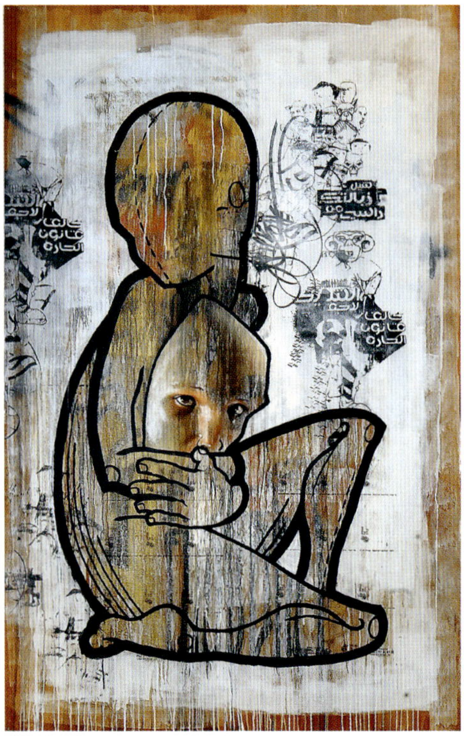

2

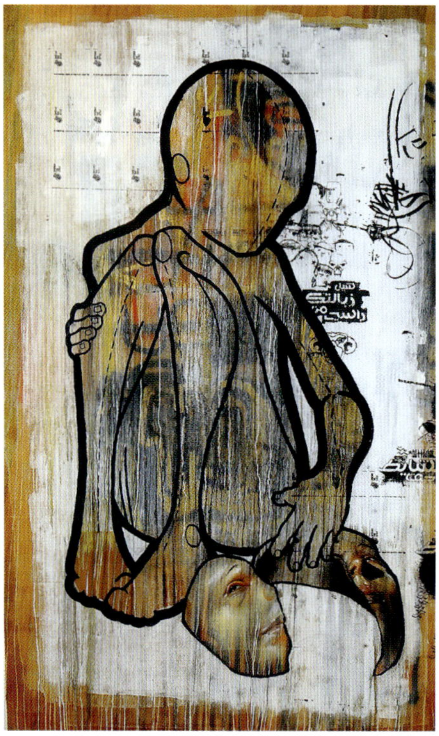

3

1./2./3. Typism & Akut, "Expired... Dying New World Exhibition", mixed media on wood, (1. 244 × 200 cm, 2./3. 122 × 200 cm), Amman, Jordan, 2009

يا غنماتي قولوا وراي
4. "My sheep, repeat after me!", Ahmad Sabbagh, "Cattle Republic Exhibition", Amman, Jordan, 2010

سمرة (كذا) ونغشة ولا بيضة (كذا) ودفشة
5. Palestinian proverb, Ahmad Sabbagh, mixed media on wood, 95 × 122 cm, "Cattle Republic Exhibition", Amman, Jordan, 2010

من في الداخل من في الخارج
6. "Who is in who is out", Ahmad Sabbagh, silk-screen print on canvas, 29 × 29 cm, "Expired... Dying New World Exhibition", Amman, Jordan, 2009

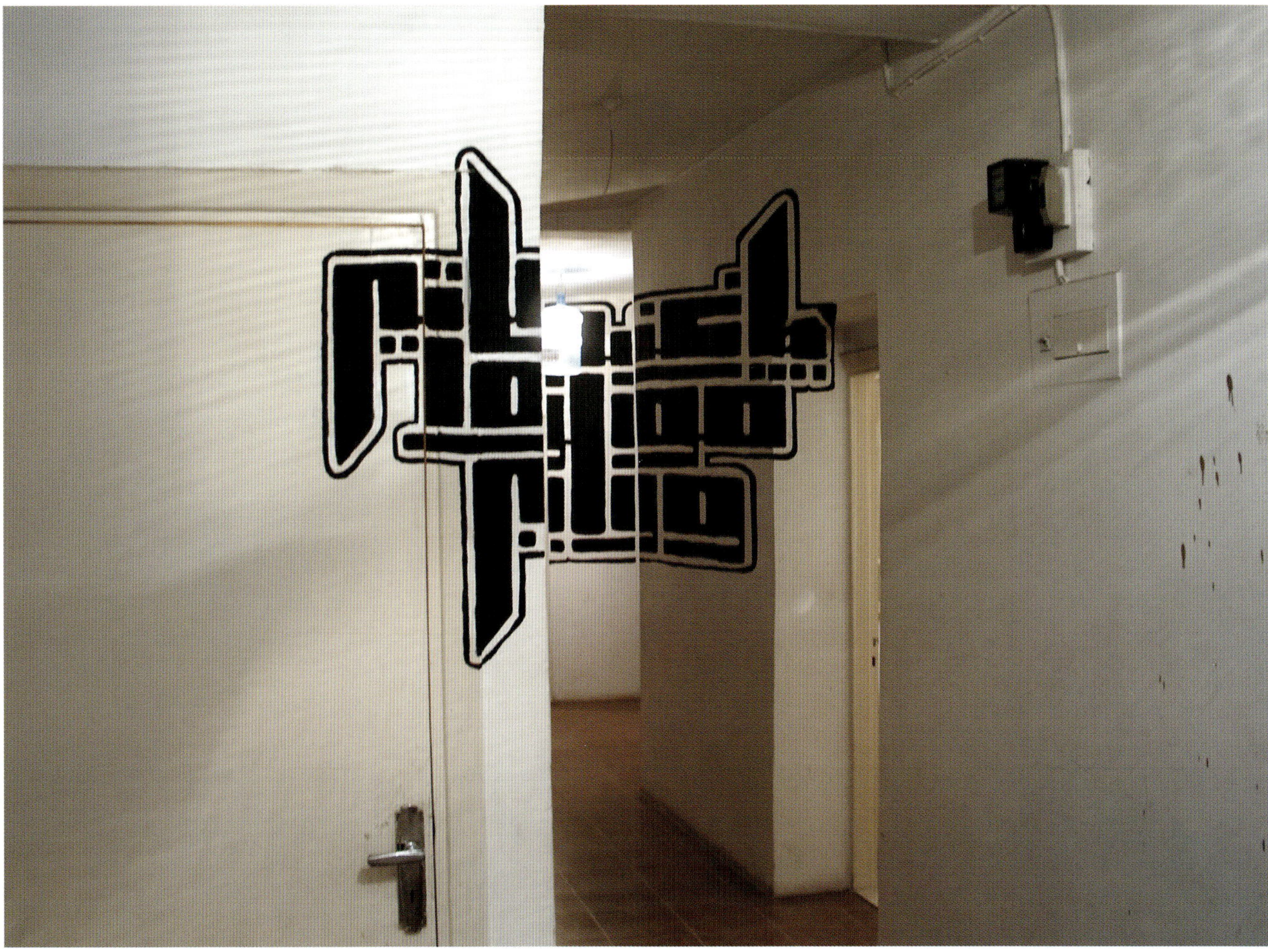

4

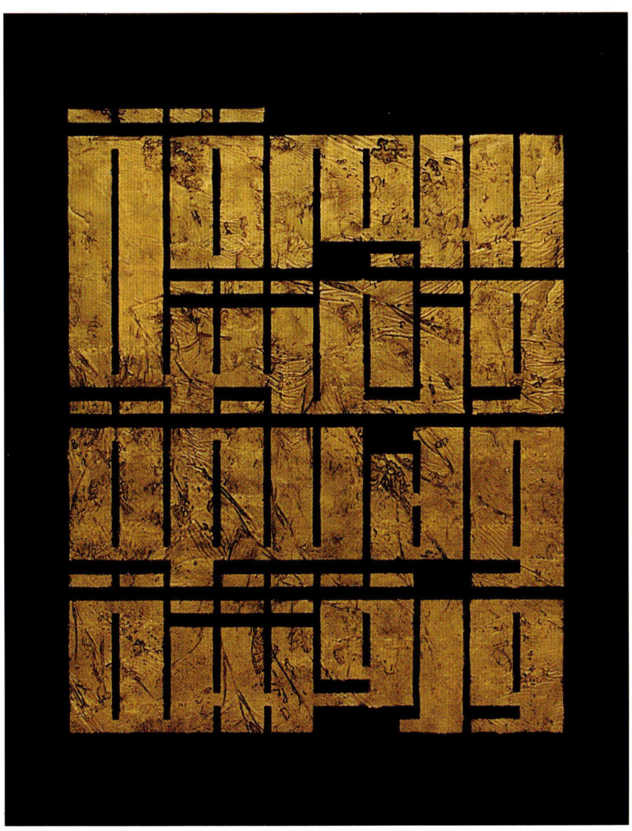

5

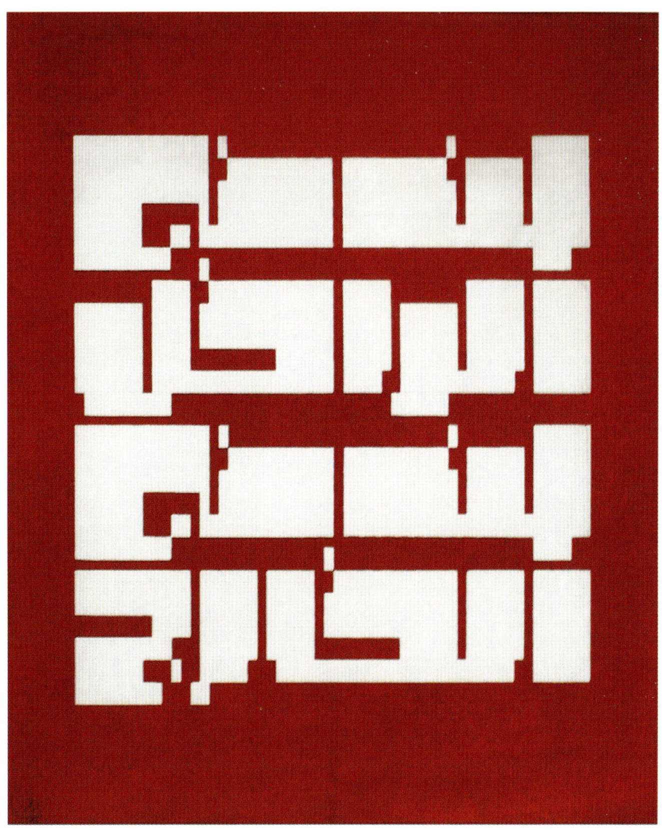

6

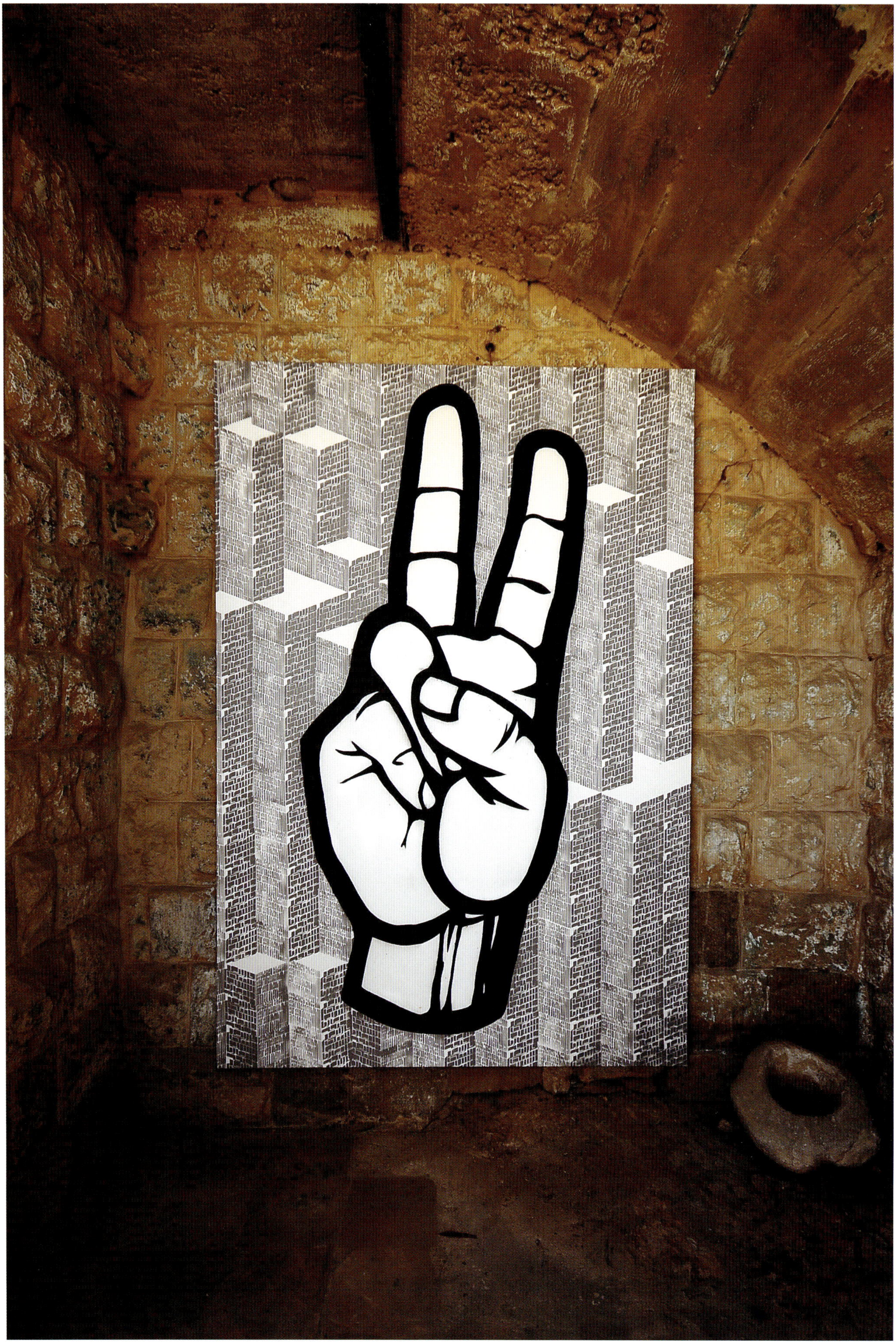

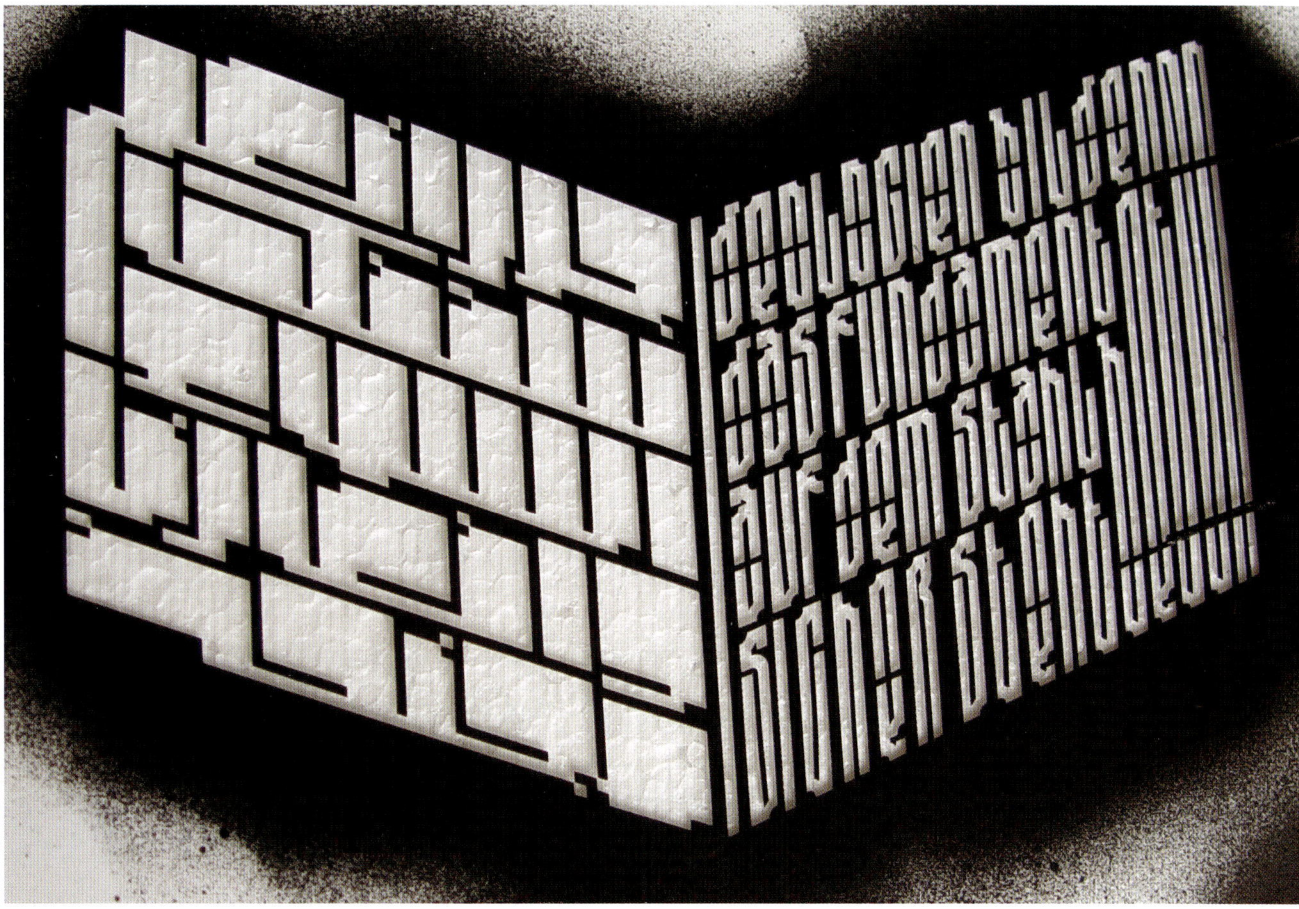

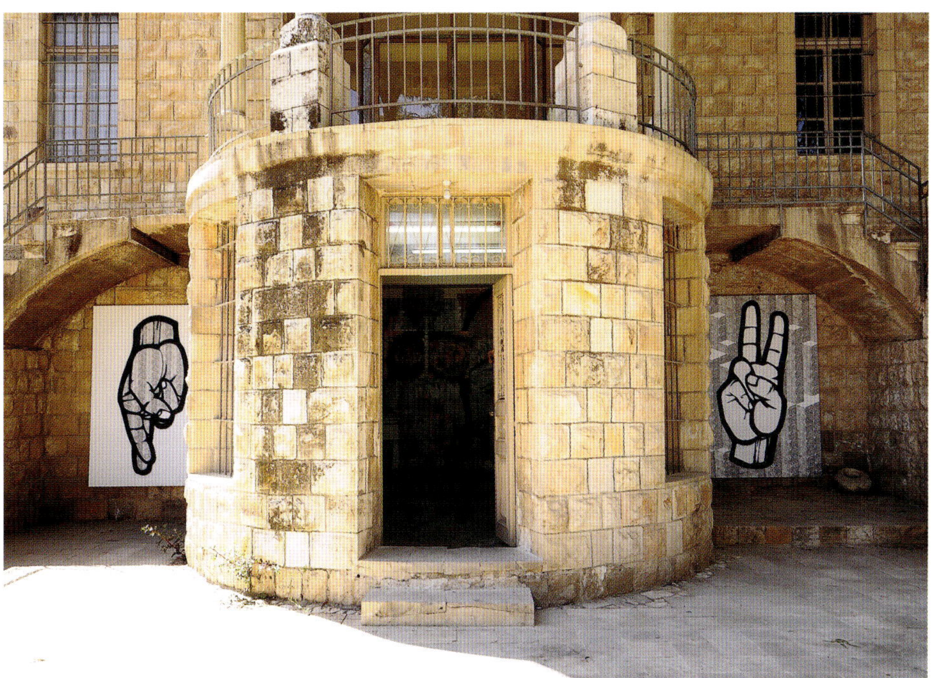

This work by Ahmad Sabbagh, Typism and Keos (aka Alexander Frank) speaks of the historic correlation that the Separation Wall built in Palestine has with the Berlin Wall.

One hand is making the victory (or peace) sign and the other is crossing its fingers, which symbolizes telling a lie. Stenciled letters make up the walls in the paintings. While the peace sign has overcome the walls, forcing the stencils into the background, the crossed fingers carry them in their hand.

The two sides of the stenciled letters, one in Arabic, the other in German, say:
Left: جدرانكم سقفها السماء وافكارنا مجنحة (Your walls seek the sky and our thoughts have wings). Right: "Ideologien bilden das Fundament auf dem Stahlbeton sicher steht" (Ideologies form the groundwork on which reiforced concrete stands securely).

Acrylic, spray paint on canvas, each 160 × 220 cm. "Expired... Dying New World Exhibition", Amman, Jordan, 2009

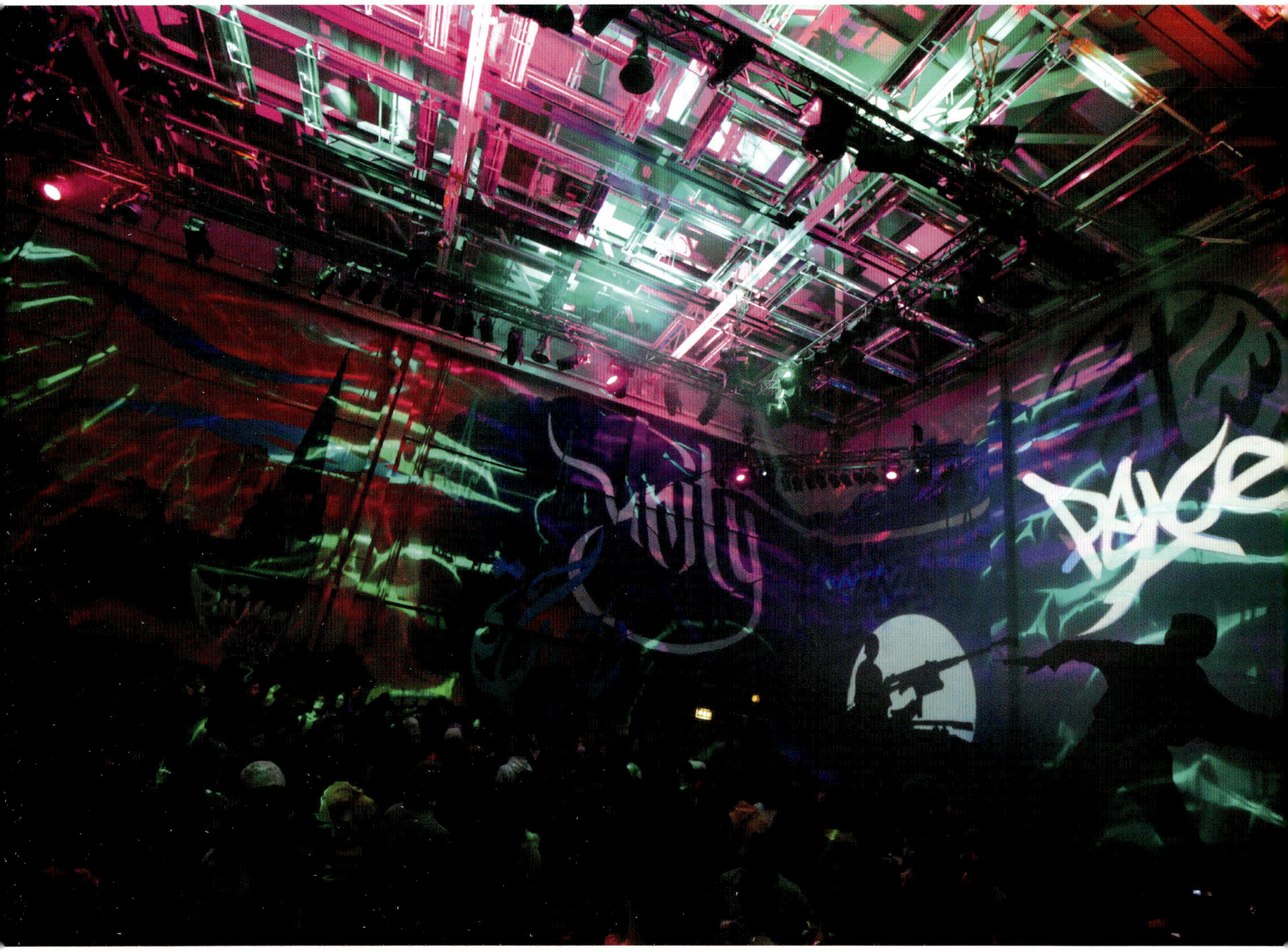

2

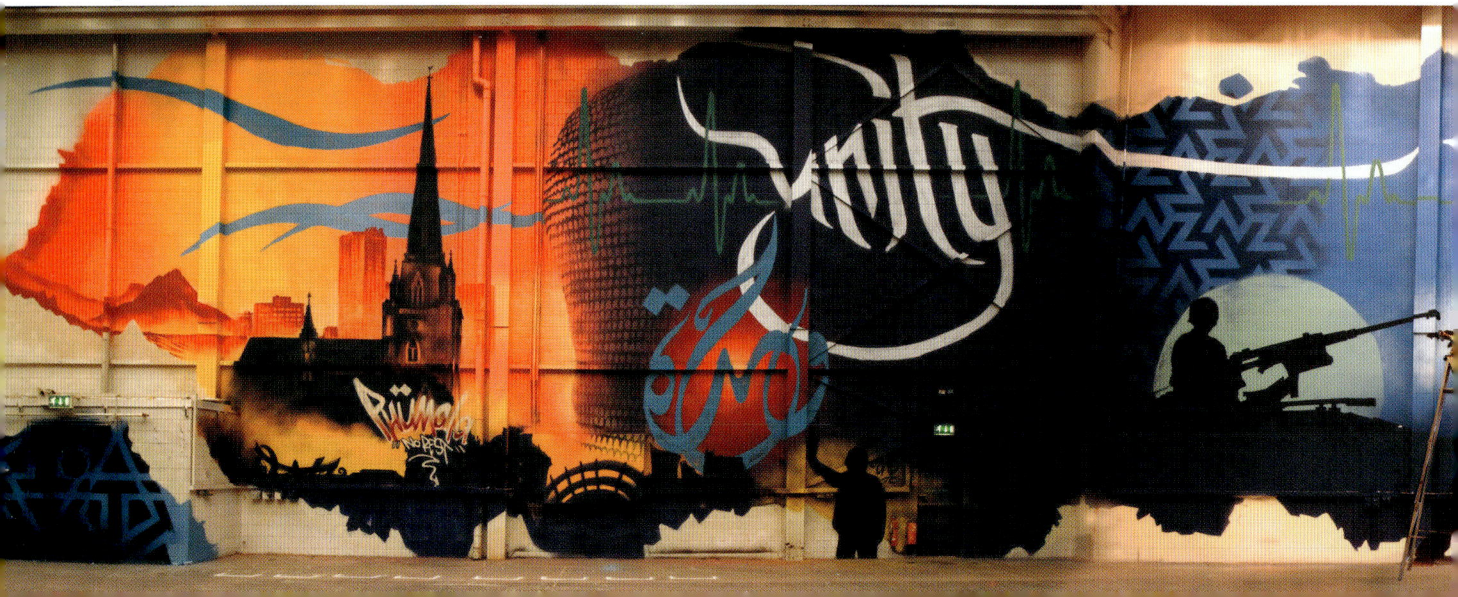

3·13
Mohammed Ali / Aerosol Arabic
محمد علي
آيروسول عربي

Born 1978 in Birmingham, UK

Mohammed Ali was drawn to the graffiti world in the early 80s, inspired by the subway art movement, and like many kids living in the UK was involved with the style writing scene. It was first after his newfound faith in Islam that he began to fuse his style writing with the grace and eloquence of sacred Islamic script and patterns.

According to Mohammed Ali, graffiti stands in clear contrast to Islamic art, but he sees that both share some fascinating parallels. For example, their focus on the use of words, or the fact that calligraphers from the Islamic art world often remained anonymous, like graffiti writers do today. But their art wasn't and isn't about self-glorification, it is rather about the word itself, and the power of words. Mohammed began exploring simple messages which at heart were still words, but words which pointed beyond the 'self', with a deeper message that spoke to the public, and was relevant to the wider society.

The art of Mohammed Ali has gone across the globe, with murals from New York to London to Melbourne. His work challenges the oft-heard term "clash of civilizations" with his fusion of graffiti writing and Islamic script, along with his conscious messages. He describes his work as "taking the best of both worlds" and bringing back to the forefront principles that are gradually fading away from our modern societies.

1. "Writing on The Wall" event opening, light projections on MOHAMMED ALI MURAL, The Rep Theatre, Birmingham, UK, 2010

حب، سلام، وحدة

2. "Unity, Peace, Love", MOHAMMED ALI, "Writing on The Wall event", The Rep Theatre, Birmingham, UK, 2010

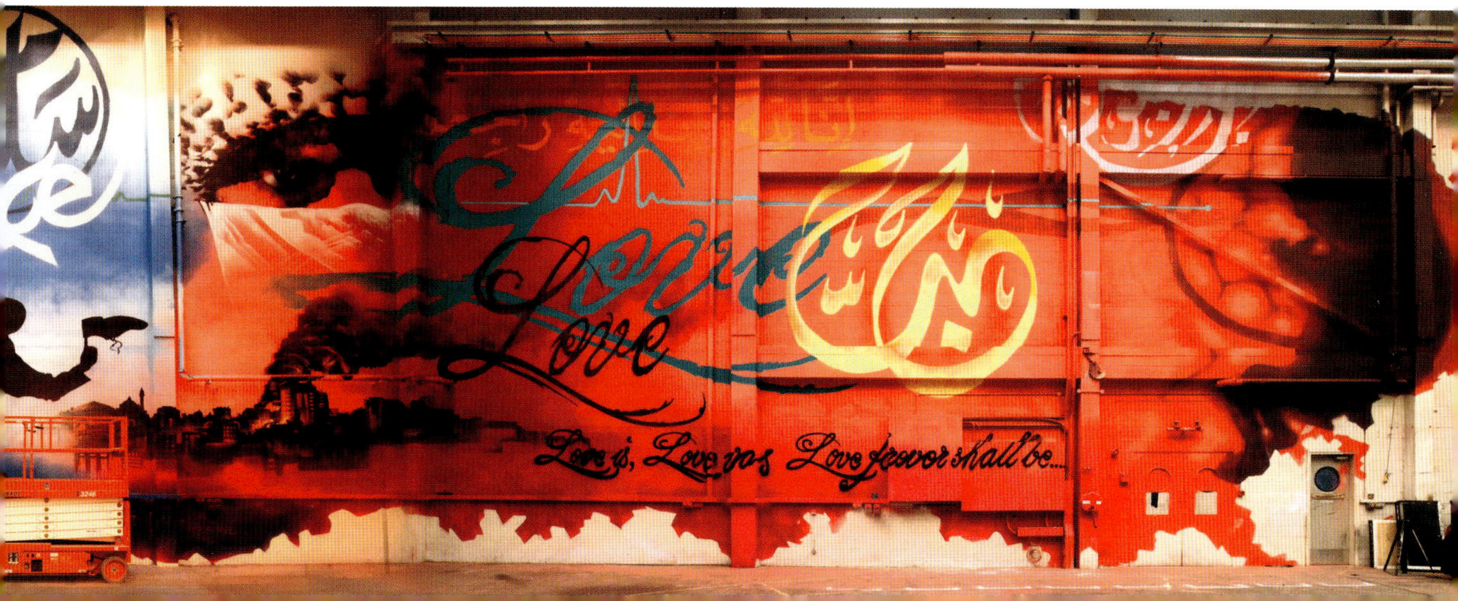

• **BUILDING BRIDGES WITH GRAFFITI ART**
Mohammed Ali

We hear government officials, academians and politicians talking about the problems of multiculturalism and community cohesion, but I feel they have left one resource untapped when it comes to finding solutions: art. In fact, I often make the bold statement that graffiti art has the power to change the world. Art that is bursting outside of conventional art spaces, outside of galleries, and is quite literally spilling onto the streets is an amazing means of connecting people. Murals I have painted on busy street corners have brought people together, as every day perhaps thousands ponder the messages of the art I create.

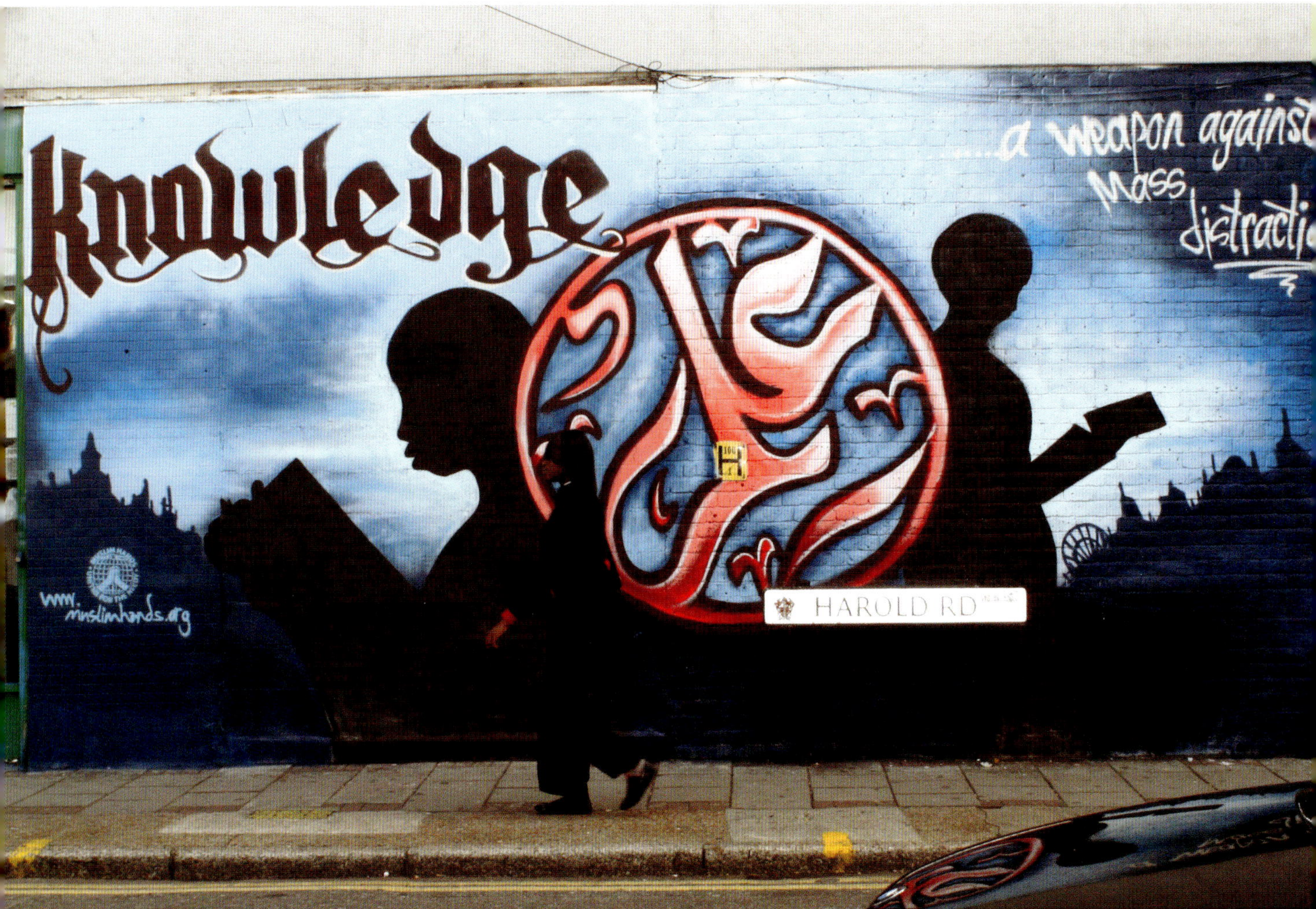

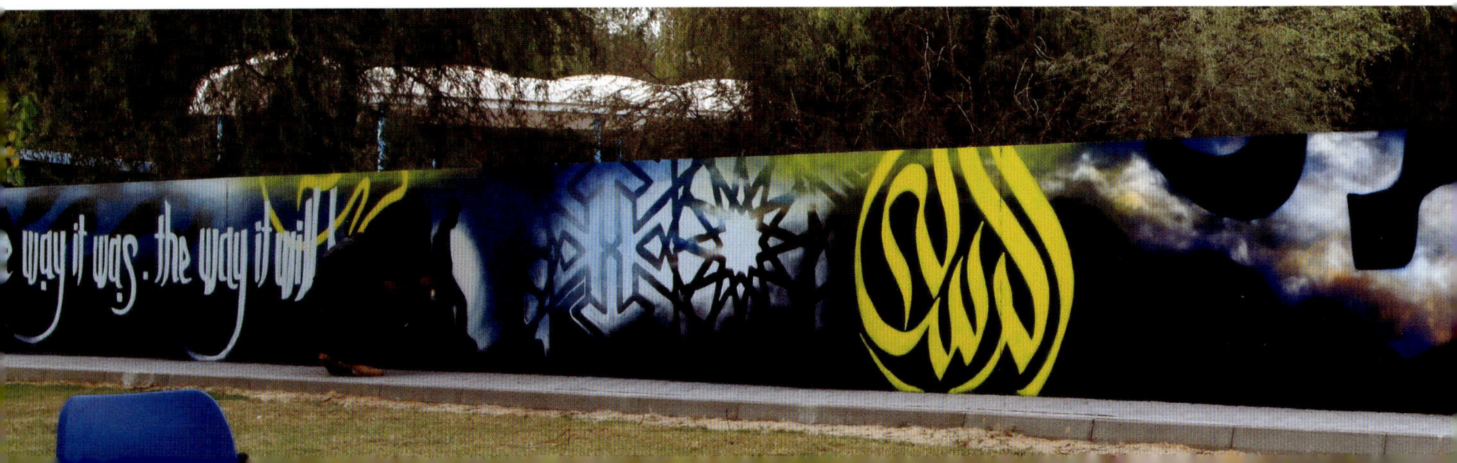

Those who have seen my work say it brings together the best of both worlds. My pieces are an amalgamation of two almost opposite extremes, in terms of art forms at least. I take street art, born on the streets of the West, and combine that with a sacred, classical style of Islamic script and patterns — introducing this art form in places where I have permission to paint.

This is my personal attempt at challenging the notion of the 'clash of civilizations'. The art I create actually merges two civilizations and communicates the unique message that we can be inspired by spirituality and faith, but that we should learn to apply these to modern life. We can deal with contemporary issues and connect with others in doing so. In the post-9/11 world, Islam has come under the spotlight and is often portrayed negatively by the media and misunderstood by non-Muslims. Amid the negativity, I feel encouraged to stick my neck out even further, go against the grain and express who I am without any insecurity hindering my efforts. Despite this hype about Islam, I feel good about being a Muslim living in the West. I can be inspired by my faith, yet also contribute to developing a harmonious society.

It's an important time to challenge these stereotypes and encourage real dialogue between ordinary people with different ideas, identities and backgrounds, not leave it to faith leaders sharing tea and biscuits. Art is one way of facilitating this dialogue. In my art, I convey principles — peace, justice, brotherhood and respect — that I believe are fading away from our modern societies, but which I highlight to make people aware that they do in fact share common principles. For the average Joe or Jane who travels to work in rush hour traffic, and for local residents who walk past a particular mural every day, I want the walls that carry my messages to come alive and remind people of these shared principles.

Man has forever told his story by carving or scratching his message onto a wall in a public space. Graffiti has been around for thousands of years, way before the spray painted subways of New York. So before we throw out the baby with the bathwater and view graffiti as something that is only for mindless youth, I ask everyone to stop and realize that we are all graffiti artists. It is an innate part of man's nature. After all, when we are on the phone and we have a pen in our hand, what do we do? We create our own graffiti.

Let's harness the energy and power of the spray can, and use our public spaces to convey something colorful and meaningful to deal with some of the problems we face in the world today.

علم
1. "Knowledge", MOHAMMED ALI, London, 2009

الرسالة
2. "The message", MOHAMMED ALI, Tashkeel Gallery, Dubai, 2010

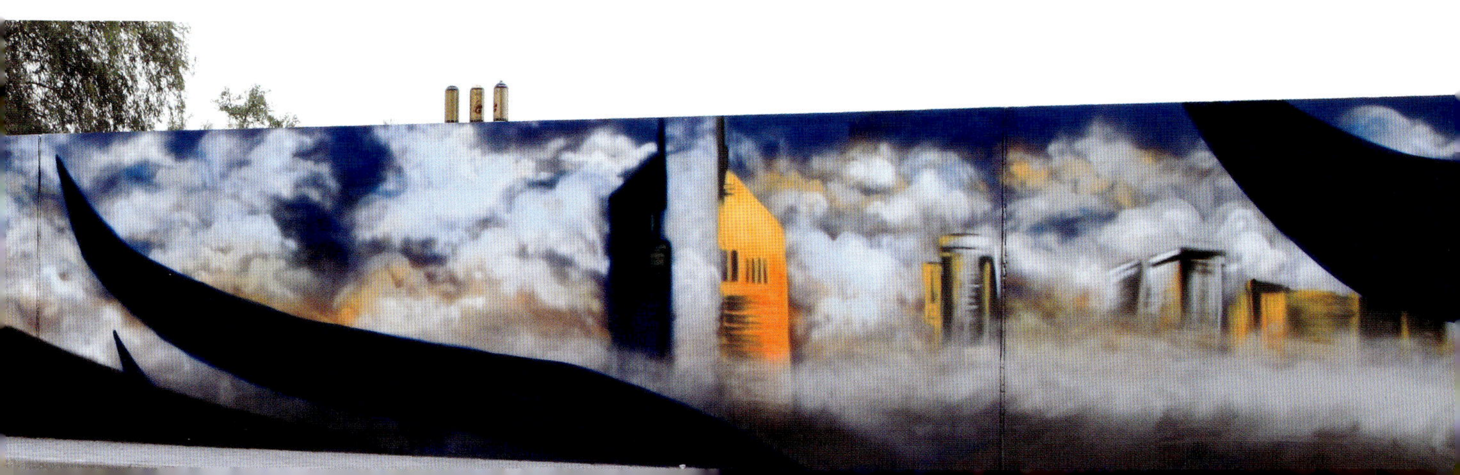

Urban Arabic Typography

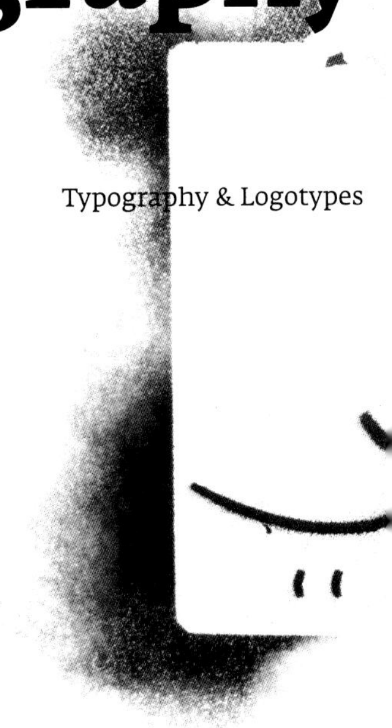

Typography & Logotypes

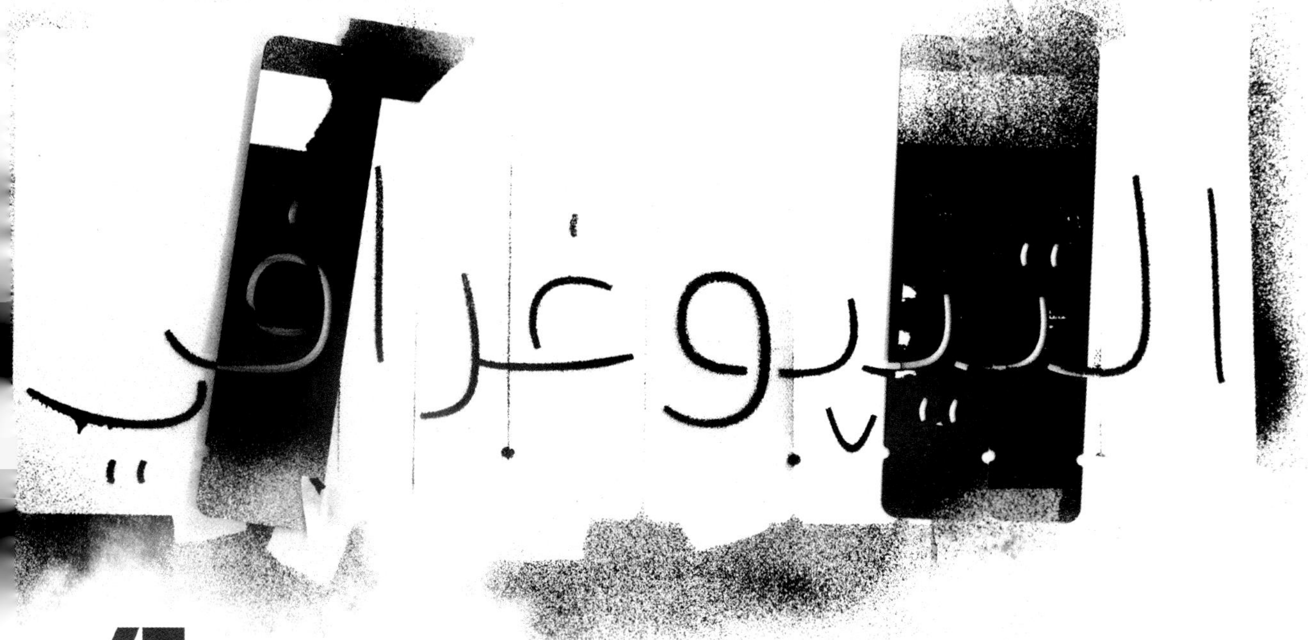

4.

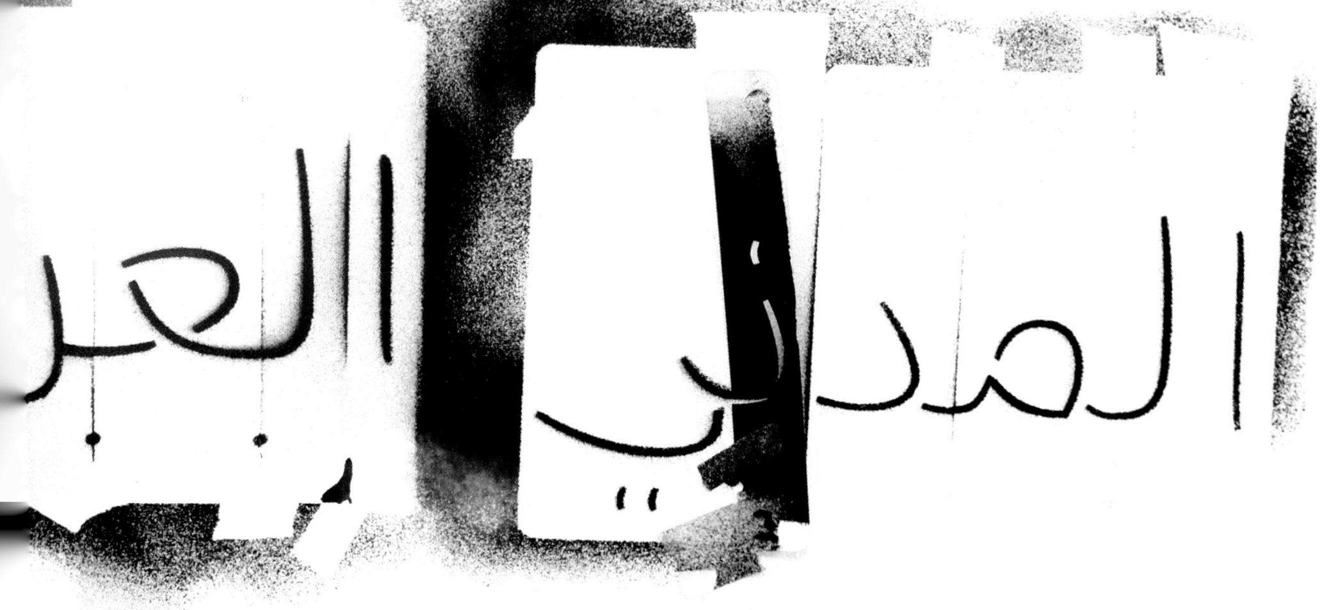

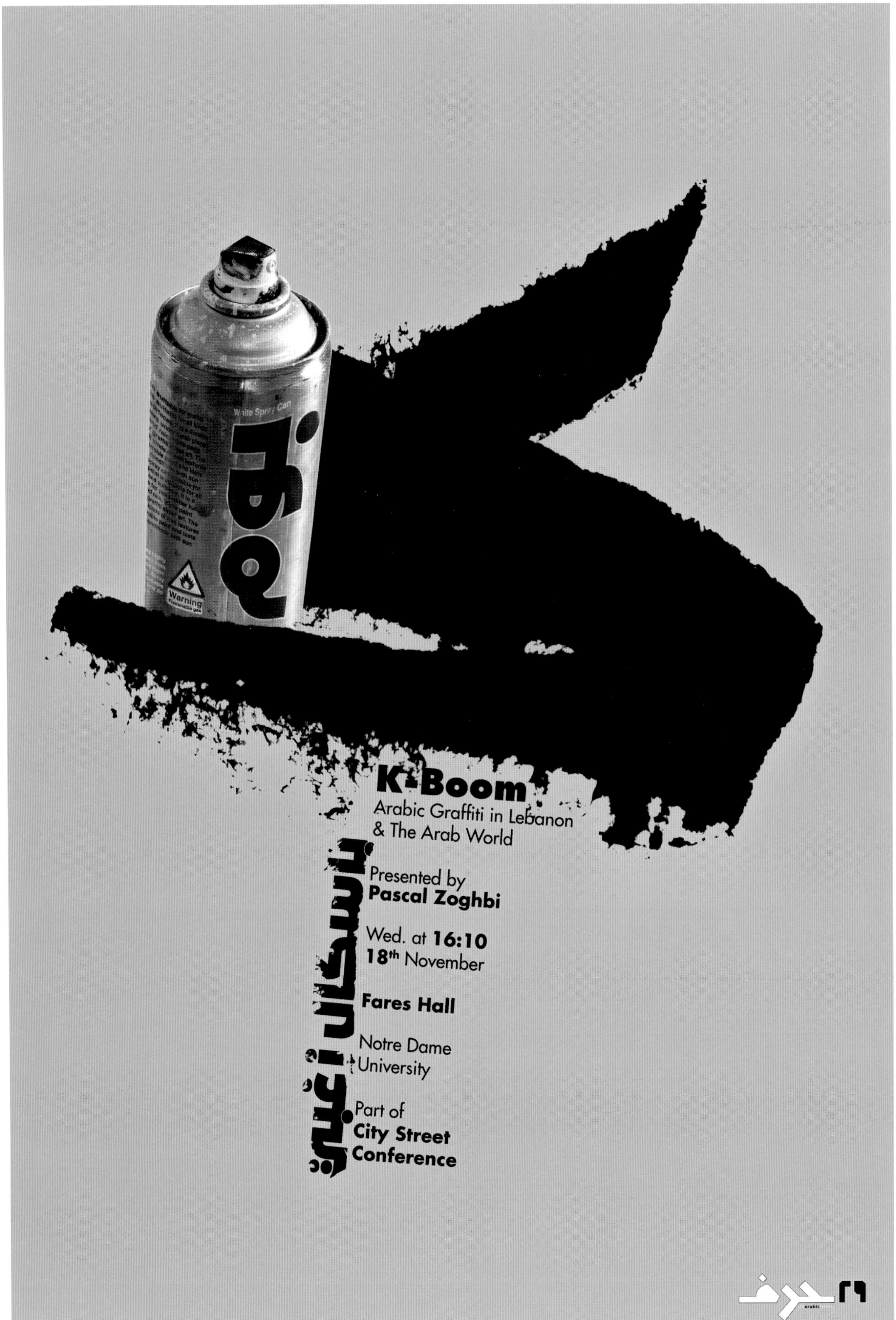
White Spray Can
Warning
K-Boom
Arabic Graffiti in Lebanon
& The Arab World
Presented by
Pascal Zoghbi
Wed. at 16:10
18th November
Fares Hall
Notre Dame
University
Part of
City Street
Conference

4·1 Typography & Logotypes
التيبوغرافية والقوالب التخطيطية

Pascal Zoghbi

The clean, Swiss design aesthetic is starting to get a traditional feel compared to the experimental, hands-on urban design trend. Our fast, chaotic lifestyle forces an untamed style on the designers. The objective, neat graphics and colors are substituted by subjective handmade drawings and color textures, which add more character to the design while incorporating the personality of designers along with their reflections and reactions in the artwork. The urban environment lends the designer new inspirational styles and design attitudes. Contemporary Arabic typographers, being part of the international design community, are merging the beauty of the Arabic script and its calligraphic characteristics with modern urban styles. The Arabic letters are drawn quickly, with rough tools in a free calligraphic style instead of following the strict traditional rules of calligraphy.

As letters and calligraphy develop over centuries, their tools and methods are also changing. We can now discern the spirit of the streets in posters, books and logos due to that evolution. The graffiti scene inspires designers, and vice versa. Designers incorporate a new set of styles in order to integrate ideas deriving from architecture, noise and urban roughness, and to illustrate messages with that new, inspiring texture. Urban design can be geometric and structured or coarse and dirty. The sturdy, concrete urban structures stand out against nature's organic formations and lend the designers a new perspective for their designs. Typefaces become roughened up and texture is added to them. The typographic work becomes a reflection of the rough environment that surrounds the typographer.

A small selection of urban designed posters and logotypes are featured in this section of the book, providing a glimpse into the urban typographic work that is present at the moment.

كبوم
1. "K-Boom", Poster for lecture about Arabic graffiti in Lebanon and the Arab world, Notre Dame University, Zouk, Lebanon, PASCAL ZOGHBI — 29letters, 2010

182

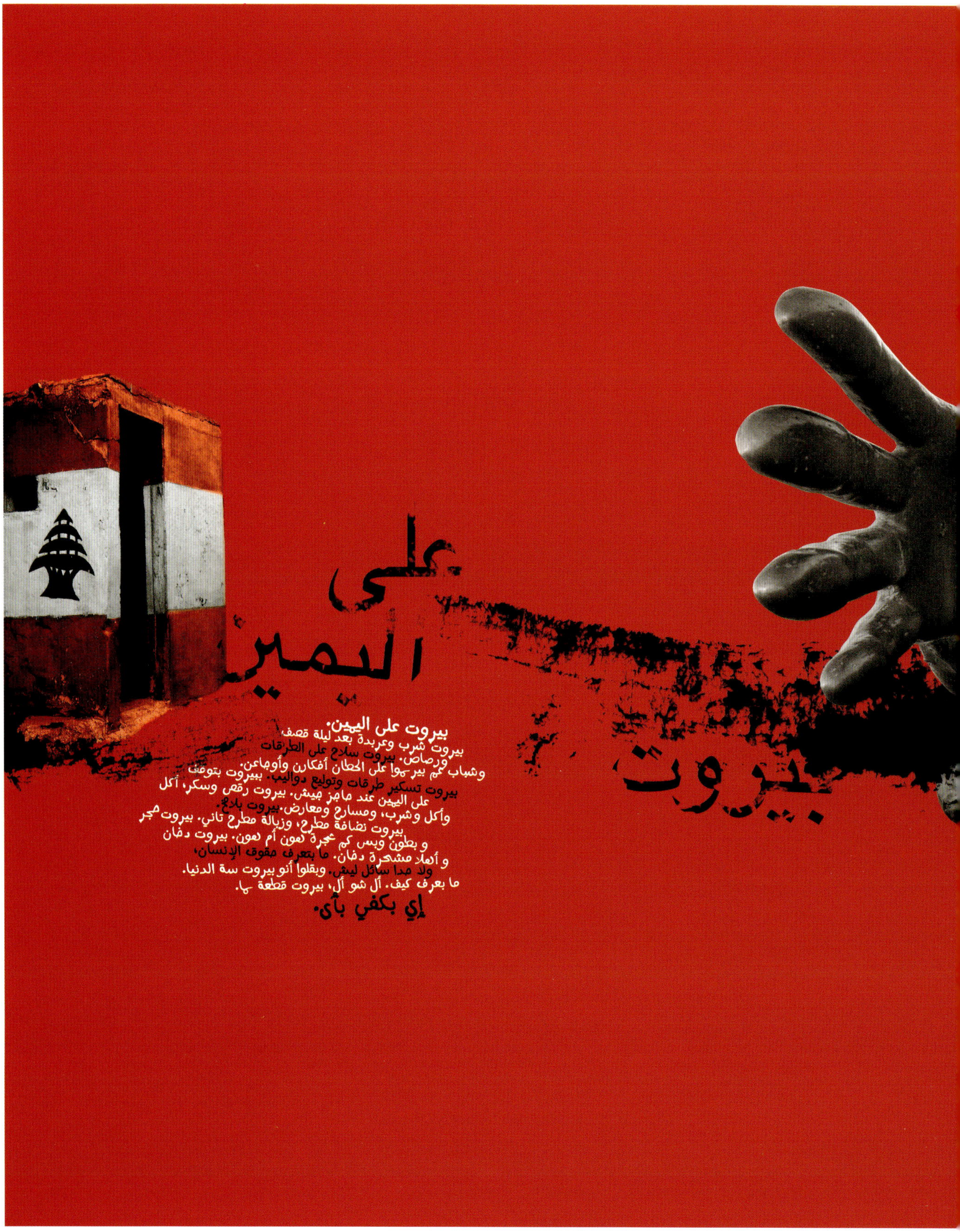
على
اليمين
بيروت
بيروت على اليمين.
بيروت شرب وعربدة بعد ليلة قصف
ورصاص. بيروت سلاح على الطرقات
وشباب عم بيرسموا على الحطان أفكارن وأوجاعن.
بيروت تسكير طرقات وتوليع دواليب. ببيروت بتوقف
على اليمين عند حاجز جيش. بيروت رقص وسكر، أكل
وأكل وشرب، ومسارح ومعارض. بيروت بلاج.
بيروت نضافة مطرح، وزبالة مطرح تاني. بيروت حجر
و بطون وبس كم شجرة لمون أم لمون. بيروت دخان
و أهلا مشحرة دخان. ما بتعرف حقوق الإنسان،
ولا حدا سائل ليش. وبقلوا أنو بيروت سة الدنيا.
ما بعرف كيف. أل شو أل، بيروت قطعة سما.
إي بكفي بأى.

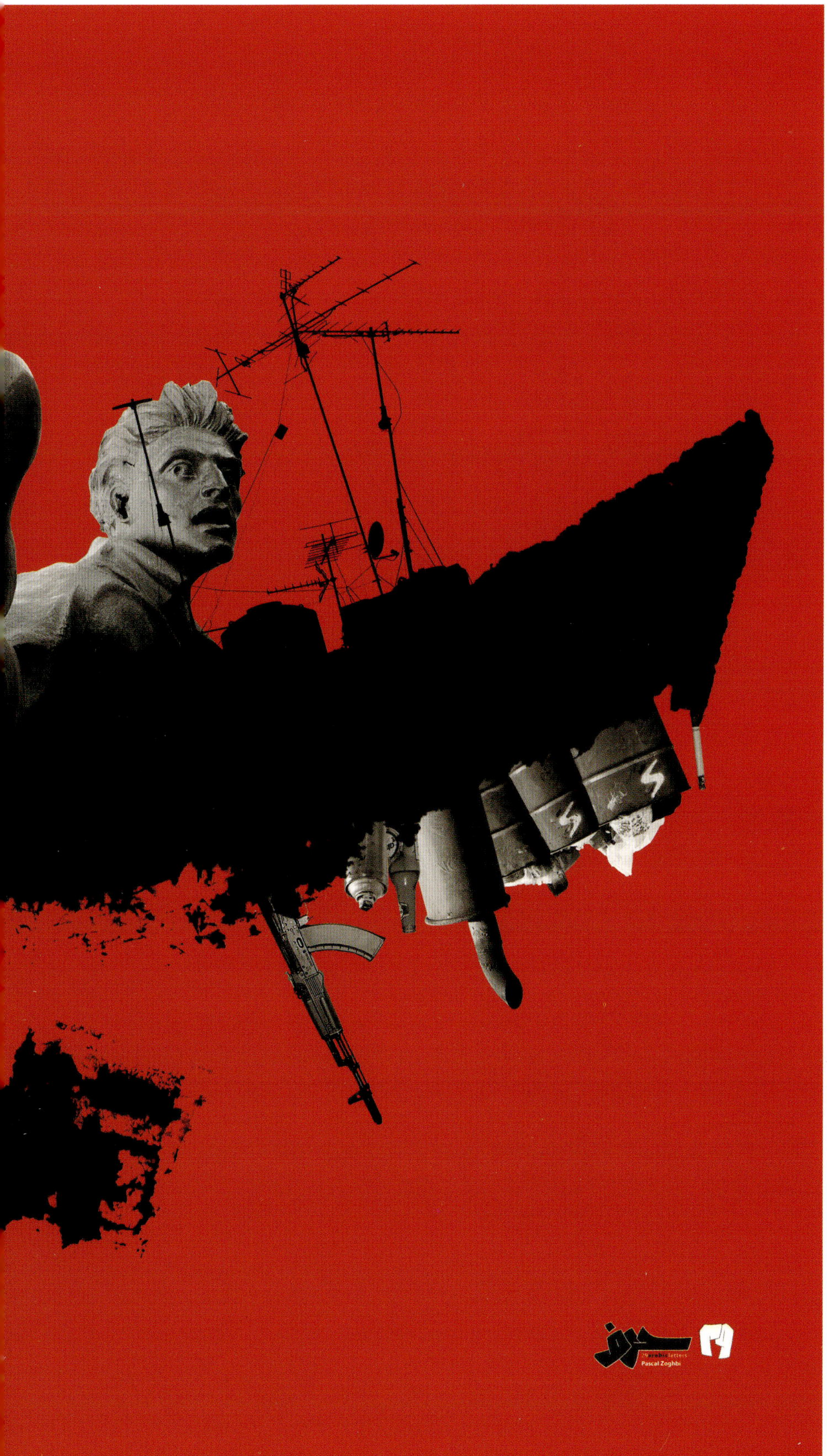

1

بيروت على اليمين
1. “Beirut to the right”, PASCAL ZOGHBI — 29letters, 2010, Lebanon

The following pages 184 & 185:

1. “Intellectual Lifestyle Magazine”, article typography, MUIZ ANWAR

2. “Intellectual Lifestyle Magazine”, cover typography, MUIZ ANWAR, 2009

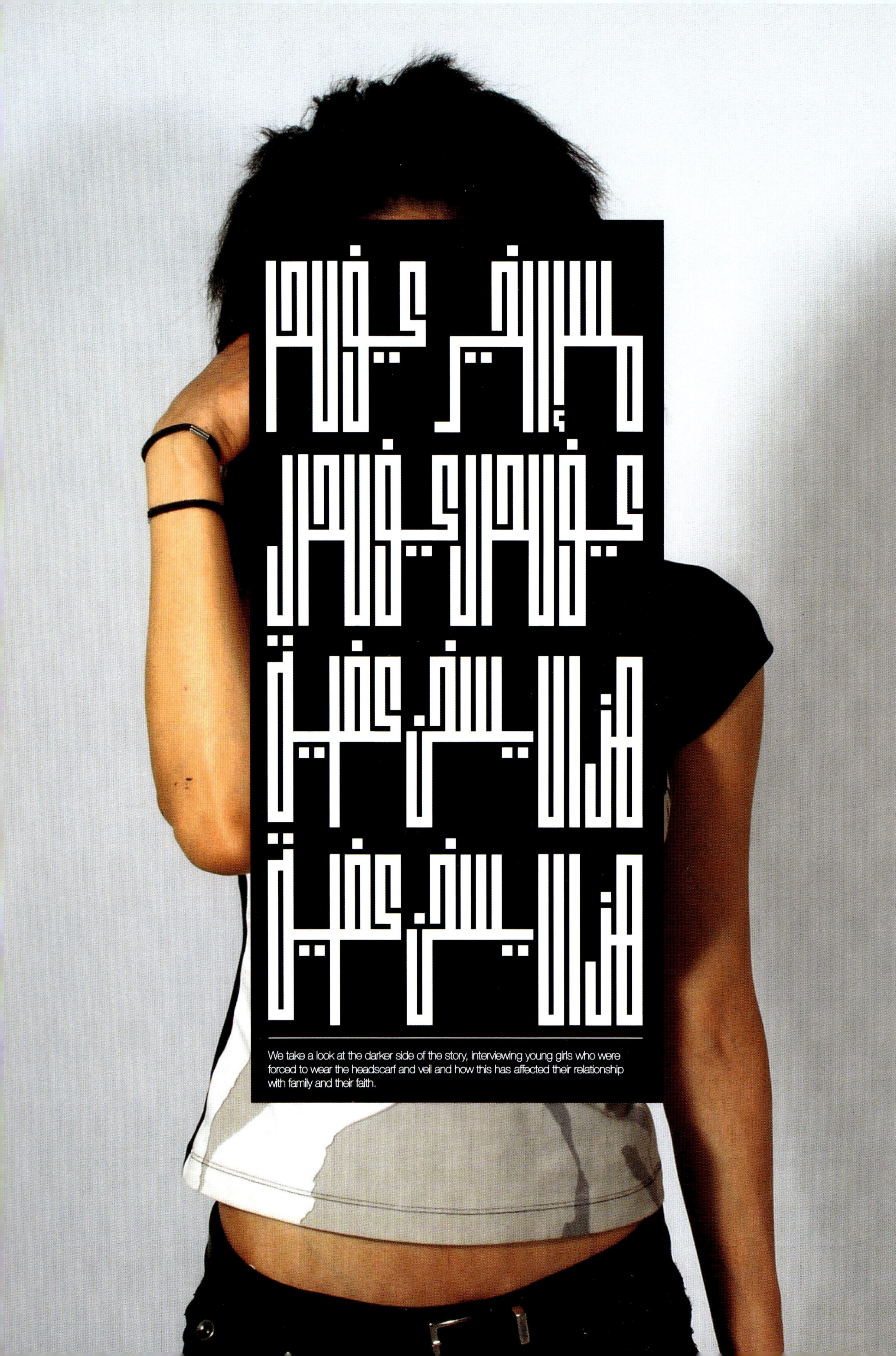

We take a look at the darker side of the story, interviewing young girls who were forced to wear the headscarf and veil and how this has affected their relationship with family and their faith.

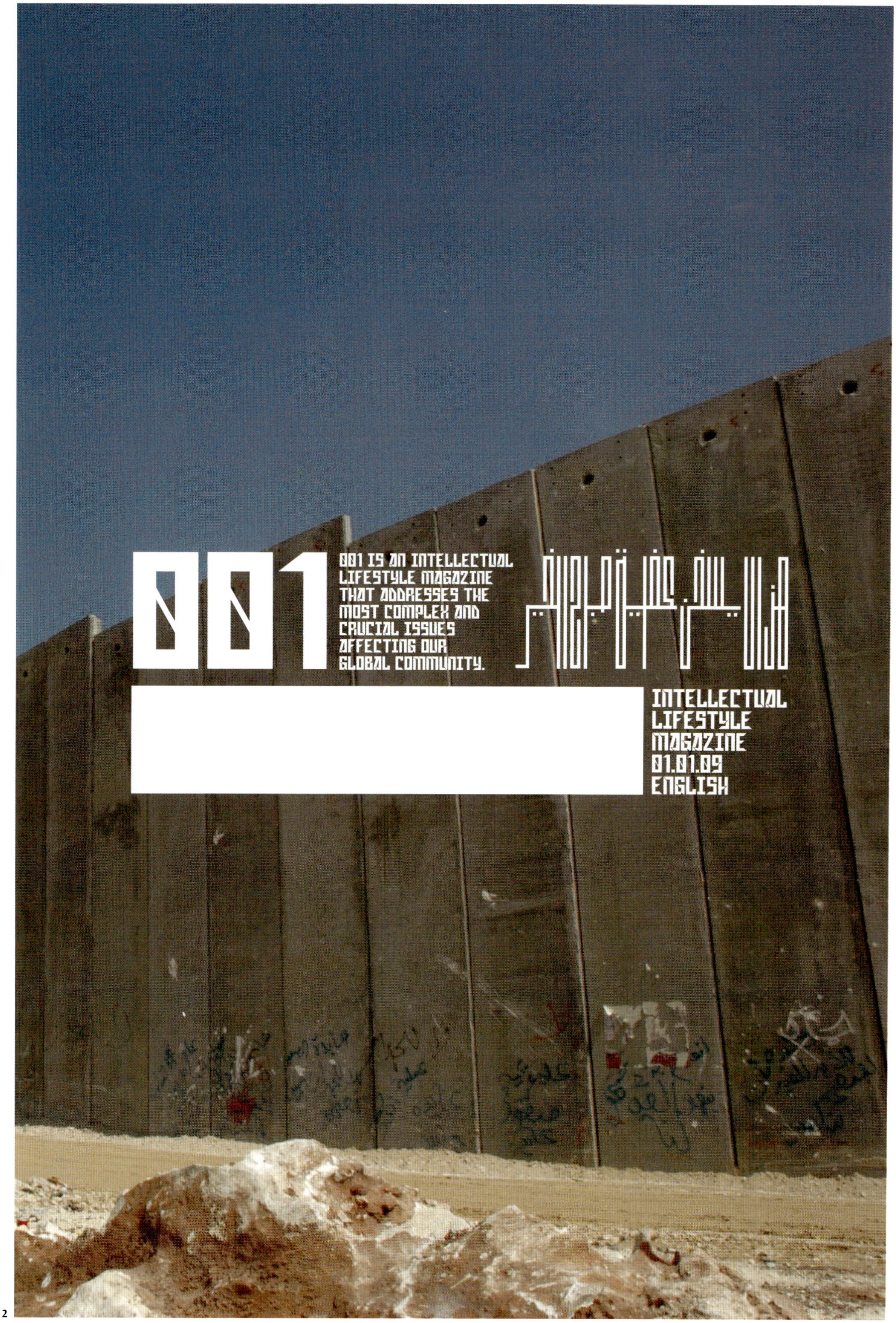
001
001 IS AN INTELLECTUAL LIFESTYLE MAGAZINE THAT ADDRESSES THE MOST COMPLEX AND CRUCIAL ISSUES AFFECTING OUR GLOBAL COMMUNITY.
INTELLECTUAL LIFESTYLE MAGAZINE 01.01.09 ENGLISH
2

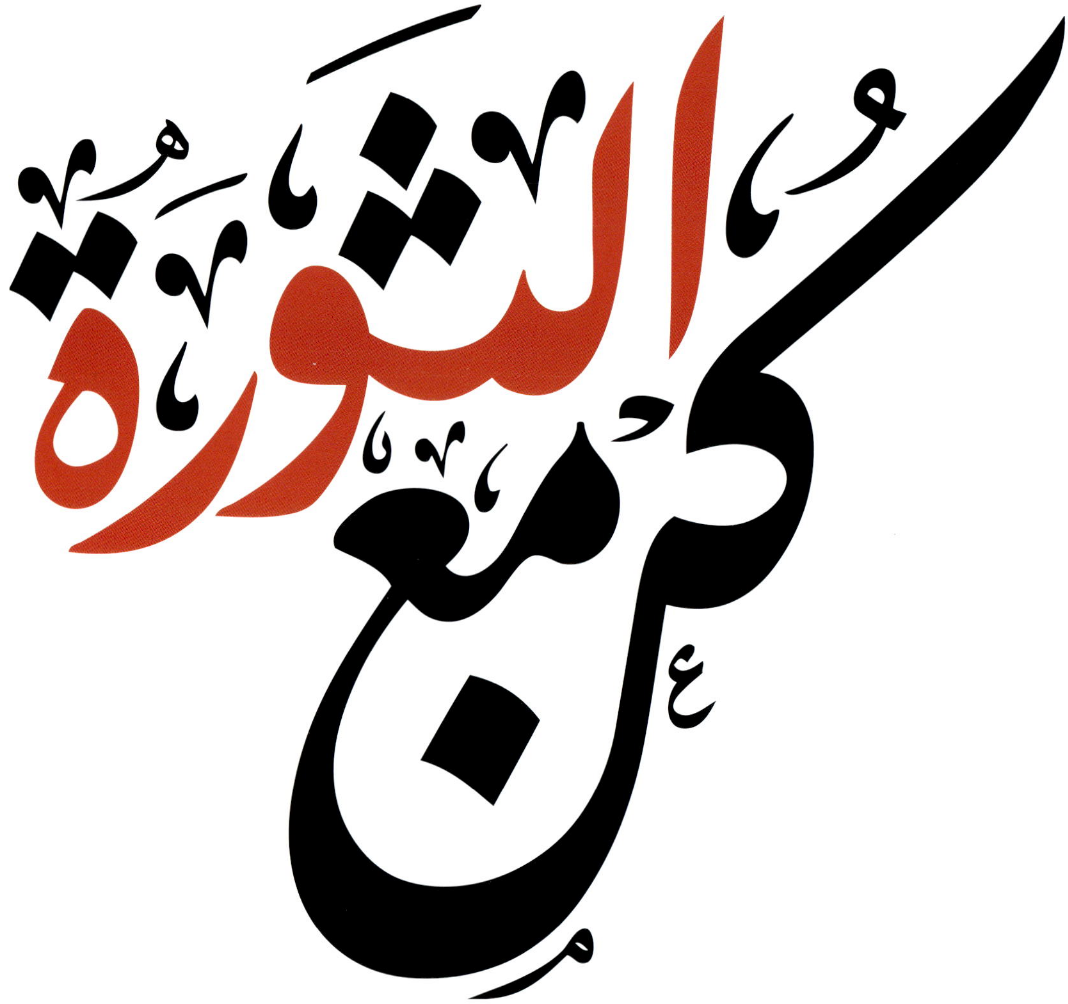

1

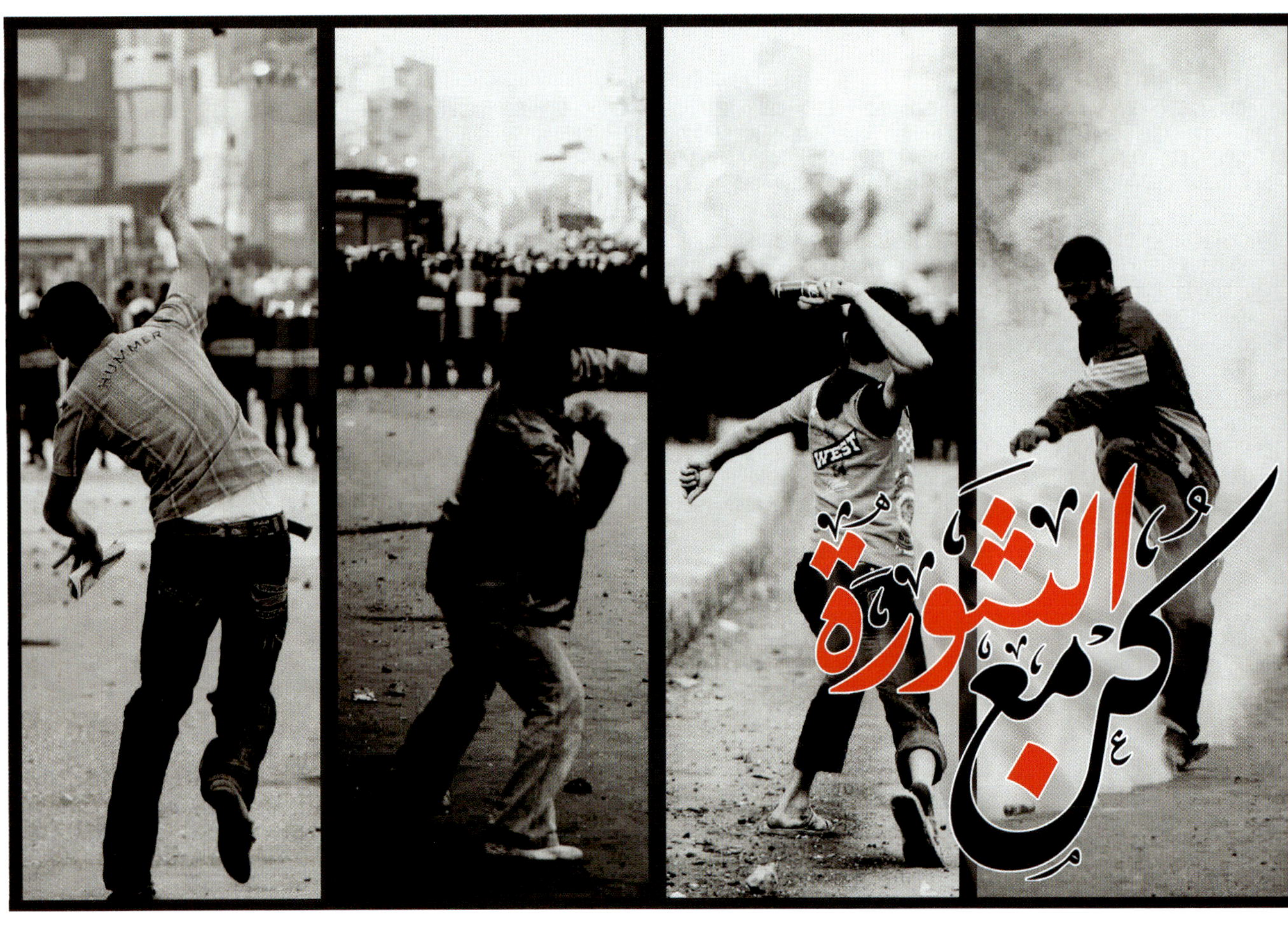

2

كن مع الثورة

1. "Be with the revolution , calligraphy by MOHAMED GABER, Cairo, Egypt, 2008

2. Poster design by MOHAMED GABER, (Photography by Nasser Nouri) Cairo, Egypt, 2008

شيل زبالتك من راسي

3. "Take your trash out my head", Blouzaat poster, TYPISM, Arabic calligraphy by HUSSEIN AL-AZAAT, 2008

The following pages 188 & 189:

صانع السلام

1. "Peace Maker" TYPISM, Arabic calligraphy by HUSSEIN AL-AZAAT

لا للحرب

2. "No War" BLOUZAAT poster in support of Gaza, 2009

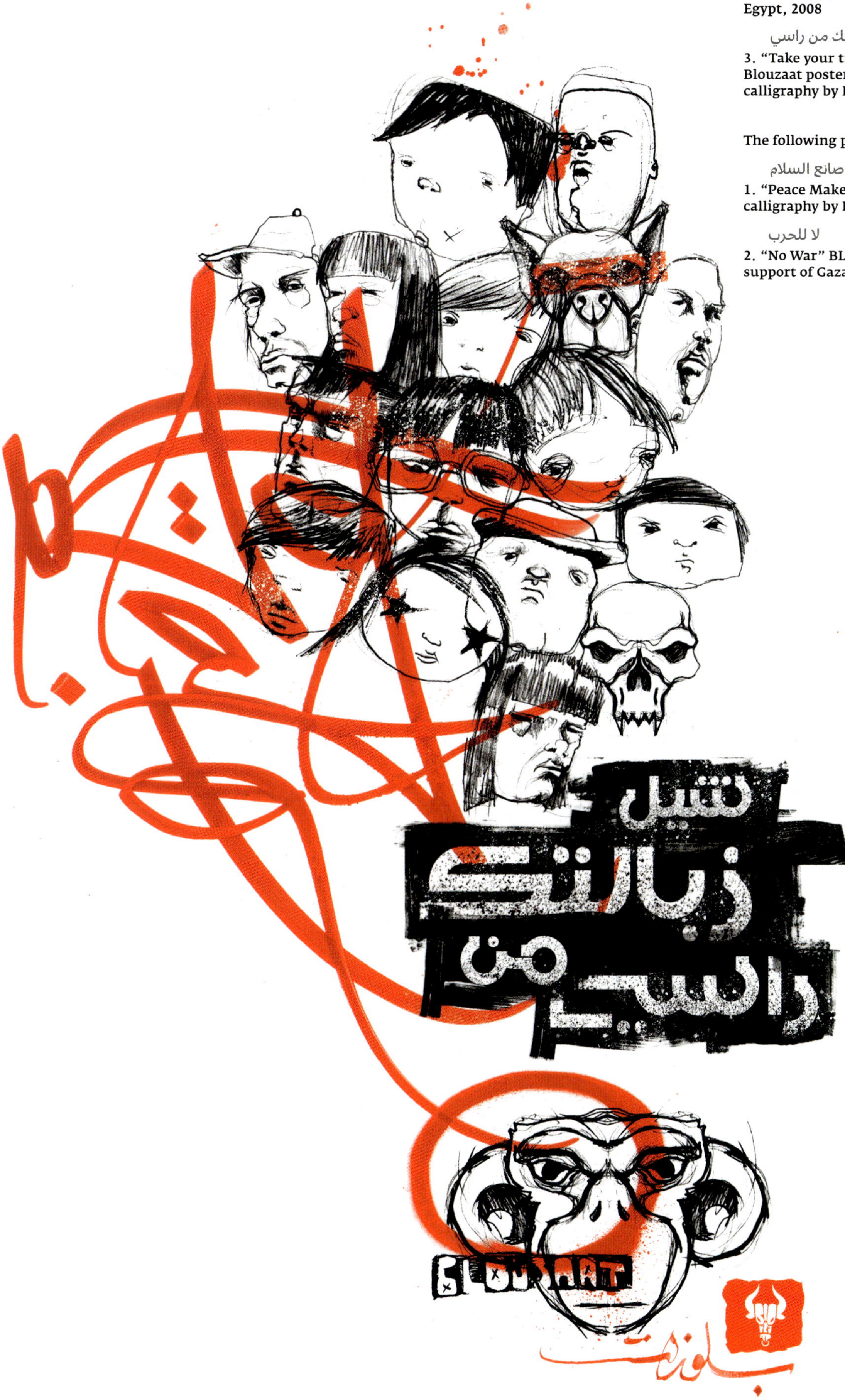

3

PEACE

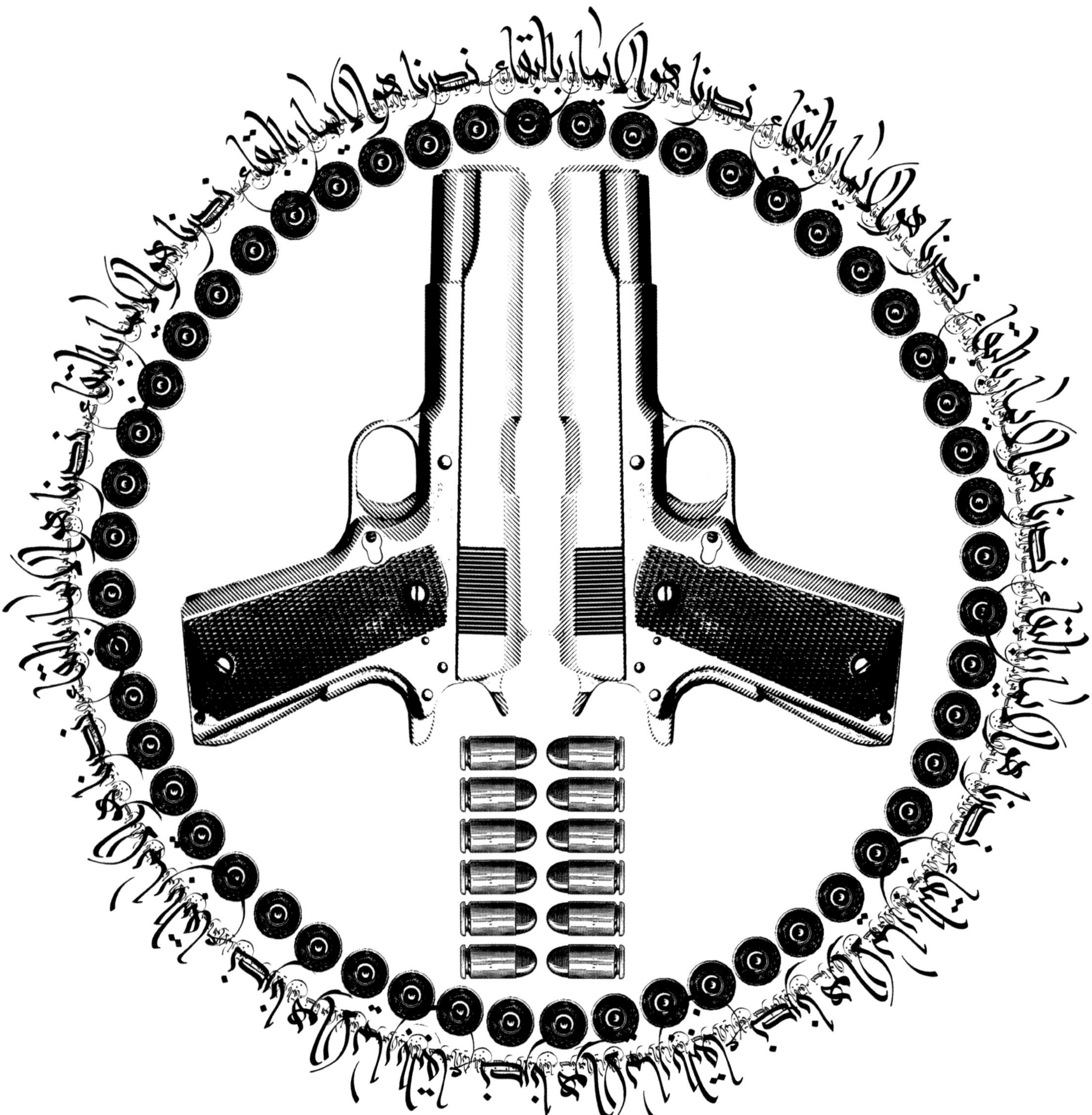

MAKER

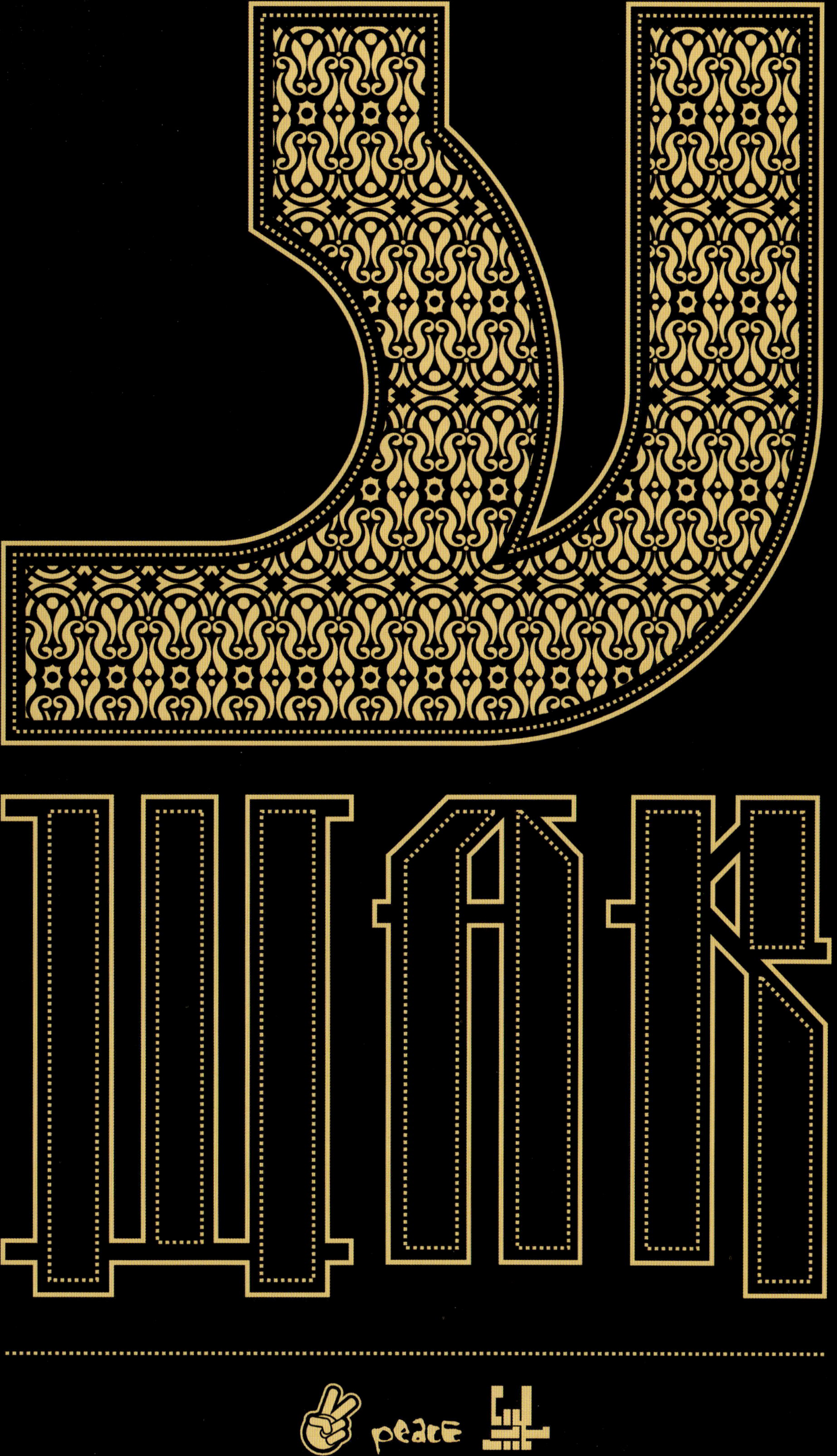
peace

1-6. Designs for BLOUZAAT T-shirt collection, 2007

7. "Khuraif" exhibition promotional poster, TYPISM, 2008

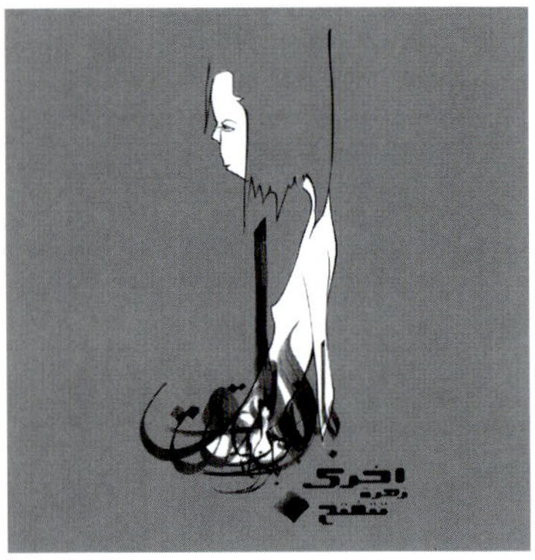

1

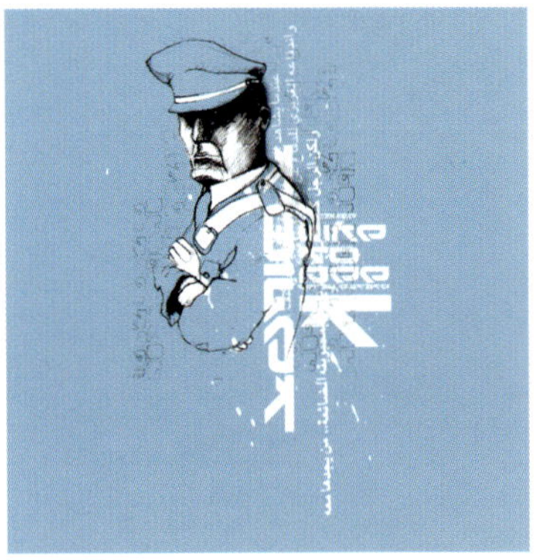

2

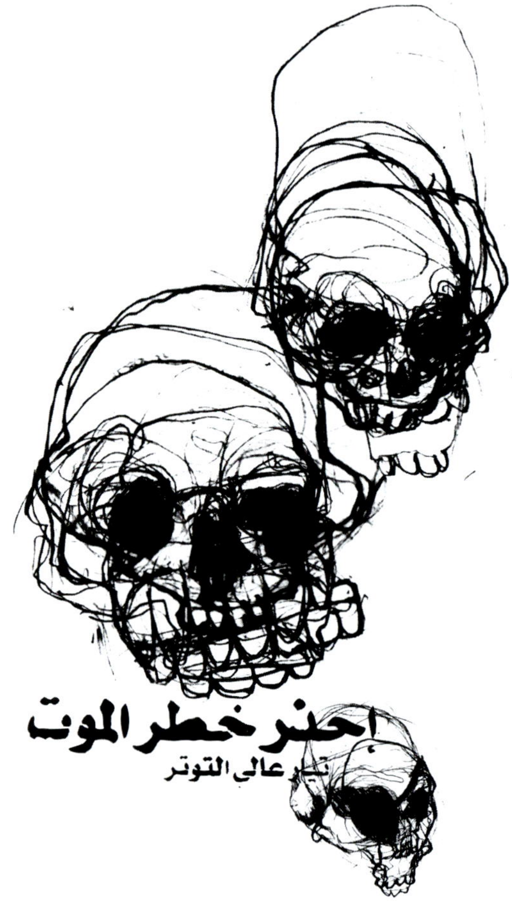

4

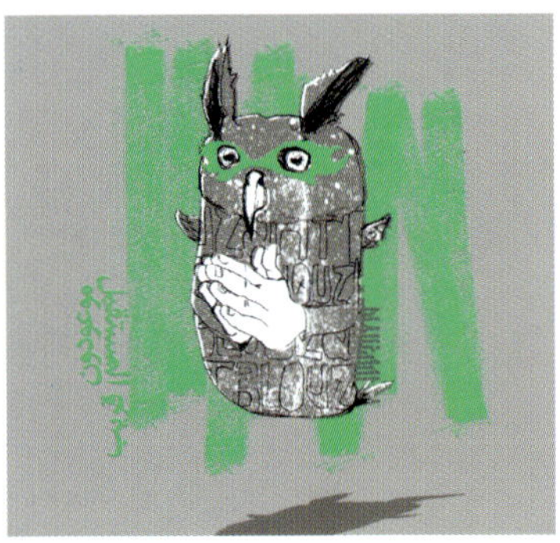

3

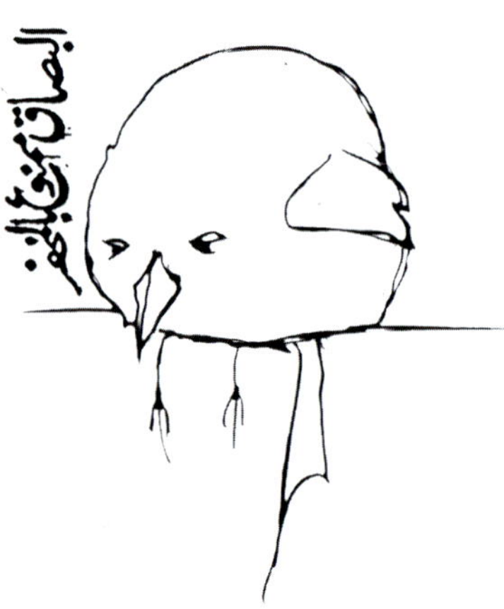

5

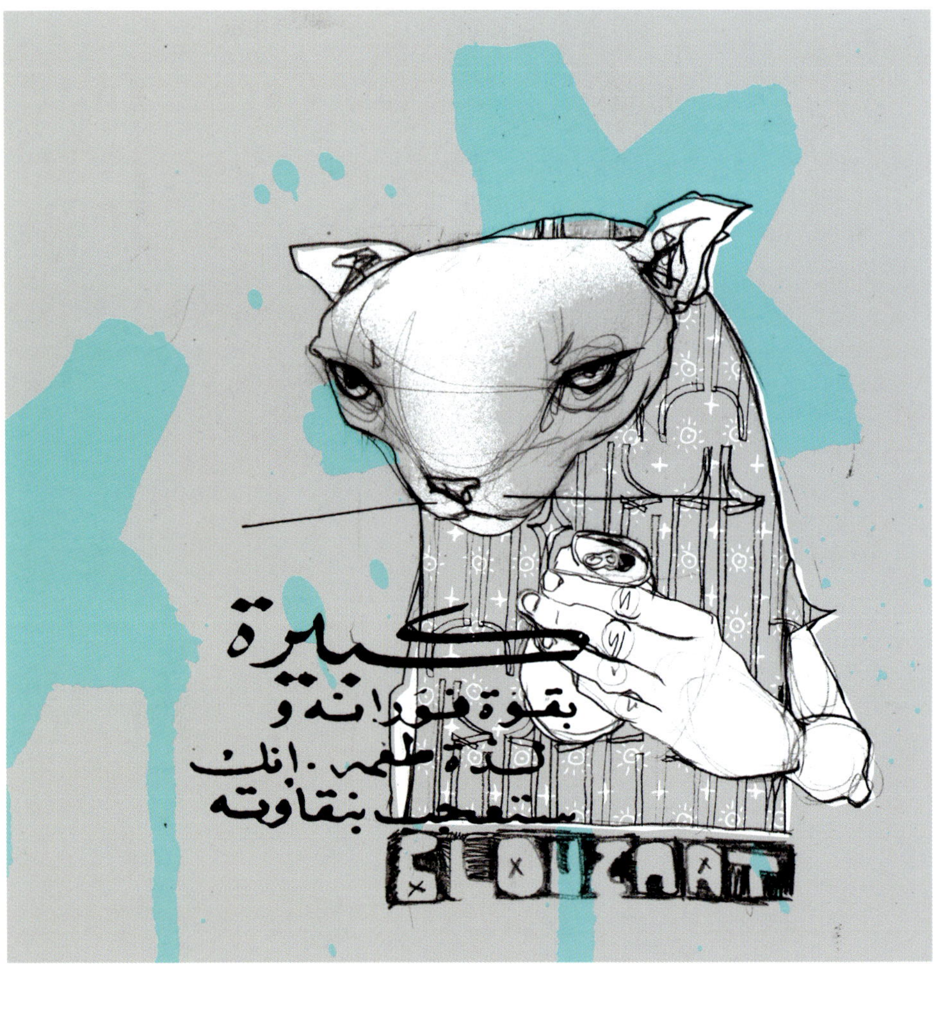

6

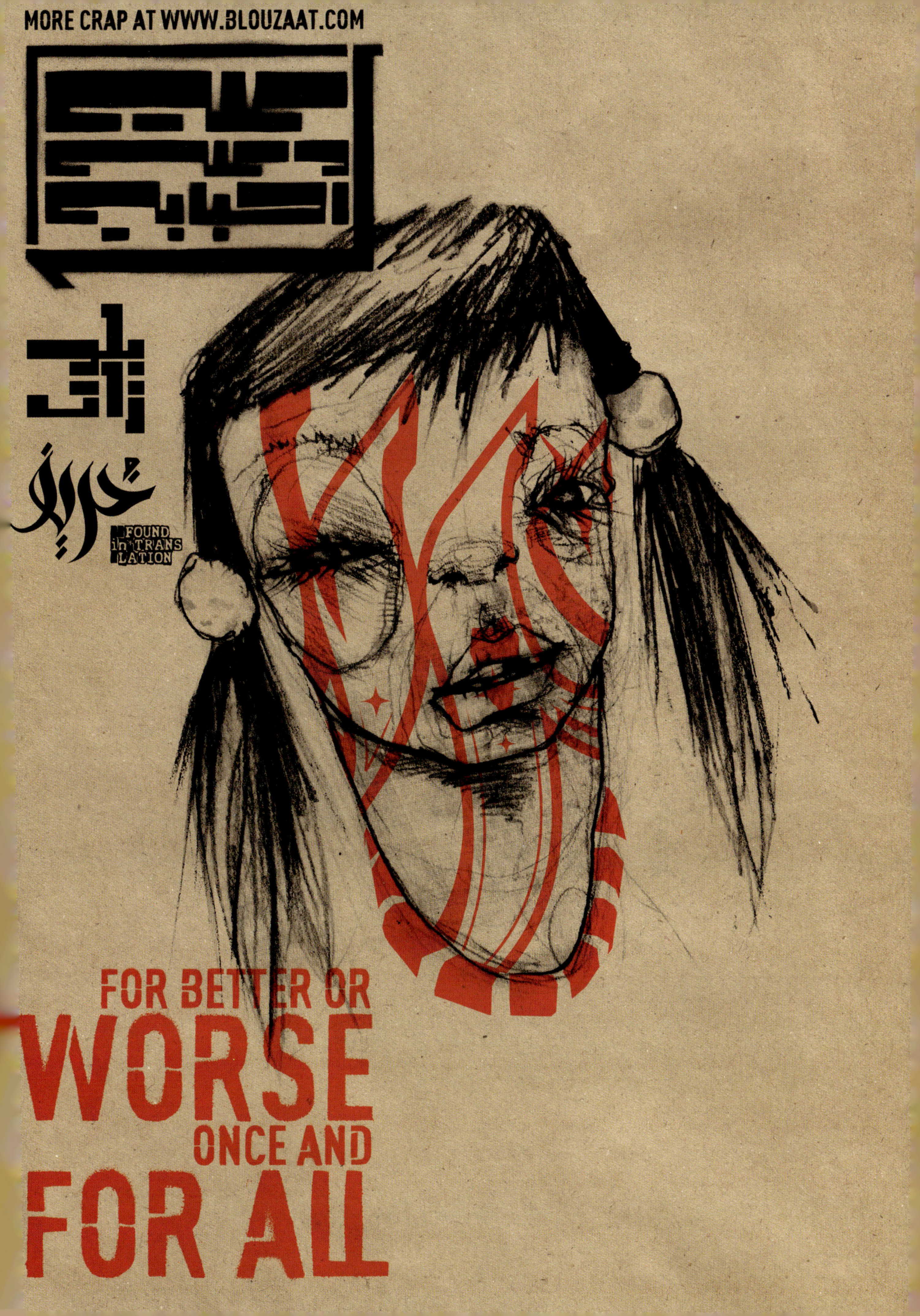
MORE CRAP AT WWW.BLOUZAAT.COM
FOUND in TRANS LATION
FOR BETTER OR
WORSE
ONCE AND
FOR ALL

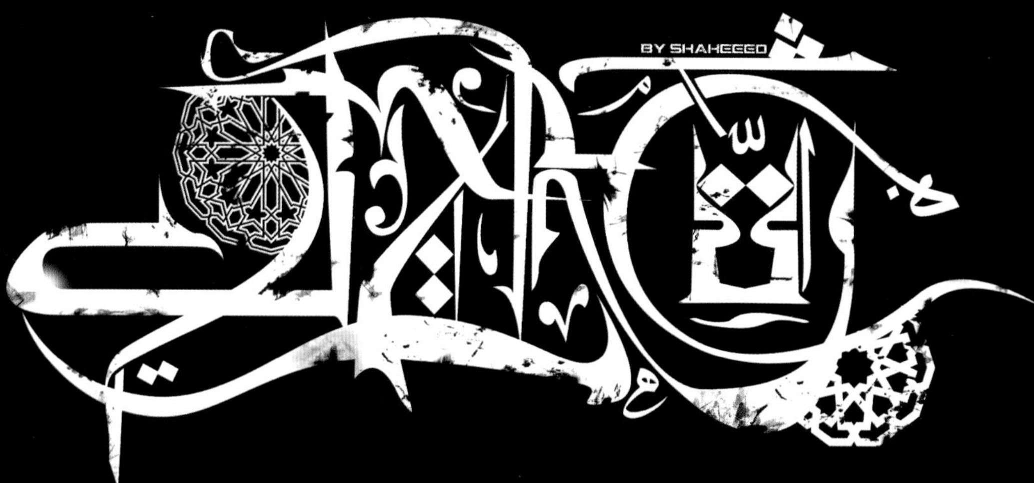

1

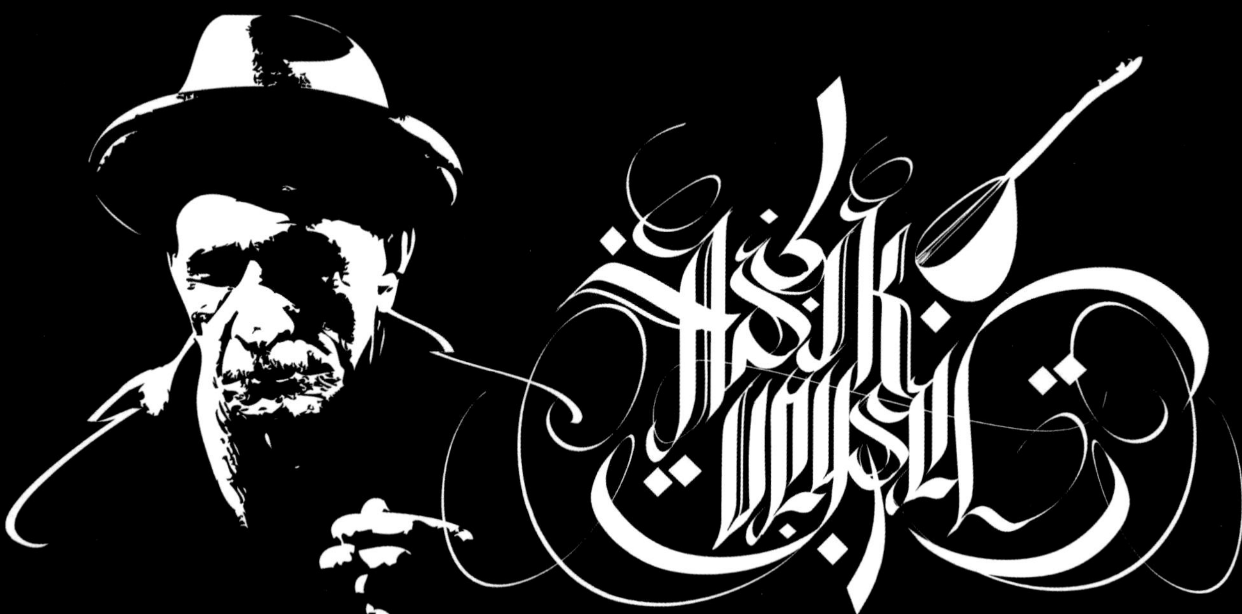

2

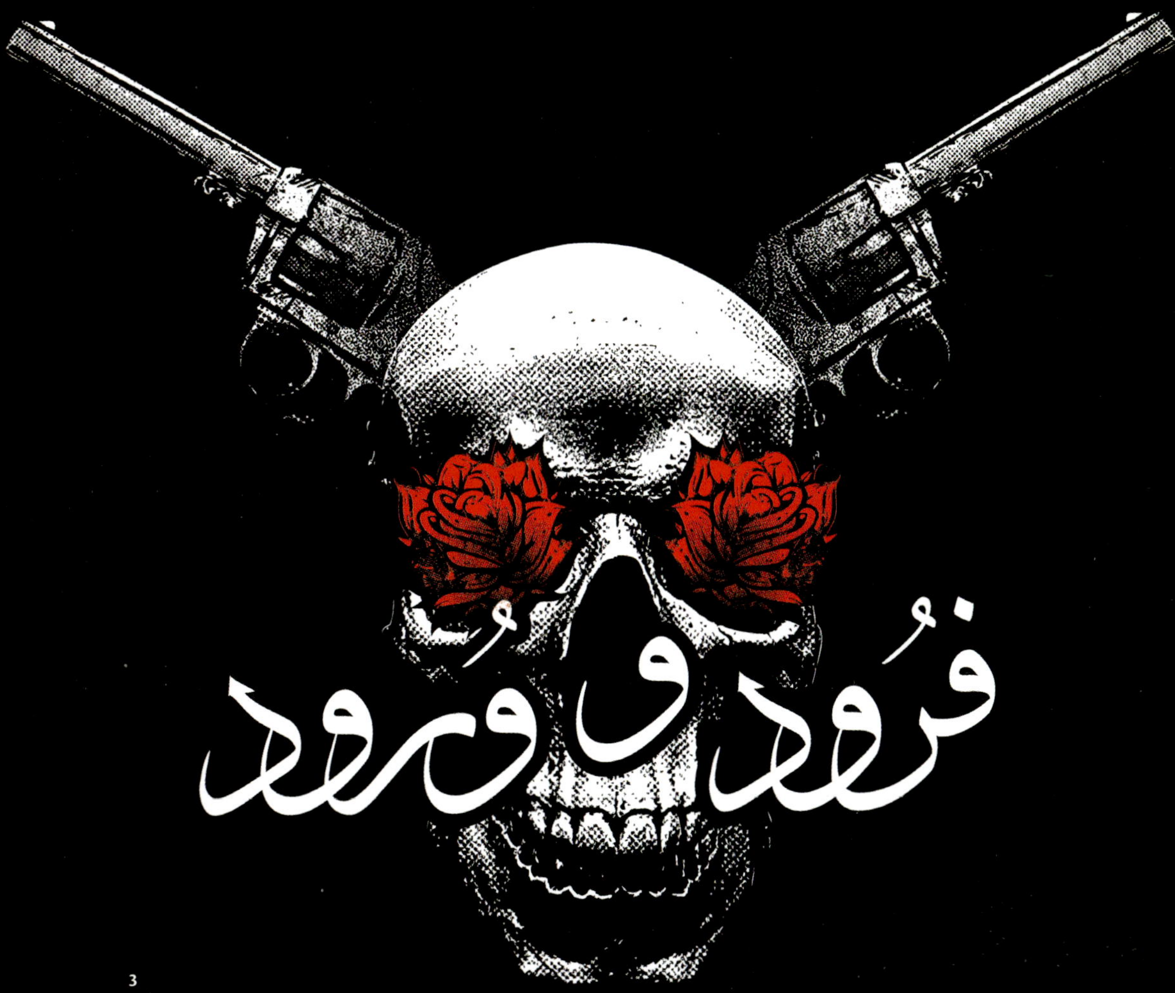

3

1. “Maroc”, typography, ZAKARIA AHMED EL AKKAF, Oujda, Morocco

2. “Asık Veysel”, poster design, KRYS2LOOPER, STREET HAT, Mersin, Turkey

فُرود و ورود
3. “Guns n' Roses”, T-shirt design, HADI ALAEDDIN, Amman, Jordan

194

1

29arabicletters

2

3

ANA FALASTINI

4

5

6

GAZA

7

AL YASSARIO

8

9

10

11

SHANKABOOT.COM

12

13

FOCUS

FOCUS ART GALLERY

14

15

16

17

18

19

20

21

DHIKR

22

23

SABR

24

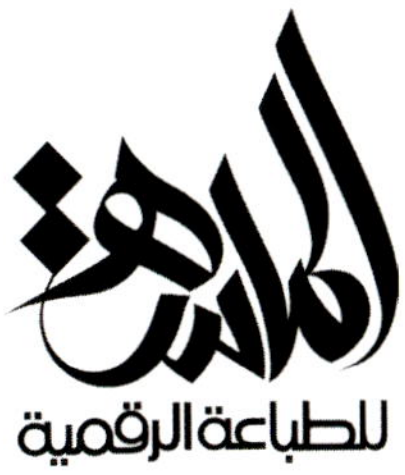

25

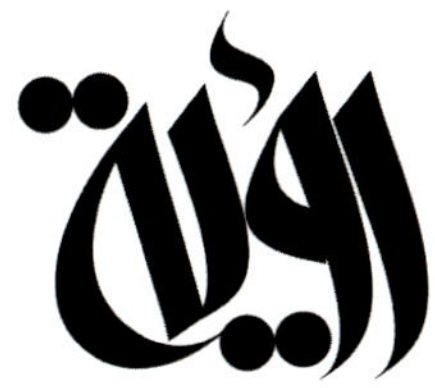

26

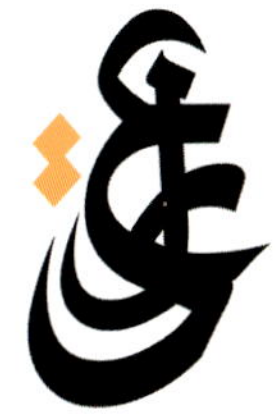

27

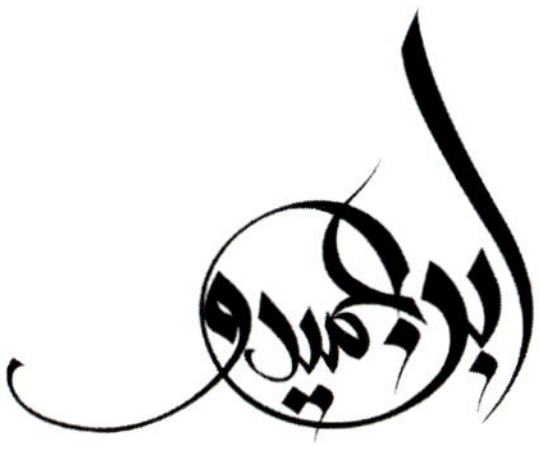

28

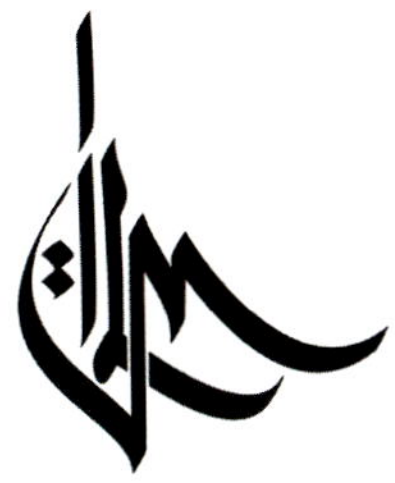

29

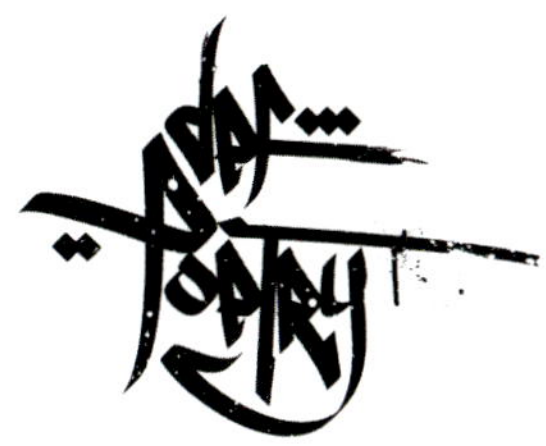

30

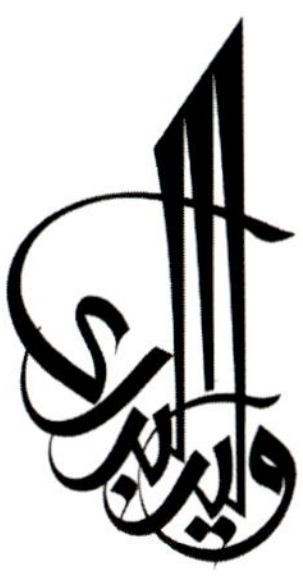

31

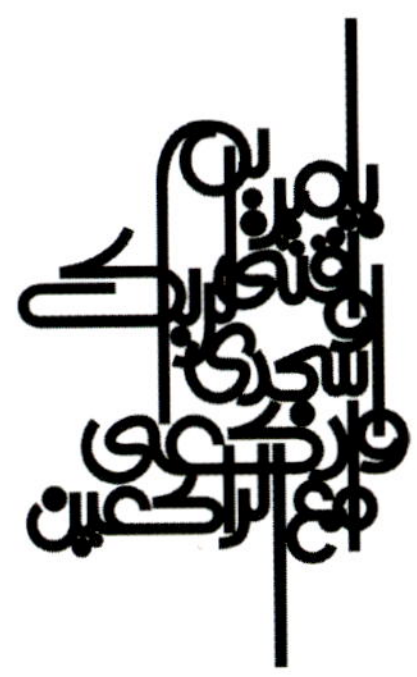

32

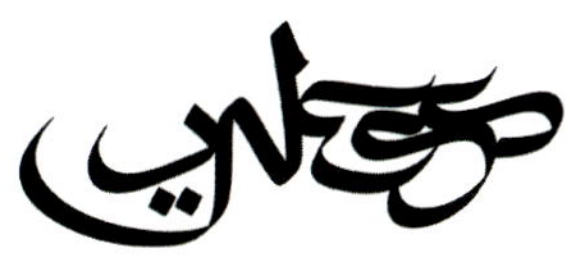

33

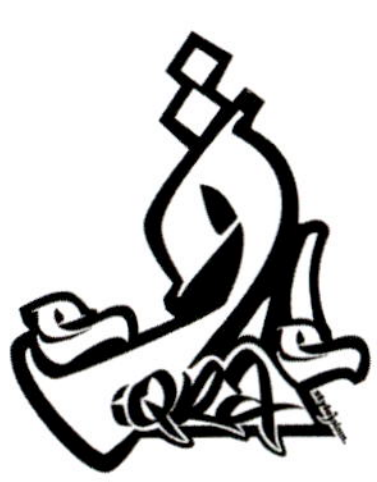

34

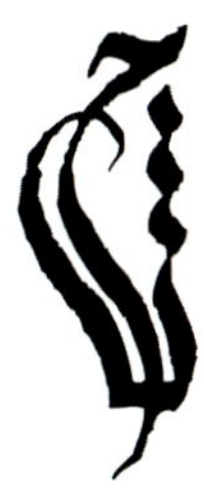

35

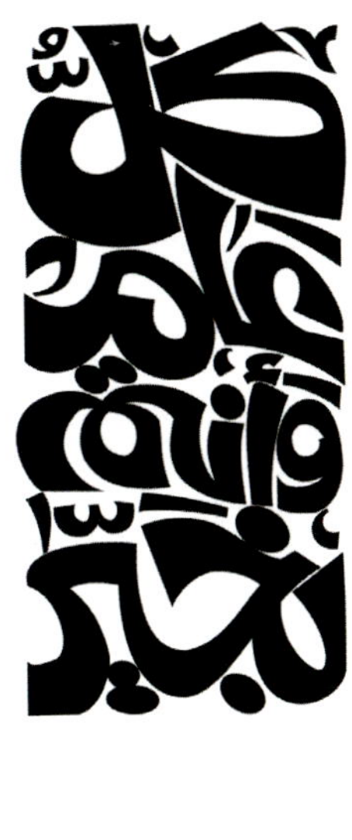

38

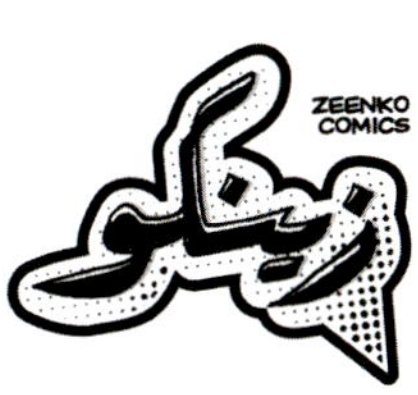

36

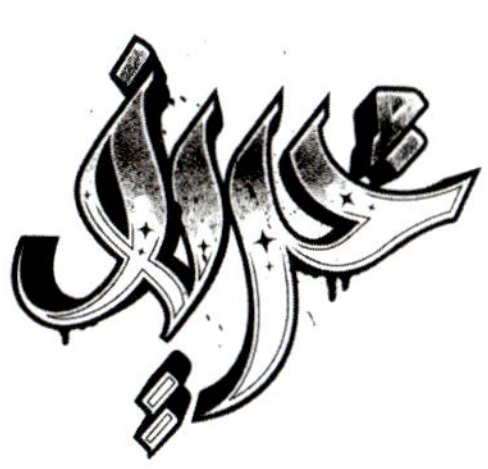

37

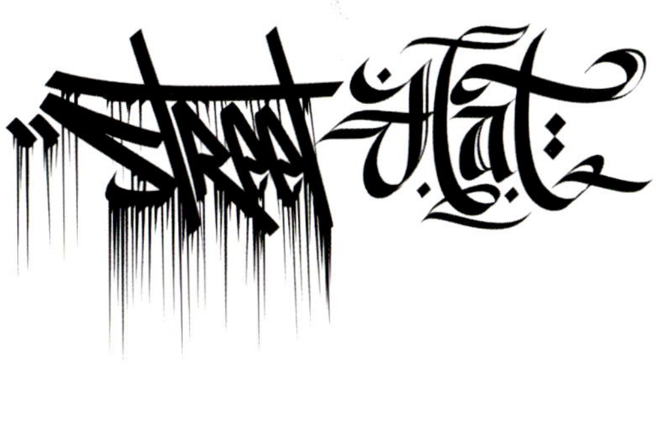

39

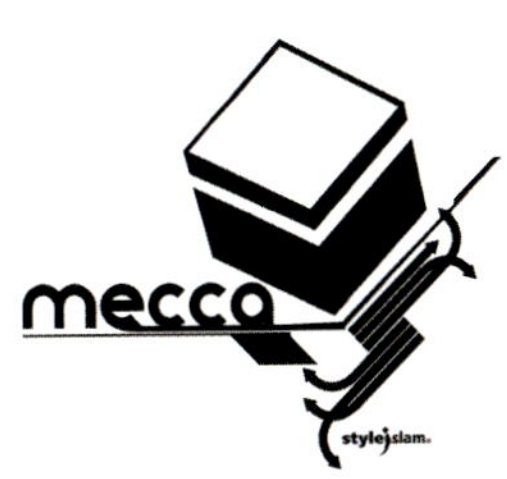

40

1. "ID Stamp", HADI ALAEDDIN, ALI MOSLEH, Jordan
2. "29arabicletters", PASCAL ZOGHBI, Lebanon
3. "Samedoon", HADI ALAEDDIN, Jordan
4. "Ana Falastini", DANA ALHANBALI, United Arab Emirates
5. "Blouzaat", BLOUZAAT, Jordan & Germany
6. "Barcode", MUIZ ANWAR, UK
7. "Gaza", ALY BCHENNATY, Lebanon
8. "Al Yassario", ALY BCHENNATY, Lebanon
9. "7 Aj", ALY BCHENNATY, Lebanon
10. "Mothanna Hussein", MOTHANNA HUSSEIN, Jordan
11. "buy or die", BLOUZAAT, Jordan & Germany
12. "Shankaboot", HAMED SINNO and TANIA SALEH, Beirut
13. "Karaj", MOTHANNA HUSSEIN, Jordan
14. "Focus Art Gallery", PASCAL ZOGHBI, Lebanon
15. MOHAMED ABDEL AZIZ, Egypt
16. "My third place", AHMAD SABBAGH, Jordan
17. "Deen Tight", PASCAL ZOGHBI, Lebanon
18. "Palestine Festival", MUIZ ANWAR, UK
19. "Geo Kufic", MUIZ ANWAR, UK
20. "Eid Mubarak", MUIZ ANWAR, UK
21. "The strongest type", AHMAD SABBAGH, Jordan
22. "Dhikr", MELIH KESMEN, SAIFU-DEEN DAG, Styleislam, Germany
23. "Most wanted", TYPISM, Germany
24. "Sabr", MELIH KESMEN, Saifudeen Dag, Styleislam, Germany
25. MOHAMED ABDEL AZIZ, Egypt
26. MOHAMED ABDEL AZIZ, Egypt
27. "Ali", ALY BCHENNATY, Lebanon
28. MOHAMED ABDEL AZIZ, Egypt
29. "ILM", QASIM ARIF, Pakistan & Holland
30. "def Poetry", QASIM ARIF, Pakistan / Holland
31. MOHAMED ABDEL AZIZ, Egypt
32. MOHAMED ABDEL AZIZ, Egypt
33. "uness", QASIM ARIF, Pakistan & Holland
34. "Iqra", MELIH KESMEN, Saifudeen Dag, Styleislam, Germany
35. "Taj", HADI ALAEDDIN, Jordan
36. "Zeenko Comics", MOTHANNA HUSSEIN, Jordan
37. "Khuraif", TYPISM, Germany
38. MOHAMED ABDEL AZIZ, Egypt
39. "Street Hat", KRYS2LOOPER, Turkey
40. "Mecca", MELIH KESMEN, Styleislam, Germany

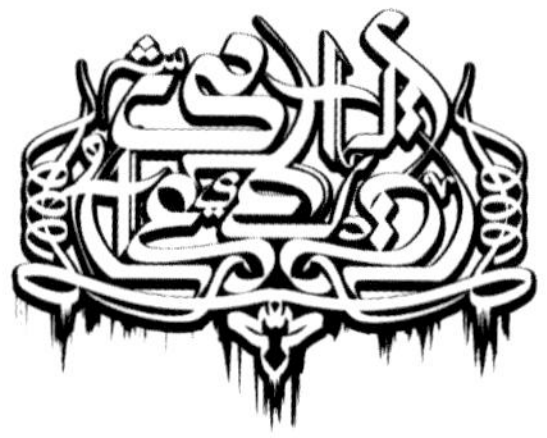

1

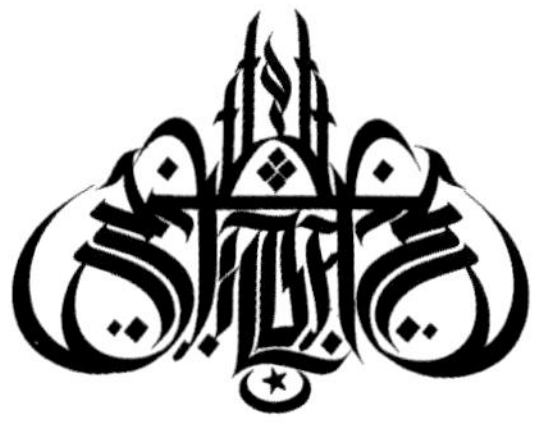

2

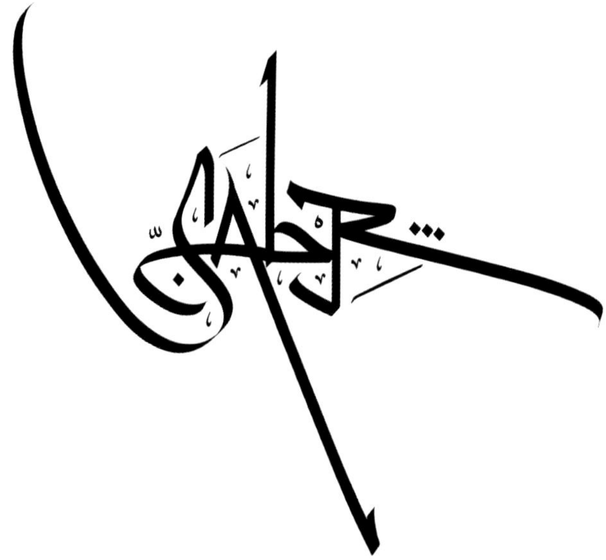

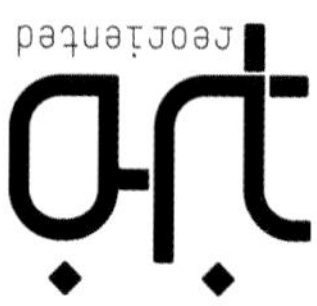

3

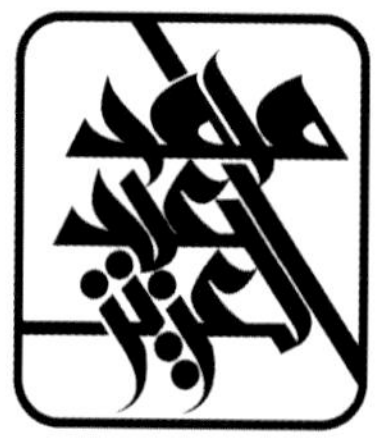

4

5

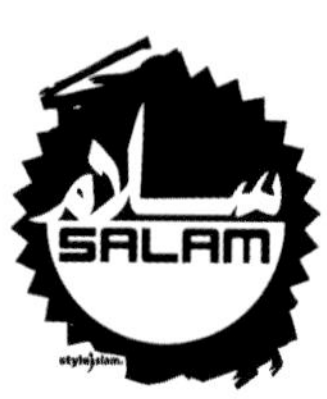

6

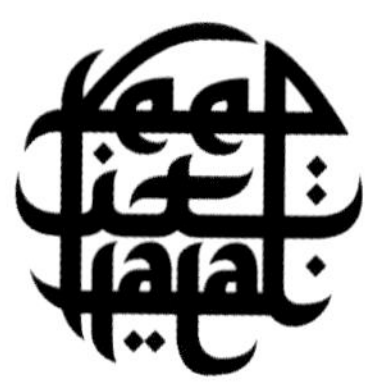

7

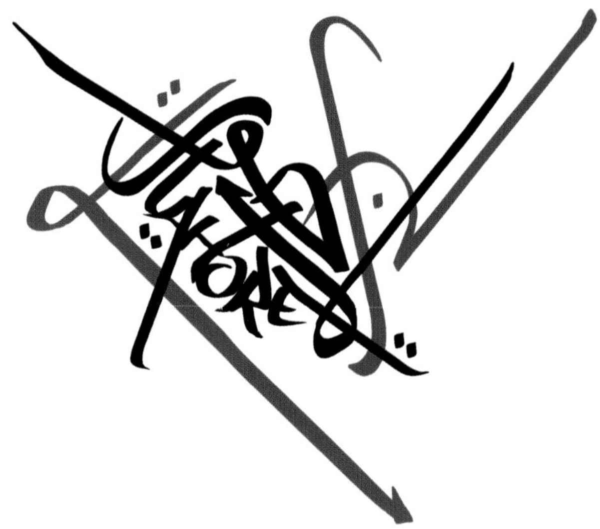

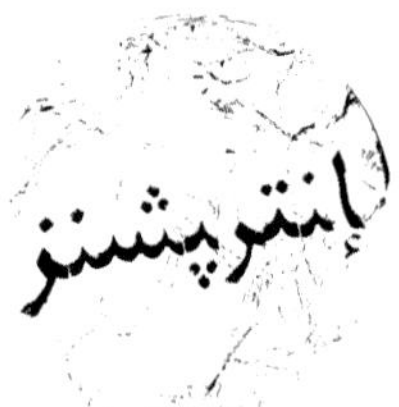

8

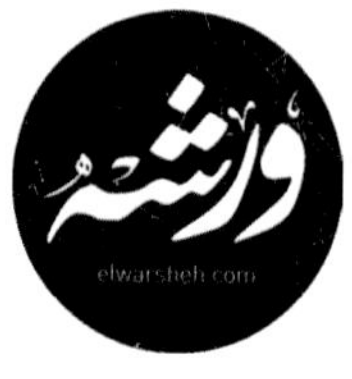

9

10

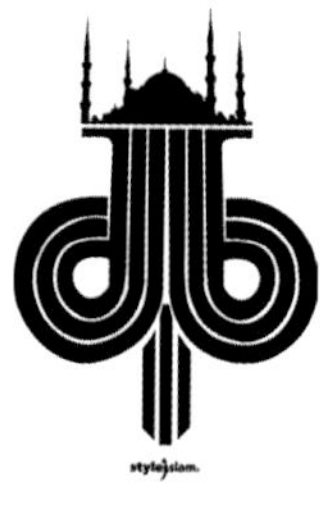

11

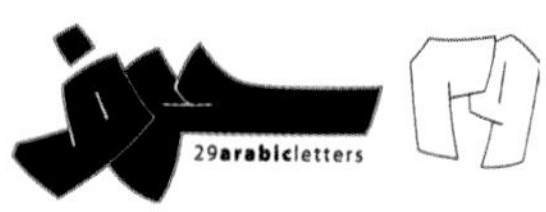

12

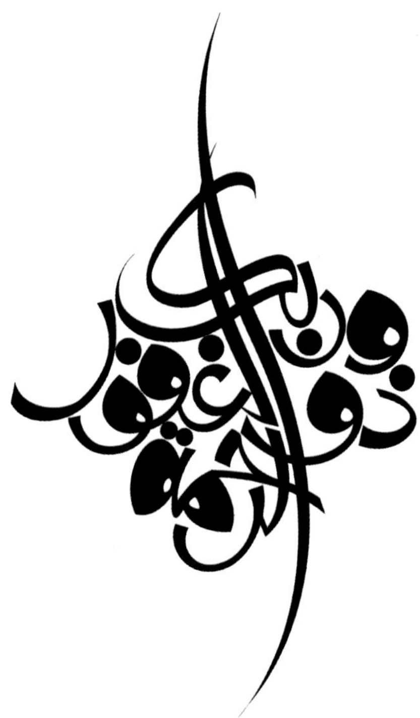

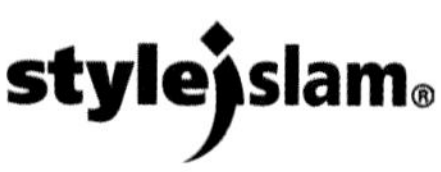

13

14

15

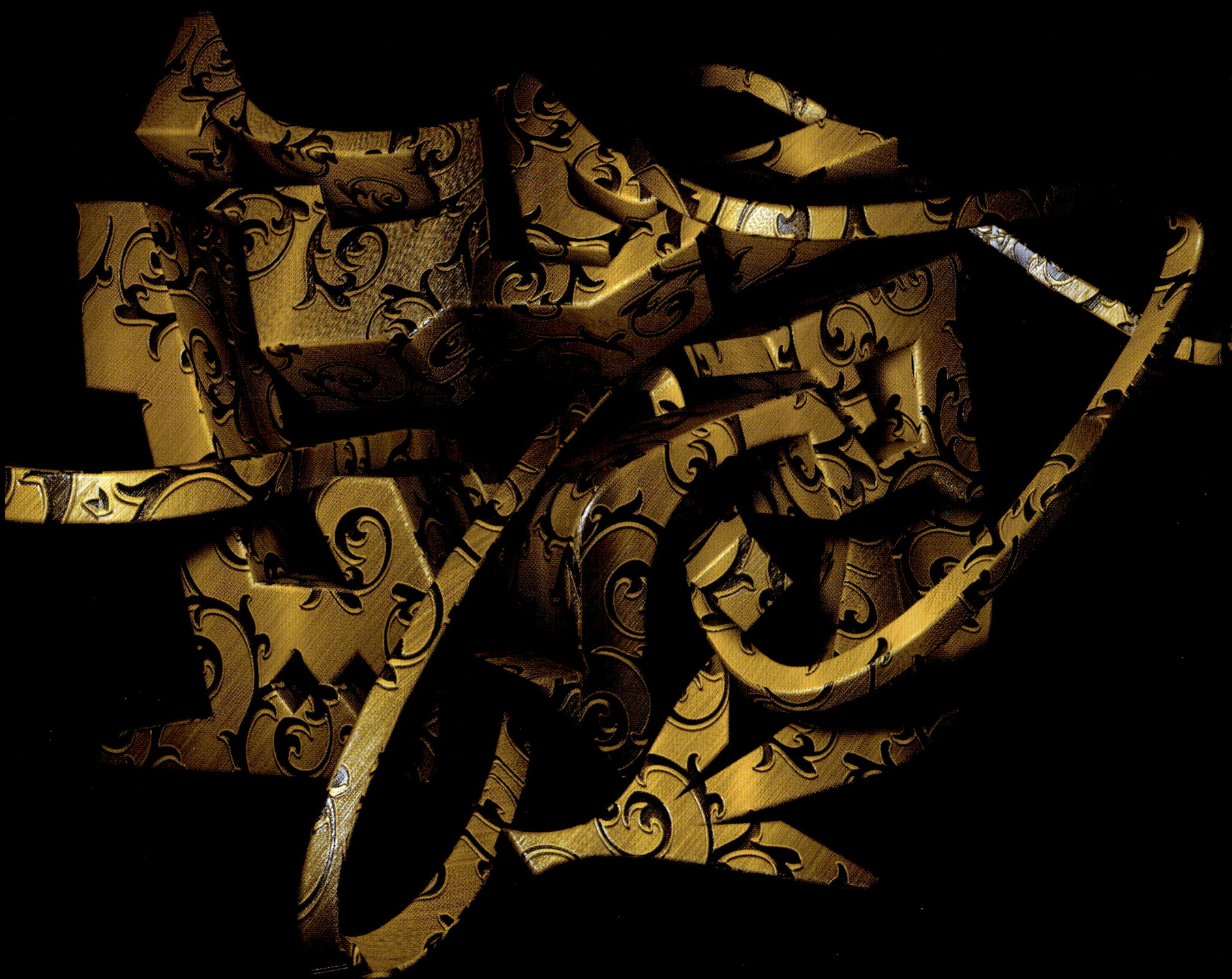

16

1. "Shaheed", ZAKARIA AHMED EL AKKAF, Morroco

2. "Stilbaz", KRYS2LOOPER, Turkey

3. "Art Reoriente", PASCAL ZOGHBI, Beirut

4. MOHAMED ABDEL AZIZ, Egypt

5. "Sabr", QASIM ARIF, Pakistan & Holland

6. "Salam", MELIH KESMEN, Styleislam, Germany

7. "Keep it Halal", QASIM ARIF, Pakistan & Holland

8. "Interruptions", Hadi Alaeddin, Jordan

9. "Elwarshe", MOTHANNA HUSSEIN, Jordan

10. "Lahore", QASIM ARIF, Pakistan / Holland

11. "Ambient Mosque", MELIH KESMEN, Styleislam, Germany

12. "29letters", PASCAL ZOGHBI, Lebanon

13. "styleislam", MELIH KESMEN, Styleislam, Germany

14. "Mustaqbali", PASCAL ZOGHBI, Lebanon

15. MOHAMED ABDEL AZIZ, Egypt

وجدة
16. "Wajda", 3-D graffiti style, ZAKARIA AHMED EL AKKAF, Oujda, Morocco

ARTISTS

AHMAD SABBAGH	BLOUZAAT.COM	sabbagh@blouzaat.com
AKUT	HERAKUT.DE	akut@herakut.de
BLOUZAAT	BLOUZAAT.COM	info@blouzaat.com
EL SEED	ELSEED-ART.COM	youwillgetareply@elseed-art.com
HASSAN MASSOUDY	MASSOUDY.NET	info@massoudy.net
HEST1	MYSPACE.COM/HEST1_THEWILDCHILD	hest1nme@yahoo.com
JULIEN BRETON AKA KAALAM	KAALAM.FREE.FR	julien.kaalam@gmail.com
KRYS2LOOPER	KRYS2LOOPER.TUMBLR.COM	contact@krys2looper.net
L'ATLAS	LATLAS.NET	latlasart@gmail.com
LIGHTGRAFF / BRUSK	LIGHTGRAFF.ORG	collectif@lightgraff.org
MALIK ANAS AL-RAJAB	MALIKANAS.COM	malikalrajab@yahoo.com
MOHAMMED ALI / AEROSOL ARABIC	AEROSOLARABIC.COM	ali@aerosolarabic.com
MONSIEUR CANA AKA ASKAR	MONSIEURCANA.COM	monsieurcana@yahoo.com
NATIVE & ZENTWO	SUPPPAFLY.COM / ZENTWO.COM	supppafly@gmail.com
SADHU	MYSPACE.COM/SADHU1	sadhu001@hotmail.com
SAIR 4	SAIR4.DE	info@sair4.de
SISKA	—	thesiskaz@googlemail.com
SUN 7 AKA JONAS BOURNAT	—	jonas.sun7@gmail.com
TYPISM	TYPISM.DE	format@typism.de
ZEPHA AKA VINCENT ABADIE HAFEZ	ABADIAFEZ.COM	abadiehafez@gmail.com

Contributors' contacts

عناوين المساهمين

DESIGNERS

ALY BCHENNATY	—	yasario_05@hotmail.com
DANA ALHANBALI	—	danahanbali@yahoo.com
HADI ALAEDDIN	BEHANCE.NET/HADIALAEDDIN	hadi.alaeddin@gmail.com
HAMED SINNO	SHANKABOOT.COM	hamsinno@googlemail.com
MELIH KESMEN	MANATWORK.COM	melih@manatwork.com
MOHAMED ABDEL AZIZ	BOYASSEEN.DEVIANTART.COM	bota_77@hotmail.com
MOHAMED GABER	GABERISM.NET	gaber@gaberism.net
MOTHANNA HUSSEIN	BEHANCE.NET/MOTHANNA	mothannahussein@yahoo.com
MUIZ ANWAR	MUIZ.CO.UK	muiz.anwar@gmail.com
PASCAL ZOGHBI	29ARABICLETTERS.COM	pascal@29arabicletters.com
QASIM ARIF	STATIQDESIGNS.COM	info@statiqdesigns.com
STYLEISLAM	STYLEISLAM.COM	salam@styleislam.com
ZAKARIA AHMED EL AKKAF	SHAHEEED.DEVIANTART.COM	illozofe@yahoo.com

AUTHORS

DON KARL	FROMHERETOFAME.COM	don@fhtf.de
HOUDA KASSATLY	—	houdakassatly@yahoo.com
HUDA SMITSHUIJZEN ABIFARÈS	KHTT.NET	huda.abifares@gmail.com
PASCAL ZOGHBI	29ARABICLETTERS.COM	pascal@29arabicletters.com
RANA JARBOU	—	rana.jarbou@gmail.com
TALA SALEH	MARKINGBEIRUT.COM	talafsaleh@gmail.com
WILLIAM PARRY	—	williamparry@yahoo.co.uk

Credits

حقوق النشر

Arabic Graffiti by Pascal Zoghbi & Don Karl aka Stone
See individual texts and essays for additional author credits

Editor: Joy Hawley
"Arabic Graffiti" cover calligraphy: eL Seed
Graphic Design & Layout: Pascal Zoghbi (29arabicletters.com) & Torge Peters (torgepeters.com)

Photo Editing: Stephan Wilke
Project Assistance and Research: Amber Grünhäuser
Arabic Editing and Proofreading: Jacques Aswad
Translation (French / English): Patrik Noll
Proofreading English: Joy Hawley

Fonts used:
Massira Spray & Hamsa Stencil by Pascal Zoghbi, Fedra Serif Arabic by Peter Bilak

Photo Credits:
Thanks to everyone who contributed photos to this book.
Texture photograph on cover: Marc L'Esperance

Chapter 1.1 – 1.3
Hassan Massoudy, Malik Anas Al-Rajab, Stone, Zurijeta, Thamer Altassan, Senk, page 34 – 35 (Montréal Mosque) by Denis McCready

Chapter 2.1 – 2.7
The following authors provided all (or most) of the photographs for their respective essays: Houda Kassatly, Rana Jarbou, Tala Saleh, William Parry
Palestinian Graffiti photos by: Monsieur Cana, William Parry, p. 59 #3 Mikhail Levit, p. 63 #4 Seedy, p. 60 #4 Mohammed Abed (AFP, Getty Images), p. 62 #1 Abid Katib (Getty Images), p. 68 #1 Joseph Melin
Beirut Graffiti & Street Art photos by: Siska, Pascal Zoghbi, Stone, Ashekman, Yaznan, Lynn Amhaz p. 96 #2 & #3 Sarah's Bag, p. 97 #4 by Raja Kanafani

Chapter 3.1 – 3.13
Photographs in this chapters are all by the artists except: 3.5 (Sair 4) all by Damian Zimmermann & Fabian Stürtz, p. 153 #3 Don Quick Shot

First published in 2011 by:

FROM HERE TO FAME PUBLISHING

Marienburger Straße 16 A
10405 Berlin / Germany
info@fhtf.de
www.fromheretofame.com

ISBN 978-3-937946-26-9

2nd Edition 2011

Printed and bound in China